*To Helen and Richard Schnaidt, my parents.*

Library of Congress Catalog Card Number: 92-85001

ISBN: 0-672-30173-3

96  95  94  93  92    8  7  6  5  4  3  2

Interpretation of the printing code: the rightmost double-digit number is the year of the book's printing; the rightmost single-digit number, the number of the book's printing. For example, a printing code of 92-1 shows that the first printing of the book occurred in 1992.

Composed in Palatino and MCPdigital typefaces by Prentice Hall Computer Publishing.

# Enterprise-Wide Networking

by Patricia Schnaidt

**SAMS**

A Division of Prentice Hall Computer Publishing

11711 North College, Carmel, Indiana 46032 USA

**Publisher**
Richard K. Swadley

**Managing Editor**
Neweleen A. Trebnik

**Acquisition Editor**
Gregg Bushyeager

**Production Editor**
Lori Cates

**Editorial Coordinators**
Becky Freeman
William Whitmer

**Editorial Assistants**
Rosemarie Graham
Lori Kelley

**Cover Designer**
Tim Amhrein

**Production Director**
Jeff Valler

**Production Manager**
Matthew Morrill

**Book Designer**
Michele Laseau

**Production Analyst**
Mary Beth Wakefield

**Proofreading/Indexing Coordinator**
Joelynn Gifford

**Graphic Image Specialists**
Dennis Sheehan
Jerry Ellis
Sue VandeWalle

**Production**
Scott Boucher
Christine Cook
Terri Edwards
Mark Enochs
Tim Groeling
Dennis Hager
Carla Hall-Batton,
    Book Shepherd
Jay Lesandrini
Juli Pavey
Linda Quigley
Michelle Self
Greg Simsic
Angie Trzepacz
Suzanne Tully
Julie Walker
Kelli Widdifield
Allan Wimmer
Alyssa Yesh

**Indexers**
John Sleeva
Loren Malloy
Jeanne Clark

# About the Series Editor

## Steven Guengerich

Mr. Guengerich is vice president of BSG's Communication division. BSG is a leading integrator of corporate computing systems, having been recognized by IDG's *The Integrator* as "Client-Server Systems Integrator of the Year." Mr. Guengerich has more than 10 years of experience in the systems integration industry, and was founder of the NetWare Advisor, a key network computing journal currently published by the COBB Group.

# About the Author

## Patricia Schnaidt

Patricia Schnaidt is editor-in-chief of *LAN Magazine,* a leading magazine for network products and technology. She has more than five years experience covering enterprise and departmental networking. She is the author of more than 100 articles on the business and technology of networking. Schnaidt is the editor of the book, *The LAN Tutorial Series and Glossary of Terms*, published by Miller Freeman, Inc. She holds a B.A. in Computer Science and English from Columbia College, Columbia University.

# Contents

## 3   Justifying and Budgeting the Enterprise-Wide Network    65

## 4 High-Level Issues of Enterprise-Wide Network Design 95

## 7 Implementing and Testing the Enterprise-Wide Network    231

## 8 Standards and Interoperability    259

## 9    Network Applications      309

## 10  Network Management: Organizational and Practical 351

## 11  The Future of Enterprise-Wide Networks 403

# Foreword

A fundamental shift is occurring in the way businesses go about using information systems for their competitive advantage. Techniques like business process reengineering are leading to systems reengineering. And as businesses decentralize and downsize, information systems are following suit. In the years ahead, we believe analysts will look back at this time as one when computing was really invented.

Along with the tremendous potential, however, there is tremendous confusion and chaos in the marketplace. Open systems, object orientation, graphical user interfaces, UNIX, OS/2, CASE, databases, and superservers—these are all terms that can impact information systems choices in various ways. But in today's rapidly changing business and computing environments, how do you decide which network computing platform is best for your needs? And how do you go about implementing that platform?

This book was written to provide answers to these and similar questions. As one would expect, the information in *Enterprise-Wide Networking* comes from the "front lines" of network computing, where battles to implement enterprise-wide networking are being won and lost regularly. As a first-hand observer to the many changes in the network computing industry and as an established editor of *LAN Magazine*, Patricia Schnaidt was our first choice to research and author *Enterprise-Wide Networking*.

We believe you will gain a much better understanding of and appreciation for the importance of this technology as you read *Enterprise-Wide Networking*, and that you will feel better prepared to ride the fundamental shifts in business and computing through the next several years.

Steven G. Papermaster
Chairman and CEO, BSG
July 1992

# Acknowledgments

I would like to thank all the people who helped me write this book by sharing their expertise, providing source material, granting interviews, and continually advising and encouraging me. I am grateful to Tom Henderson of Corporate Networks for his information, help, and support. And a special thanks is due Melanie McMullen, who encouraged me throughout the whole process of writing and editing.

I would also like to thank the following people for their contributions to this book: Pete Abene, Electronic Data Services; Dan Burger, Proteon; Dave Korf, Digital Equipment Corporation; Mike New, Attachmate; Stan Levine, Levine Consulting; and Leo Spiegel, LANSystems.

# Trademarks

All terms mentioned in this book that are known to be trademarks or service marks have been appropriately capitalized. Sams Publishing cannot attest to the accuracy of this information. Use of a term in this book should not be regarded as affecting the validity of any trademark or service mark.

# Introduction

The cooperation of individuals produces the finest end results, yet balancing cooperation and individualism is a never-ending challenge. The 1980s delivered a revolution in work and computing: the personal computer freed workers to compute independently. The information systems revolution of the 1990s is the local area network. Networks encourage people to work individually while fostering cooperation among them.

Empower a business with a network that spans every location, and that organization can operate more efficiently and more creatively. By electronically linking workers, a network enables all employees to work together as efficiently as if they were in the same workgroup. A network allows people to make decisions based on the most current information; they don't have to rely on a report that was generated yesterday. This leads to better decisions and higher productivity. Propelled by the right corporate philosophy, an enterprise-wide network can help even a monolithic corporation act like an agile start-up company.

A network can also reduce a company's operations costs. Networks don't lock companies into purchasing equipment from a single vendor. Rather, networks inherently contain equipment from many different vendors, and that equipment can use dissimilar protocols and operating systems. Yet, with the right plan, this dissimilar network can operate smoothly and efficiently. Networks can reduce your company's reliance on expensive mainframe systems. Networks are less expensive to purchase, to maintain, and to develop applications for.

Although local area networks have existed throughout the 1980s, the critical change is that companies no longer use networks to increase worker productivity or reduce costs. Corporations use networks to run their businesses, from manufacturing to inventory control to transaction processing to employee communication. Companies use networks to reduce their inventory and tie up less money in stock. Other companies use their networks to better manage their projects, enabling them to meet deadlines and ensure a good reputation and additional business. Many companies use networks to foster better communication among employees. Whatever the specific reason, corporations use their networks as a strategic advantage, one that can gain them an edge over their competitors. Networks have become an integral and essential part of a company's business.

When a company relies on its enterprise-wide network as a critical business tool, it must carefully plan, design, implement, and manage the network, considering both the business and technology issues. The business issues elude many. Networks are not technology toys; they are competitive, strategic advantages. You must construct your enterprise-wide network with the business functions at the forefront, because ultimately, its ability to solve the corporation's and users' problems will determine its success.

You must choose the network technology so that it meets the company's business functions and solves the company's problems. Whether your "enterprise" is contained within a single location or spans five continents, your technology decisions are of paramount importance to the company's business strategy. Whether you choose the oldest or the newest in local area network technology and designs, wide area network services, applications, and network management will be determined by your company's requirements, global competitiveness, corporate philosophy, budgets, and willingness to take risks.

This book teaches the network professional and business executive how to turn the power of individual networks into a cooperating organism—an enterprise-wide network that spans every location in a company, connecting all computers, and by extension, all of its workers. This book explores the process of building an enterprise-wide network from start to finish.

By reading this book, you will learn how to identify your company's network and business needs, determine a solid network strategy, and cost-justify the network. You will understand how to select the network topologies and types, build an internetwork with wide-area connections, and enable interoperability among dissimilar computers. You will learn how to install and test the network for optimal success. You will gain an understanding of the possibilities for network applications and network management.

# The Emergence of Enterprise-Wide Networks

## CHAPTER 1

*Objectives:*

1. To introduce the concept of enterprise-wide networks, explaining why corporations are installing them in record numbers.

2. To propose the objectives of enterprise-wide networks, which include the ability to accommodate a wide variety of computing equipment, including existing systems.

3. To define departmental, campus, enterprise, and global networks, and trace the rise of networks.

## Adapting Information Systems to Fit a Changing Market

Increased productivity at a lower cost is the Holy Grail of modern corporations. In today's highly competitive and increasingly global marketplace, corporations are striving to produce more products with less capital investment. Today's sharper focus on profitability and productivity has several sources. First, the world is rapidly becoming a single market. Foreign corporations now bid on more and more contracts within the United States and vice versa, thereby requiring companies everywhere to react more quickly and operate more efficiently than they have in the past.

Second, Eastern Bloc countries and other developing nations present new market opportunities never before available to Western firms. Opportunities are exploding in the former communist countries, in the Pacific Rim, and in South America. Competition to sell to this huge, largely untapped market comes not only from United States companies, but also from corporations abroad. To compete in Europe, the Pacific Rim, and beyond, United States businesses must build an international presence.

Third, within the United States, the bull market of the 1980s enabled many companies to tolerate waste in their corporate structures. The economy slowed significantly in the early 1990s, exposing these excesses. Many corporations found themselves supporting many more tiers of management than were necessary. Many other companies were burdened with huge debts to repay. Companies can no longer tolerate waste if they are to remain profitable and make their interest payments—or even stay in business.

Consequently, companies are examining their business practices to identify sources of waste, low productivity, and unprofitable operations. They strive to eliminate unprofitable ventures and maximize their profitable undertakings. To streamline their operations, companies must examine their methods of doing business, from the reception desk to the loading dock. They are improving business practices and supporting operations. Companies are trying to make information more easily available to employees. They are downsizing information-processing systems and moving applications from mainframes to PC servers in an effort to reduce costs.

Businesses must consider information to be an asset in the same way they consider a manufacturing plant to be an asset. To an automotive manufacturer, knowing precisely how many bumpers are in stock is as important as having them in stock when it needs them. Keeping as many bumpers in stock as are needed enables the manufacturer to tie up less money in inventory. Keeping too few bumpers in stock can stop the assembly line. Thus, having information about how many bumpers are stocked at any given time and using this information with the ordering process can be considered an asset.

Faster and easier access to information can increase worker productivity, which in turn can increase corporate profitability. When workers have easy access to information and have the power to act on the information, corporations can react more quickly to market shifts. Reacting quickly—whether it's preparing a bid in three days instead of three weeks, or automatically ordering more materials when inventory drops to a certain level—is essential to ensuring productivity, and therefore profitability, in today's market.

The productivity of the information worker has come under special scrutiny. During the 1980s, host computers and personal computers eased the tasks of clerks, typists, and administrative assistants by giving them databases, spreadsheets, and word processors to automate the tedium of data entry and manipulation. In the 1990s, the focus is on the information worker, or the white-collar office worker. A new class of software, constructed around networks, promises to free white-collar workers from the drudgery of managing their work, maintaining a work flow, and communicating with people in different locations. This software, however, requires a complete information flow from all computing sources.

Computers are the vital business tools that store and manipulate business information. Computer networks can place information in the hands of workers. With information, people can make decisions more quickly and do their jobs more efficiently, thus becoming more productive. Companies use computers and networks to increase productivity and remain competitive.

# Why Corporations Install Networks

Organizations are installing networks in record numbers across a broad spectrum of industries. Corporations (both large and small), universities, and the government and its agencies are installing networks. Market research firms offer differing estimates on the size of this growing LAN market, but they agree on one thing: people are installing networks, and they will continue to install them.

Market Intelligence Research Corporation (MIRC), a computer market research firm located in Mountain View, CA, expects that the total worldwide
PC LAN market will be $5 billion by the end of 1991. By 1992, MIRC expects
the market to grow to $6 billion; by 1993, the market will be $7.1 billion. By
1994, MIRC expects the market will be $8.1 million, and by 1995, the market
will be twice 1991's size, at $9.2 billion (see Figure 1.1).[1]

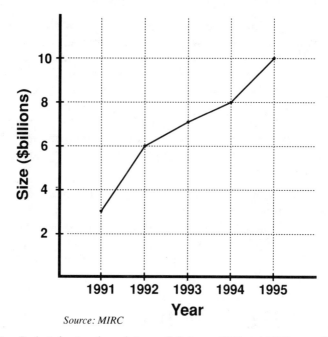

Source: MIRC

**Figure 1.1.**   *Projected network market growth between 1991 and 1995, according to*
*MIRC.*

The Gartner Group, a computer market research firm based in Stamford, CT,
projects that by 1992, 67 percent of the PCs in the United States will be
connected to a LAN. This is a significant growth, considering that in 1988
only 32 percent of PCs were networked and that the personal computer is
little more than a decade old.

---

[1]Market Intelligence Research Corp. "World Personal Computer Local Area Network Marketplace." MIRC, 1990.

Networks are found across industry types, although networks are more prevalent in certain industries. According to MIRC's research, manufacturing firms and government agencies are the primary purchasers of networks (see Figure 1.2).[2] In 1989, manufacturers bought 31 percent of the PC LAN equipment sold worldwide. Engineering companies bought 13 percent, financial companies bought 11 percent, airlines bought 10 percent, and small businesses and educational institutions purchased the remaining 10 percent.

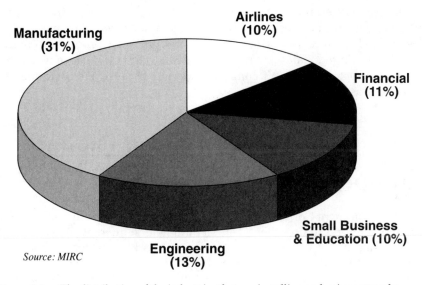

Source: MIRC

***Figure 1.2.*** *The distribution of the industries that are installing and using networks, according to MIRC.*

These statistics suggest that an increasing number of companies will use networks as a strategic advantage. Networks have unique advantages over mainframes, minicomputers, and stand-alone PCs. First, they accommodate existing types of computing equipment, so users don't have to discard one computing technology in favor of another. Second, networks not only enable users to communicate and share information, but also they give users freedom and individuality. The market numbers point out also that more and more people will have to understand how to design, install, manage, and justify networks.

---

[2]*Ibid.*

# Three Case Studies of Enterprise-Wide Networks

The following three case studies are examples of some reasons for deploying an enterprise-wide network, and demonstrate how networks are used to run businesses. For example, Digital Equipment Corporation's network enables it to deliver products faster and reduce inventory levels. Advanced Micro Devices relies on its network to get its semiconductor products to market faster. The United States Air Force installed a network because its existing computer systems couldn't communicate and because a thrown-together solution was too costly.

## Worldwide Networking at Digital Equipment Corporation

Digital Equipment Corporation (DEC, Maynard, MA) not only sells computers and networks, it uses them. Digital built its first internal networks in the 1970s using dial-up lines; today, a single network, managed by one team, links the entire corporation, making Digital the owner of one of the largest private networks in the world. Digital's enterprise-wide network has reduced costly time delays that once plagued the minicomputer manufacturer. Digital's business units depend on the network to achieve their business goals, making the network a utility as essential as heat and running water.

Digital uses its network to speed up the order-management process. It handles every customer order over the network, from the entry point in the local sales office, to fulfillment, to invoicing. Digital has reduced its inventory levels by coupling sales forecasts with its manufacturing schedules and by more effectively coordinating requirements from the manufacturing plants that supply parts. Over a two-year period, inventory turns improved from 2.0 to 3.6 times, resulting in a decrease of $700 million in assets previously tied up in inventory.[3] Digital uses its network to put information in the hands of decision-makers (see Figure 1.3).

---

[3]Wayne Hall and Robert McCauley. "Planning and Managing a Corporate Network Utility." Digital Equipment Corp., 1987.

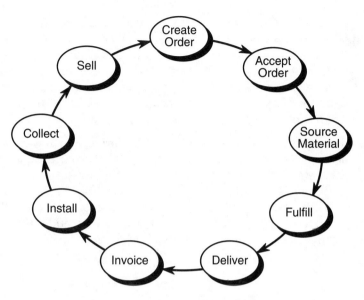

***Figure 1.3.*** *Networking order management at Digital Equipment Corporation.*

Digital's network connects more than 64,000 computer systems worldwide, with more than 111,000 employees in 800 locations using an electronic mail system. A private packet-switching network delivers network services to remote terminal users. EtherNet LANs connect smaller offices to their district and regional headquarters. Digital's network services go beyond data; the company has a private telephone network and a broadcast satellite network. E-mail, computer conferencing, and videotext are integral network applications.

# At AMD, the Chips Are Up with Networks

The quick exchange of information is just as vital to success at Advanced Micro Devices (AMD, Sunnyvale, CA) as it is at Digital Equipment Corporation. AMD, a semiconductor manufacturer, was the first to ship 100Mbps Fiber Distributed Data Interface (FDDI) chips, enabling it to garner the largest market share for high-speed fiber network chip sets. AMD has also cloned Intel's 386 chip, and threatens to become a formidable competitor in the PC CPU market. Much of AMD's continued success hinges on its ability to maintain the significant advantage of being the first to market.

AMD's network provides support and service for its engineering and manufacturing groups—the heart of the business. AMD cites interoperability and cooperative networking between host computers and organizations as the chief benefits of its enterprise-wide network, which is primarily used for computer-aided design. Integrating departmental and campus networks with a minimum of management demands is essential as AMD moves toward computer-integrated and paperless manufacturing.

The network, which connects sites in Texas, California, and Singapore, crosses 11 time zones (see Figure 1.4). Using the TCP/IP protocol suite, AMD's network delivers peer-to-peer interoperability to users of a multitude of operating systems, including DOS, IBM VM/CMS, IBM MVS, UNIX, DEC VMS, DEC Ultrix, and Apple Macintosh. AMD's network includes EtherNet and FDDI network hardware as well as T-1, leased lines, and satellite transmission facilities for wide-area connectivity. More than 1,550 TCP/IP hosts are online.

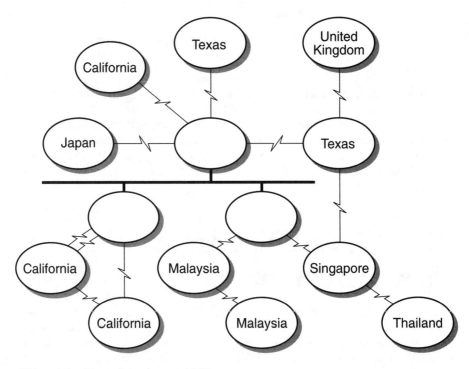

*Figure 1.4.*  *Network topology at AMD.*

# United States Air Force Flies with LANs

Lower inventory and better communication are just two reasons to install networks. The United States Air Force Logistics Command (AFLC) uses its network to more efficiently service and maintain its planes. Each year, the AFLC overhauls 1,300 aircraft, rebuilds 3,400 engines, processes four million materials requisitions, and repairs two million components, with the help of the largest broadband network in the United States.

The AFLC network spans five Air Logistic Centers from Texas to California, plus the AFLC headquarters and the Aerospace Guidance and Meteorology Center in Ohio. The network provides connectivity for 35,000 terminal and PC users, as well as host-to-host connectivity.

In 1986, the Air Force did not have an organized, efficient way to collect and distribute information as materials were ordered and received and as equipment was serviced. Information stored in one type of computer could not be easily entered into another, dissimilar computer. Data often had to be rekeyed into a different computer system, greatly increasing the possibility of error. To speed the process of materials management, the Air Force modernized its computers in a $1.5 billion, 10-year undertaking.

The Air Force designed eight VAX-based applications to manage supply acquisition and distribution. The largest of these applications controls the storage, allocation, and distribution of all AFLC supplies. A second application determines what supplies are needed and prepares budget requests. Another application manages the transportation of materials by Air Force planes.

# Why Should You Network?

As these three case studies show, corporations install enterprise-wide networks to increase communication, eliminate some of the problems inherent in communicating across large distances, and share resources. There are as many reasons to network as there are businesses themselves.

Whatever the reason, the right reason to install a network is a business one. Networks are business tools, not technology toys. A savvy information systems manager doesn't install a network because it's great fun to figure out a new technology. A savvy IS manager installs an enterprise-wide network because it makes the company more productive and thus more profitable. Enterprise-wide networks must be conceived and built with the business of the company in mind. Here is a summary of reasons to network, followed by an in-depth look at each reason.

- *Sharing costly resources.* A network can be used to share expensive resources, such as color printers and plotters. A network can be used also to share resources such as faxes, modems, and optical disks.

- *Improving communication.* Networks improve information exchange and communications among employees, customers, and suppliers.

- *Reducing the barriers of time and distance.* Even when the workers are located in different offices, a network helps workers share information and communicate as if they were in the same workgroup.

- *Increasing workers' access to information.* Employees can access many different sources of information, all the while using their familiar desktop computers.

- *Reducing the cost of doing business.* By giving workers ready access to information, they can make decisions more quickly and efficiently. Networks reduce a company's reliance on other forms of information delivery, such as the telephone or mail.

- *Reducing the cost of MIS operations.* LANs are less expensive to operate than mainframes, and LAN servers and applications are continually increasing in power.

- *Giving companies the freedom of location.* Networks enable companies to locate their divisions and operations where they are most efficient, rather than according to the convenience or demands of the computing systems.

- *Building an inter-company network.* By connecting a company's suppliers and customers via an inter-company network, a corporation can act more quickly and gain a significant advantage over its competitors.

# Sharing Costly Resources

Companies install networks to share expensive resources, such as high-speed laser printers, color printers, plotters, fax machines, and high-speed modems. Networks can be used also to share the expense of high-end storage devices, such as optical disk jukeboxes. By enabling many users to access such peripheral resources, companies can distribute the cost of those systems among the users. File and printer sharing were the original motivators for installing a network; however, many more important reasons exist today. These newer reasons may be more difficult to quantify, yet they can contribute significantly to a company's bottom-line competitiveness. A network is often considered a strategic tool rather than a cost-saving device.

# Improving Communication

Companies install networks to improve communication among employees. A network and its accompanying software enable employees to share information more easily. Networks let workers exchange information and messages through file transfer, electronic mail, and shared applications. Without a network, workers may have to exchange floppy disks or magnetic tapes to share files. Without a network, users of different computer systems may have to rely on the telephone, letters, and facsimiles for communication, rather than electronic mail. Because networks take care of the details of communication, they enable people to collaborate more easily.

# Reducing the Barriers of Time and Distance

With networks, workers can share information and ideas regardless of geographical distance and time differences, which otherwise would impede communication. For example, when a company connects its offices in New York and San Francisco, workers in those offices can share information more easily, quickly, and reliably than via interoffice mail, express mail, facsimile, or telephone. Workers are more likely to double-check a number if the information is readily available. Employees in different workgroups are more likely to share ideas and information if it is convenient. Orders can be booked more quickly, and products can be shipped more quickly. Networks can reduce the complications introduced by time zones and geographical distance.

# Increasing Worker Access to Information

Companies install networks to give workers quicker access to more information, even data residing on different computer systems. For example, users can access mainframe-based data while still using their personal computers. Workers can access information residing in different locations and on different types of computers. Because networks enable different types of computers to communicate, workers have access to a variety of information sources while still using their own familiar computers.

# Reducing Costs

Networks can reduce the cost of business operations. With better access to information, companies can reduce the cost of doing business, as Digital Equipment has with its inventory turns. If a company is spending too much money on overnight package delivery, couriers, and facsimiles, an enterprise-wide network used primarily for exchanging electronic mail reduces the need to ship paper-based information.

A network can also help a company reduce the cost of its MIS operations. Mainframes are costly to purchase and operate. PCs have always been relatively inexpensive; however, until recently, they were not powerful enough to be serious business tools. As PC-based computing increases in power, functionality, and reliability, however, the LAN becomes a critical tool in MIS. Companies are now moving mission-critical applications from the mainframe to the LAN, in an effort that is called *downsizing* or *rightsizing*. Some companies are downsizing completely; in other words, they are throwing out their mainframes in favor of PC LANs. But many more companies are using networks in conjunction with their existing host computers. A network's modularity is also key in this process, because a network can accommodate existing equipment while providing a path to tomorrow's technology.

# Giving Companies the Freedom of Location

Networks give companies new freedom in locating their divisions and operations so that they are suited to the business needs. If a company's business lends itself to a widely distributed operation, a network can accommodate this structure. A network has no one set configuration or architecture; networks are inherently flexible. Networks don't lock a company into a central business organization, which enables the company's business practices—rather than its computing systems—to dictate its structure.

# Building an Inter-Company Network

Networks don't exist just within a corporate entity; inter-company networks are emerging. A company may connect its customers via a network, enabling customers to place orders, pay for products, and perform other business activities electronically that once required paper and long delays. Similarly, a company may connect its suppliers via a network, enabling it to order more parts, often automatically as their inventory level drops. Building inter-company networks, together with electronic document interchange (EDI) and just-in-time (JIT) manufacturing, can give a company a significant strategic advantage over its competitors. An inter-company network enables a corporation to act more quickly.

Companies have installed networks for these same reasons—with varying degrees of ease and success—since networks were invented in the 1970s. But today, more companies are installing networks on a grander scale, and they are installing them a little differently; they are emphasizing the business reasons for networking and enlisting the help of the MIS department.

To successfully deploy an enterprise-wide network, business unit managers and MIS managers must work together. In many cases, this is a revolutionary change. LANs, like PCs themselves, have often been outside MIS's control. Today, networks are moving under MIS's umbrella, but the rules must change. The LAN is gaining equal footing with the traditional computers of MIS. Additionally, MIS has become more than a service department; it works in partnership with a company's business units. When the MIS and business unit managers work together to solve business problems, the enterprise-wide network can be overwhelmingly successful.

In many companies, MIS must now be as frugal as all other departments. In the past, many firms permitted MIS to purchase the latest mainframe, the newest software revision, or the fastest PCs without justifying whether these technology advances made real business sense. More and more, however, organizations require MIS to prove that it needs the latest technology to serve the needs of the business units. *Do more with less* is the new motto of MIS.

# Defining Networks

Five years ago, the word *network* didn't conjure up images of PC LANs, and certainly not of enterprise-wide networks. To people working in telecommunications, the network meant the telephone network. To those in data communications, it meant a terminal-to-host network.

Now, a local area network (LAN) refers to a group of computers, each equipped with the appropriate network adapter card and software, connected by cable, that share applications, data, and peripherals. A LAN, by definition, is local, without remote-access services. It typically spans a single building or campus. A wide area network (WAN) is made up of multiple LANs tied together, usually via telephone services or fiber-optic cabling. WANs may span a city, state, country, or even the world.

Five or more years ago, the standard computing architecture was comprised of a three-tiered hierarchy. At the pinnacle was the mainframe, the vital corporate data storehouse that ran the payroll, accounting, and inventory applications. Minicomputers were at the second tier; some were directly connected to the mainframe. The minis ran manufacturing, invoicing, and other departmental applications. At the bottom of the hierarchy were personal computers, which ran office-automation applications such as word processors and spreadsheets. The personal computers and PC LANs were connected directly to the minis in some instances, but not directly to the mainframe (see Figure 1.5).

This structure emerged because the different kinds of computers—mainframes, minis, and personal computers—required different levels of tending and expertise. Mainframes needed to be isolated in rooms with special cooling and raised floors—the so-called glass house. Mainframes were the repository of mission-critical information, data so important that the company could not survive without it. Minicomputers were used in the individual business departments. They did not require quite as much "care and feeding" as mainframes, and their applications were important but not mission-critical. PCs popped up virtually everywhere, and one primary benefit was that you didn't need to be a programmer or a computer scientist to use the PC and its applications.

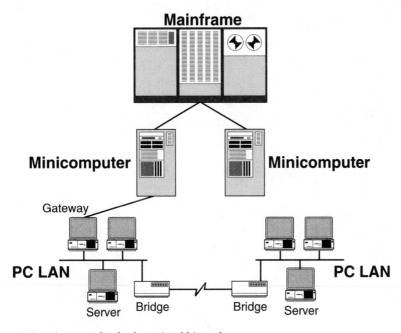

**Figure 1.5.** *An example of a three-tiered hierarchy.*

Over time, companies began to implement a two-tiered network architecture. The minicomputer was no longer the middle man, connecting PCs to mainframes. All devices, whether personal computers, terminals, or minicomputers, were connected directly to the mainframe. Mission-critical applications were still run on the mainframe or minicomputer, however, rather than on the PC LAN (see Figure 1.6).

The two-tiered architecture is gradually flattening, with PC LANs taking on greater importance. In some companies, the PC LAN has gained equal footing with the mainframe. Today's computing architecture is in transition from host-based to distributed. Tomorrow's computing architecture is likely to be client/server or distributed. Client/server computing, unlike hierarchical computing, offers more flexibility. Information sources and computing power are placed where they are best utilized—at the workers' desks, in the department, or in the MIS room.

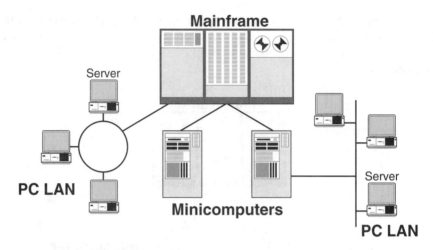

*Figure 1.6.*   *An example of two-tiered network architecture.*

Distributed computing takes advantage of the CPU power of desktop computers as well as the server computers. Instead of assuming that the user has a dumb terminal, as the hierarchical model does, the distributed computing model assumes that the user has an intelligent personal computer. Under this assumption, you can divide the applications and the data and distribute the portions among the server and client computers.

This division enables processing to occur at the more appropriate location—the client or the server. Note that in the older model, all applications and data reside on the same computer—the mainframe. In client/server computing, a company's accounting system may reside on the mainframe, for example, but sales are entered in an application running on a departmental LAN. To invoice customers, the mainframe application asks the LAN server to upload the sales information so that invoicing can be run. The accounting system remains on the mainframe, where it is controlled and managed by MIS. The salespeople can use an application that meets their specific needs—as long as it can communicate with the mainframe application. The needs of both groups can be satisfied. The client/server model enables companies to tailor their computing systems to their needs in each location. Figure 1.7 is an example of client/server computing architecture.

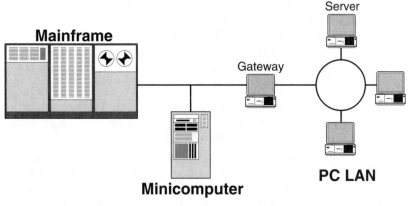

***Figure 1.7.*** *Client/server computing architecture.*

Another benefit of this division of labor is specialization. Computers can be designed for a specific function, such as serving the needs of the users who want to print, fax, or use a database. In the older model, the same machine serves all of the users' needs. Software and hardware can be specialized to the different needs of the tasks. A database server can be designed for I/O, whereas a printer server can be designed for processing batch jobs and fonts, for example.

The client/server architecture can also reduce the overall network traffic. In a network that does not implement client/server computing, traffic can be quite high, as applications and data are downloaded from the server or host to the user. With the client/server architecture, however, the front-end application resides on the users' computers. Also, the traffic that traverses the LAN cable is primarily queries and responses rather than program code and unnecessary data.

The client/server model scales easily from small to medium-sized systems (and improvements are being made at the high end). For example, a network is appropriate for a workgroup environment, but it can also be an appropriate solution for an enterprise-wide system. The client/server model also accommodates computer systems from one end of the scale—the personal computer—to the other—the mainframe.

Networks take advantage of the rapid technology developments in personal computing. Even as personal computers and workstations become increasingly more powerful, blurring the demarcation between a high-end workstation or server and a low-end minicomputer, the price is dropping. Companies can purchase powerful RISC-based workstations and Intel-based servers for only a few thousand dollars.

But networks aren't without their difficulties. Maturity is perhaps the biggest problem. Networks are a relatively new technology, and although developments are occurring rapidly, much more work needs to be accomplished. Networks began in the business department rather than in the MIS room. Reliability and robustness weren't the most important features as they are with minis and mainframes; rather, usability and flexibility were paramount, because those were the end users' primary concerns. Now those qualities must come together.

Because the network components come from so many different vendors, integrating the pieces is a large-scale project. Unlike with mainframes or host computers, you don't buy the entire system from a single vendor. With networks, the end user companies are left to integrate the systems themselves. So, not only must MIS monitor and manage the computer systems, it must integrate the pieces.

Network management is another area of immaturity. Today, the tools to truly manage networks—not just monitor them—are lacking. However, developments are occurring, enabling managers to better monitor, configure, and control computer systems, even when those systems are remote. Technology improvements are occurring, and IS people are gaining a greater understanding of networks, which ultimately will ease the network management crisis.

As one considers the evolution from mainframes to LANs, one wonders if networks are the "end of the line." Will something else replace networks, as minis came after mainframes, and PCs and PC LANs came next? Perhaps. It's likely, however, that the client/server, networked computing architecture will reign for some time, given that it is the only type of computing that can accommodate other types of computing, both past and future. As Ray Noorda, president and CEO of Novell, said, it will be networks forever, but the performance, facility, and utilization will become more sophisticated and useful.[4]

---

[4]Patricia Schnaidt. "Ray Noorda." *LAN Magazine*, October 1991: 26.

# Types of Networks

Distinguishing between local area networks and wide area networks is relatively simple. Unfortunately, the distinctions among types of networks have become much more complex. We classify networks into *departmental*, *campus*, *enterprise*, and *global* varieties. These classifications are guidelines, but you should use them to identify your company's network type so that you can better assess the scope of the networking project that stands before you.

- *Departmental networks* are used by a small group of people working toward a similar goal. The primary goal of a departmental is to share local resources, such as applications, data, laser printers, and modems. Departmental networks usually aren't partitioned into subnetworks unless they are part of a larger, enterprise-wide network.

- *Campus networks* connect multiple departmental LANs within a single building or campus of a corporation. They are still local area networks, but may cover several miles. Services include connectivity among the departmental networks, access to corporate databases, and access to fax servers, high-speed modems, and high-speed printers.

- *Enterprise networks* connect all computers in all locations of a particular company. They may span a city, a state, or a continent. Users want to share information and applications with their workgroup, other departments, branch offices, and corporate headquarters. They require all the applications and services used on departmental and campus networks, plus access to mainframes and minicomputers.

- *Global networks* span all departments, campuses, branch offices, and subsidiaries of a corporation. They are international in scope, and bring with them the challenges of dealing with multiple languages, cultures, standards, and telephone companies.

## Departmental Networks

A departmental network, or *workgroup network*, is used by a group of people working toward a similar goal, such as in accounting or marketing. A departmental LAN's primary goal is to share local resources, such as applications, data, laser printers, and perhaps low-speed modems. Departmental networks typically have one or two file servers and fewer than 30 users. Departmental LANs usually aren't partitioned by bridges into subnetworks, unless they are part of a larger, enterprise-wide network. Even when departmental LANs are connected into an enterprise-wide network, the majority of the traffic remains on the departmental LAN, because that's where the majority of people's work is performed. As a rule of thumb, a user will need local resources 80 percent of the time, and will need remote resources only 20 percent of the time. Figure 1.8 is an example of a departmental LAN.

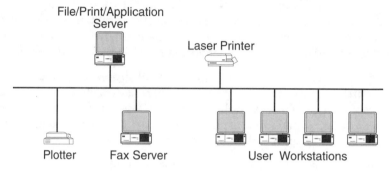

*Figure 1.8.*   *A departmental network.*

Departmental networks require little management. Tasks are relatively simple: administrative tasks include adding new users, performing simple trouble-shooting, and perhaps installing new nodes and software upgrades. Difficult tasks, such as major upgrades, are usually performed by a consultant or value-added reseller. Management tools are relatively mature and quite plentiful, because departmental LANs are also relatively mature. A part-time adminis-trator can easily manage such a network. In most cases, the LAN manager rarely receives formal training, but probably is the person in the department or small business who knows the most about PCs and gets the job by default.

## Campus Networks

Departmental LAN users and managers soon realized that they could im-prove efficiency by gaining access to information in other departments of the same company. If a salesperson could gain access to the specifications of a particular product and incorporate them into a presentation, the information could be more up-to-date, and therefore would have more impact. This might help close deals more quickly, for example. If the marketing department could access the latest specifications of a product under development, it could have the marketing materials ready shortly after the specifications are final-ized by engineering.

The next step in network evolution is to campus networks. A campus network connects LANs in multiple departments within a single building or campus of a corporation. Campus networks may cover several miles, but wide area connections are not required. Campus networks have a *backbone* or main network, with subnetworks attached to the backbone like ribs. In a few cases, companies may use routers to improve performance; more frequently, however, they use bridges to connect the subnetworks to the backbone.

In a campus network, each department retains control of its file server or servers, but it gains access to some files and resources on other departments' networks. Services available go beyond simple file and print sharing; campus networking facilities often include facsimile servers and high-speed modem servers. Multiprocessing servers may be necessary to handle the communications load. Access to corporate databases, whether they reside on database servers or minicomputers, becomes essential. Figure 1.9 is an example of a campus network.

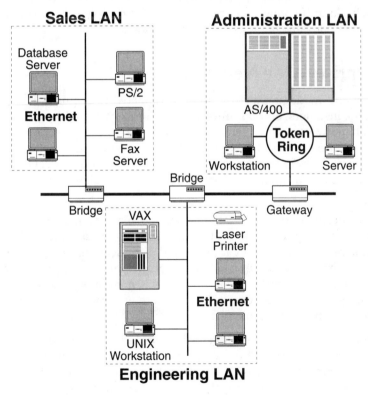

*Figure 1.9.* *A campus network.*

The problems of integrating networks begin at the campus level. Generally, individual departments have chosen the application and computer, and therefore the network, that best suited them. What best suits the sales department, however, is not likely to suit engineering, for instance. Computer types, network operating systems, and network hardware may be different in each department. For example, the engineering department may use UNIX and EtherNet, the sales department may use DOS, NetWare, and ARCnet, and the marketing people may use Macintoshes, AppleShare, and LocalTalk. Very often, campus networks connect dissimilar computer systems, whereas departmental networks are often made up of similar computers. Campus networks are also often haphazardly patched together. For example, two departments that often work together might connect their computer systems, and then a third group might want connection.

These increasingly complex departmental networks make network management difficult. Administrators must be more skilled, and as a result, need more training. No longer can the administrator walk around to troubleshoot, easily checking if connectors are tight or if the troubled PC is plugged in. Sophisticated on-line network management tools are important.

# Enterprise-Wide Networks

Building and managing an enterprise-wide network requires enterprising designers, installers, and administrators. An enterprise-wide network connects all networks in a company's organizational units—departments, campuses, and branch offices—regardless of geographical location. Enterprise-wide networks may span a city, a state, or a continent. They involve wide area links to other locations or long-distance fiber connections (see Figure 1.10).

Users of enterprise networks want to share information and applications with their workgroup or department, other departments, and all branch offices and corporate headquarters. They require all the applications and services used on departmental and campus networks, plus some unique ones. Access to mainframe and minicomputer applications is mandatory. No recipe exists for building an enterprise network. Corporate-wide networking is the leading edge of network technology.

Enterprise networks run mission-critical applications. These applications, which are the heart of the business, were formerly run on mainframes and minicomputers. The increasing sophistication, performance, and reliability of PC LANs has made it possible to move these applications down from the host computers to the network, in the *downsizing* process.

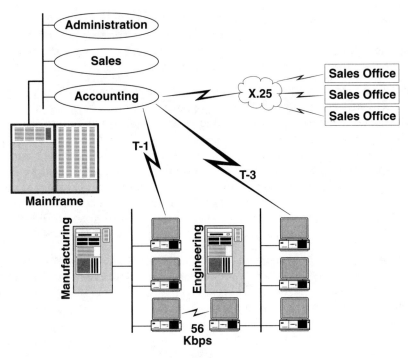

*Figure 1.10.* *An enterprise-wide network.*

Users want access to all information all the time, but information and applications reside on a wide variety of computer types and locations. Nevertheless, applications must work efficiently and seamlessly. Access to these information sources should be provided transparently.

Enterprise-wide networks include the pantheon of end-user devices: intelligent workstations such as PCs, Macs, and UNIX workstations, as well as terminals for minis or mainframes. Multiple operating systems are also used, and the integrator may be faced with making DOS, UNIX, OS/2, Macintosh, VMS, and other operating systems work to share data. Network designers can use a variety of protocols, proprietary and standard, to facilitate connections to workstations. They may be faced with a multitude of network hardware types, including EtherNet, Token Ring, ARCnet, LocalTalk, and FDDI as well as network software and protocols, including SNA, DECnet, NetWare, AppleShare, and TCP/IP. All of these must be transparently integrated into a single network.

Enterprise networks include departmental and campus networks that may be many miles apart. One challenge of building enterprise-wide networks is cost-effectively connecting LANs over WAN links. Emerging wide area networking services may make these connections more efficient.

This multivendor, multiprotocol network must be managed. Managing an enterprise network encompasses the problems of managing departmental and campus networks, plus some unique challenges. In an enterprise-wide network, users can tolerate little downtime. Equipment redundancy and disaster recovery planning are essential. Because administration is complex, network managers require complete systems, not just individual tools, to change their roles from reactive to proactive. Administrators can use these management systems to discern network performance trends and spot problems before they become failures. Managers also need complex troubleshooting and configuration tools.

Although you may be able to build campus networks without the help of MIS, an enterprise network cannot be patched together. The expertise, discipline, and training available from MIS is crucial. Formulating a plan that accommodates the business and technology aspects is essential to building a successful enterprise-wide network.

## Global Networks

A global network spans all departments, campuses, branch offices, and subsidiaries of a corporation. Global networks, as the name suggests, are international in scope, and bring with them the problems of dealing with multiple languages, cultures, standards, and telephone companies (see Figure 1.11).

Requirements for a global network include complete connectivity, high performance, zero downtime, and ease of management. Global networks are even more difficult to build and manage than enterprise-wide networks, because they network the computing systems of multiple subsidiaries of a corporation. Whereas a company may have computing standards for a single location or even within a single country, different types of computers are the de facto standards in different countries. Designers have to deal with the problems of connecting computers over international telephone lines, which often offer low bandwidth and high error rates. Plus, the designers must deal with the people issues of culture and language.

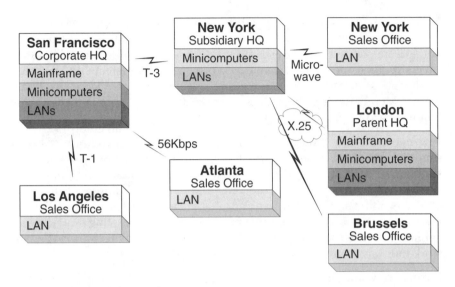

*Figure 1.11.* *A global network.*

With each progression—from departmental to enterprise—the network must be more reliable and more robust, despite the added performance demands placed on it. As the network grows in size, it also tends to grow in functionality. More data—and more important data—is placed on the network, where it must be secured and protected, yet available. The connections that facilitate communications must be more transparent. Yet, with each progression, the computing equipment is more diverse and the geographical distance is greater, making these goals more difficult to achieve. Also, managing those connections becomes more problematic and costly.

# Enterprise-Wide Networks Accommodate Existing and Disparate Systems

Networks offer a means of connecting existing computers, from mainframes to PCs, as well as a way to incorporate the latest computer technology. Businesses continue to install networks because they provide a growth path for the future while accommodating existing equipment.

Networking promises the integration of all computer types into a single transparent organism. If networks are based on standards, they promise transparent connectivity and seamless interoperability of a variety of different computers, operating systems, network operating systems, and network hardware. *Transparent connectivity* and *seamless interoperability* are buzzwords. Merely saying them doesn't make them true; making them true requires hard work.

Few networks are *homogenous*. A homogeneous network is comprised of similar components from a single manufacturer. Today, few networks are made up of products from one manufacturer. Few organizations have networks made up of equipment from only IBM or Digital Equipment anymore. The days of the single-manufacturer LAN are gone. *Heterogeneous networks*, which are made up of a multitude of workstations, operating systems, and applications, are the norm in today's computing. An enterprise-wide network must accommodate these diverse systems.

Because networking began as a grass-roots effort, people bought computers and networks to suit their individual needs, without regard to company standards (if standards existed). Departmental networks are thus designed to solve a particular group's computing problem. For example, an engineering department may have chosen Sun Microsystems' SPARC workstations connected by an EtherNet network because it needed an application that ran only on UNIX. File sharing is accomplished through TCP/IP and NFS.

The same company's sales department may have bought IBM PS/2s, Token Ring, and NetWare to manage its client database, write letters, and make proposals. Then the marketing department chose Macintoshes, because its priority is designing presentation materials. The Macs are connected by LocalTalk, and file and printer sharing is accomplished through AppleTalk. The computer services department must integrate these disparate systems into a transparent organism.

Mergers and acquisitions have also introduced a variety of computing systems into networks. When a company is acquired, the computer systems, like the employees, can be "laid off," but commonly the company has invested too much in its hardware and software to discard the computer systems. The acquiring company gains unfamiliar computer systems that often are unable to communicate with the company's own computers.

A network should mask the differences between operating systems and computer types. A Macintosh user should be able to use UNIX-based resources. A UNIX user should be able to share information with DOS users. Users don't want to—and shouldn't have to—know about file formats and

UNIX commands. A user at an IBM 3270 terminal should be able to exchange mail with PC network users without having to enter an arcane (and impossible-to-remember) address.

With networks, the location of the data should be hidden. Users shouldn't have to know that the sales database resides on a file server on the third floor of building 2 on the north campus. They simply should be able to find out how many widgets the company sold last month. Geographical distance should be invisible. Users in New York should not know that the information they need resides in a database in the Los Angeles office.

No matter how the equipment was acquired, an enterprise network must accommodate existing computer systems. Relegating existing equipment to the dustbin is simply too expensive. Fortunately, microcomputers are "recyclable." As more powerful processors come along, older equipment can be "demoted" from a server to a workstation, for example. Although a 286 PC is inadequate as a server, it can serve an individual user's needs if the user is not a power user. When network demands require a 486 server, the 386 can act as the server for a less-busy network or be given to a power user as a workstation. DEC VAXstations can act as servers when they are no longer useful as workstations.

Companies should continue to give their workers the right tools for the job. If a department's mission is best helped by Macintosh software, the company should buy Macintoshes and install a network. Similarly, if computer-aided design is the department's mission, a UNIX network with Sun workstations may be the best choice. Companies should choose the application first, then the computer system, and finally the network.

MIS departments must also establish and follow corporate standards for the "right tools for the job." Although it is very important to allow strategic groups and departments to use the hardware and software that best meets their needs, MIS must also define and implement standards for equipment. This way, a company can create a "menu" of hardware and software for departments to choose from, rather than having each department research and purchase its favorites. Standards can still include multiple choices; however, by narrowing the choices, the company can reduce the complexity of the network and ultimately increase the reliability.

Networks should be designed to solve a specific business unit's or department's problem. One network design will not serve the needs of the entire enterprise. A network designed for manufacturing is very different from one designed to solve the problems of communicating with a company's retail locations. Although both publishers and lawyers process words, a network for producing a newspaper is very different from one used to produce legal briefs. A network should be designed toward solving specific business problems.

Most computers can be made to talk to each other, given the right combination of network hardware and software. Sometimes, however, it makes more sense to throw out the old hardware or software that cannot communicate easily and start fresh. Along the same lines, if your company uses 75 types of word processing software, set a corporate standard and get rid of the other 74 word processors.

A successful enterprise network accommodates existing equipment. The challenge is that the integration process is now left to MIS and to the user.

# Is an Enterprise-Wide Network Worth the Risk?

An enterprise network can give a company significant strategic advantages. Its improvements can be small—such as more efficiently using MIS resources—or great—enabling a company to interact more quickly and flexibly with its suppliers and customers. An enterprise network can save your company money, both in MIS and in the business units.

A network can deliver information into worker's hands, empowering them to make better, faster decisions. It can foster communication so that decisions are not made with old information. It can reduce inventories, thereby freeing up cash. Powered by the right corporate philosophy, a network can help a large corporation act like an agile, small company. When a company relies heavily on its network as a critical business tool, however, it must properly and carefully plan, design, deploy, and manage the network, considering the business and technology issues involved.

The challenge is that an enterprise-wide network is not a cookie-cutter endeavor. Although it's relatively simple to install a 40-node NetWare LAN, there are no similar time-tested recipes for building a corporate-wide network. Each network must be tailored to a company's business goals, corporate structure, and philosophy. If implemented properly, however, the rewards of an enterprise network are great.

This book guides you through the steps of building an enterprise network for a competitive advantage. The network must be carefully planned and designed, involving not only the IS managers but also the business managers and key end users. The company must carefully analyze the requirements, write a request for proposal (RFP), and evaluate the costs, benefits, and risks of the proposed solutions. The network must be budgeted and justified.

Every aspect of an enterprise network must be planned, from the cabling system to applications to the management. Every aspect must be selected carefully, with an eye toward accommodating existing and future systems and applications. Interoperability among dissimilar types of computers is crucial, so that users gain access to a transparent network. This way, they can freely access information stored in different formats and locations. Wide area services must be considered carefully, because the WAN is the key aspect of an enterprise network. Users will judge the network by how quickly and easily they can access remote resources.

Applications are the lifeblood of the network, and designers should pay particular attention here. Workers should be able to retain their existing applications, as well as reap the benefits of the client/server architecture, by gaining access to databases and E-mail company-wide, as well as to the new class of work-flow and imaging applications. Because of the client/server architecture, the core of the application can stay on the mainframe, while portions are offloaded to the end users' computers.

Management of the network is particularly important. Because an enterprise network runs mission-critical applications, downtime is not easily tolerated. Because money is lost when the network fails, the network must be managed proactively rather than reactively. Tools, techniques, and strategies are crucial; yet the reality of management is a far cry from what is needed.

A network can offer a company a significant competitive advantage that no company should be without. Although building an enterprise network is a challenge requiring the involvement of many different groups of people, it can bring your company considerable cost savings and business advantages.

# Identifying the Business Issues and Requirements of Networking

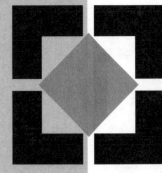

## CHAPTER 2

*Objectives:*

1. To explain why as companies deploy networks across their corporate structures, requirement analyses, requests for proposal, and formal bidding on network prospects become the norm.

2. To describe the motivations and benefits of a requirements analysis.

3. To lead you step-by-step through the requirements analysis, request for proposal, and contracting processes.

# The Requirements Analysis

An enterprise-wide network built without a clear understanding of your company's business problems and without a plan to solve these problems is doomed to fail. Quite simply, you can't efficiently solve a problem if you don't fully grasp the situation. If you don't know what you want to do or how to get there, you won't arrive at the correct end point.

Let's say you want to build a tool shed in your backyard. You decide that the shed should be 20 feet long, 15 feet wide, and 10 feet high. If you draw plans for the shed, figure the precise length of the beams, and carefully measure the wood before you cut, your shed has a good chance of being square and plumb. If, however, you decide that you don't need to carefully plan and measure the dimensions, your shed is quite likely to be lopsided, unless you've built a similar shed many times before. You'll wish you had bought a kit for a pre-fabricated shed instead of building it from scratch.

Building an enterprise-wide network without a plan will lead to a similar end result. An unplanned network will be patched and ill-fitted, not elegant and efficient. In the end, an ill-fitting network will be unstable, unreliable, and cost your company money instead of saving it money.

The first step in defining the problems—and therefore the goals—of your network is to perform a *requirements analysis*. A requirements analysis helps you evaluate the business value of a technology decision. Formulating the requirements analysis defines the goals and benefits of the network for you, which then helps you design the network. The analysis helps you pinpoint and prioritize the portions of the computing system you want to improve or expand. Defining your requirements can help you focus your efforts so that you save the company money by building an enterprise-wide network, rather than wasting it by including unnecessary features. After you define the goals, you can better outline the benefits and justify the purchase to upper management. A thorough analysis is the basis for a well-written request-for-proposal document, from which systems integrators will work to propose network designs. Finally, a clear understanding of the goals provides a measure for the network's success.

A requirement analysis is an alien concept to many traditional (or departmental) LAN people. Many departmental LANs and LAN managers fly by the seat of their pants. Quite often, a departmental LAN administrator purchases the network operating system and applications from the software store around the corner and buys the network hardware through mail-order catalogues. The administrator may also enlist the help of a value-added reseller. Either way, the departmental LAN manager probably won't perform a thorough requirement analysis, because he or she is buying a single network for the department rather than for the entire corporation. In this case, a haphazard approach suffices because the network doesn't affect the corporation's business-line functions. If the network fails, only the users in the department are affected, not the majority of a company's employees. Additionally, the purchase price of the network is inexpensive enough that the manager probably won't need upper management's approval.

Today, MIS personnel—rather than workgroup LAN managers or department heads—typically install an enterprise-wide network. MIS managers perform careful analyses and follow formalized procedures before installing new mainframe or minicomputer hardware or software. They are accustomed to planning for complex hardware and software upgrades.

Although MIS managers understand the steps to planning and deploying mission-critical, mainframe-based applications, they may find that networks can be more confusing and complex than mainframes because of the wide variety of hardware, software, and protocols used and the multitude of vendors providing them. Often, MIS people have little experience with the issues that LAN administrators face daily, such as how to make clone PCs talk to a mainframe. MIS needs to evaluate its current requirements analysis procedures to ensure that they meet the needs of an enterprise-wide network. Information systems are a key underpinning of business, as important as the manufacturing systems and workers (see Figure 2.1). As such, computing systems must be considered a strategic asset.

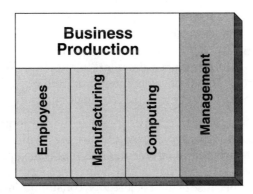

*Figure 2.1.* *Computing as a strategic business component.*

# Why You Should Perform a Requirements Analysis

A requirements analysis helps you to:

- Evaluate the networks' and computers' current state so that you know what problems need to be solved.
- Define the goals and benefits of the network, which helps you design the network.
- Focus on the goals of the network, which enables you to build a cost-effective network.
- Pinpoint and prioritize the systems to be improved or expanded.
- Justify the network's purchase to upper management.
- Write an effective request for proposal.
- Define a metric for the network's success.

# How to Perform a Requirements Analysis

Various companies perform requirements analyses in different ways and in varying depths, according to their corporate policies and cultures. Your requirements analysis document may be anywhere from 10 to 150 pages long. Some companies perform the requirements analysis themselves. Others enlist the aid of a consultant or system integrator. Still other companies hire a management consultant to define their strategic computing directions.

Unless your MIS department is very experienced in designing and installing enterprise-wide networks, you should enlist the help of a consultant or integrator to perform your requirements analysis. Because of their experience in building networks, consultants can help you clarify the business and technology issues. Because of their objectivity, consultants may help you view issues and solutions differently. Consultants can ensure that you design a network that can be built and managed efficiently. Consultants can be integral in helping you select the best design.

A consultant's role can be adapted to your needs. You may need a consultant for only one part of building the enterprise-wide network, or you may need different consultants for different aspects. Network integrators are changing how they sell their services, enabling you to contract for whatever service you need, whether it is analysis, design, procurement, or management and support. For example, you may contract with a consultant to help you define your system requirements, and then bid the network design to systems integrators. The integrators then design the network and procure the equipment, and the consultant helps you select the best proposal. You may also contract with a systems integrator's consulting division for the requirements analysis and with its integration group for the network design. Your company's purchasing department can procure the equipment, which the integrator installs.

# Building a Business Model

An enterprise-wide network is a corporate asset rather than a technology plaything. It exists only to perform business functions. As such, you must factor the network's role into your company's business structure. To successfully build an enterprise-wide network, you must build a business model from which you derive the technological and physical models of the network. Most large, successful integration firms employ this or a similar strategy, including Electronic Data Systems.

Application and computing architectures play a key role in the business architecture (see Figure 2.2). A company's business is based on its data management architecture, its applications, and network architecture. Successfully analyzing the requirements, and ultimately, successfully building the enterprise-wide network, requires you, a technologist at heart, to think like a businessperson. A common mistake some managers make is thinking only in terms of technology.

Before you can begin to assess the enterprise-wide network's requirements, you need to gain a general understanding of the unit's business. Start by building a business model of the network. A business model is a written description of how the company's business is performed. It usually does not mention the computing systems, but rather focuses on the business practices and work flow. First build a model that is an overview of the entire company's work flow, then build models for each department's work flow. Describe in detail how the work flows, who performs the work, and the dependencies among the workgroups and departments.

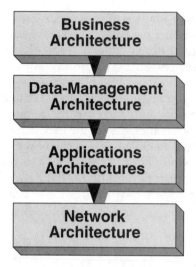

**Figure 2.2.** *The relationship between the business and MIS.*

To illustrate its points, this chapter refers to a fictitious publishing company, Animate Publishing. Its business model and project object are shown in the section called "Publishing at Animate." A work-flow diagram of a business model for this publishing company is shown in Figure 2.3.

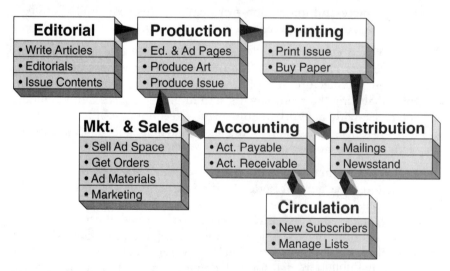

**Figure 2.3.** *Animate Publishing's business model, showing how a magazine is produced and the involvement and responsibilities of the individual departments, suppliers, and customers.*

You should also write a business model for each department in an organization, showing the work flow in detail. The model in Figure 2.4 is for an editorial/production department of a publishing company, and it shows how words and pictures are combined to form magazine pages.

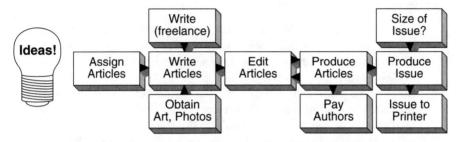

*Figure 2.4.* *The business model of the magazine publishing company's editorial/production department.*

To write the business model, designate a project team made up of key managers, users, and MIS personnel. Name a project leader. Interview the business units' managers and key end users in each division to determine their functions and how their computer systems help them perform their jobs. Find out how the business functions flow from one department to another. How do the information and tasks flow from one employee to another? What are the dependencies—who needs to approve what and what work must be accomplished first? Where are the bottlenecks in the existing system—is the response time slow, and is the process inefficient? Interviewing end users is an essential but often overlooked step in determining a network's needs. Ultimately, you build the network for the end users, so it's critical to get their insight on many issues.

# Publishing at Animate

To illustrate the process of defining an enterprise-wide network's project goals and systems requirements, this chapter uses a fictitious company, Animate Publishing Company, as an example. The business description is as follows:

> Animate Publishing Company is a trade magazine publisher. It publishes 15 magazines on the topic of animal care and veterinarian issues. Animate is headquartered in New York, with sales and editorial offices in San Francisco, Chicago, Atlanta, and Seattle. The

company employs 500 people. Editorial, advertising sales, and magazine production occur in New York, although bureau writers and regional salespeople are located around the country. Accounting is centralized in New York.

The project goal is as follows:

> It is the intent of the Animate management, with the aid of its MIS department and outside consultants, to network all locations of Animate. Animate management hopes to shorten the production cycles, enabling its advertising salespeople to book ads closer to the magazine's printer date, which the magazine hopes will increase ad revenues by giving the advertiser greater flexibility. The computerized production system also would make the magazine content less dated, which in the long run will increase subscriptions. The magazine expects this flexibility to increase advertising bookings, and ultimately to increase revenue.

> Additionally, Animate expects to gain efficiency and improve accuracy by moving to a computer-based, advertising sales booking system rather than the current quasi-automated system. Animate expects to gain efficiency by moving to a computer-based production system, instead of requiring much of it to be done manually. The system is expected to increase productivity while freeing up workers for other projects.

# Improve the Existing System

Interview the business unit managers and key users to discover what they want the networked computing system to accomplish. Their answers will run the gamut from "I want exactly what I have today" to forward-thinking, cutting-edge ideas such as just-in-time (JIT) manufacturing or electronic document interchange (EDI). Do the department heads want to reduce the amount of money spent on express delivery and messenger services while improving communication? Do they want to decrease inventory turns? Do they want to communicate electronically with suppliers and customers?

These early stages are the times for imagination and brainstorming. Ask the managers what features and services they would want if price were no object and the sky were the limit. Ask what displeases managers and key end users about the existing computing system. Is the system down too much? Is it too slow? What information sources would they like to access? Next, ask the business unit managers to prioritize their business requirements. Which are wish list items and which are essential? This list of priorities will help you identify the phases in which the network will be installed.

During this stage, business unit managers should examine their manual and computer-based procedures for efficiency. Automating an inefficient business procedure results in an inefficient computer system. Many economies can be gained by automating a paper-based process, but the actual process may need to change. Do the business managers want to change procedures or will alterations too greatly disrupt the business practices?

# Business Under the New Paradigm

Once you understand the unit's business, you must explain to the unit managers how a network could fundamentally change and improve their business. Client/server computing, and the enterprise-wide network that enables it, are the new paradigms of computing, quite unlike the mainframes and minicomputers familiar to most business managers. A network is far different than dumb terminals wired back to an intelligent host, functionally and technically. You will spend more time explaining how a network can change a business unit if your company is entrenched in the traditional hierarchical mainframe architecture than if departmental networks are the norm.

When explaining how a network can change the business, talk in terms the manager understands. A common failing is to talk in technology terms rather than productivity terms. Business managers do not understand or care about the benefits of 100Mbps Fiber Distributed Data Interface (FDDI) versus the 16Mbps Token Ring. They don't care about collision detection versus token passing. They do, however, care if the network can enable them to manufacture more valves, sell more cars, or reduce the company's inventory. Using Animate Publishing as an example, explain that with a network, workers not only will be able to move text, but also video and graphics, from user to user. Information will move as a unit rather than as disjointed words, numbers, and pictures. Explain how the business unit manager can reduce the time customers wait on the phone, which will ultimately increase customer satisfaction. Give specific, descriptive examples to make them understand what impact the network will have on business processes and productivity.

Building a business model of the computing system isn't a simple task. There is a shortage of technical people who can understand the business issues. Most technology people understand only technology, and most business people firmly grasp only the business aspects. This lack of understanding is one of the deadly failings of building networks, whether departmental or global. Business and technology people must be "cross-trained" to build efficient and useful enterprise-wide networks. Therefore, build the business model with careful attention to the business issues.

Building a business model also helps you gain upper management's support and shows that you understand the business side of the situation as well as the technology side. It enables you to quantify the benefits of the enterprise-wide network in terms a business manager can understand: improved customer satisfaction, faster turnaround, improved worker productivity, decreased MIS spending, and so on. A common strategy is to find a business unit manager who will benefit or find the opportunity to benefit from the enterprise-wide network you want to build. The manager then acts as your "sponsor" to upper management.

# Successfully Dealing with Users

An enterprise-wide network is built for business. End users accomplish the everyday demands of the business. So ultimately, you'll have to please your users with your network. The users, however, are often forgotten during the planning, designing, and implementation phases of an enterprise-wide network. When the system is completely installed, the users complain that it "doesn't work" or is "always down." They'll say that printing takes longer than before and they don't like the network. Instead of using the network system as a tool, they view it as an impediment.

The key to successfully dealing with users is communication. MIS and users don't talk enough to each other. Often, they don't tell the whole story. The MIS manager tells the users, "We're putting in a corporate network, and it's going to be great!" But that's not enough.

During the requirements analysis phase, talk to key end users as well as the business units' managers to identify their requirements for the jobs. You should talk to the users who are the most savvy about computer systems or who have the greatest computer-dependent workload. Because they use the network every day, the end users often have the best insight into how the business functions and computer systems interrelate. Then it's up to MIS to choose the equipment that best meets the users' business requirements, instead of merely choosing the newest or fastest products available.

Designate at least one user to be the liaison between the user community and MIS so that users are ensured of representation during the planning, design, and implementation phases. Invite the user liaison to planning meetings with other users in each department. The liaison should hold meetings with the end users, notifying them of developments and progress. This chain of feedback maintains a constant flow of information between MIS and users, and increases the chance that users will be happy with the enterprise-wide networks that MIS builds.

Users' discontent is often rooted in the wrong expectations. MIS must ensure that users' expectations meet their own. Give users a realistic picture of what the network can do. Tell them how much downtime you expect. (During the requirements analysis, you should ask how much downtime they can tolerate.) Give users honest estimates of the installation schedule. MIS often "sells" the whole network at once to users. When MIS tells the users that a corporate-wide network will be installed, but doesn't tell them that VAX connectivity won't be put in for a year, the users who need the VAX connectivity will be unhappy. Tell users if their piece of the connectivity puzzle is last.

Keep in mind that you have two groups of users when you install a network. The first group of users, the *MIS users*, is made up of the people who maintain and operate the network. The second group, the *end users*, is comprised of those who use the network for the applications. The goals and needs of the MIS users and end users can be diametrically opposed. The MIS users are cost-conscious; they want an efficient and easily managed network. End users don't care about cost; they want the network to help them do their jobs better. Assure both groups that you will train them to use the new system, because the end users may be fearful that the network will be difficult and strange to use, and the MIS users may be rooted in mainframes and may fear that they'll lose their jobs.

Also keep in mind that most people don't like change. They've become familiar with their applications and computers; many don't want to deviate from their memorized procedures. When designing how the users will interact with the system, you may want to simulate the existing interaction (provided that it makes sense in the new environment). Also remember that you cannot take functionality away from users without dissatisfying many of them. You must add to existing functionality without taking anything away.

# The Technology Model

Once you've constructed a business model of the network and determined what procedures need to be changed or streamlined, you are ready to build a technology model of the network. The technology model describes in broad terms how computing equipment will be used to achieve the business model. To build the technology model, you must audit the existing equipment, determine the system requirements, and assess the state of today's and tomorrow's technology.

# Audit the Existing Equipment

Few companies have the luxury of building an enterprise-wide network from scratch. Instead, they must accommodate the computer systems in place, some of which may have been used for 10 years. You must evaluate which of these systems will continue to have strategic value for the company, and which can be safely discarded. Before you can begin, however, you must find out exactly what you have.

For each department in each office location, inventory the existing computer equipment to determine what is used. Do the employees have IBM personal computers, Macintoshes, Sun workstations, VAXs, Hewlett-Packards, AS/400s, System/3Xs, and 370 mainframes, for example? What networks are used: SNA, DECnet, TCP/IP, NetWare, AppleShare, Apollo Domain, or VINES? Where is this equipment located? What is the condition of this equipment?

Does it make financial sense to continue to use the older technologies, or is it more cost-effective to upgrade to newer technologies? For example, your company's IBM mainframes may use bisync, a decades-old protocol. If you have a significant amount of money invested in the software and the system isn't having problems, however, there's probably little reason to change it. The enterprise-wide network will have to accommodate the bisync network. Similarly, you may have a computer system whose cost of maintenance far outweighs its usefulness.

After you've audited the hardware systems, do the same for the applications. What applications are used in each office? How many people use each application, and how much traffic do they generate? Will (and can) these applications be used in the enterprise-wide network? Where are these applications located and how will users access them in the new environment? Do better or more efficient applications exist, and do the business units want to upgrade?

## Automating the Tedium of Inventory

Regardless of whether you are counting nuts and bolts, designer fashions, or computer equipment, taking inventory is a tedious, time-consuming, error-prone, and ultimately dated exercise in futility. It's easy to miss items or incorrectly count them. As soon as you've finished and one item is changed or moved, the result of many days of labor is out-of-date.

Soon, a clipboard and a pencil may be the outmoded tools of inventory. A bar code wand or even software may replace the tried-and-true tools.

Every piece of equipment—from cable segment to memory card—on the enterprise-wide network should be labeled. Keeping a precise inventory of network and computing equipment enables you to account for the computer equipment purchased. It also enables you to better assess what you need to purchase. Label every piece of equipment with an identification numbering scheme that takes into account the equipment's location in the department and in the company.

The older method is to write these codes on labels and affix them to the equipment. With bar code labels and readers, however, the process can be simplified to the swipe of a wand. Although bar codes simplify the tracking of equipment, technicians must still walk around the office and physically locate every piece of equipment.

Another improvement is software that automatically takes inventory for you. Several software publishers sell packages that automatically inventory the network hardware, software, and applications installed on users' computers. Functionality is still rather limited, although it is improving. Packages for the Macintosh generally offer more functionality than the packages for the PC, primarily because the Mac is capable of providing more information about itself than the PC or DOS is.

Inventory software works by querying the nodes on the network, asking for information such as CPU type, available memory, available disk storage, disk drives, add-in adapter cards—such as network interface cards, fax boards, and memory boards— graphics capabilities, applications on the workstations (including version numbers), operating system versions, and network operating system drivers.

The software compiles a database of this information, which can be used for reference as well as for troubleshooting. Administrators can periodically run automatic inventory software, giving them a weekly, monthly, or quarterly snapshot of the network resources.

# Determine the System Requirements

After you've assessed the current computer inventory, you must determine the requirements of the new system. To determine the technical parameters of the network, view the system requirements from the businessperson's perspective rather than the technologist's perspective. Most MIS people attack the problem from a technological viewpoint when they should take it from a business tack.

Questions to determine the system requirements phase include:

- *What needs to be connected?* Do the units need to talk to a small (or large) number of people over a small area, or do they need to talk to a small (or large) number of people over a geographically large area? The volume and distribution of traffic will help you determine the computing power of the computer systems, as well as the types and speeds of connectivity equipment and services.

- *What existing hardware and software will be used in the new environment?* Of the existing systems, which ones will be retained in the enterprise-wide network? Can these systems be networked? Does the existing hardware and software operate gracefully on a network? Are there any corporate standards for hardware and software, or do any applications predominate? What hardware and software must be added to achieve the business goals?

- *How much information will be transferred?* The amount of information transferred determines the amount of network bandwidth required. Will more or less information be transferred over the enterprise-wide network than is currently transmitted? Determine this by calculating the number of users, how many transactions they commit per day, and the average size of the transaction. This determines the type and speed of media-access technology and wide area network services.

- *What network response time is needed?* Can users tolerate one second, a half-second, or two seconds of delay? This measurement determines the required speed of the hardware, software, and communications links.

- *What network availability is required?* Determine how critical the network is to the success of the business. Does the network need to be available 24 hours a day, seven days a week (24 x 7) or just 8 hours a day, 5 days a week (8 x 5)? Does the current uptime need to be increased?

- *What service response time is needed?* Again, assess the network's criticality to determine the necessary service response time. How important is the network's service to the operation of the business? Will the company lose $5 million or $100,000 if the network is down for one hour? How much money will the company lose if the network is down for two hours?

- *How much growth is projected?* What is the current volume of usage and how is that expected to change over the next six months, one year, and two years? Even if you carefully plan the network and anticipate growth, the requirements are likely to change and increase. Plan that the system will grow before you have to react to the fact that it grew.

# The System Requirements of Animate Publishing

■ *Connectivity*—Animate management and its MIS department have decided to network the entire corporation in phases over the next 12 months. The New York headquarters will be networked first, because that is where the majority of work occurs and where the most people work. When the New York network is up and running, the remote offices will be networked in the following order: San Francisco, Chicago, Seattle, and Atlanta. The order has been determined by the number of people who work in each office. Additionally, the San Francisco office is astute with computers and is willing to work out the quirks of connecting the remote offices to New York.

■ *Existing equipment*—Although MIS wants to retain as much investment in existing equipment as possible, it is aware that much of the technology is quite old and may need to be replaced.

The designers must evaluate whether they will impose standards on what types of desktop computers are used and what applications will be run. For example, the workers in this company use a combination of PCs and Macintoshes and a range of applications. Do they impose standards in the headquarters? In the remote offices? As for network hardware, the designers must decide if the older or slower technologies will be retained, or if a corporate standard will be retroactive. What network operating system is best in this environment?

■ *Volume of data transmitted*—Currently, data is split among mini-computer and LAN systems. Traffic in the new network is expected to be medium to heavy. Most applications are traditional office automation applications: spreadsheets, word processing, sales bookings, electronic mail, and printing, which place low demands on the network bandwidth. The nature of publishing, however, demands large graphic files. The company publishes 15 magazines; each monthly magazine averages 150 pages in length. Each page ranges from 8MB to 10MB in size. This places a heavy demand on network availability, although this takes place only in New York—on a local network.

■ *Response time*—In New York, the best case is less than one minute, and the worst case is two minutes, as agreed on by the publishers of each of the magazines. For the remote offices accessing New York, the best case is two minutes and the worst case is seven minutes.

■ *Availability*—New York network and remote connections must be available six days a week, 18 hours a day. Night shifts are run in New York. System availability in the remote offices is five days a week, nine hours a day.

- *Service response time*—Two hours.

- *Growth*—The company plans to acquire or start five more magazines in the next year. The network must accommodate, at minimum, one-third more load without any effects on response time or availability.

# Existing Systems and Inventory at Animate Publishing

Currently Animate uses minicomputers and personal computers. Accounting and magazine production are host-based; sales and editorial are accomplished through PCs and Macintoshes. Overall, networks are still in departmental/workgroup state, and there are many stand-alone PCs. There is quite a bit of old computing equipment. There are few corporate standards for networks, applications, and hardware. The inventory list is as follows:

- *New York headquarters:*

   *Editorial Production*—Atex publishing system, six CPUs (mirrored), four disk drives, eight Atex laser printers, and 100 terminals. Film output machine connected to Editorial network via gateway. Two 9600-baud modems for dial-in for authors.

   *Editorial*—NetWare LAN, Atex terminals. 80-user NetWare 3.11, 25MHz 386 server, 1GB drive (mirrored), EtherNet hardware. Gateway between NetWare and Atex. Four laser printers, 20 dot-matrix printers. Of the 80 nodes, 70 are 286s, 20 are XTs, and 10 are 386s. Comm server, fax server. Applications: Xywrite word processing, cc:mail electronic mail, Paradox databases, and Intel LANspool print spooling software.

   *Art*—Eight-node Sitka/TOPS network with EtherNet hardware. Of the eight nodes, five are Mac IIcxi, three are Mac IIsi, and all have color monitors. Two LaserWriters. One 9600-baud modem. Applications: Quark Express, PhotoShop, Aldus PageMaker.

   *Sales and Marketing*—Workgroup PC networks for each magazine: AppleShare, Novell NetWare, Sitka/TOPS, Artisoft LANtastic. One Wang system. Two NetWare networks (one ELS, one NetWare 286), three and ten users, respectively, running a mixture of XTs, ATs (on ARCnet), and Macintoshes (on LocalTalk). Two laser printers, five dot-matrix printers. Ten 2400- and 9600-baud modems. Applications: WordPerfect, Symantec Timeline, ACT contact-management software, Paradox, desktop presentation software.

One AppleShare network on LocalTalk with five users, one LaserWriter, three AppleShare networks on EtherNet with six, seven, and eight users respectively, and two LaserWriters. All of the preceding items are networked together. Applications: Microsoft Word, CE Software QuickMail, and presentation graphics software.

One TOPS network with LocalTalk hardware, five users, and one LaserWriter. Applications: Microsoft Word, Sitka InBox mail, and presentation graphics software.

Two LANtastic networks with five AT users, one laser printer, and three dot-matrix printers. Five modems. Applications: WordPerfect, Lotus 1-2-3, Foxbase, and presentation graphics software.

*Administration*—One Wang system, 10 stand-alone PCs. Applications: WordStar, WordPerfect, Word, Human Resources software (non-networked), Lotus 1-2-3, Borland Quattro, and Microsoft Excel.

*Circulation*—22-node LANtastic network with 12 ATs, 10 386s, 20 dot-matrix printers, and one laser printer. Applications: WordPerfect, Lotus 1-2-3, circulation-projection software.

*Accounting*—HP 8000 with accounting software. Twenty users.

■ *Remote sales offices and editorial bureaus:*

*San Francisco*—Five editorial people and five salespeople. Two editors have 286s with dot-matrix printers, and three have 386s with laser printers. Two sales people have Mac IIs with LaserWriters, and three have PS/2s. There are no networks, and everyone has a stand-alone modem.

*Chicago*—Twenty editorial people and ten salespeople. NetWare LAN with ten 286s, 15 Macs, all on EtherNet. Applications: WordPerfect, Xywrite, ACT, Castelle fax server, J&L comm server, Network Courier electronic mail, LANspool.

*Atlanta*—One sales person and two editorial people. All have 386s with laser printers and modems.

*Seattle*—One sales person working from home. One 386, one laser printer, one fax board, and one modem.

# Building the Technology Model

Once you've determined the system requirements, you're ready to build the technology model. In this step, you determine how you are going to meet the business requirements from a technology point of view. Most network designers are most familiar with building the technology model.

First examine the existing systems. What will you keep in the enterprise-wide network? What is not suitable? How will you reconcile the different network hardware, operating systems, and application software currently in place?

Next examine the technology currently available. What is the state of the art? Do you want to use a state-of-the-art design? Do you even need the state-of-the-art? For example, if you are building a network for a purchasing department, FDDI is probably overkill, even if the department processes a large number of requisitions. However, FDDI makes more sense in an engineering department, where large files are common. But you could also build a hub-and-spoke EtherNet LAN where each user essentially has his or her own subnetwork. Building a good technology model means you must carefully balance the company's needs and your wants. Use only as much technology as necessary. Don't buy a Ferrari when a Hyundai will do.

Consider the ramifications of using state-of-the-art technology versus proven technology. Are you willing to be on the cutting edge? For example, EtherNet and Token Ring are proven technologies. FDDI, although it entices with huge capacities, is still new. Few designers and technicians are familiar with fiber and FDDI. Troubleshooting tools are rare and expensive. The investment could, however, pay off.

Evaluate which product families meet your business requirements. For example, will bridges or routers best suit your needs? (It depends on the volume of network traffic, the number of subnetworks, the distribution of subnetworks, and the experience level of the managers.) Should you design a network with a mesh or star topology? (It depends on your company's organization.) What speed communications links does the network need? (It depends on what will travel over the network. Do you want to combine voice and data services?) Determining these requirements means you must have an understanding of the values of the different types of technologies as well as a thorough understanding of the volumes and types of traffic that traverse the network.

Next, research what technologies will become available in the near-term. What are the long-term projections for these technologies? How will your network design accommodate tomorrow's technology evolution? For example, what about running voice, video, and data over FDDI instead of just data today? What is the next speed increment for FDDI? Will there be a faster EtherNet, or is the upgrade path directly to FDDI?

The technologist's skill is evaluating what is available today, projecting what will be available tomorrow, and merging them into an elegant, efficient network design. For example, today you can run EtherNet and a 4Mbps Token Ring over unshielded twisted-pair or telephone wire. Many manufacturers market products that run a 16Mbps Token Ring over unshielded twisted-pair wire, including IBM. Some vendors have demonstrated FDDI over unshielded twisted-pair wire, although it is an untried technology. It's a likely conclusion that you can run twisted-pair wiring for the department up to the wiring closet, rather than coaxial cable.

# Animate's Technology Model

In the previous steps, Animate corporate and MIS management determined the system requirements for the enterprise-wide network and evaluated the state of its existing equipment. The next step is to build a technology model of the network. In this exercise, the Animate MIS department evaluates the existing technology in an attempt to find the one system design that will best fit the business needs of the network.

Animate's enterprise-wide network can be built using client/server or host-based technologies. Both are currently in use at the company, but the designers must determine which technology will carry them into the next decade as well as provide good performance and service at a good price.

The designers start with the core of the business—the publishing/production system. Editorial currently uses Atex, a host-based system; however, an alternative is desktop publishing with Macintoshes or UNIX workstations. The graphic artists currently use Macs.

The designers must evaluate the state of the art in each case. Atex runs on proprietary hardware (modified DEC hosts), although it is being ported to a newer hardware platform, which will soon be available. The company's existing investment and expertise is host-based production; however, it is becoming increasingly difficult to hire new employees with Atex experience because the market has shifted toward desktop publishing. The proprietary system is costly, because Animate is locked into a single-vendor solution. It is becoming increasingly difficult to find parts and get service.

The quality of desktop publishing systems is rapidly improving and the price is rapidly dropping. Currently, only the graphic artists have desktop publishing experience. Moving to desktop publishing would require all new hardware and complete retraining of personnel. The editorial and production staffs could use either Macintosh or UNIX desktop systems.

After the designers have outlined the technology models—Atex, Macintosh, or UNIX—they must decide which is the most appropriate. The designers must be familiar with each type of system's capabilities and costs. For example, Quark and PageMaker can both be used for Macintosh systems. Similarly, Frame and Intergraf make UNIX-based systems. The designers must decide, based on the system requirements and budgets, which direction is most appropriate.

The designers must go through a similar process for the other systems used: accounting, sales, circulation, and so on. (For the sake of brevity, we cover only the editorial and production system here.) Similarly, the designers must evaluate the feasibility of systems such as electronic mail, fax servers, databases, and print sharing.

The designers must decide the network topology and how the remote offices will be connected to headquarters. Some of the things they must consider include the following:

- Should the network take on a star topology, where all remote sites are connected directly back to the New York hub? Would some of the offices benefit from connecting directly to each other without going through New York?

- What technology will be used for the network connectivity—bridges or routers? Is the traffic on the network in New York high enough to warrant local bridges or routers? Which technology is more appropriate?

- What network hardware is necessary? Will the existing hardware types be retained? Does EtherNet or Token Ring provide sufficient bandwidth, or is a high-speed network like FDDI warranted? Will the network be efficient if it uses many small subnetworks?

The designers must also meet the availability and service requirements. For example, because the network must be available on most nights and weekends, redundant disks and uninterruptible power supplies will be placed on critical file servers to ensure that lost work can be recovered quickly and that downtime can be minimized. Are mirrored disks enough, or is a disk array warranted? How much battery power is needed on the uninterruptible power supply?

# Building the Physical Model

When you've decided on the proper technology for the network, you must evaluate how it meets the business requirements. Work backward from the technology model, matching its solutions to the business needs. No technology solution will meet all your business requirements. That means it's up to the integrator, whether in-house or hired, to weigh the options and match the technology available to the business requirements.

Does the proposed technology solution meet the business requirements? For example, if your business moves its employees around often, one business requirement would be high mobility. Can you disconnect and reconnect workstations to the network quickly and easily? Other issues include flexibility and low cost. Does the network design meet the corporate standards? Can it be built and managed within budget? Does the new network accommodate the existing computer systems and networks?

After you've determined that the technology model is sound, you can build the physical network model. The physical model describes the specifics of the technology model. The physical model is a very detailed description of the network, whereas the technology model talks in more general terms.

Although the designers need to be quite familiar with each technology and only generally familiar with products, the physical modeling phase requires them to be intimate with available products. From here, the designers evaluate the features and functions of the appropriate products and determine which best fit the systems' needs. After doing basic research to determine what is available, designers will get products in-house to test that they truly work as their manufacturers claim. To find appropriate products, the designers should look to the experience of consultants, fellow MIS people, and integrators, as well as to secondary resources such as product reviews in magazines and journals.

In the physical modeling phase, the designers describe exactly what components are needed, how many pieces are required, where they will be located, and how the pieces fit together into an enterprise-wide network. This can be achieved through the request for proposal (RFP) process.

# The Physical Network Model at Animate

After the Animate Publishing Company designers have determined which of the technology models is best for the company—Mac, UNIX, or Atex—they must begin to design the details of the network. They must build a model of the physical network. The designers must thoroughly research and evaluate the products available for the technology model they've chosen. For example, if Animate MIS and corporate management chose a UNIX-based editorial/production system, the designers would then examine the features and functionality of the available production systems, such as Intergraf's Interleaf and Frame's FrameMaker.

Then the designers must evaluate which bridges or routers will be used. Should routers or bridges be used at points of connection to the wide area network? Does the San Francisco office need local bridging? Similarly, the designers must determine the brands of the network operating system, applications, server hardware, desktop computers, backup, uninterruptible power supply, and so on. The designers do so by evaluating the leading products in each category and choosing the one that provides the best performance at the best price.

# Writing the Request for Proposal

Once you've built the business and technology models, you must write a *request for proposal* (RFP). Your RFP is largely based on the information gathered in the requirements analysis phase. In essence, the RFP tells the integrator, "Here's our company's business and computing problem. How would you, as a network designer and integrator, solve it? How many of these pieces can you solve yourself and how many will you contract to other vendors?" You distribute the RFP to several (usually at least three) network integrators to obtain their opinions on how to design and build the enterprise-wide network. The vendors will propose solutions based on the RFP you wrote. The enterprise-wide network's complexity and your company's culture determine the depth and scope of the RFP. RFPs may be five or 50 pages—or longer.

A second type of RFP is one where the company doesn't know what it wants. Instead, it asks the integrators and vendors to help it determine its needs and design the network. This type of proposal is often called a *request for information*, or RFI. If your company does not exactly know its requirements, it is better off with this type of proposal, because it enables you to capitalize on the expertise of an integrator or consultant.

As with the requirements analysis, you may prepare the RFP yourself or with the help of a consultant. If a consultant is involved, the RFP probably will be more detailed and complete than one you prepare alone. The RFP prepared by a consultant should include a fairly complete network design and a list of equipment you need to buy, so that the proposers will bid primarily on price. If you prepare your own RFP, you may want to rely more heavily on the integrators' design proposals and less on bottom-line cost. If you don't have the answers to all of the questions that follow, don't worry—an integrator can help you define these requirements.

The following section assumes that you are procuring consulting and integrators for your enterprise-wide network. Even if your network is designed and constructed in-house, you should go through the steps of writing proposal documents, because they not only help you justify the project to your superiors, but they also help you define the problems at hand.

# What Should Your RFP Include?

The following procedure, based on actual RFP documents prepared by consultants and in-house MIS staff, outlines what your RFP should cover.

## Introduction

The introduction outlines the scope of the RFP. It briefly describes your company, its network and business goals, and a tentative schedule for network installation.

■ *Scope*—Is the RFP for the complete planning, implementation, and post-installation support and maintenance of the enterprise-wide network? Does this exclude any offices or equipment types, such as cabling? Do you want the integrators to bid on the procurement, installation, configuration, burn-in, testing, maintenance, and support charges or a combination of these?

- *Schedule*—What is the schedule of events? List a tentative timetable for RFP release, response deadline, proposal evaluation, integrator presentations and demonstrations, contract negotiation, and installation.

- *Confidentiality*—You may want to include a statement about the RFP's confidentiality status. Your RFP contains information that your competitors would very much like to have; the bidding integrators should not divulge its contents to anyone who will use it for any purposes other than quotation.

- *Company background and goals*—In general terms, what does your company do? A law firm's business is very different than a manufacturing company's; therefore, its networks are different. To properly bid on your network, the integrators must understand your business. This section should also describe the number of employees and locations of the offices to be networked.

## The Company's Business and Network Goals

This section describes your company's vision of how a network can make its business more productive. What do you want the network to accomplish? Also, you should indicate if there are related MIS projects under way that are not covered by the RFP.

- *Network requirements*—Outline the network requirements as defined by your needs analysis. For example, you may want corporate-wide communication, but require compatibility with the existing equipment and software base, communications with host computers, a new transaction-processing application, ease of use and management, redundancy, and high performance.

- *Equipment currently used*—Enumerate the computer types and quantities used in each office. Include everything from mainframes and internetwork devices to the workstations' operating systems and memory-management software. Get this information from the inventory performed during the requirements analysis.

- *Cabling issues*—What cable types exist and how much of each is available at each location? Will the network use the existing cabling plant or should the integrator propose cabling solutions? Is a site visit required?

- *Compliance with corporate standards*—State your corporate hardware and software standards. For example, your company may have standardized on Compaq SystemPros for file servers. Can the integrator make any exceptions to your standards?

■ *Implementation schedule*—Most enterprise-wide networks are installed in phases, because of the network's complexity and budgetary restrictions. Describe the order in which departments will be networked. Include target dates.

## Proposal Requirements

What do you want the integrators to include in their bids? This will help you to compare the proposed solutions on the basis of quality, timeliness, and price. The requirements vary according to your corporate culture, but include the following:

■ *Technical requirements*—The RFP asks the bidding integrators to include the names, model numbers, and prices for all proposed hardware, as well as the names, release numbers, and prices of all proposed software. The integrators should also provide you with diagrams of the proposed network. The RFP asks for delivery dates.

■ *Integrator requirements*—Along with the technical requirements, the RFP asks for references from the bidding integrators. The integrators should include in their proposal a description of their history, the personnel most likely to work on the design and installation (and a description of their experience), corporate financial statements, and references from clients with similar installations.

## Network Objectives

This section of the RFP outlines your objectives for the network.

■ *Qualifications for selecting the integrator*—An integrator's experience with building enterprise-wide networks, particularly ones in your business area, is essential. Other criteria include the quality of the design, installation services, training, and support. References, financial stability, and price competitiveness are very important. Also, specify if you are willing to work with multiple integrators or if you want one integrator to act as the general contractor.

■ *Technical network requirements*—This section should be based on your technology model. What components of the network are included? For example, do you specifically want to use routers as the internetworking device, or should the integrators suggest alternatives?

If a consultant prepared the RFP or the requirements analysis, this section will be quite detailed. If, however, you prepared the RFP yourself, this section should be more general, because you are relying on the integrators' expertise to design a network that meets your business needs.

■ *Application requirements*—For each application type, set forth your requirements. What applications do you need: electronic mail, client/server databases, work-flow software, and communication software? Do you want applications that use a graphical user interface? Do the applications need to work across multiple operating systems and network operating systems? Will you allow gateways to integrate different manufacturers' packages? What is an acceptable speed?

■ *Communications requirements*—Do users need to communicate with other offices, mainframes, minicomputers, or on-line sources? Do they subscribe to public electronic mail such as MIC Mail or on-line information sources such as Dow Jones News Service? Specify whether you require a certain operating system, network operating system, or user interface. How heavily are the applications used?

## System Specifications

The system specifications section of the RFP describes the technical specifications of the network components.

■ *Departmental level*—The RFP describes the specifications for workstations, printers, file servers, applications, print software, communications software, and electronic mail. If redundancy is needed, specify the components you want, such as duplexed servers, uninterruptible power supplies, and tape backup. The RFP should specify an acceptable amount of downtime.

■ *Enterprise and campus levels*—The RFP lays out the acceptable specifications for bridges, routers, modem servers, fax servers, and mini- or mainframe gateways, communications software and system-wide applications such as electronic mail. Specify the necessary network availability. What is an acceptable amount of downtime?

# Network Issues

This section outlines the physical model of the technology model.

- *Network operating system*—The RFP asks the integrators' proposals to specify the network operating system used in the enterprise, if a corporate standard doesn't exist. What is the network's release version, and why has the integrator specified this product over its competition?

- *Network and communications hardware*—Will a different access method be used for departmental networks than for the backbone? The RFP should require the proposals to justify the choice of Token Ring, EtherNet, or FDDI, including discussions of the transmission rate and how technology developments may affect the rate in the future.

- *Wiring concentrators*—Ask the integrator to describe the specifications of the proposed wiring hub. The integrator should defend the choice of the manufacturer, with attention to expansion, management, and cost.

- *Internetworking*—How will the departmental networks be joined? The RFP asks the integrator to defend the choice of the internetworking method as well as the product manufacturer.

- *Mini- and mainframe communication*—The RFP specifies what equipment is currently used to access the mainframes and minicomputers and asks for alternatives. The proposal should specify the hardware and software needed on the host and workstations. How many simultaneous sessions are supported? What are the limitations?

- *Wide-area communication links*—What WAN links will be used to join the different offices? The proposal should describe the wide-area connectivity requirements for each location and defend the choice according to bandwidth, cost, and manageability. Are these public or private services?

- *Remote communications*—The proposal should describe how remote communications will be accomplished. This is especially important if employees use laptops or travel extensively but require network access. What direct dial-in and dial-out access is required? Will users dial in through public data networks such as BT/Tymnet? Will users connect to public networks such as CompuServe or the Internet? Will they connect to other companies' networks?

- *Security*—What security scheme will be used to protect the network from accidental and intentional security breaches? How is external access handled and what security is provided to protect against viruses and break-ins?

■ *Network availability*—What is the network availability? Is it 24 x 7 or less? What redundancy will be included? What is the required mean time between failure on critical network components? What is the service response time from vendors and carriers? What are the carrier's uptime statistics?

■ *Network management*—How will the network be managed? How will troubleshooting be done? What tools are needed? Can management be done remotely? How many people will be required to support the network? What is the integrator's response time (if you are purchasing a maintenance contract)?

■ *Network scalability*—The proposal should address how the network will meet your company's needs in the future. Estimate corporate and network growth for the next year in the RFP, thereby enabling integrators to propose a solution that will grow with your needs. The proposal should specify the maximum number of users for the applications, servers, bridges, routers, and gateways that will be supported without significant performance degradation.

■ *Disaster recovery*—You may want to specify several scenarios of failure. For example, what happens when a wiring concentrator or bridge fails? What happens to the network if the power fails? What are the recovery procedures for a natural disaster, such as an earthquake or a tornado?

## Maintenance

Maintenance encompasses hardware and software, setting out the requirements for the network management.

■ *Consider how the hardware will be supported*—The integrator should describe where it will support your hardware. If it does not have support offices in each location where you need support, will it contract to another integrator? Define the terms of this relationship. Does the integrator maintain an on-site inventory of core components? How many hardware technicians are in each of these offices? What is the guaranteed response time? Can the integrator remotely diagnose hardware problems in your offices? What are the warranties on the proposed products?

■ *The RFP probes the software maintenance issues*—What are the warranties on the software used? What is the cost of a maintenance contract when the warranties expire? Is source code available? Again, can the integrator perform remote diagnostics and problem resolution? How many of the integrator's employees are trained in software maintenance for each office that will support your enterprise-wide network?

■ *Reliability*—Do moves, adds, and changes require system downtime? How much? Can this be done at night or on the weekends? Will the network be able to grow and change modularly and without impacting the users?

# Training

■ *Scope of training*—Specify how many people in your office need training, their skill levels, the types of training they need, and whether it can be done off-site or on-site. Estimate the number of hours of training needed. In its proposal, the integrator should describe how it will train your end users and MIS people and the cost.

■ *Documentation*—How many user manuals are included at no charge? What is the charge for additional manuals? How will special features of your network be documented and by whom?

■ *Hot-line support*—The RFP asks for the cost of the integrator's support hot-line and on-line diagnostic service.

# Network Installation Issues

Installation issues include delivery schedule, the physical requirements of the equipment, and the cost by phase of installation.

■ *Delivery schedule*—The RFP should request the estimated delivery schedule for the proposed system.

■ *Physical layout*—The proposal should also describe the physical layout, including the requirements for floor space, electrical wiring and plug connections, air conditioning, heat output, humidity, and floor load capabilities. For each product used, the proposal should describe its dimensions, weight, floor loading, voltage, amperage, wattage, phasing, plug requirements, heat dissipation per hour, and recommended temperature and humidity range.

■ *Costs by phase*—The RFP should ask for installation costs by phase. Include overtime charges for work performed on the weekend and at night. The RFP asks for shipping and freight charges by phase.

## Proposal Evaluation

The RFP should outline the criteria you will use to select the hardware and software. Hardware criteria may include price, speed, installation support, ease of operation, reliability, scalability, support, manufacturer, and maintenance costs. Software criteria may include price, flexibility and integration with existing software, reliability, maintenance support, experience of the integrator, documentation, and speed.

# Choosing an Integrator's Proposal

Depending on the integrator's expertise, each proposal will present a different physical model of your technology and business models. Compare these proposed networks to determine whether they match your technology and business models. Work backward from the physical model to your technology model, and finally to your business model. Perform a cost/benefit analysis to determine which proposal gives the best price/performance ratio. Ask the integrators for a demonstration of the network design or a small pilot network.

Check your integrator's references, which were required in the RFP. Examine the integrator's history. Has the integrator demonstrated the capability and the technical competence to install the network it proposed? Is the integrator committed to you? Does it have the engineering discipline to do revision changes? Has it met schedules in the past?

The actual selection criteria differs from company to company. If you performed your own requirements analysis, your selection of the integrator and proposal will probably be based on the design, the integrator's experience, and the price. If a consultant helped you analyze your requirements and prepare the RFP, you are more likely to base your decision on price.

# Getting the Most for Your Money

Once you've received the vendors' responses to your RFP, you should perform a cost-benefit analysis to see which one best fits your business model. You can perform a hard or soft cost-benefit analysis. A *hard cost-benefit analysis* defines—in dollars and cents—the price of installing the network and how much it will save the company. A *soft cost-benefit analysis* is more difficult to determine, and is perhaps the more important one. It extrapolates the business advantages of building an enterprise-wide network, and it projects the costs of *not* building one. Procedures for completing a cost-benefit analysis are outlined in Chapter 3, "Justifying and Budgeting the Enterprise-Wide Network."

Pricing on network products is volatile. You need to comprehend the costs of building the different technology solutions through the requirements analysis; however, pricing, whether performed by your integrator or by your purchasing department, should be done last. Because network product prices change almost daily, you can often shave large amounts off the final price.

You can use two methods to purchase the network components. The integrator can procure the equipment as well as install the network. Or you can use the integrator as a consultant only, and have your company's purchasing department procure your own hardware and software. The procurer sends a *request for quotation* (RFQ) to hardware and software suppliers. Some companies may want to bid on only the hardware and allow the integrator to procure the software.

Handling your own purchasing forces you to act as your own integrator. You must deal with multiple manufacturers rather than a single integrator. Writing contracts and assigning responsibility are more difficult; however, you may be able to save a great deal of money.

If you choose to do your own purchasing, you are safest when bidding out the hardware and software, but not the service. Service is more difficult to purchase in price only; even more than with "hard goods," with service, you get what you pay for.

# Writing the Contract: Your Insurance Policy

When you have chosen an integrator and a proposal, you must negotiate a contract. The contract sets the expectations between the integrator and your company. It outlines the terms of warranty, maintenance, payment, product licensing, ownership, and purchasing. The contract is your network's "insurance" policy. If it takes six weeks to negotiate the contract, spend the six weeks, because it's better than being unhappy after the system is installed and you discover that the contract doesn't cover the disputed item.

The contract formalizes the proposal. It legally sets the terms of the acceptance for the hardware and software, maintenance, documentation, installation schedule, network design and implementation, price, and acceptance testing.

- *Network hardware, system software, and applications*—The contract enumerates the quantities and specifications of the network and communications hardware to be used. It outlines the office's physical environment for the hardware, including temperature, humidity, and electrical requirements. The contract also covers the cabling.

  The contract includes the licenses for the system and application software used. It should specify the contact point for software problems, because multiple companies are involved. If you want access to source code, write it into the contract.

- *Maintenance*—If you are purchasing maintenance from the integrator, the contract should specify the terms, including the number of technicians available to your company and the guaranteed response time. Items to consider include the following: Does the maintenance contract cover network hardware, communications hardware, systems software, and application software?

- *Schedule of events*—Write into the contract the time schedule for installation. What is the schedule for each installation phase? What will happen if this timetable is not met?

- *Documentation*—The contract should define what constitutes documentation. It should include a statement of work, which is a diagram of the logical network, including the location of core components such as bridges and routers. It should include third-party hardware and software documentation. Will the integrator revise the documentation at no cost if changes are made during the installation process? Determine the cost for changes to the documentation after this period.

- *Implementation*—The contract describes the technical specifications of the network design. It outlines what components will be connected and how. You should base this component on the technical aspects of the integrator's proposal.

  The contract may specify that the integrator guarantees a certain system response time, expansion capability, and compatibility with certain key applications, if necessary. For example, you may want to ensure that the new network works with old DEC minis. The contract should also specify the integrator's project manager for your installation.

■ *Testing*—Installation and acceptance tests are very important, but often overlooked, elements of the requirements analysis and contract phases. An installation test is basic; it ensures that the network's components work alone and together. It is generally done with a small group of people using a pilot network. An acceptance test assures that the integrator's system meets the business and technology requirements. An acceptance test defines what it means when the network is "finished."

Write the terms of installation and acceptance testing into the contract. For example, what happens if the network does not pass the installation test within 10 days after failing the test? Who fixes the problems uncovered by the functional tests? (Chapter 5, "Designing the Local and Campus Internetwork," discusses implementation and testing in detail.)

■ *Price*—The contract specifies the price, the terms of a price adjustment, and terms of payment. After signing the contract, the price may change if you specify additional work. Understand that you may realize that you've omitted a crucial element or you need to tweak a concept. Allow for a way to renegotiate changes in your network plan, either within the planning process or in the contract.

For terms of payment, you may want to give the integrator 30 percent on signing the contract, 40 percent on delivery of the equipment, and the remaining 30 percent on successful completion of the acceptance testing.

Also, write overtime charges into the contract. The contract should specify also whether you can purchase equipment for the installation from a company other than the integrator.

# A Business Asset

In an enterprise-wide network, the business considerations are as important as the technology issues; however, they are often ignored because computer professionals are typically technologists rather than businesspeople. However, a corporation conducts its business using computer systems and networks, and therefore the designers must keep the business needs in the forefront of their minds.

A successful enterprise-wide network must be founded on a successful business plan. Performing a requirements analysis is the first step in this plan. In a requirements analysis, a team of MIS, LAN, business managers, and key users define the business goals of the network. They also identify the deficiencies in the current system. These business needs are then formalized into a requirements analysis document.

From the requirements analysis, your team should prepare a request for proposal, which is a document asking network designers and integrators to suggest solutions. Be as complete as possible when you prepare the RFP so that you can give the designers the maximum amount of information with which to work. Network designers and integrators use the request for proposal to assess the project's scope and goals, and ultimately to design the network according to your specifications.

The RFP can be used also as the basis for bidding the network to product suppliers. From there, you must carefully write the contract, because it is your insurance policy that the network will meet your business needs.

# Justifying and Budgeting the Enterprise-Wide Network

*Objectives:*

1. To prepare and establish a budget for an enterprise-wide network, and justify the associated purchases to your corporation's upper management.

2. To evaluate the different models of cost accounting, describe the economic impact of networks, expose the hidden costs of networks, and discuss how to evaluate return on investment and perform other risk-analysis measurements.

Just as companies must implement more stringent procedures for analyzing business requirements before designing enterprise-wide networks, so must they formalize the procedures to justify network expenditures. In the era of departmental and workgroup networks, many department business managers independently purchased the computer equipment they needed. The stand-alone departmental network did not affect the company's business-line functions and therefore was not managed by MIS. Because the costs were generally relatively low, the manager could include it in the department's budget. As long as expenditures did not exceed the budgeted amount, the manager could continue to improve the network.

Cost accounting and justification is rarely performed for workgroup or departmental networks, because the cost of performing this analysis outweighs the benefits. Cost accounting and justification are essential, however, if an enterprise-wide network will be a strategic part of a corporation's business. Then, these standard business practices make good business sense. MIS can determine how much the network costs so that it can budget expenditures and justify the network to management. The cost information can be used also to calculate the network's return on investment.

A conflict can arise when departments *do* cost-justify their networks, and then MIS installs an enterprise-wide network. For example, finance may have an SNA network which it budgets and cost-justifies, and engineering may have a TCP/IP network that it also budgets and cost-justifies (out of a different budget and on a different schedule). Yet these departments may both need to talk to the same remote location. A connection between these two networks is then warranted and put into place, but who pays for the link? What cost-justification scheme is used? Who manages it? This is a problem many corporations face.

# Models of Cost Accounting

Under the practice of cost accounting, the business units and departments must pay for the computing services that MIS provides. Cost accounting is a standard practice for mainframes. The typical mainframe-centric MIS department bills the users for every transaction the mainframe computes in a process called *charge-back*. Today, these cost accounting models are well-applied to networks.

As opposed to the charge-back model, you can use the *corporate utility* model to account for network costs. Under a utility model, all departments are charged equally for network service in much the same way as a company's facilities department charges for air conditioning, electricity, and so on as overhead. Which model you choose depends on your company management's philosophy. Charge-back may be easier to justify; however, considering the network as a utility provides some clear benefits in a networked computing environment.

# Charge-Back Cost Accounting

Charge-back is the traditional model of cost accounting. Each department or business unit pays for a portion of the network and computing systems. In this model, MIS is considered a zero-sum gain department; it does not make any money, nor does it get any money. MIS must gain from other departments the money it spends. If a department wants a computing project, it must fund MIS. MIS salaries are absorbed as overhead.

Charge-back can be designed around several models. MIS may charge the departments per transaction. Departments may be charged for items such as transactions processed, service and support, equipment acquisition, and maintenance. MIS calculates how much it costs to provide each service to the departments, and charges them accordingly. For example, MIS may charge each department $20 per hour for a technical support call and $50 plus an hourly rate for an on-site call. It charges a certain rate for access to the VAX, and another rate for access to the IBM mainframe.

A variation of charge-back is to charge a flat rate instead of charging per service event. For example, MIS may charge a set fee monthly or quarterly, depending on the company's accounting structures. MIS may charge the departments $10 per month for each EtherNet port and $100 per month for each WordPerfect user. These amounts include the installation and mainte-nance of the system. These amounts, too, depend on what it costs MIS to run and support these services.

In some cases, it may be quite difficult to cost-justify according to a flat rate. Networks and products do not provide facilities for accounting and cost-justification. Some provide only limited facilities. Mainframe networks, telephone networks, and public packet switching networks can easily be cost-justified, but PC LANs are usually more difficult. The best facility available may be to charge users by the megabyte of data stored on the server, which does nothing to measure the processing cycles used or the network band-width consumed.

Using the charge-back model may slow the progress of upgrades. For ex-ample, if an upgrade or an additional feature will benefit two departments, each with their own budgets and cost systems, much of your time will be spent trying to figure out who owns how much of the cost. For example, a finance department and an engineering department may both need a link to an international office. But who pays how much for that link? Your energy is distracted from the real focus—providing the best service—to accounting.

This impedes the speed at which you can upgrade the network and provide service to your users.

These methods of charging departments per kilobyte of data transmitted or per megabyte of data stored may be shortsighted. The traditional charge-back model may not be suitable for an enterprise-wide, client/server network. Instead of calculating how much the network *costs* each department, MIS should calculate how much the network enables the department to *produce*. MIS personnel should be able to tell the business unit managers that the enterprise-wide network will enable them to grow their business by a certain percentage, and within that context, that the network will cost a certain amount per transaction. The emphasis, however, should be on how the network can grow the business. The cost should be in terms of the business unit, whether it's orders processed or widgets manufactured. (It is, however, more comforting for management to know that MIS will zero-balance at the end of the year through direct-usage balance.)

Forcing business unit managers to think of the network in terms of cost per megabyte stored may cause them to lose sight of their goal: improving productivity. The MIS manager, rather than the business unit manager, should be concerned with the actual cost of the network, whether it costs $10 or $12 per month for an EtherNet port. The specific amount is related to accounting structures. The idea is to encourage business users and managers to use the network to increase productivity. Focusing too much on charge-back schemes and data accounting—especially during the start-up years on the network—can be counter-productive. Networking can help a company be more effective, more efficient and more competitive. MIS personnel must also view the network cost in terms of productivity, because this helps them develop a better understanding of the business units' needs. This enables them to maintain the business model of the network technology, which was developed during the request for proposal phase (see Chapter 2, "Identifying the Business Issues and Requirements of Networking").

# The Network as a Corporate Utility

Budgeting the network as a *corporate utility* is a newer—and in most instances better—model. In this model, the cost of the network is considered part of the cost of doing business. The network is valued as a utility, just as electricity, heating, air conditioning, and water are utilities. This model recognizes that the motivation for installing an enterprise-wide network is to solve business problems.

Regarding the enterprise-wide network as a utility enables MIS to provide network services similar to the way a company's facilities management department provides heat and water as part of corporate services. When users move into new offices, their phones are already plugged in, the electricity works, and air conditioning is available. Similarly, the network connection is in place. When the users come in, they flip on the lights, turn on the computer, and pick up the phone—they are ready to work.

Under this model, the company's management gives MIS a budget to install and maintain the enterprise portion of the network. In essence, the network becomes part of the corporate overhead. Each department then pays MIS for using the enterprise portion of the network. The departments retain cost responsibility for their departmental networks. In another model, MIS can take cost and construction responsibility for both the enterprise and the departmental network. Which one is more appropriate depends on your company's philosophy.

The actual cost can be determined by calculating the cost of designing, installing, and maintaining the enterprise system over its lifetime, depreciating that cost, and then dividing that sum among the departments. For example, MIS determines what it costs to support a NetWare network, a VAX system, or a Hewlett-Packard mini, and charges accordingly.

The utility model solves some problems endemic in many MIS departments. With the charge-back model, the department with the most money typically is able to "purchase" the best connectivity from MIS, even if it doesn't need the most complete connectivity. In reality, the department with the least funding may actually need the best connectivity; however, unless it is well-funded, it may find itself stifled under the traditional charge-back model.

With the utility model, MIS can take into account the corporation's strategic interests and needs. MIS is able to serve departments according to their greatest needs, not on the priorities of those departments that have the greatest amounts of funding. MIS, along with the corporation's business management, can prioritize the different departments' requirements, and hopefully, create the best connectivity strategy. For example, connecting the New York office to the remote offices may be the most important connectivity piece, so MIS can start there, instead of networking the offices with the largest computing budgets.

The utility model provides a more stable cost infrastructure. The network is considered a necessary entity, which the MIS department oversees. Departments can come and go, using the network as necessary. This model better accommodates a company that changes rapidly, as corporations are merged and departments are consolidated, eliminated, or created.

Regarding the cost of an enterprise-wide network as part of the cost of doing business also increases the flexibility of the system. For instance, your company may need to reroute all data normally sent to the New York office to the Philadelphia office because of a power outage or natural disaster. Similarly, the network could be rerouted according to inexpensive WAN services on an ad hoc basis. Although it may be technologically easy for the network technicians to change the physical routing paths, properly charging back the New York and Philadelphia users for the packets they transmitted can be quite difficult under the charge-back model. In this situation, considering the network a utility would avoid this difficulty and increase corporate flexibility and perhaps even reduce costs.

The utility model can be more difficult to manage than the charge-back model. Because departments are charged back for a certain portion of the enterprise-wide network, the business units and MIS must agree on what constitutes an "enterprise-wide network." The enterprise-wide network could include everything beyond the departmental wiring hub, including the internetworking device, the backbone, and telecommunications services. Or it may include the departmental wiring hub but not the departmental router or bridge. They must also agree on the depreciation schedule.

Making the transition from a charge-back model to a corporate utility model can be challenging. MIS must define the parameters of the enterprise-wide network, then calculate the costs, and then depreciate them. MIS may use data collected from its existing charge-back accounting system to determine the new costs. It then must build a cost structure for the utility model and apply it. Building this model requires the expertise and cooperation of the company's accountants. It also requires the department managers to learn a new way of reading their budget reports. And as tax laws and financial reporting structures change, the cost-accounting model must evolve.

The difficulty of defining and managing the network-as-utility model may be worth the extra work because networks are fast becoming essential utilities. When it comes time to trim the budget, department heads can tell their staffs to eliminate unnecessary travel or cut down on express delivery services, but they can't tell them to use the telephone less or reduce the amount of time they spend on their computers, if that is how they do their work.

MIS must *amortize* or *depreciate* the computer systems over several years. Depreciation determines your network's return on investment. How quickly you can depreciate equipment purchases will determine how successful your decisions seem to management. For example, if you purchase a minicomputer and plan to depreciate it over five years, but discover that it's obsolete in three, you can't throw it out, because the mini has two years of value left. Depreciation largely determines if you must retain an old system (even in a new role) in the new enterprise-wide network or if you can throw it out.

Although your company's accounting policies and the government's tax laws set the depreciation schedule, most companies depreciate hardware over a three- to five-year period. Some technology-driven companies depreciate equipment faster, perhaps over a two- to three-year period, in an attempt to gain a higher return on investment. Cable plants are typically written off over a longer period of time, for instance five to 10 years, because they are more stable and less subject to technology developments.

# Pros and Cons of Cost Accounting Models

The following lists the pros and cons of the charge-back and corporate utility models.

## Charge-Back Model

*Pros:*

- The ability to account for the cost of every bit and byte processed provides a clear-cut cost structure for the accounting department. MIS will have a zero-balance at the end of the year.

- The charge-back model is a well-established model used for mainframes, public data networks, and telephone companies. Accounting and MIS departments are familiar with it.

*Cons:*

- Departments with the most money often get the best service.

- It is difficult to use this model for PC LANs because they often lack sophisticated accounting features.

- Upgrades and enhancements do not always point to one specific group, making rapid upgrades more difficult.

- The charge-back model requires support from the products themselves.

## Corporate Utility Model

*Pros:*

- Considering the network as a utility provides a more stable structure.

- This model enables MIS to prioritize projects according to business need rather than according to funding from the department.

- The corporate utility model is more flexible than the charge-back model, which makes it easier to accommodate new projects, developments, and departments.

*Cons:*

- The corporate utility model is more difficult to define and to manage.

- Management is unfamiliar with this model, which may make its initial acceptance more difficult.

# Evaluating a Network's Economic Impact

Determining a network's cost is difficult, especially because little hard data exists on the cost of enterprise-wide networks. Whereas rigorous cost analyses are often performed on minicomputer and mainframe systems, up to now, LANs and WANs have usually been exempt from heavy economic evaluations.

This is partially because networks, until now, haven't been a central part of many organizations' strategic computing plans. It's also because networks include so many components that it is difficult to perform accurate cost modeling. Additionally, the expense of conducting a cost evaluation can surpass the costs of purchasing the actual equipment. Whereas it is easy to ascertain the purchase price of network components, it's much more difficult to calculate the maintenance costs. The difficulty in determining costs can result from something as simple as not tracking whether the long-distance calls are from computer or voice traffic.

Note that networks are much more costly to maintain than to install. Maintaining and supporting a network costs three to four times the purchase price, according to various market research studies and anecdotal evidence.

When purchasing a network, consider how much it is going to cost your department to maintain and support the equipment. Don't focus too narrowly on the purchase price. A few extra dollars spent up-front may save four times that amount later. If you are too price-sensitive during the acquisition phase, you may spend a great deal later on recurring costs.

# Networks Cost More to Run Than to Buy

In its study "The Costs of Network Ownership," The Index Group found that the initial cost of a network is a fraction of the overall cost.[1] Because operating and incremental change costs can be substantial, justifying a network based on purchase price alone can be misleading.

The study, written by Dr. Michael Treacy of The Index Group (Cambridge, MA) and commissioned by Digital Equipment Corp., followed the cost structures of 11 corporate IBM and DEC host-and-terminal networks over a period of five years. These networks used either a centralized or distributed topology. Although the research group studied terminal networks rather than networks with intelligent clients, the methodology is sound, and the results can be extrapolated. (Client/server networks tend to be less expensive than host-based networks, because they are based on inexpensive PC technology and are largely not based on proprietary systems.)

The Index Group's study also found that personnel costs are higher than expected. Because they can reach even 50 percent of the total network cost, controlling personnel costs is key. Third, the choice of a vendor affects more than the initial acquisition costs; it affects also the personnel costs for routine operation and change. Finally, the effects of topology on network cost are great. Centralized networks are more costly than distributed networks.

The Index Group placed costs in five line-item categories: equipment, software, personnel, communications, and facilities. The study mapped these costs over the three phases of the network's life cycle: acquisition, routine operations and troubleshooting, and the support of incremental network changes (see Figure 3.1).

---

[1]Dr. Michael Treacy and The Index Group. "The Costs of Network Ownership." Cambridge, MA: The Index Group, 1989.

|  | Acquisition Costs | Operations Costs | Incremental Change Costs |
|---|---|---|---|
| **Equipment** |  |  |  |
| **Software** |  |  |  |
| **Personnel** |  |  |  |
| **Communications** |  |  |  |
| **Facilities** |  |  |  |

*(Source: The Index Group)*

**Figure 3.1.**  *The Index Group's model for the cost of network ownership.*

Acquisition costs relate to a network's initial planning, purchasing, and installation. During the acquisition phase, MIS purchases the network equipment, purchases or licenses the software, pays the initial communications hookup charges, builds the facilities, and runs the cabling. Personnel costs stem from the planning, design, and selection as well as the equipment and software installation.

■ *Operations costs* concern the price of operating, supporting, and maintaining the network over a certain period. MIS must maintain the hardware and software. MIS personnel must routinely monitor and operate network hardware and software and correct network problems. Also, personnel charges stem from the user liaison and administration. Communications costs are the monthly telecommunications tariff charges. The company's facilities-management group also charges for the space the network occupies.

■ *Incremental costs* are associated with changes to the network over time. Incremental changes include adding equipment, purchasing additional software licenses, and changes in tariff charges for communication links. Incremental costs also include personnel charges that stem from making changes to the network. (See Figure 3.2).

In its study, The Index Group found that on average, only one-third of the five-year ownership charges are related to the network's acquisition, whereas two-thirds are related to operations and routine changes. The Index

Group discovered that the operations and incremental change costs were almost twice as large as the acquisition costs. Incremental change costs are closely related to the operations costs.

| | Acquisition Costs | Operations Costs | Incremental Change Costs |
|---|---|---|---|
| **Equipment** | Equipment Purchase | Maintenance | |
| **Software** | Software Purchase and License | Annual License Software Maintenance | |
| **Personnel** | Planning, Design and Selection<br><br>Equipment and Software Installation | Routine Monitoring & Operation<br><br>Problem Correction<br><br>User Liaison, Administration | User and Software Version Changes |
| **Communications** | Initial Hookup Charges | Monthly Tariff Charges | |
| **Facilities** | Facilities Development<br><br>Wiring Costs | Space Expense | |

*(Source: The Index Group)*

***Figure 3.2.*** *Contributors to network costs.*

The study found that equipment costs comprise 33 percent of the network's total per-port cost over its five-year life cycle. Software costs about 8 percent. Communications cost about 26 percent. Personnel costs account for 25 percent of the five-year costs. (This figure does not include the personnel costs of acquiring the network.) Facilities costs, at 7 percent, are the least significant (see Figure 3.3).

Although the specific dollar amounts shown in Figure 3.3 will change over time, the ratios are sound. You can make adjustments to this model according to your own network structure. This model is built around a centralized corporate terminal-to-host network. For distributed client/server networks, anticipate higher equipment and communications costs.

|  | Acquisition Costs | Operation Costs | Incremental Change Costs | |
|---|---|---|---|---|
| **Equipment** | $1,258 (25.3%) | $413 (8.3%) | | **$1,671 (33.6%)** |
| **Software** | 214 (4.3%) | 179 (3.6%) | | **$393 (7.9%)** |
| **Personnel** | N/A | 847 (17%) | 39 (8%) | **$1,244 (25%)** |
| **Communications** | 58 (1.2%) | 1,252 (25.2%) | | **$1,310 (26.4%)** |
| **Facilities** | 261 (5.2%) | 90 (1.8%) | | **$351 (7.1%)** |
| *(Source: The Index Group)* | **$1,791 (36.1%)** | **$3,178 (63.9%)** | | **$4,696 (100%)** |

*Figure 3.3.* *Corporate network cost structure.*

## The Cost of Networking

One-third of a network's five-year ownership costs relate to acquisition. Two-thirds are related to operations and routine changes. The operations and incremental change costs are almost twice as large as the acquisition costs. Incremental change costs are closely related to the operations costs.

# Discerning PC Networking's Costs

Ferris Networks, a San Francisco network consulting and research firm that studied networking costs, reached similar conclusions to The Index Group's. In 1991, Ferris examined the cost of installing and operating PC networks ranging from 20 to 1,000 nodes.[2] Ferris has calculated the cost to install and operate networks for the first year and over three years, showing that you achieve economies of scale as your network grows.

Larger networks are relatively less expensive to install and maintain than smaller networks, Ferris found. Smaller networks are more expensive because the end-user company mounts the steep learning curve of network design, implementation, operation, and management of networks. Once

---

[2]David Ferris. "Indepth Cost Analysis of PC Networks." Networld Boston Conference Manual. Englewood Cliffs, NJ: Bruno Blenheim, 1991.

these systems are in place, you can reap the benefits—at least for a while—of the initial investment cost. At a certain size, however, the network's size and complexity increase the administrative costs.

The Ferris study used two models. In the first, each full-time (or equivalent) administrator supports 40 workstations. In the second, each full-time administrator supports 75 workstations. For both models, the study makes the following assumptions: each user has one PC. The basic hardware and software costs $4,000 per year, plus $500 per year in new products and 10 percent in maintenance. The study assumed that cable installation costs $300 per workstation. The study also assumed that each user spends 30 minutes unproductively each week. It assumes also that the computer staff cost averages $40 per hour, or $80,000 per year. User education requires two days of classes per year at $225 per day, plus three days per year learning on the job. The annual cost of communication lines per user per year is $500.

According to Ferris' data, it costs $7,608 per workstation to install and operate a 20-node network, with one administrator for every 40 users. A 100-node network, at $7,494 per workstation, costs 1.5 percent less to install and maintain than a 20-node network does. A 1,000-node network, at $7,426 per workstation, costs 2.4 percent less to install and maintain than a 20-node network.

Ferris calculates that a 40-node network with one network administrator costs the company $222,650 to install and maintain the first year, for a total of $900,300 over three years, or $7,503 per PC per year. Of that amount, products and installation comprise 31.1 percent, system management is 27.3 percent, and user training is 24.1 percent. Unproductive time is 9.6 percent of the total cost. Wide area network line costs comprise 6.7 percent, whereas design and planning account for 1.2 percent (see Figure 3.4). As shown earlier, the cost of system management is surprisingly high. Unlike product acquisition, the costs of network management are ongoing.

Figure 3.5 shows the PC LAN costs if each administrator supports 75 users. Over a three-year period, a 40-node PC LAN costs $6,569 per PC per year. Using this scenario enables you to reduce the cost of system management in relation to the price of hardware, software, and installation. By decreasing the support ratio, you can decrease overall costs even though some costs rise, because the portion spent on network management is so large. It is notable that user training rises (to 27.5 percent) and unproductive time rises slightly (to 11 percent), because the network is not supported as well. WAN line costs increase to 7.6 percent because as the network grows, users need more contact with outside data sources.

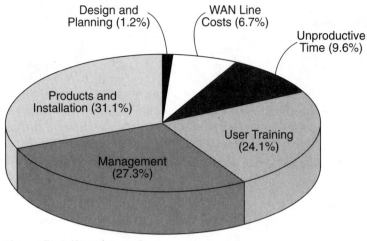

*(Source: Ferris Networks)*

**Figure 3.4.**   *PC LAN costs at a 1:40 support ratio.*

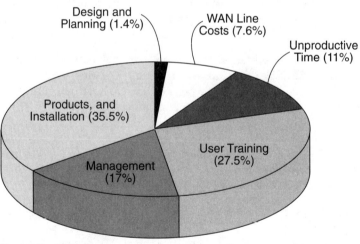

*(Source: Ferris Networks)*

**Figure 3.5.**   *PC LAN costs at a 1:75 support ratio.*

A 20-node network costs $7,608 per workstation, according to Ferris. The price of a 40-node network decreases slightly, to $7,503. A 100-node network decreases to $7,494 per workstation. A 500-node network costs $7,435 per workstation. The cost per workstation decreases slightly as the staff gains expertise and builds a base of management tools.

At a 1:75 support ratio, a 20-node network costs $6,674 per workstation. A 40-node network has an annual cost per workstation of $6,569. A 100-node network costs $6,541 per workstation. Continuing the downward trend, a 500-node network costs $6,478 per workstation. You can achieve an economy of scale as your network grows in size. Users and managers master the learning curve. The size and complexity, however, finally overtake the efficiency gained. (See Figure 3.6 and Tables 3.1 and 3.2.)

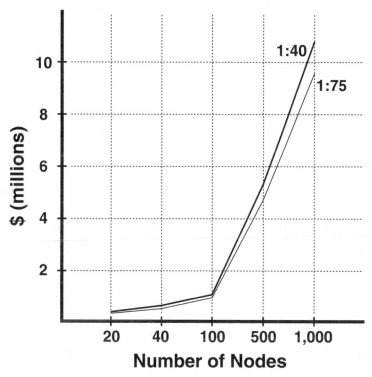

*(Source: Ferris Networks)*

***Figure 3.6.*** *The cost of LAN installation in the first year.*

By decreasing the support ratio, you can save money; however, users will spend more time waiting for service. According to Ferris' figures, at a 71:1 ratio a 20-node network will cost 12.2 percent less than a network supported at 40:1. A 40-node network costs 12.4 less, a 100-node network costs 12.7 percent less, and 500 nodes costs 12.8 percent less (see Figures 3.6 and 3.7).

**Table 3.1.**  Network costs at a 1:40 support ratio, according to Ferris.

| Installation Costs | Number of Workstations | | | | | |
| --- | --- | --- | --- | --- | --- | --- |
| | 20 | 40 | 100 | 500 | 1,000 | |
| Network design and planning | $8,800 | $11,000 | $22,000 | $33,000 | $44,000 | |
| Hardware and software | 80,000 | 160,000 | 400,000 | 2,000,000 | 4,000,000 | |
| Cabling and installation | 6,000 | 12,000 | 30,000 | 150,000 | 300,000 | |
| **Systems management** | | | | | | |
| Training class fees | 1,500 | 1,500 | 4,500 | 19,500 | 37,500 | |
| **User training** | | | | | | |
| Time | 7,200 | 14,400 | 36,000 | 180,000 | 360,000 | |
| Class fees | 2,250 | 4,500 | 11,250 | 56,250 | 112,500 | |
| **Total Installation Costs** | **$108,750** | **$203,400** | **$503,750** | **$2,438,750** | **$4,854,000** | |

*continues*

**Table 3.1.  continued**

| Annual Operating Costs | Number of Workstations | | | | | |
|---|---|---|---|---|---|---|
| | 20 | 40 | 100 | 500 | 1,000 | |
| **Systems management** | | | | | | |
| Salaries | $40,000 | $80,000 | $200,000 | $1,000,000 | $2,000,000 | |
| Class fees | 1,500 | 1,500 | 4,500 | 19,500 | 37,500 | |
| **User training** | | | | | | |
| Time | 24,000 | 48,000 | 120,000 | 600,000 | 1,200,000 | |
| Class fees | 9,000 | 18,000 | 45,000 | 225,000 | 450,000 | |
| Unproductive time | 14,400 | 28,800 | 72,000 | 360,000 | 720,000 | |
| Additional products | 10,000 | 20,000 | 50,000 | 250,000 | 500,000 | |
| WAN line costs | 10,000 | 20,000 | 50,000 | 250,000 | 500,000 | |
| Product maintenance | 8,000 | 16,000 | 40,000 | 200,000 | 400,000 | |
| Product applications maintenance | 0 | 0 | 0 | 0 | 0 | |
| **Total Operating Costs** | **$116,000** | **$232,300** | **$581,500** | **$2,904,500** | **$5,807,500** | |

Total Installation and Operating Costs

| | | | | | | |
|---|---|---|---|---|---|---|
| First-year cost | $222,650 | $435,700 | $1,085,250 | $5,343,250 | $10,661,500 | |
| Three-year cost | 456,450 | 900,300 | 2,248,250 | 11,152,250 | 22,276,500 | |
| Annual cost per workstation | $7,608 | $7,503 | $7,494 | $7,435 | $7,426 | |

Table 3.2. Network costs at a 1:75 support ratio, according to Ferris.

| Installation Costs | Number of Workstations | | | | |
|---|---|---|---|---|---|
| | 20 | 40 | 100 | 500 | 1,000 |
| Network design and planning | $8,800 | $11,000 | $22,000 | $33,000 | $44,000 |
| Hardware and software | 80,000 | 160,000 | 400,000 | 2,000,000 | 4,000,000 |
| Cabling and installation | 6,000 | 12,000 | 30,000 | 150,000 | 300,000 |
| **Systems management training** | | | | | |
| Class fees | 1,500 | 1,500 | 3,000 | 10,500 | 21,000 |
| **User training** | | | | | |
| Time | 7,200 | 14,400 | 36,000 | 180,000 | 360,000 |
| Class fees | 2,250 | 4,500 | 11,250 | 56,250 | 112,500 |
| **Total Installation Costs** | **$105,750** | **$203,400** | **$502,250** | **$2,429,750** | **$4,837,500** |

*continues*

**Table 3.2.** continued

| Annual Operating Costs | Number of Workstations | | | | | |
|---|---|---|---|---|---|---|
| | 20 | 40 | 100 | 500 | 1,000 |
| **Systems management** | | | | | |
| Salaries | $21,333 | $42,667 | $106,667 | $533,333 | $1,066,667 |
| Class fees | 1,500 | 1,500 | 3,000 | 10,500 | 21,000 |
| **User training** | | | | | |
| Time | 24,000 | 48,000 | 120,000 | 600,000 | 1,200,000 |
| Class fees | 9,000 | 18,000 | 45,000 | 225,000 | 450,000 |
| Unproductive time | 14,400 | 28,800 | 72,000 | 360,000 | 720,000 |
| Additional Products | 10,000 | 20,000 | 50,000 | 250,000 | 500,000 |
| WAN line costs | 10,000 | 20,000 | 50,000 | 250,000 | 500,000 |
| Product maintenance | 8,000 | 16,000 | 40,000 | 200,000 | 400,000 |
| Product applications maintenance | 0 | 0 | 0 | 0 | 0 |
| **Total Operating Costs** | $98,233 | $194,967 | $486,667 | $2,428,833 | $4,857,667 |

Total Installation and Operating Costs

| | | | | | |
|---|---|---|---|---|---|
| First-year cost | $203,983 | $398,367 | $988,917 | $4,858,583 | $9,695,167 |
| Three-year cost | 400,450 | 788,300 | 1,962,250 | 9,716,250 | 19,410,500 |
| Annual cost per workstation | $6,674 | $6,569 | $6,541 | $6,478 | $6,470 |

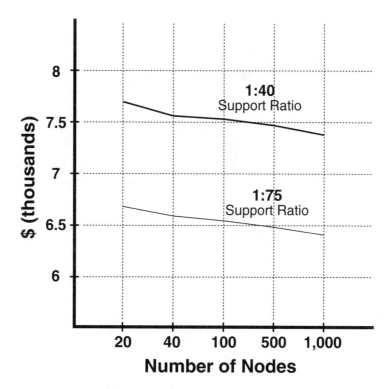

*(Source: Ferris Networks)*

**Figure 3.7.** *Annual cost of a PC LAN by workstation.*

When you estimate support ratios, the following rules of thumb apply: you'll need one network administrator for every 100 workstations on a homogenous network, whether the network is remote or local. Heterogeneous networks require one administrator per 50 workstations. One hardware or software technician can support 100 users, and one administrator can support 50 stand-alone PCs.

# How to Figure Your Network's Costs

Calculating the cost of your network is extremely beneficial. As The Index Group points out, "Once a manager applies the model to in-house network costs, the most significant candidates for management attention can be identified and targeted." The report also writes, "An important element of any ongoing cost-management strategy is the tracking of progress over time. Correspondingly, the use of the model in analyzing the costs needs to be an ongoing activity." You can calculate the cost of running your network using the worksheet shown in Figure 3.8a. and 3.8b.

| Cost Category | Enter Value Here |
|---|---|
| **Design and Planning** | |
| In-house salaries | |
| Consultants | |
| **Hardware** | |
| Servers | |
| Workstations | |
| Bridges | |
| Routers | |
| Gateways | |
| Faxes | |
| Printers | |
| Storage | |
| Management hardware | |
| **Software** | |
| Network operating system | |
| Electronic mail | |
| Database | |
| Print spooling software | |
| Word processing | |
| Spreadsheets | |
| Project management | |
| Applications development | |
| Management software | |
| Project management | |
| **Cabling** | |
| Backbone | |
| Departmental | |
| **Installation** | |
| **Training** | |
| Systems management | |
| End users | |
| **Total Installation Costs** | |

*(Table rows from "Design and Planning" through "End users" are grouped under the vertical label* **Installation Costs***.)*

*Figure 3.8a.* *A worksheet for figuring network costs.*

| Cost Category | | Enter Value Here |
|---|---|---|
| **Operating Costs** | **Systems Management** | |
| | Salaries | |
| | Overhead | |
| | **Training** | |
| | Ongoing sys. management | |
| | Ongoing end user | |
| | **WAN Line Costs** | |
| | **Maintenance** | |
| | Service contracts | |
| | T&M service | |
| **Total Operating Costs** | | |
| **Total Installation Costs** | | |
| **Total Costs** | | |

**Figure 3.8b.** *A worksheet for figuring network costs.*

Once you have performed cost modeling on your network, you can perform a competitive analysis of the cost structure of networks in other companies or within your company. This analysis will enable you to gauge the networks' cost effectiveness, allowing your company to distribute its resources as wisely as possible.

Price sensitivity alone should not determine your network's value. Take into consideration intangible factors, such as the network's functionality, flexibility, and manageability. Evaluate how well the network performs services on demand. Determine how gracefully it can evolve to meet tomorrow's needs. How easy or difficult is it to monitor, maintain and assure the security of the network? Finally, and perhaps most importantly, how much does it cost to run the network?

# Exposing the Hidden Costs of Networking

The "hidden" costs of networking are the recurring costs of training, mainte-nance, and staffing. In the past, managers focused too heavily on the costs of the wiring, the adapter cards, and the servers. It's easier to focus on the costs of hardware and software acquisition, because they are easily quantifiable. Now, managers have a growing awareness of the significant costs of admin-istration, configuration, service management, changes, upgrades, and train-ing. As a rule of thumb, every time you buy a piece of hardware, triple or quadruple the purchase price to figure out how much it will cost to maintain it over the life of the equipment.

Consider how much time and money your company has invested in develop-ing applications and training MIS to manage them and users to use them. This is a significant percentage. Can you protect this investment as you move to an enterprise-wide, client/server system?

You must consider the costs of training both the end users and the MIS staff. The users have learned how to use their applications. Forcing them to learn a new E-mail package, for example, distracts them from the real business of doing their jobs. Changing systems introduces a learning curve. To minimize the learning curve, allow users to keep existing systems and applications wherever possible. When it is necessary to introduce new technologies and applications, train the users thoroughly.

Similarly, the MIS department has learned how to make the existing systems work. Can you protect this investment of learning and knowledge? Tradition-ally, VAX managers only know how to maintain the VAXs; NetWare admin-istrators are strictly NetWare experts. Most companies find it difficult to maintain individual experts in each system type. What enterprise-wide network managers need is a knowledge of how disparate systems interact. What can happen, for instance, when you interconnect DECnet and NetWare? Support people need more experience in multiple disciplines.

One key way to ensure a return on investment is to have your MIS people work closely with the consultants and integrators. By working as partners, your in-house MIS people can make sure that existing investments are preserved in the new system.

Fortunately, technology tends to become less expensive to support over time. As technology becomes more intelligent, it requires fewer people to support it; however, those people must be more intelligent, better trained, and consequently, more highly paid. Instead of hiring three administrators at $30,000 each per year, you may need one full-time person and one part-time person at a total cost of $60,000. Also, when a problem arises, it is likely to be catastrophic, whereas on smaller networks, which are inherently simpler, problems are easier to solve.

During the acquisitions phase, one often-overlooked cost is overtime. Plan and budget for overtime charges for the in-house people and your integrator. Ask the integrator how much it charges to work after 5 p.m. and on weekends. You'll need your internal facilities management people and MIS people around while the integrator is installing the network, even if that is on Saturdays and Sundays. Integrators have to pay their own people overtime when they work on weekends; they're going to pass that cost along to you. Write your amount of projected overtime into the contract.

# Getting a Return on Your Investment

Calculating a *return on investment* (ROI) enables MIS to gauge the networks from a business profit-and-loss standpoint. You calculate a ROI by subtracting the total cost of the network from the total benefit. To do this, you must perform a cost-benefit analysis.

You can measure the ROI qualitatively or quantitatively. Quantitatively measuring ROI is simpler, but does not always provide a true measure of the network's value. In this method, calculate the "hard" costs of the system. For example, how much does it cost to acquire the new hardware, software, wiring, training, and installation? What are the ongoing operational costs? You can determine these prices from the request-for-proposal submitted (if you are installing an enterprise-wide network from scratch), or you can determine these prices by checking past purchasing records. You should add in also the cost due to interruption of employees' work flow. From this, you can determine the network's costs.

To determine the network's value, you should calculate how much the existing system would cost if it remained in place. The difference, when amortized over the system's life span, is the real cost of the network. The depreciation schedule determines when the enterprise-wide network starts paying for itself.

Sometimes this is a straightforward calculation. For example, a network may save the company a vast amount of money in telephone or express delivery charges. For example, by bundling data and voice traffic on the same T-3 lines, you may be able to spread the cost of the higher-speed line among many different departments, instead of each department justifying its own T-1 line. You may also justify a network on the basis that it eliminates the need for data-entry clerks to rekey data from one computer system into another.

If you choose to perform a cost-benefit analysis on an applications basis, be very clear about what you are going to quantify and hold to it so that you can know when you've achieved your goal.

A purely quantitative cost justification, however, doesn't always provide the most accurate picture. A network does more than save money; it enables a company to produce more (given that the network and applications are properly designed). If you build your enterprise-wide network on the principle that it is part of the business strategy, you calculate your ROI based on the production value of the network. The cost, then, is not only the hard costs—the acquisition and operational costs—but "soft" costs as well. The soft costs are those that aren't so easily placed into a double-entry ledger sheet. For example, you may be able to show that the enterprise-wide network enables better communication, which enables the departments to turn business around faster, which gives your company a service edge. The network may help the company increase sales. In addition, as productivity continues to increase through the use of networking, the use of the network will increase. Innovative ideas about how the network can be used will be generated by application planners and users.

You can also factor into the ROI calculation what would happen to the company if it *does not* install an enterprise-wide network. Will the company remain competitive, or will it lose its edge? Will the network enable the company to gain a competitive edge it never enjoyed before? This cost of lost opportunity is more difficult to determine. In this case, the purchase of an enterprise-wide network is justified on the cost of doing business.

You can use the tables in Figure 3.9a. and 3.9b. to calculate a network's costs and benefits. An analysis of a network's costs and benefits helps MIS to justify the network's purchase to upper management. It also enables MIS to calculate the return on the investment.

| Type of Cost | Projected Cost |
|---|---|
| **Hardware** | |
| Systems hardware | |
| LAN hardware | |
| **Software** | |
| Application software | |
| LAN system software | |
| **Installation** | |
| LAN installation | |
| WAN installation | |
| **Personnel** | |
| **Wide Area Network** | |
| Services | |
| Acquisition | |
| **Training** | |
| MIS personnel | |
| End users | |
| **Ongoing Costs** | |
| Maintenance | |
| WAN services | |
| **Total Projected Costs** | |

*Figure 3.9a.* *A cost/benefit worksheet.*

| Type of Benefit | Projected Benefit ($) |
|---|---|
| **Hard Benefits** | |
| Due to increased efficiency | |
| Due to automation of manual procedures | |
| Personnel reduction | |
| **Cost Avoidance** | |
| By not acquiring new systems for each department | |
| By not hiring personnel | |
| **Soft Benefits** | |
| Goodwill and reputation | |
| Enhanced decision-making | |
| Improvements in efficiency | |
| **Total Projected Benefits** | |
| **Total Projected Cost** | |
| **(Cost)/Benefit of Project** | |

**Figure 3.9b.** *A cost/benefit worksheet.*

# Performing a Risk Analysis

Most corporations install networks without any thought or analysis of the risks involved or any definite contingency plans. Whether you perform a *risk analysis* depends on your corporation's size, function, and philosophy. Approximately 20 percent of companies perform risk analyses. If your company's business depends on an enterprise-wide network, however, you should perform a careful risk analysis.

You can perform either a *technology risk analysis* or a *business risk analysis*. A technology risk analysis is fairly straightforward. You must consider the external risks to the system, evaluate their severity, and calculate the costs of losing network services. Calculate how much it would cost the company to have one of these disasters occur, then calculate how much it costs to have a backup solution in place. This will help you determine how much risk prevention you should take.

In examining the external risks, look at the consequences of data loss, system failure, and security breaches. Consider also the stability of the environment itself. What is the cost of replacing lost data? Will data have to be rekeyed or can it be restored from tape? How often are the servers backed up? How much data can the users afford to lose? Is tape backup sufficient or do the departments need continuous online backup? Is backup stored off-site and on-site? What precautions are taken for users who are dialing into or out of the enterprise-wide network? What security policies are in place and who is assigned to enforce them?

What happens if a server, a wiring hub, a router, or a bridge fails? Determine the effects and the cost on productivity. How much downtime can the users afford? Is the amount of lost work greater than the cost of a duplexed server or redundant bridges or routers? What fault-tolerant features are built into critical components?

Next, consider the security of the system. Many unnecessary risks are taken because the system is not properly secured. Are the servers in a secure room? Is the data protected? Does the security scheme sufficiently protect the data? What precautions are placed on users dialing into the network?

Analyze the stability of the environment. Consider the issues related to basic building services such as power, lights, and water. Is the power stabilized? Does the power need conditioning? Is the power backed up with uninterruptible power supplies? Do the business units need an orderly shutdown of servers if the power fails?

In addition to issues related to the costs of downtime, evaluate the risk of managing the system. For example, if you have 27 software packages and you decide to upgrade one, what is the cost and the risk of upgrading the other 26? Do they all depend on that one package? Will they necessarily work with the upgraded software?

# Performing a Vulnerability Analysis

A more sophisticated form of risk analysis is on the business level, and is often called a *vulnerability analysis*. You must determine how successful the project will be. Your gut reaction is "It's not going to fail." But the project might. Despite your careful attention to identifying the users' requirements, designing the network to meet the business needs, selecting the best vendor, and deploying the system, the enterprise-wide network might not live up to your or the CEO's every expectation.

If the system completely fails, the CIO is usually held responsible, and often is terminated. Unfortunately, making a scapegoat out of the CIO won't solve the network problems left behind. It's essential to plan for what happens when the network is not installed on schedule, or worse, does not work as planned when installed. When projects are late, it generally isn't because people aren't good or didn't do their job. Integrating networks is complex. It's difficult to plan for all contingencies, but it's essential. Contingency planning can prevent embarrassment, at the least, so have your answers and plans ready.

As with technology-level risk analyses, vulnerability analyses are done to different depths, depending on the corporate culture and network's function. Issues to consider include the following: Formulate your responses if milestones are not met. For example, what happens if the network fails its installation testing? What happens if it fails the acceptance testing? Will you run the old and new systems in tandem until you can safely cut over to the new system? What happens if data is lost during the cutover?

If you are new to vulnerability and risk analyses, integrators and consultants can help you. Integrators, especially those who commonly work with Fortune 1000 firms, are accustomed to performing risk analysis and can help streamline the process for you. You may want to discuss the analysis procedure and the results with your insurance company so that you are adequately insured.

# Justifying the Network's Existence

Networking can be a costly proposition, and many companies spend money needlessly. Yet by carefully defining the network's requirements and controlling costs, you can build a useful and cost-efficient enterprise-wide network. Key to this success is a cost-benefit analysis, a cost-accounting model, and a good understanding of network costs.

Calculating a network's cost is quite difficult, because little hard data exists. Networks are relatively new, and enterprise-wide networks are uncharted territory. One appropriate cost-accounting model is a utility model, in which your accounting department considers the network as overhead, thereby allowing each department equal access to the network resources and giving MIS guaranteed funding for its mission.

It is also important to periodically reevaluate the network's cost algorithm, because different cost-modeling methods may be appropriate for the network in its various stages of life. For example, in the first few years, the cost model should be flexible enough to accommodate the network's rapid growth and high cost, the new and unplanned uses for the network, the innovative and creative ideas being raised by users and application planners, and the slow-going cultural acceptance. As the network matures, however, the pace of growth and innovative use will slow, and the network will become politically accepted within the company's structure.

When evaluating a product's cost, consider not only the cost of acquisition, but also the cost of maintenance, because the ongoing costs are typically two-thirds of a device's cost over its lifetime. Choose products that will be low-cost to maintain, even if they are a little more expensive at the initial purchase, because they will save you money in the long run.

# High-Level Issues of Enterprise-Wide Network Design

## CHAPTER 4

*Objectives:*

1. To design an enterprise-wide network in a modular fashion so that it can accommodate existing technologies as well as emerging ones.

2. To design your network using standards-based products to maximize the network's modularity. Establishing corporate standards also aids in achieving modularity.

3. To select a network topology and network operating system that match your company's business and computing structures.

## Modular Networks

One advantage of networks over previous forms of computing, including mainframes and minicomputers, is their independence from any single manufacturer. By nature, networks are made up of components from a myriad of vendors. Consider even a seemingly simple network, such as a 50-node NetWare and EtherNet LAN that is designed for word processing. The end users' computers run DOS and Windows, but even these two operating systems can run on Intel-based machines from hundreds of manufacturers. The EtherNet adapter cards can come from any of more than 250 different vendors. Add to that list of possible incompatibilities the many makers of printers. Then consider the myriad software applications, from word processing to electronic mail, from which the designers must choose, and which all vie for memory, processing power, and interrupts.

With networks, no one vendor provides a total solution, from wiring to applications software. Instead, a company's MIS department or systems integrator must select and integrate the various components from many manufacturers into a functioning network system. Without the integrator's skill, the pieces of the network are dismembered parts unconnected to the network brain. The advantage of this method is flexibility; the disadvantage is complexity.

# Benefits of Modular Networks

Modular, standards-based networks have a number of benefits and drawbacks. The benefits include the following:

- Designers can specify a network that exactly fits a company's needs, instead of retrofitting an existing computer system to the company's business and computing needs.

- You can easily swap standard components in and out of the system, thereby reducing your reliance on any one vendor to provide the total solution.

- A modular network more easily accommodates existing technologies as well as emerging ones. You can also increase your different systems' ability to interoperate. You may find it easier to hire network experts who understand your network.

- You can change the individual pieces without impacting the other layers, and therefore minimize the impact on the users.

- A modular network accommodates growth and new technologies.

## Fitting the Company's Needs

If designed properly, a network is inherently modular, enabling designers to mix and match the parts to fit the business need. Designers can specify a network that exactly fits a company's needs, instead of trying to retrofit an existing computer system to the company's business and computing requirements. Because you build a network piece by piece, it can adapt to a company's business problems and solutions.

For example, you can design the network used in the accounting department separately from the one used in the marketing department. You can select the applications, desktop computers, printers, and network hardware and software that best suit each department. Although the two networks may be quite different, they will still be able to communicate with each other.

## Reducing Reliance on a Single Vendor

By designing the network so that you can easily swap components, you reduce your reliance on any one vendor. No longer is a customer subject to the supplier's development priorities. The more companies that supply a particular product, the lower the prices, according to the law of supply and demand. Ultimately, the buyer benefits by saving tremendous amounts of money. For example, 10BaseT EtherNet was three years in the making. Now, more than a hundred vendors manufacture and sell standard 10BaseT adapter cards and hubs. With such competition, prices drop rapidly. Contrast this with the token ring market, which is dominated by IBM. Far fewer companies manufacture token ring products, and prices are considerably higher. (Royalty payments on the patent also partially explain the higher token ring prices.)

For example, you can purchase MAC-layer bridges from a variety of vendors and gain the same level of functionality, given that you've designed your network carefully and selected the products equally as carefully. Buying components from more than one source gives you the flexibility to shop elsewhere if a vendor can't provide the performance or price you require. This can enable you to gain the same levels of performance while reducing the overall cost of your network.

## Accommodating Existing Technologies

Modularity enables your network to more easily accommodate existing technologies as well as developing ones. By designing your network to be modular and relying on standards-based products, you can reduce the speed at which your network becomes technologically obsolete. You can also increase your system's ability to interoperate—or meaningfully share data and programs—with other computer systems, even if the two systems use fundamentally different means of communication.

## Changing Pieces without Affecting the Other Layers

If your network is built modularly, you can change the individual pieces without impacting the other layers, and therefore minimize the impact on the users. For example, you can change the medium-access method from EtherNet to Token Ring without changing the cable plant (if you used unshielded twisted-pair and fiber cabling and if the network operating system supports both). You can also switch the network operating system without impacting the medium-access method (if the network operating system is independent of the underlying hardware). Finally, you can switch the users' applications (if the applications run across multiple operating systems and protocols).

## A Wider Experience Base

By building a network from standard components, you may find it easier to hire network experts who understand your network. Network technicians and managers will be able to use what they've already learned from other networks when they are building and managing yours. With a proprietary network, there will be fewer people who understand the technology and are experts on it, and therefore there will be a smaller pool of expertise for you to choose from. For example, many people are knowledgable about bridges and routers, because these are "standard" network components.

# Drawbacks of Modular Networks

Modular, standards-based networks also have a number of drawbacks, including the following:

- There is no single source of network products, network support, or network expertise.

- Because each network is unique, identifying and isolating problems can be difficult. Supporting and managing networks can be complex.

- Because of each network's uniqueness, personnel's expertise cannot always be easily transferred from one installation or problem to another.

## Scattering Responsibility

Not relying on any single vendor to provide a network solution creates complexity. There is no single source of network products, network support, or network expertise. When there is a problem, no single company can take total responsibility. There are more than a thousand manufacturers of network products. There are some 250 manufacturers of EtherNet, more than 100 manufacturers of MAC-layer bridges, and nearly 100 manufacturers of routers. The combinations and permutations of network products are nearly endless. That means the combinations and permutations of problems and incompatibility also are endless. When a network product is a commodity, as adapter cards are, choosing among hundreds of suppliers is fairly straightforward. When you are choosing among versions of a relatively complex product, such as a router, however, selecting network components becomes more difficult. Choosing from standards-based products at least limits the number of technologies in a network.

## Making Problem Isolation Difficult

Supporting and managing networks can be complex. Like fingerprints, no two networks are the same. Each has been custom-designed to fit the company's needs and existing computing systems. Mixing many different network components may cause an unpredictable and unstable reaction. Isolating the cause of the problem can be very difficult when so many factors are involved. Because there is no clear-cut product source, MIS administration and the different product manufacturers frequently point the fingers of blame at each other, none willing to accept responsibility for solving the problem. Again, standards-based products reduce the number of different technologies used.

## Transferring Expertise Among Installations

Because each network is unique, expertise cannot always be easily transferred from one installation or problem to another. An expert in one installation is not necessarily an expert in another installation. Designers, managers, and operators must gain expertise in many different areas. Consider even the rather limited field of network operating systems: understanding Novell's NetWare requires a completely different skill set than Banyan's VINES or

Microsoft's LAN Manager, although the principles of design and operation are the same. In the quickly expanding network marketplace, people with experience and expertise are difficult to find and hire.

# The OSI Model Explained

Much of the modularity of network products is due to the *Open Systems Interconnection* (OSI) model, which was established in 1984 by the International Standards Organization. The OSI model divides computer communication into distinct functions, logically represented as layers. Although products that exactly conform to all of the conventions of the OSI model are not common in commercial implementations, many manufacturers have adopted the conventions, especially at the lower layers. This significantly aids in the ability to build modular networks.

As with all layered protocols, each OSI layer functions independently of the layers immediately above and below it. At the same time, each layer can communicate directly with each layer above and below through a communications programming interface. For example, layer 2, the data-link layer, can communicate directly with layer 1, the physical layer, as well as with layer 3, the network layer. A layer cannot, however, "skip" its neighboring layer and communicate directly with its neighbor's neighbor. For example, layer 1 cannot directly communicate with layer 3; it must go through layer 2. This structure enables layers to be functionally independent of one another, while providing a stable set of services. Designers can implement the mechanics of each layer independently, as long as the layer provides the standard set of services and the interface.

The OSI model has seven layers: physical, data-link, network, transport, session, presentation, and application. The lower layers—physical, data-link, network, and transport—are concerned with providing real-time data communications services. The upper layers—session, presentation, and application—are concerned with providing end user-oriented services. The specific roles of each layer are outlined in Table 4.1.

**Table 4.1. The seven-layer OSI model.**

| Layer Number | Layer | Function |
|---|---|---|
| 7 | Application | File transfer, access and management, document and message interchange, and job transfer and manipulation. |
| 6 | Presentation | Transfer syntax negotiation and data representation transformations. |
| 5 | Session | Dialog and synchronization control for application entities. |
| 4 | Transport | End-to-end message transfer, including connection management, error control, fragmentation, and flow control. |
| 3 | Network | Network routing, addressing, call setup and clearing. |
| 2 | Data-Link | Data link control, including framing, data transparency, and error control. |
| 1 | Physical | Mechanical and electrical network interface definitions. |

■ *Layer 1, Physical*—The physical layer provides the mechanical and electrical interface specification for how a computer attaches to a physical medium, so that the computer can transmit bit-oriented data. Examples of physical media include coaxial and twisted-pair cable. This layer includes aspects such as physical connectors to the electrical voltage to be used to transmit bits.

Common physical layer standards include: 802.3 EtherNet running over thick coax, thin coax, unshielded twisted-pair or shielded twisted-pair, and fiber optics; 802.5 Token Ring running over unshielded twisted-pair, shielded twisted-pair, or fiber optics; 802.4 Token Bus running over coax; ANSI Fiber Distributed Data Interface (FDDI) running over fiber optics.

- *Layer 2, Data-Link*—The data-link layer organizes the bits to be sent and received into frames of data so that they can be transmitted as electrical signals by the physical layer. Error detection and correction occurs at this layer. The data-link layer is often divided into two sublayers to deal with the differences in the physical networks used for LAN and WAN communications. The lower sublayer is the *medium access control* (MAC) and the upper sublayer is the *logical link control* (LLC). The MAC layer governs access to the particular type of transmission media, and it is media-specific. The LLC, which is independent of the underlying access method, handles packet framing issues. It interfaces directly with the MAC layer.

  Common data link standards include: Logical Link Control with CSMA/CD, Token Bus, Token Ring, or FDDI as well as High-Level data link control and Link Access Protocol B.

- *Layer 3, Network*—The network layer uses the underlying data link services to provide data transmission services across networks. The network layer provides the rules that dictate how computers communicate across multiple network segments, including the containment of messages into packets with addresses. It is responsible for reliably transmitting the data from end to end. The network layer is particularly concerned with routing, and provides data transmission services to the transport layer.

  Common network layer protocols include: OSI's Connectionless (CNLS) and Connection-Oriented (CONS) network protocols, the Internet's Internet Protocol (IP), and Novell's Internetwork Packet Exchange (IPX).

- *Layer 4, Transport*—The transport layer ensures that the data will be reliably handled, regardless of the reliability of the underlying layers. It handles end-to-end, or node-to-node, connection management, error control, and flow control. Transport layer service is either connection-oriented or connectionless. Connection-oriented transport services operate by establishing connections. Whereas connection-oriented transport services generally provide high reliability, they usually offer low speeds. Connectionless transport services do not establish connections, switches, or pipes before transmitting. They tend to offer higher speeds with less reliability.

  Common transport layer protocols include: OSI's Transport Class 0, Class 1, and Class 4; the Internet's Transmission Control Protocol (TCP), and Novell's Sequenced Packet Exchange (SPX).

- *Layer 5, Session*—The session layer inhabits the ground between the upper layers, which are oriented toward applications, and the lower layers, which are oriented toward real-time data communications. The session layer provides services for the management and control of data flow between two communicating systems. It establishes and maintains multiple simultaneous connections, synchronizing and managing the dialog between communicating applications. Session layer management services include the ability to start, halt, abandon, or restart activities.

- *Layer 6, Presentation*—The presentation layer provides a common representation of information that is being transferred between two computer systems. For example, the translation between ASCII and EBCDIC character encoding is performed at this layer. The presentation layer ensures that any information exchanged between two systems is commonly understood.

- *Layer 7, Application*—The application layer provides communication-based services to end users. High-level system-independent activities occur at this layer, and such activities are managed by a component of the local operating system. Unlike the other layers of the OSI model, the services of the application layer are directly available to the end users. Functions include file transfer, message handling, directory management, remote job execution, and terminal emulation.

  Common OSI application layer standards include: X.400 Message Handling Service, X.500 Directory Management, FTAM file transfer access and management, and VTAM virtual terminal access and management.

# What the OSI Model Really Means

Your network can achieve a higher degree of modularity if it follows the lead of layered protocols in general and the OSI model specifically. Achieving this modularity is much easier at the lower layers, which are oriented toward data communications. The services at the physical, data-link, and network layers have been separated into different products more quickly than at the upper application-service layers.

For example, you can more easily swap among the different network hardware—Token Ring, EtherNet, and FDDI—than you can swap out session layer or presentation layer services. Changing network hardware types is merely a matter of changing the network interface card and network operating system driver software. The same interface card can work with a variety of network operating systems, simply by writing a software driver that mediates the differences. These lower layers are implemented in hardware or firmware today, and their services are more clear-cut. As networks develop, however, modularity should increase at the upper layers, as well. For example, the network layer became more modular in 1991, as network operating systems offered customers the option of choosing among different Network and transport layer protocols, instead of offering only one protocol.

## Lack of Conformity

Few networks completely conform to the OSI model's layers and conventions. This has happened for several reasons. First, many manufacturers designed and implemented their network structures before ISO specified the OSI model. For example, Digital Equipment Corporation designed its Digital Network Architecture and IBM designed its Systems Network Architecture frameworks before ISO finalized the OSI model. Nevertheless, both are layered protocol stacks and are moving toward the ISO conventions. For example, Digital's fifth phase of DECnet includes support for TCP/IP and OSI protocols as well as DECnet. Similarly, IBM has included support for TCP/IP and OSI as well as its own SNA into its Systems Application Architecture.

Second, the International Standards Organization has also specified protocols at each of the OSI model layers, but OSI networks in production environments are still rare today. Commercial OSI products are still immature and offer limited functionality at high purchase and implementation prices. OSI is implemented more widely in Europe than in the United States, although the United States government has mandated either OSI compliance or a migration path to OSI support. (For more on the specifics of OSI protocols and interoperability among different protocol stacks, see Chapter 8, "Standards and Interoperability.")

# Choosing Among Official and Industry Standards

There are two types of standards: *de facto* and *de jure*. De jure standards are endorsed by official standards organizations. De facto standards are widely used and implemented, but controlled by a single vendor or group. For example, Novell's NetWare and the Internet Engineering Task Force's TCP/IP are industry standards; the ISO's OSI suite is an official standard.

# Official Standards

Official standards bodies include the Institute of Electrical and Electronics Engineers (IEEE), the American National Standards Institute (ANSI), the International Consultative Committee for Telegraphy and Telephony (CCITT), and the International Standards Organization (ISO). Individual companies and countries participate in these standards-making bodies to decide on the specifics of computers and computer communications.

The IEEE is a professional society of electronics and electrical engineers. Within the computer communication industry, the 802 is the best-known IEEE group. The 802 group defines many of the computer communications standards, ranging from network management to metropolitan area networks to wireless networks (see Table 4.2).

**Table 4.2. A guide to the IEEE 802 standards.**

| Standard Number | Specification |
| --- | --- |
| 802.1 | *Higher Layer Interface standard*. This standard is concerned with specifications such as the Spanning Tree Algorithm for transparent MAC-layer bridges and the Heterogeneous LAN Management specification for a common set of management objects for Token Ring and EtherNet networks. |
| 802.2 | *Logical Link Control (LLC) standard*. This standard is concerned with the specification that enables the physical layer of LANs to be independent of the upper layers. The LLC is the upper sublayer of the data-link layer. |
| 802.3 | *Carrier Sense Multiple Access with Collision Detection (CMSA/CD)*. This standard is concerned with the specification of CSMA/CD networks, more commonly known as EtherNet. Specifications exist for 1Base5 Starlan, 10Base5 thick EtherNet, 10Base2 thin EtherNet, 10BaseT telephone wire EtherNet, and 10Base36 broadband EtherNet. A draft exists for fiber EtherNet (10BaseF and 10BaseF-FO). |

*continues*

**Table 4.2.  continued**

| Standard Number | Specification |
| --- | --- |
| 802.4 | *Token Bus*. This standard is concerned with the specification of 10Mbps token-passing, bus-based networks. |
| 802.5 | *Token Ring*. This standard is concerned with the specification for token-passing, ring-based networks. Specifications exist for 4Mbps and 16Mbps transmission speeds over shielded twisted-pair and unshielded twisted-pair wire. A draft standard exists for a fiber-optic Token Ring. |
| 802.6 | *Metropolitan Area Network*. This standard is concerned with the specification of a distributed-queue, dual-bus access method over fiber-optic cable. |
| 802.7 | *Broadband Technical Advisory Group*. This standard is concerned with the specification of broadband transmissions over multifrequency coaxial cable. |
| 802.8 | *Fiber-Optic Technical Advisory Group*. This standard is concerned with specifying fiber-optic networks. |
| 802.9 | *Integrated Voice-Data Terminals*. This standard is concerned with the integration of voice, video, and data networking. A standard exists. |
| 802.11 | *Wireless Networks*. This standard is concerned with wireless transmission methods for local area networks. Work is under way to define a draft standard. |

ANSI is another source of computer communications standards. ANSI is not an arm of the United States government; it is instead an independent organization that is funded primarily through the sale of standards. ANSI forwards many of the IEEE standards to ISO, as well as defining its own, such as FDDI.

The CCITT is primarily concerned with establishing telecommunications standards. The CCITT is part of the International Telecommunications Union (ITU), which is under the aegis of the United Nations. The CCITT is made up of individuals representing the public and private telecommunications organizations. The CCITT establishes standards for interconnecting different countries' telephone networks and for the signaling systems used by modems. For example, ISDN, X.25, frame relay, cell relay, and T-1 are CCITT standards.

The world's largest standards body is the ISO, which issues standards on nearly every topic, including film speeds, screw threads, humane animal traps, and network connections. The OSI series of ISO computer standards includes at least one specification for every layer of the OSI model. ISO and CCITT try to work closely together, so as not to duplicate their efforts. For example, both organizations publish the OSI model. Under the CCITT, it is Recommendation X.200; under the ISO, it is ISO 7498. Similarly, the ISO publishes the same specification for store-and-forward electronic messaging as ISO 10021, and CCITT publishes it as Recommendation X.400.

# Industry Standards

Many other widely used protocols are not endorsed by a vendor-neutral body. These de facto standards are generally controlled by a particular manufacturer instead. For example, Apple Computer controls the AppleTalk specifications, Digital Equipment Corporation controls DECnet, IBM controls SAA and SNA, the Internet controls TCP/IP, and Novell controls NetWare. A fine line exists between a proprietary system and a de facto standard. The line is usually crossed when the vendor's installed base hits critical mass and the protocols and devices can no longer be dismissed.

A protocol isn't necessarily better because it is an official standard. Nor is a protocol or specification necessarily better because it has hit critical mass. OSI and TCP/IP are the prime examples of the official standard and the existing solution that came to the rescue. De facto standards are often quicker in the making than official standards, simply because they are "thrown out" into the public and evolve as needed. For a standard to be officially blessed often means years of debate and argument among the members of the standards organizations, which are vendors and even countries, each with their own interests to protect. Nevertheless, de facto standards typically indicate industry or widespread acceptance and that the technology or protocol meets the needs of those who are using it. In any case, de facto standards are powerful statements.

# Are More Standards Better?

Standards are both beneficial and detrimental. They're beneficial, supporters claim, because they help simplify the interconnection of computers and drive down the price of products. They're detrimental, detractors say, because they take too long to develop and stifle engineering creativity.

Standards usually take a long time to develop. Often the problem has been solved by an "interim" solution by the time the standards are formally recognized. A long lead time is partially the nature of the beast—getting hundreds of companies, each with their individual agendas, to agree on a single specification takes a long time. In the worst case, uncooperative vendors—who want to sell proprietary products in the interim while no official standard exists—will purposefully slow the standard's progress. The last stages of 10BaseT's progress largely consisted of debating the signal values—something most end users don't care about. Manufacturers with existing products, however, did.

Often, by the time a specification is finally standardized, the need has been filled by another solution. For example, a standard for fiber-optic EtherNet has been in development for six years. In that time, proprietary solutions have solved the problem and FDDI, a 100Mbps fiber LAN, has emerged. The wide-area service frame relay is a rare exception to the slow process of standards-making. Frame relay is standardized and available in time for end-user companies to get maximum use of it.

Standards are often criticized for blocking engineering creativity, because the protocol skeletons are set, and the vendors and engineers add the dressing. For example, the hundreds of companies manufacturing 10BaseT products could have had their engineers working on different solutions that could be a better way to use unshielded twisted-pair wire for high-speed data transmission. If the engineers worked in a hundred different directions, however, the problems of multivendor networks would be far greater.

In the end, standards help the end user. Vendors don't develop as many proprietary solutions, and end users will have an easier time building a network using different vendors' equipment. Using standards-based products reduces the complexity of multivendor networks. Standards provide a level playing field from which manufacturers can innovate new features.

# Why Corporate Standards Are Important

Although it seems that more industry standards exist than could ever be needed, reasonable standards are essential for building a manageable enterprise-wide network. Without standards for what can be attached to the backbone, the network is an uncontrolled, unmanageable melting pot of devices and protocols.

The network is like a beaker in a chemistry laboratory. Mixing substances carelessly might result in an explosion, a fire, or worse. At the very best, you'll have a beaker filled with an unknown, and probably useless, substance. Without standards on the enterprise-wide network, chaos will result.

Establishing corporate standards requires you to walk a fine line between too much control and not enough control. Standards are necessary: the support desk can't adequately support 17 different word processing packages, nor can MIS manage 10 protocols on the enterprise backbone. Without any standards, MIS spends too much of its resources supporting users, juggling file formats, and putting out incompatibility fires.

Too much control is detrimental to the users and the business-line functions, however. In the past, some MIS departments controlled computer resources too tightly, causing users to seek other solutions. Users aren't about to relinquish the flexibility they gained, nor should they. Productivity losses are the result of overly strict standardization policies. Before mandating that everyone give up his favorite spreadsheet or word processor in favor of the official packages, make sure that the corporate standard meets the departments' business needs. While users are learning a new software package, their productivity decreases. When you establish a corporate standard, make sure that the user ultimately benefits.

The right amount of control enables you to build an enterprise-wide network that can be managed and expanded in a graceful manner. MIS can concentrate on doing a few things well, instead of many things adequately. A network that spans multiple protocols, vendors, and locations is, by definition, complex. By reducing some of the variables, MIS can better control the network.

Your company philosophy will dictate whether MIS standardizes the products used on the departmental level, such as workstations, printers, and applications. Many companies leave the choice of the desktop computer up to the individual departments or users, allowing them to choose the computing devices that best help them do their jobs. As long as they can connect to the enterprise-wide network, the individual departments are often permitted to use whatever equipment helps them achieve their business line functions. Although this approach creates a heterogeneous network that can be quite difficult to support, it greatly benefits the users.

Corporate standards are also essential in maintaining a cost-effective network. MIS departments should define a list of accepted applications, giving users a choice where possible. Departments do not have to waste their efforts in researching applications that are suitable in the network environment, because MIS gives them a menu of options. Corporate standards enable MIS to control what is placed on the network, so that they can ensure that only reliable, tested, and proven components are placed on the mission-critical enterprise-wide network. The fewer different types of network components there are, the more reliable and stable the network will be, because there are fewer variables introduced into the networking equation. Also, MIS can concentrate its efforts on learning how to integrate, manage, and support these applications, so that users can be readily helped. These benefits ultimately lead to cost savings.

When MIS establishes corporate computing standards, it should publish them to the users wherever it makes sense to do so. For example, users may not care about rules such as "all file servers should be connected to the backbone" but they will care about standards such as "nothing less than an IBM 386 with 2MB of RAM will be placed on the network." MIS should publish a list of "approved" products and make it clear that it will support only the items on the list.

Corporate standards can be a source of tension between the departments and MIS. The departments want whatever computers they need to get their jobs done (and they should be permitted to have them), but MIS has to support them. One way to resolve this tension is to draw a line of demarcation between the enterprise-wide network and the departmental LANs, and to give the departments responsibility for managing their own networks. This strategy is often an equitable way to mediate between departmental and central MIS control. The enterprise-wide backbone is MIS' domain; the departmental LANs are the local LAN managers' and users' domain.

When establishing corporate standards:

- ■ Choose products that conform to official or industry standards and will increase your network's flexibility and modularity.

■ Consider the scope of what you will standardize. Will you specify what can be connected to the departmental networks, or will you leave that to the departmental LAN managers?

■ Consider your company's existing computing infrastructure. How do the corporate standards fit with the existing systems?

■ Consider your MIS department's expertise and how the corporate standard will affect it.

■ Consider the component's ability to scale into the enterprise. Will it work gracefully in a large wide area network or will it be an awkward solution?

■ Consider where the technology is in its life cycle. Is it a new technology with a long life span or an older technology that will be obsolete in a year or two?

# Which Components Your Company Should Standardize

Reducing the variables isn't simple. Choosing the right products isn't the hardest part of establishing corporate standards. That's a matter of choosing several likely products, testing their functionality, and then choosing the ones that perform well and that you can afford. This is a straightforward exercise, where you scientifically choose products and test their features. The most difficult part of defining corporate standards is establishing who gets control and whose needs take priority. Often, business units, users, network administrators, and vendors all vie for control. The political aspects of establishing corporate standards are far more tricky.

When establishing corporate standards for network products, consider the technology and physical network models you constructed during the requirements analysis phase. As described in Chapter 2, the technology model describes, in technical terms, how the network will accomplish the business functions of the company. The physical model describes the specifics of the implementation. For example, during the technology modeling phase for a network in a magazine publishing company, the designers will decide whether to use a desktop or host-based publishing system and what the operating system should be. Then in the physical modeling phase, they decide which specific product implementation should be used. Your corporate standards should be in line with your physical and technology models.

Your company should establish rules or standards for network design. For example, your MIS department may decide that end-user workstations cannot be connected directly to the backbone; end-user computers must be connected to a segment. Designing a network in this manner will reduce the amount of traffic on the backbone as well as help localize failures. Or, for example, the MIS department may decide that all file servers must be connected directly to a high-speed backbone to speed up users' access to server-based resources.

Your company should also establish standards for the specific network components, from wiring, to the network protocols, to the operating systems, to the network applications. Keep in mind that different hardware and cable types are easier to accommodate; multiple network protocols and applications are more difficult to support.

When defining your company's computing standards, you should choose products that adhere to industry or official standards, and you will gain the benefits of a modular, standards-based network. A sample of standard network products appears in Table 4.3.

**Table 4.3.   Sample approved list for a company's supported network products.**

| Category | Product |
| --- | --- |
| Desktop Hardware | Compaq 386/25 or 386/33 with 80MB hard disk, 4MB RAM, SuperVGA monitor. |
| | Northgate 386/25 or 386/33 with 80Mb hard disk, 4Mb RAM, SuperVGA. |
| | Compaq 486/33 with 80Mb hard disk, 8Mb RAM, SuperVGA monitor. |
| | Macintosh IIgs |
| | Macintosh Quadra |
| Desktop Software | DOS 5.0 or 3.1 |
| | Windows 3.0 or 3.1 |
| | OS/2 1.2 Extended Edition |
| | System 7.0 |

| Category | Product |
| --- | --- |
| LAN Hardware | EtherNet (thin coaxial or twisted-pair). 10BaseT EtherNet for all new EtherNet installations. 16-bit cards—SMC or 3Com. 4/16 Mbps Token Ring using STP. 16-bit cards—Madge or Olicom. |
| Servers | NetFrame or Compaq SystemPro. 320Mb disk, 8Mb RAM. Remote management. |
| Network Operating Systems | NetWare for Mac for all Mac users. NetWare 3.11 running IPX for all DOS and OS/2 users. |
| | NetWare Lite for DOS workgroups that don't want connectivity to any other department. |
| | AppleShare for Mac workgroups that don't want connectivity to any other department. |
| Network Services and Utilities | Castelle as second-source. Optus FacSys with CAS-compatible fax modem for faxing. |
| | Intel LANspool for print spooling. Alternatively, Fresh Technology is supported. |
| | Insight Mosaic for printer font management. |
| | XtreeNet for end-user file management. Alternatively, Norton Utilities is supported. |
| | McAfee anti-viral software. |
| Applications | WordPerfect 5.0 for DOS users. Alternatively, Microsoft Word is supported. |
| | Microsoft Word for Mac users. Alternatively, WordPerfect is supported. |

*continues*

**113**

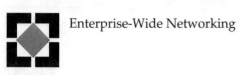

**Table 4.3.   continued**

| Category | Product |
| --- | --- |
| Applications (continued) | Excel for DOS or Mac users. |
| | Lotus 1-2-3 for DOS users. Alternatively QuattroPro 4.0 for DOS users is supported. |
| | Paradox 3.5 for DOS users in workgroup applications. |
| | Oracle 5.0 for DOS and Mac users and for strategic applications. |
| | Forest & Trees for database query tool for DOS users. |
| | OracleCard also supported. |
| | Aldus PageMaker |
| | Aldus Persuasion |
| | cc:Mail for DOS, OS/2, and Mac users. Alternatively, CE Software QuickMail supported for Mac users. |
| | Co/Session or CloseUp for remote access. |
| | Attachmate Extra! or Wall Data Rumba for 3270 terminal emulation. |
| Internetworking | Retix local EtherNet bridges. RAD local EtherNet bridges. Madge local Token-Ring bridges. Proteon local Token-Ring bridges. |
| | cisco routers. |
| | Attachmate 3270 gateways. Wall Data is second-source. |
| WAN Services | Dial-up modems/lines up to 19.2 Kbps. USRobotics or Telebit preferred. Call-back security must be implemented on any modem attached to the network. |

| Category | Product |
|---|---|
| WAN Services (continued) | T-1, fractional T-1 supported. |
| | X.25 supported. |
| | J&L Information Systems Chatterbox asynchronous communication servers. Network Products is second-source. |

# Consider the Scalability

Consider the component's ability to scale into the enterprise. Products and technologies designed into the enterprise network must accommodate the scope and goals of the network. Choose standards with an eye toward a product's manageability, reliability, functionality, and reputation. Key is a product's ability to perform consistently even under high loads. For example, Apple's LocalTalk operates at 230Kbps, which is much too slow for an enterprise backbone. Similarly, the routing system used by AppleTalk causes a high number of broadcasts to be transmitted, which can quickly flood the limited bandwidth of a network operating system. A network protocol designed for operation in a wide area network, such as TCP/IP, is more suitable.

# Consider Your MIS Department's Expertise

Also consider your company's existing computing equipment and MIS personnel's expertise. As much as possible, your corporate standards should enable you to preserve your investment in computing equipment. For example, if you are primarily a DEC shop, it probably does not make sense to go entirely to an IBM implementation. For one, your MIS personnel will be well-versed in the existing system, and you should try to use as much of that knowledge as possible.

As the computing infrastructure moves from mainframe-based, it is imperative that MIS, LAN, and telecom personnel are cross-trained on each others' systems. A computer person can no longer afford to be ignorant of telecommunications, because multisite wide area networks are becoming the norm rather than the exception.

# Consider the Life Cycle

Consider the technology's life cycle. When establishing standards, examine where the technology is in its life cycle. For example, FDDI is at the very beginning of its implementation life cycle. ARCnet is toward the end (except in departmental or workgroup networks). EtherNet and Token Ring are in the middle of their cycles. Newer technologies will be more expensive, both in terms of purchasing products and hiring expertise, but they thwart technological obsolescence longer.

It is also important to regulate which network layer protocols run on the backbone. The network layer protocols are determined by your primary computer systems and their network types. The network protocols are usually tuned to their specific environment so that you usually get the best performance and greatest functionality. You may choose to deviate from the "native" network protocols, however, if there is no clear-cut native protocol, if your company lacks expertise in that protocol, or for many other reasons.

Sometimes the choice is simple. For instance, if the users primarily have Sun workstations, then TCP/IP is probably the network protocol of choice, because TCP/IP runs natively with the operating system. TCP/IP has the best performance and functionality in this instance. Novell's NetWare probably won't provide the best set of features and services. If the departmental LANs are primarily NetWare, you may chose from IPX/SPX or TCP/IP. If the desktop computers are primarily PCs, IPX/SPX is most likely; however, if your desktop computers are UNIX, you must choose IPX or TCP/IP (or run both).

In practice, an enterprise-wide network often must accommodate a variety of network layer protocols, but you should select the few most important protocols to run over the backbone network. This reduces the management complexities because there are fewer variables. For example, you may determine that only TCP/IP, IPX/SPX, DECnet, and LAT traffic may run on the backbone. All other protocols must be encapsulated into one of these "standard" protocols.

Not all protocols are suitable for the enterprise backbone. Backbone protocols should provide good performance, the ability to be routed, good error recovery, good flow control, and the ability to operate efficiently in a wide area network. Such protocols include TCP/IP, DECnet, SAA/SNA, and OSI. Protocols such as NetWare's IPX, NetBIOS, and Apple's AppleTalk are not designed specifically for wide area network communications, and are often encapsulated or translated into a protocol better suited to wide area network routing. As mentioned, IPX/SPX is not efficient on a WAN. NetBIOS is intended to be a local protocol, and does not include routing functionality; AppleTalk incurs a great deal of overhead because of how frequently its routers dynamically update their address tables.

If you run multiple native protocols on the backbone, interconnect the systems with multiprotocol routers. Multiprotocol routers deliver higher performance but at a price. A multiplicity of protocols makes the network harder to manage.

An alternative to multiprotocol routers is encapsulation. When one protocol is encased in another protocol's format, it is called *encapsulation* or *tunneling*. Encapsulation slows the overall network performance by anywhere from 20 to 200 percent. Also, no standard method of encapsulation exists. Despite encapsulation's drawbacks, it reduces the number of protocols on the backbone, which translates into easier management.

# Selecting the Network Operating System

A hand saw and a power saw both accomplish the same end, but with different degrees of ease. A hand saw is suitable for small jobs. A power saw, however, can cut the same piece of wood much more quickly and efficiently, and is better suited to large jobs. Likewise, your Network Operating System (NOS) must fit the job at hand. Network operating systems fall into two categories: *departmental* and *enterprise*. Departmental, or workgroup, network operating systems provide an array of network services, including file, application, and printer sharing. They should also offer fault-tolerant features, such as server mirroring and disk mirroring. Typically, departmental network operating systems are simpler to install and manage as enterprise-wide network operating systems, but offer fewer features and less security, poorer connectivity to other types of systems, and slower performance.

A network operating system suitable for an enterprise-wide network must offer more sophisticated services. Like a workgroup NOS, an enterprise-wide NOS enables users to share files, applications, and printers, but it does so for a larger volume of users and data and at higher performance. Furthermore, an enterprise-wide NOS offers the ability to connect to disparate systems, both workstation and server. For example, even if the NOS runs on an Intel-based platform, it should accommodate UNIX workstations. Similarly, a RISC-based server operating system should accommodate DOS, Windows, Macintosh, and OS/2. An enterprise-wide network operating system must accommodate multiple protocols (such as TCP/IP, IPX/SPX, NetBIOS, DECnet, and OSI), enable easy access to remote resources, and offer sophisticated management services, including hooks to enterprise-wide management systems.

Network operating systems such as Banyan's VINES, Novell's NetWare 3.X, Microsoft's LAN Manager, or Sun's NFS are well suited to enterprise-wide networks, whereas network operating systems such as NetWare 2.X, Artisoft's LANtastic, or Tiara's 10net are suitable for smaller workgroups.

Standardizing on a single network operating system greatly simplifies the enterprise-wide network and benefits both users and MIS. Whereas the lower layers of the OSI model are fairly modular and easy to mix and match, the software layers are not. Using a single NOS that can scale from the department up to the enterprise provides a unified platform from which to run applications and manage the network.

Settling on a single NOS facilitates communication, because gateways between network operating systems are rudimentary at best, offering users little more than a way to transfer files between servers running dissimilar network operating systems. A NetWare user trying to access resources on a VINES network, for instance, might as well be trying to use VAX resources. Service will be limited and slow. Improvements in this area are happening, albeit slowly. For example, under LAN Manager 2.1, users can access LAN Manager and NetWare servers simultaneously. Some third-party products enable users to load multiple network operating system drivers at their workstations, enabling them to access two different NOSs at the same time.

An integration problem arises if dissimilar network operating systems are already in use, as they are in most enterprise-wide networks. If the applications were properly selected, you may be able to change the network operating system without affecting the applications. If not, you may need to weigh the cost of limited communication against the price of pulling the plug on one NOS and replacing it with a new one. Switching network operating systems is painful. Do it only when it is truly essential.

Some criteria for choosing an enterprise-wide network operating system follow. Because a single network operating system currently does not satisfy all of these criteria, you'll have to make tradeoffs based on your business needs and computing experience. Figure 4.1 illustrates the services of such an ideal network operating system. The ideal network operating system should support a variety of desktop operating systems, transport interfaces, and computing environments. Using one NOS that can reach from the desktop to the glass house enables you to build a common computing infrastructure.

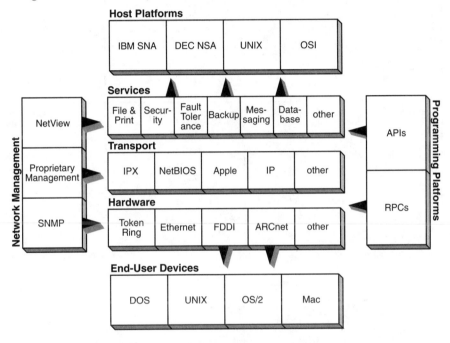

***Figure 4.1.*** *Network operating system architecture.*

Table 4.4 summarizes the features of the major network operating systems, as evaluated against these criteria. The major PC LAN network operating systems are compared on a variety of fronts, including native operating systems support, desktop workstation support, and management functionality.

Table 4.4. Network operating systems compared.

| Network Operating System | Server Operating System | Workstation Operating System | Other Host Platforms | Network Hardware | Network Protocols | Directory Services | Management | Programming Interface |
|---|---|---|---|---|---|---|---|---|
| Novell NetWare 3.X | 32-bit NetWare single processing | DOS, OS/2, Macintosh, UNIX | UNIX, VM/MVS, AS/400, RISC, VAX | Ethernet, Token Ring, FDDI, ARCNet, all through ODI & IPX | IPX/SPX IP, AFP | Naming | proprietary SNMP Netview hooks | APIs, RPCs |
| Microsoft LAN Manager 2.X | 16-bit OS/2 single processing asymmetrical multiproc. available | DOS, OS/2, Macintosh | UNIX, VAX | Ethernet, Token Ring, NDIS-Compatible | NetBEUI, IP | Naming | proprietary SNMP Netview hooks | APIs, RPCs |
| Banyan VINES 4.X | 32-bit UNIX single processing symmetrical multiproc. available | DOS, OS/2, Macintosh | UNIX | Ethernet, Token Ring, ARCNet, NDIS-Compatible | VINES IP, AFP | distributed global directory | proprietary | APIs, RPCs |
| IBM LAN Server | 16-bit OS/2 | DOS, OS/2 | | Ethernet, Token Ring, PC Network | NetBEUI | | proprietary | APIs |

# End-User Services

The NOS should provide a wide array of end-user services. The NOS should provide high-performance file and print serving on a local and remote basis. It should also ensure data security and integrity though strict security and fault-tolerant schemes. Backup facilities should be integrated directly into the network operating system.

Application-layer services such as database and messaging are beginning to be integrated into the NOS itself, rather than running as an add-on application. Such integration will afford higher performance.

# High Performance

The server operating system must be a high-performance operating system. A NOS is analogous to a desktop computer operating system such as DOS or OS/2, except a NOS controls the operations of many computers. A NOS "tricks" an operating system into thinking that it is a multi-user operating system. The network operating system must provide higher performance to meet the needs of many users. Consider whether the NOS is a 16-bit or 32-bit implementation. A 32-bit NOS, such as NetWare or VINES, crunches bytes more quickly than a 16-bit NOS such as LAN Manager or LAN Server.

In some network operating systems, the server runs both the NOS and the OS. When a user makes a request, the NOS intercepts and interprets it, then hands it to the OS for execution. The OS services the request, and hands it back to the NOS, which hands it back to the user. Such network operating systems include Microsoft's MS-Net (and all of its variations) as well as Microsoft's LAN Manager and IBM's LAN Server.

Many high-performance network operating systems bypass this slow process by running a proprietary operating system on the server, instead of a standard OS plus redirector software. VINES is built around a proprietary version of UNIX. NetWare's server OS is a proprietary multitasking OS that has interfaces, called *shells*, to standard operating systems such as DOS, OS/2, and UNIX. Using a single-layer architecture greatly improves network performance. Whereas a LAN Manager server runs two layers of software, a NetWare server runs only one. NetWare is widely regarded as the fastest NOS.

Multiprocessing is another way to deliver performance to operating systems. To date, Banyan and Microsoft ship multiprocessing versions of their network operating systems; Novell has only announced a strategic direction. Multiprocessing network operating systems, which run on servers with multiple CPUs, provide higher throughput and support larger processing volumes by running unrelated tasks on separate CPUs. In a *symmetrical multiprocessing* implementation, either processor can be used for any task. In an *asymmetrical* implementation, one processor must be used for I/O, and the other may be used for an application.

NOS vendors are currently moving toward combining the desktop and server operating systems. This tighter integration will decrease the layers of software and therefore increase the performance and services offered by the server. It will enable them to better integrate messaging, directory, and security services into the NOS. For example, Microsoft is developing Windows NT (for

*New Technology*), a 32-bit operating system due out in 1992. Because Windows NT uses a 32-bit kernel rather than a 16-bit kernel, it will be able to deliver higher performance than 16-bit operating systems such as OS/2 version 2.0, Windows 3.x, and DOS. In addition, Microsoft is incorporating networking services in both Windows NT and Windows 3.x.

# Support for Desktop Operating Systems

The NOS must support an array of desktop operating systems. To be suitable for the enterprise, the network operating system must support the gamut of desktop computer operating systems, including DOS, Macintosh OS, UNIX, and OS/2. Users should have the applications and workstations that best enable them to do their jobs, and the NOS must support the resulting array of workstation types.

The different workstations should be able to view files and resources in their native OS formats, even if the files or resources reside on a server type different than the workstation. For example, Mac users should see network resources in their familiar folder format, even if the resources reside on a NetWare server. Differences in file naming formats must be overcome. The different lengths and conventions of DOS, OS/2 High Performance Filing System, UNIX, and Macintosh file names must be resolved.

NetWare offers the broadest workstation support—DOS, OS/2, Macintosh, and UNIX clients—and offers "name spaces" of native filing conventions for each. To do so, NetWare hashes and caches file names as they are requested by users. VINES supports DOS, Macintosh, and OS/2, but OS/2 is not as well integrated as DOS. In VINES 4.x, Macs are supported through a third-party product, so they are not as well integrated either; however, Mac support will be native in VINES 5.x. LAN Manager supports OS/2, DOS, and Macintosh workstations, but IBM's version, LAN Server, supports only OS/2 and DOS workstations.

# Independence from Hardware

The NOS must operate independently of hardware. An enterprise-wide NOS should not be tied to any particular network hardware or server, which enables you to preserve your investment in existing equipment.

A NOS should run on the array of hardware suitable for enterprise-wide and departmental networks including FDDI, EtherNet, Token Ring, LocalTalk, and ARCnet. Network hardware independence is delivered through two driver interface specifications: Network Driver Interface Specification (NDIS) and Open Data-Link Interface (ODI), which act as a "buffer" between the adapter card and the network operating system. NDIS is used on LAN Manager networks and is optionally supported on VINES; ODI and NDIS are used on NetWare.

Much of Novell's success results from NetWare's ability to run virtually any type of network hardware, even rare types. NetWare can run on EtherNet, ARCnet, Token Ring, FDDI, PC Network broadband, and a slew of older, slower hardware types, using IPX or ODI drivers. LAN Manager runs on EtherNet and Token Ring via NDIS drivers. VINES runs on ARCnet, EtherNet, and Token Ring, plus optionally supports NDIS drivers. LAN Server runs on Token Ring and IBM PC Network broadband.

The NOS should also run independently of the server type and scale across the range of hardware types. It should be able to run on Industry Standard Architecture (ISA), Extended Industry Standard Architecture (EISA), and Micro Channel Architecture (MCA) Intel 8X86 bus servers. Some network operating systems can also run on Motorola 68000-based servers as well. In the past, vendors such as 3Com and Banyan optimized their network operating systems to run on their proprietary file servers. Although their servers were better designed for network needs than a standard PC, this arrangement locked customers into buying a single-source, proprietary solution. Both companies have since discontinued their hardware lines.

# Support for Communication Protocols

The NOS must support a variety of communication protocols. All network operating systems have native transport and session protocols; however, an enterprise-wide NOS must provide support for other types. Support for a variety of protocols is key to having a single NOS on the enterprise because it enables you to accommodate multiple types of workstations and file systems.

For example, NetWare uses IPX/SPX at its core but can run TCP/IP. LAN Server and LAN Manager use NetBEUI (which is a variation of NetBIOS);

however, Microsoft has announced that LAN Manager 2.1 will support TCP/IP. Version 2.1 is due to ship in 1992. VINES uses VINES IP, a Banyan-specific version of the industry-standard IP.

Carefully examine the session and transport protocols, because they largely determine network traffic patterns. Check how often the protocol sends updates to its routers. If the messages are sent too frequently, it may overburden wide-area links. Consider also the performance penalty of running multiple protocols in the network's file servers.

# Access to Resources

The NOS must offer a way for users to easily find and access resources. Usually, the enabling technology is a directory service or a naming service. Naming services or domains are less sophisticated than directory services. With a directory service, users no longer have to know where the desired resource is located and type an arcane set of characters to reach it. Users need to know only that they want to print to the plotter in New York, for example. A directory system identifies network users and resources by associating names with attributes.

NetWare and LAN Manager both have domains, which are groupings of servers that can be treated as one unit to facilitate network management. Banyan offers StreetTalk directory services for its VINES. Since its inception, StreetTalk has been the benchmark of directory services. StreetTalk makes it exceptionally easy to locate and manage resources in a far-flung network, which is key to VINES's viability in a large-scale network.

The directory service's naming convention should be convenient to the user rather than to the computer system. For example, it should support normal rules of case and permit embedded spaces and punctuation. Support for multilingual names is important if your enterprise-wide network spans countries. The directory service must also be distributed across the network.

Essential to any company's directory service offering is its migration to the emerging OSI's X.500 directory services standard. Although X.500 won't be deployed until 1995, the vendor should have a migration strategy that will enable it to connect its existing directory service to the OSI standard.

# Resource Management and Enterprise Management

The NOS must provide a way to manage its resources, as well as hook into enterprise management systems. The enterprise-wide NOS must deliver tools that enable its management. The vendor must not only provide server-based management tools so that the departmental administrators can manage server resources such as disk space and print queues, but the vendor must provide hooks to an enterprise manager. This is usually done through the Simple Network Management Protocol (SNMP) or through hooks to an enterprise management system such as IBM's NetView.

Novell offers some server-based management tools, and many third-party companies fill in the gaps. Both Novell and Microsoft have integrated SNMP support into their network operating systems so that they can report alarms and other information to an SNMP console. Both can also send alerts to NetView. To date, Banyan supports only proprietary management.

# Scalability to Other Platforms

The NOS must scale to other computer platforms. If one NOS is to serve users' needs across an enterprise, it must scale to computer platforms beyond the PC. Network operating systems, therefore, need to run on minicomputer host OSs such as UNIX and VMS, as well as mainframe OSs such as VM and MVS.

Systems developers have ported Novell's Portable NetWare to run on various implementations of UNIX as well as IBM host OSs. For example, versions of Portable NetWare run on Data General's line of minis as well as NCR hosts. Microsoft has codeveloped versions of LAN Manager that run on UNIX, called LM/X. (Hewlett-Packard originally developed LM/X with Microsoft, but in 1991 Microsoft forged a development agreement with AT&T to develop the next generation.) Digital Equipment has also ported LAN Manager to run on its line of VAXs.

If native versions of the NOS are not available, the vendor should support gateways to dissimilar host types. Gateways are slower than running the software directly on the host, but many MIS departments prefer having the intermediate devices so as not to "corrupt" the host.

# Published APIs

The NOS should have published APIs. The NOS vendor should publish the NOS's application programming interfaces (APIs), which enable third-party developers to write applications that augment the network operating systems' native services. The NOS should also support remote procedure call (RPC) programming toolkits as a way to ease the development of applications that run across a multitude of protocols. Novell, Microsoft, and Banyan have published their APIs and support RPCs through third-party products.

# Choosing the Network's Topology

After you have built a business model of your enterprise-wide network, you must construct a technology model, which serves as a blueprint of the network's architecture. This model lays out the network's ground rules that define the basic network structure, describes how information will be distributed, and specifies allowable network components. The technology model should allow for modular construction of the network.

The first step in determining the enterprise-wide network's topology is deciding where the resources will be located in the infrastructure. During the requirements analysis phase, you identified the resources and applications that are needed as well as the resources that are available. During this phase, you've also identified the shortcomings of the existing system. During the design phase, you should evaluate how you will improve access to these resources, applications, and services.

Resources on an enterprise-wide network can be *centralized* or *distributed*. In a centralized network, one site is designated as the central data center. The remote sites maintain minimal local computer services instead of relying on the services at the central site. In a distributed network, the computing resources are spread more evenly through the local sites. Departments have control over their computing systems and their applications. Both models have advantages and disadvantages, and which architecture is appropriate depends on your company's business goals, distribution of offices, management philosophy, network expertise, and budget.

# Centralized Networks

A centralized network is physically configured as a star (see Figure 4.2). This configuration is most similar to the traditional mainframe model. One site, designated the *hub*, is the central location of the computer hosts, networking hardware, telecommunications equipment, management and support services, and other related equipment and services. With a star-configured network, the remote end-user sites communicate back to the central site; they do not directly communicate with each other, but rather indirectly talk through the hub. Although some computing equipment may be distributed to the departments, all of the shared resources are maintained centrally.

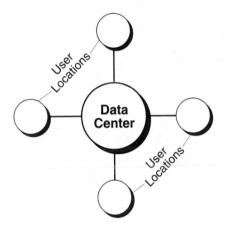

**Figure 4.2.** *A centralized network topology.*

A variation of this architecture is a *cascaded star* or *tree*, where several data centers or hubs are often set up for redundancy's sake. This way, if a disaster occurs and one data center is disabled, the other data centers can continue operation.

A centralized network is most appropriate if your company is comprised of a central headquarters with many branch offices. Retail stores, branch banks, and sales organizations typically build centralized networks. A centralized client/server network may also be appropriate if your company has already implemented a mainframe-oriented, data-center computing infrastructure, so that all of your computing resources and expertise are already centrally located.

A star configuration enables you to concentrate all of your computer and telecommunications equipment and expertise in a few locations, which eases management and troubleshooting. This reduces the number of technicians and managers necessary, because they are localized. Also, an equipment failure in a local site affects only those users, rather than affecting all of the users in the enterprise.

A star-configured network has its disadvantages as well. It requires one link for each remote site, which can be costly. The number and the cost of wide-area links increase linearly as the network grows.

Also, a star network has a single point of failure. If a fire, tornado, or other natural disaster destroys the data center, the remote offices will be left without any means of communication, because they depended on the data center to provide services. Even failures of telephone services can disable the enterprise-wide network. In an imperfect world, redundancy of data centers and critical equipment is essential to protect against total network failure. Redundancy significantly adds to (and often doubles) the cost of the enterprise-wide network.

## A Star Network at Springfield Public Schools

Networking at the Springfield, Oregon public schools is educational. The public school district relies on networked databases to track student behavior and testing results, to monitor the special needs of its elementary students, and to aid nurses in maintaining information on students' health problems.

Students, administrators, and teachers use the network. Students use PCs in the library to locate books in any of the school district's libraries. Students can quickly find the book's location, and because the information is kept electronically, cards aren't missing or damaged, and the space that would otherwise be occupied by drawers of cards is freed up for books, tables, and other library essentials. Scheduling software helps the school administrators efficiently schedule meetings and allocate space, so they spend taxpayers' dollars wisely. Electronic mail eliminates phone tag and helps bring the latest news to administrators and teachers.

The Springfield schools tap into the Oregon Total Information Service's databases, which are maintained by a consortium of 78 school districts. The Oregon Total Information Service furnishes databases for human resources, fiscal management, payroll, purchasing, and inventory management. By sharing resources, this database service helps eliminate redundant administrations and services among the school districts.[1]

The center of the Springfield Public Schools' star-shaped enterprise-wide network—and business operations—is the district office. The school system's network topology matches its business organization. The central network is primarily comprised of 10BaseT EtherNet over unshielded twisted-pair, but some older 1Mbps Starlan and Corvus Omninet exists. The individual schools are connected to the main site via bridge/routers. T-1 lines run to each high school; one 56Kbps channel is used for data, whereas the rest of the bandwidth is used for voice traffic. Each high school has a file server and network for its own applications. The elementary and middle schools and the maintenance center are connected to the district office via 56Kbps dedicated leased lines (see Figure 4.3).

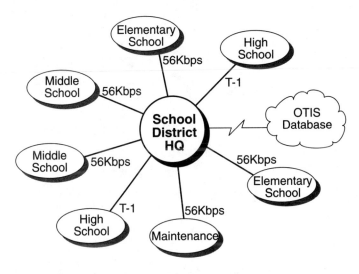

*Figure 4.3.  The Springfield Public Schools' star network.*

---

[1]Dan Matthews, Springfield Oregon Public Schools. "Interop Achievement Award Application." Mountain View, CA: Interop, 1991.

In this application, a star topology is appropriate because the individual schools communicate almost exclusively with the central administration and have little need to communicate with each other. LANs at each site take care of local computing needs.

# Distributed Network

The approach that better fits the distributed, client/server or network computing model is to decentralize the computer and telecommunications services. In a distributed network, locally used resources are distributed to the local sites and shared resources are maintained centrally. Each site communicates with other sites via a *mesh* topology (see Figure 4.4). In a distributed network, communication is many-to-many, whereas communication in a centralized network is point-to-point. A mesh network provides any-to-any connectivity.

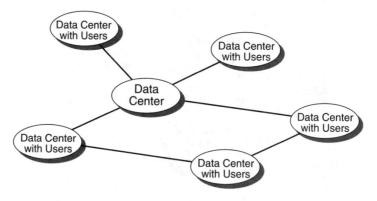

**Figure 4.4.** *A distributed network topology.*

A distributed network architecture is appropriate if your company's offices are also distributed and each carries on an equally important business function and therefore needs to communicate with any other office. For example, if your company has a manufacturing site in one city, corporate headquarters in another, and research and development in a third, a distributed network is best. Mesh networks are also appropriate for law offices or financial institutions or for any company that wants peer-to-peer connectivity.

Distributed networks place the resources where the users can have immediate access to them. In centralized networks, users have to send jobs off to a remote mainframe and wait for the results. In distributed networks, processing is primarily performed locally. A mesh network is more flexible for the users and therefore the business, but it can be more difficult to manage, especially for individuals trained in centralized network management. A mesh network ensures redundancy; because more than one path exists between any two points, the loss of service at one site shouldn't affect other sites.

# Hybrid Networks

Your company's distribution of offices and management philosophy largely determines the architecture of your enterprise-wide network. Keep in mind that although your industry may affect your company's structure, business goals are the ultimate determinants of the network architecture.

An extreme version of either star or mesh topology is rarely the best solution. A strict star implementation brings back the days of tight control over information and applications and slow improvements in information services. On the other hand, any-to-any connectivity can be costly and a challenge to manage. The best design is often a mix of star and mesh designs, or a *hybrid* (see Figure 4.5). A series of hierarchical stars or a partial mesh may best fit your corporation's distribution of power and offices.

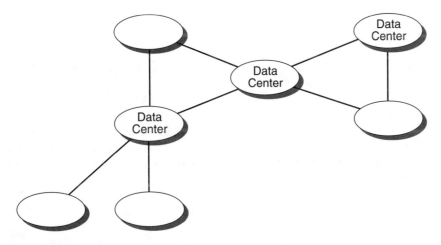

*Figure 4.5.* *Hybrid network topology.*

Consider the impact of traffic flow on the enterprise backbone. Do most user sites have information that must be reported back to a central location, or do they perform most of their work locally and ship only some information back to another location? Perhaps your network is a combination. Pay more attention to how work and information flow in the company than to strict architectures.

When bringing connectivity to each site in the enterprise, consider how you will manage the network. If you build a centrally controlled network, you may want to manage it centrally as well. If you build a distributed network, distributed management may be appropriate. The strategy depends on your corporate culture, staffing, and the quality of available tools. In addition, compare the costs against your available budget.

The enterprise-wide network's architecture does not have to match the campus networks' topology. For example, two campuses may be FDDI rings, three may be star-wired EtherNets, two may be bus-based EtherNets, and four may be star-wired Token Rings. A campus network often uses a *bus* or a *star*. A bus-based backbone has bridges or routers "hanging" off it to connect the departmental LAN "ribs." An *inverted backbone*, or star, is the newer architecture and it enables MIS to centralize the wiring concentrators, bridges and routers into a central location, which eases management. In an inverted backbone, a high-powered wiring hub and router become the center of the network, and all cable runs back to this hub. (For more on structured wiring and the use of internetworking devices, see Chapter 5, "Designing the Local and Campus Internetwork.")

## A Hybrid Network at SUNY

The State University of New York (SUNY) implemented a modified star architecture to connect 34 state-operated campuses and eight county-supported community colleges with each other and to SUNY Central Administration (see Figure 4.6). SUNYNet's charter is to provide and maintain a communications infrastructure for its member campuses to use at a reasonable cost. Applications include SUNY business administration, academic research, software distribution, training support, electronic mail, and file transfers.[2]

---

[2]Tom Neiss, State University of New York Central Administration. "Interop Achievement Award Application." Mountain View, CA: Interop, 1991.

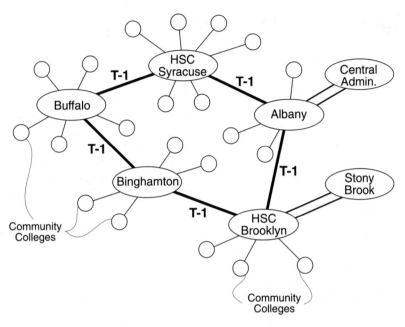

*Figure 4.6.* *SUNY's hybrid network.*

In addition to providing services to New York's state universities, SUNYNet also connects to other networks and organizations, including Bitnet, New York State Department of Audit and Control, the Department of Labor, the Higher Education Services Corporation, the Department of Motor Vehicles, and the Department of Labor.

Six SUNY schools connect to Central Administration in Albany: Albany, Binghamton, Brooklyn, Buffalo, Stony Brook, and Syracuse. Each is also the center of a star that connects its local community colleges. Additionally, each campus has an extensive local network. The SUNY star networks are connected by T-1 lines in a ring topology to facilitate communication. Although the business center of the network is Albany, the network is supported from Buffalo, which is across the state.

SUNY uses a hierarchical star to achieve this communication. The community colleges need only to communicate with the state university in their areas, but the state-run universities' applications necessitate that they communicate with each other as well as with the central administration in Albany. As the SUNY topology shows, however, the network's logical center (Albany) does not have to coincide with the management center (Buffalo).

# The Cost of Distributing and Centralizing Services

Although some think that distributed networks are more expensive to build and maintain than traditional host-based systems, they are actually less so, according to a study conducted by the Index Group, "The Costs of Network Ownership." The study defines a distributed computing network as one "in which users obtain most of their services from a local processor. The job of the network in these cases is to support access to remote processors when and as it is needed." The study, conducted in 1989, examined host-based minicomputer networks.[3]

The study found that a distributed network costs $2,741 per port over a five-year period, whereas a centralized network costs $6,242 per port over the same period (see Table 4.5). The largest differential is communication line costs. In a distributed network, the line costs are 6.5 percent of the total, whereas in a centralized network they are 31.3 percent of the total cost. Line costs are higher in a centralized network because every site must rely on the central data center for its data processing. With a distributed network, the majority of the processing occurs locally, and only a small percentage will be sent over the network. Also, because a centralized approach requires a high degree of redundancy, the average equipment and software costs differed by nearly $1,000 per port.

Table 4.5.   Corporate network costs by topology.

|                | Distributed     | Centralized     |
| -------------- | --------------- | --------------- |
| Equipment      | $1,157  (42.2%) | $1,965  (31.5%) |
| Software       | 267  (9.7%)     | 465  (7.5%)     |
| Personnel      | 846  (30.9%)    | 4,471  (23.6%)  |
| Communications | 179  (6.5%)     | 1,957  (31.3%)  |

[3]Dr. Michael Treacy and The Index Group. "The Costs of Network Ownership." Cambridge, MA: The Index Group, 1989.

|  | Distributed | Centralized |
|---|---|---|
| Facilities | 292 (10.7%) | 384 (6.1%) |
| Total | $2,741* | $6,242* |

*Dollars per port over a five-year period

# Plan Before You Leap

More than one company has spent millions of dollars installing a new network or computer system only to discover that the system doesn't work properly. The system may be so difficult to use that it's essentially useless. It may never quite get up and running in every location, and only bits and pieces function. Whatever the particular ill, the workers are frustrated by the system's failure to help them do their jobs. Corporate management is displeased with the waste of money. IS is embarrassed, and ultimately held responsible for a system that should never have been approved. The company must decide: scrap the investment and start over, or patch a poor system?

Installing a network or connecting existing networks into an enterprise-wide system is always a risky proposition, but you can minimize your exposure by planning carefully. Can the business process itself be improved before you automate it? Carefully identify the shortcomings of the existing system and enumerate the goals of the new system.

The architecture of the network depends on the business function, the geographical nature of the company, and the corporate philosophy and culture. The architecture may be distributed or centralized. Whatever architecture is appropriate for your company, you must define corporate standards.

Although difficult to accomplish, defining standards will help you to better control the network's growth and management. Standards reduce the infinite number of combinations of network products that can manifest themselves in your network, which ultimately leads to a more stable, manageable LAN. With standards, you can ensure a minimum level of support and service for your users.

Consider standardizing on a network operating system, because it can effectively serve as the network infrastructure. Standardize on the network-layer protocols and internetworking devices. From there, you can vary the users' computers and their applications according to their business needs.

# Designing the Local and Campus Internetwork

*Objectives:*

1. To examine the design and physical aspects of the building, campus, and LAN portions of an enterprise-wide network, including the motivation for and design of a structured wiring cabling plant.

2. To examine how to choose appropriate network types for the enterprise-wide network.

3. To learn how to integrate departmental or proprietary technologies into the enterprise.

4. To examine the use of hubs, repeaters, bridges, routers, and gateways as internetworking devices.

# Designing the Physical Network

A garden left untended soon becomes overgrown. Birds drop seeds and weeds spring up. The grass from the yard creeps over the garden's edge, blurring the carefully cut shape. The shrubs grow too large and block the sun from the flowers growing below. The flowers die out and the weeds grow strong.

Gardeners fight the forces of nature. They spread down peat moss to squelch the weeds. They pull out the unwanted plants and cut back the grass. They prune the shrubs so that all of the plants get enough light. They make the soil more acidic or sandier, depending on the plants' preferences. They kill the bugs and grubs that bore at the plants' roots and leaves.

Like a garden, a network must be well-tended. Left alone, entropy prevails. The network grows haphazardly and chaos ensues. Users attach devices to the network at any time and any place. Subnetworks seem to appear out of nowhere. Such a haphazardly grown network is unmanageable and prone to failure. The problems of early EtherNet networks, which were grown in this fashion, are well-documented. Too many taps, bad splices, and unterminated cables cause intermittent problems. Hunting down these intermittent problems is time-consuming and frustrating. A haphazardly grown network is neither efficient nor elegant. MIS must carefully plan and structure the enterprise-wide network, carefully choosing the right cable types, network types, and internetwork devices.

Although your business applications dictate your specific network architecture, network type, and cable type, today's time-tested network design calls for a star-wired EtherNet or Token Ring over unshielded twisted-pair for the departmental networks and FDDI over fiber for the campus network, linked to various WAN services to connect the multiple campuses. Departmental and campus networks are joined via bridges and routers. Wiring concentrators are used at the different levels to ease the task of running and managing wiring. Gateways are used to connect dissimilar computer systems, such as LANs and mainframes.

# Logical and Physical Designs

Enterprise-wide networks must be designed on two levels: physical and logical. The logical design specifies in general terms where resources are located, where applications reside, and how users will access them. Your company's network can be centralized or distributed, as discussed in Chapter 4. For example, your company's network may be centralized at its headquarters, with the branch offices linked in a star-like fashion. If your company's business structure is decentralized, a distributed network, where any office can communicate directly with any other office, may best fit.

Underneath the logical design, however, is the physical design. The physical design specifies exactly what will be used to build the logical network, for example, what internetworking devices will be used, precisely where the wiring will be run, and what wide area networking services will be used. Chapter 6, "Building the Wide Area Network," covers the wide area networking services, whereas this chapter discusses the concerns of the campus portion of an enterprise-wide network.

# Structured Wiring Defined

A *structured wiring plant* is the underpinning of a well-tended network. Structured wiring assumes that every location in the corporation needs voice and data service eventually, if not immediately. Therefore, MIS wires the entire campus—every building, every conference room, every office, and every cubicle—for data and voice services. You should implement a structured wiring system, because it will ultimately make your network more flexible as well as save your company money.

A structured wiring system is planned and built hierarchically, with a main backbone and multiple branches extending from the backbone (see Figure 5.1). Its structure was adopted from cable plants used in voice networks. As with telephone system wiring, wiring runs across the campus, into the buildings, up the risers, into wiring closets on each floor, through the conduits and cable trays, and out to punch-down blocks and finally to the users' desktops. Every office has network outlets, just as they have telephone jacks.

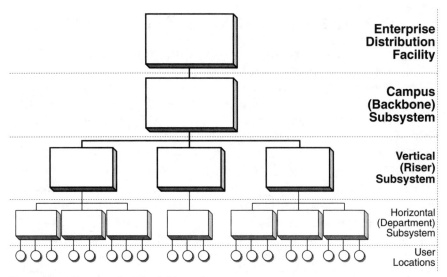

Enterprise
Distribution
Facility

Campus
(Backbone)
Subsystem

Vertical
(Riser)
Subsystem

Horizontal
(Department)
Subsystem

User
Locations

*Figure 5.1.* *Structured wiring's hierarchy.*

Structured wiring is also called *premises distributed wiring*. Different manufacturers call their systems by different names, but the general principles and architectures remain the same. For example, IBM calls its structured wiring system the IBM Cabling System; AT&T has the Premises Distributed System, and Digital has DECconnect. All accomplish the same purpose, but use different wiring specifications.

# Why You Should Use Structured Wiring on the Network

If you implement a structured wiring system, you can increase the life of your cable plant; reduce the cost of adds, moves, and changes; gain easier management and improve network uptime; grow your network gracefully; and simplity documenting the cable plant.

If you implement a structured wiring system, you can:

- Increase the life of the cable plant.

- Reduce the cost of adding, moving, and changing network drops and workstation locations.

- Grow the network gracefully.
- Gain easier management and improve network uptime.
- Simplify documenting the cable plant.

## Increasing the Life of the Cable Plant

Structured wiring increases the life of your cable plant. By implementing structured wiring, you can extend the life of your cable plant. The cable plant is the very skeleton of your network. If properly planned and designed, a structured cabling plant can last 8 to 10 years.

It's difficult to anticipate where users will be located in six months; it's virtually impossible to guess how many users will need network services (and where they will be located) even five years from now. Yet your company's cable plant should be viable for 10 years. With premises distributed wiring, MIS doesn't have to anticipate and guestimate future wiring needs because its managers have anticipated that every user and every location will be networked. Structured wiring gives you a fighting chance at keeping up with a network's relentless growth.

## Reducing Costs

Structured wiring reduces the cost of adds, moves, and changes. For a 100-node network, installing a cable plant costs about 6 percent of the network's total price. As the network grows, so does the cost of installing the cable plant. You do not achieve economies of scale with cabling plants. Although the cable itself is inexpensive, pulling wire is labor-intensive and therefore costly. Pulling wire becomes even more expensive when you have to repeatedly call the cable installer back to add new segments or outlets.

The cost of acquiring the cable plant is relatively small compared to the price of maintaining and adding devices and segments. The average employee moves three times each year. Plus, new people are hired. Offices are expanded. Offices are closed. The cost of adding, moving, and changing users is a significant portion of the network's cost.

The cost of adds, moves, and changes in a structured cable plant is lower than in one grown haphazardly. In a structured cable plant, all the technician has to do is pick up the device, move it to its new location, and plug it in. The department head doesn't have to call in the cable installer to pull a new length of cable or set up 50 new outlets. Connectivity is immediate and already paid for.

## Enabling Graceful Growth

Structured wiring enables graceful network growth. Because a structured wiring plant is modular, it is easier to upgrade. The network can expand in a controlled, graceful manner. For example, you can add a new subnetwork to the backbone with little effect on the network's existing users. You can also replace the type of cable used in one department without affecting the rest of the users. Structured wiring makes it easier to segment your network into manageable and efficient units, because the network is already divided into units.

## Enabling Easier Management and Improved Uptime

Structured wiring enables easier management and improved uptime. The problems of bus-based networks are well documented. The failure of one device can affect the rest of the network. Troubleshooting must be done station by station. Technicians cannot efficiently troubleshoot remote bus networks.

Because a structured wiring system is a series of hierarchical stars built with wiring concentrators, a problem on one segment affects only that segment. Problems are localized; a failure in the engineering department's subnetwork, for example, does not affect the accounting subnetwork. Technicians will find troubleshooting simpler because problems are localized. However, the concentrator becomes a single point of failure; redundant power supplies and repeater logic are essential. This chapter later covers concentrator requirements.

## Simplifying Documentation

Structured wiring simplifies documenting the cable plant. Cable plants are notoriously poorly documented. Often, technicians root through wiring closets and risers for hours in search of the right cable to test. A prewired, structured system is simpler to document. It's easier to label each cable and document its location in a computer-aided design or even a word processing program. Also, the cable plant is relatively stable. With the proper documentation, technicians can quickly find the right cable to test.

# The Structure of Structured Wiring

A structured wiring system is physically configured as a modified hierarchical star, with all locations pre-wired for voice and data. It is comprised of a central main distribution facility, campus system, vertical subsystem, and horizontal subsystem. The *horizontal subsystem* runs from the telecommunications wiring closets to the users' outlets. This cabling runs out to the departments on the floors of a building. The *vertical subsystem* is the cable plant that runs from the wiring closets on each floor to the building's main equipment room. This cable, which typically runs through a building's risers, connects the main wiring closets located on each floor. The next step up in the wiring hierarchy is the *campus subsystem*, which connects multiple buildings to a centralized main distribution facility, local exchange carrier, or some other point of demarcation. This portion is commonly referred to as the *backbone*.

The distribution facilities may be connected by cross-connect patch panels, as is done in telecommunication wiring, or they may be connected via internetwork devices such as bridges or routers (see Figure 5.2). The main distribution facility is located in the computer room. From this wiring room extends the campus subsystem (which is usually fiber) that runs to each building. Each building has a vertical subsystem (which is also usually fiber). Each floor has its own segment, called the horizontal subsystem, that is connected to the vertical system. Horizontal wiring is usually twisted-pair. WAN services are concentrated in the main distribution facility.

# Structured Wiring Design Considerations

If you are designing a structured cabling plant for a new building, discuss networking needs with the building architects as early as possible. Most architects and facilities managers are unfamiliar with a network's cabling requirements. This means they may not allow enough room in the cable raceways or design the wiring closets large enough or with the proper ventilation. If you are augmenting an existing cable plant or running a new cable plant in an existing building, you may be constrained by the cable choices already made, available space, and your budget.

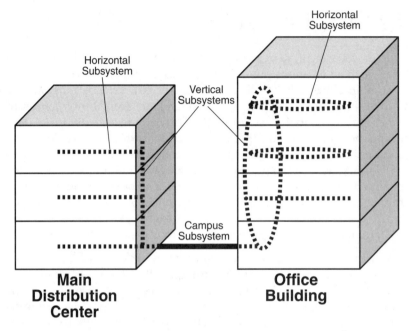

*Figure 5.2.* *A structured wiring system.*

During the requirements analysis phase, you inventoried the existing cable as well as the network and computing hardware and software. Go back to these documents and answer the following questions:

1. What type of cable is installed? Is it unshielded twisted-pair, shielded twisted-pair, thin coaxial cable, thick coaxial, fiber-optic, ARCnet co-axial, or SNA coaxial? Assess this for each location.

2. For each type of cable, measure the length of the run (you can use a TDR or time-domain reflectometer to help).

3. How much of the existing cable is currently in use and how much is currently unused?

4. What is the condition of the existing cable? Examine it visually and with a TDR. Are the wires and jacket in good condition? Use a TDR to measure if the quality is appropriate to be used to carry high-speed data traffic. Is it suitable for terminal, voice, and video traffic? Will the existing cable plant accommodate network growth for the next 5 or 10 years?

5. Examine the conditions and locations of the wiring closets. Are they sufficient? Is there proper ventilation and enough space? Is there a telephone in each wiring closet so that technicians can call back to the central support room?

6. Where does the cable plant need to be replaced or augmented?

7. Does the cable run in a return air space, therefore requiring the use of plenum-rated cable or running the cable in a conduit?

8. Does the cable run outdoors, either in the ground or aerially? What sort of protection is required—concrete, PVC pipes, and so on.

In designing the cable plant, you must balance the cable's bandwidth and ability to support services with its cost and complexity. For example, fiber-optic cable can carry huge amounts of data over vast distances, but it is expensive to install and terminate. Copper cable, including telephone wire, has a smaller bandwidth and is less expensive to install. Although fiber has always been considered advantageous because of its high bandwidth, immunity to electrical and radio frequency interference, and ability to carry signals long distances, advancements in technology are now permitting high-speed data to be transmitted over the twisted-pair copper wire. Price and lack of familiarity usually limits fiber's usage to the backbone, rather than to the desktop. The inexpensive twisted-pair copper is widely used for departmental LAN and for customer-premise telephone networks.

Whether you choose copper or fiber cable, if the cables are to be run in a plenum space or an area that serves as a duct for recirculating air in a building, they must be plenum-rated or contained in a conduit for the entire run. When burned, the polyvinyl chloride (PVC) jacketing used on cables gives off noxious fumes that could poison people. The National Electric Code (NEC) does not permit the installation of PVC cables in a return-air ceiling. Although plenum cables are more expensive than conduits, they provide greater flexibility, and as a result are worth the extra cost.

The key to the cable plant's success is distance. Although you should generously estimate the users' bandwidth needs, you should conservatively restrict the distances of the wiring runs. An AT&T study concluded that 99 percent of devices are located within 100 meters (or 330 feet) of a wiring closet, 95 percent are located within 90 meters (roughly 300 feet), and 90 percent are located within 80 meters (approximately 260 feet).[1] (See Figure 5.3.)

[1]Lindsey Vereen. "High Speed Twist." *Lan Magazine*, November 1991.

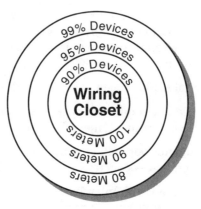

**Figure 5.3.** *Devices' average proximity to the wiring closet.*

You might want to be more conservative than the industry average distances between the users' devices and the wiring closet to ensure that your cable plant will have a long life. In this case, you should place all of the users' devices within 90 meters of the wiring closet. Similarly, the wiring runs in the vertical subsystem should be no longer than 500 meters. The campus distribution facility should be no longer than 1,500 meters. Violating these distances may make your network more prone to errors and failure.[2] (See Table 5.1.)

**Table 5.1.   Maximum distances for structured wiring.**

| Subsystem | Maximum Cable Length |
| --- | --- |
| Horizontal (Terminal device to telecommunications closet) | 90 meters |
| Vertical (Telecommunications closet to equipment room or building entrance facility) | 500 meters |
| Campus (Building entrance facility to campus main distribution facility) | 1,500 meters |

[2]Tony Nuciforo. "Winning By Design." *LAN Magazine*, November 1989.

Whatever type of cable you choose for the horizontal, vertical, and campus distribution systems, it's essential to follow the IEEE specifications for the medium-access method and cable type. Unless you know the precise effect of changing variables in the specification, don't do it. You'll only end up with problems.

Cable runs terminate in *wiring closets* located on each floor and building. Each floor should have a wiring closet, and each building should have a central wiring facility. The wiring closets should be located in the same position on different floors to minimize the cable run when connecting the building's wiring closets. The wiring distribution frames, concentrators, bridges, routers, and other data communications equipment are located in wiring closets.

# Choosing the Wiring Type for the Horizontal Subsystem

Because users' first point of contact is the horizontal cable plant, and because changing it causes the greatest disruption to users, most designers begin by writing the specifications for this portion first. Your cabling choices include: unshielded twisted-pair, shielded twisted-pair, coax, broadband, and fiber. You might avoid cable completely and use a wireless medium.

Copper wire, specifically unshielded twisted-pair, is the preferred medium for the horizontal wiring system, although fiber-optic cable is viable when users need very high bandwidth or when the wiring system is in hostile environments. Coax-based broadband wiring is an older technology that you should probably avoid, unless you have a large broadband network in existence. Wireless networking is a new and promising technology; however, because of its relative newness it is best suited in limited, non-mission-critical environments.

Influences on your choice of cable include bandwidth, distance, security, electromagnetic and radio frequency interference, cost, the existing cable plant, and market direction. Cable choices include twisted-pair, coaxial, fiber, or no cable at all. The benefits and liabilities of each are as follows:

■ *Unshielded twisted-pair*—Inexpensive. Easy to work with. Is a large base of technical experience from telephone installations. Can be used with voice and data. Satisfactory resistance to electromagnetic interference. Quickly becoming departmental wiring medium of choice.

- *Shielded twisted-pair*—Can be pricey. Relatively easy to work with. Used primarily in IBM ships. Good immunity to electromagnetic interference.

- *Thick coax*—Expensive and difficult to work with. Good immunity to electromagnetic interference. Not really appropriate for departmental LANs.

- *Thin coax*—Easier to work with than thick coax. Difficult to troubleshoot. Inexpensive.

- *Fiber*—Expensive. Excellent immunity to electromagnetic interference. Excellent distances and bandwidth. Can carry voice, video, and data.

- *Wireless*—Relatively expensive. Not subject to restraints of cabling, but distances and transmission speeds are often limited. This is a new technology with promise.

## Twisted-Pair Wire

Twisted-pair comes in shielded and unshielded varieties. Shielded twisted-pair (STP) is a pair of foil-encased copper wires twisted around each other and wrapped in an insulating shield (see Figure 5.4). Unshielded twisted-pair (UTP), or ordinary telephone wiring, is a pair of foil-encased copper wires twisted around each other (see Figure 5.5). Most twisted-pair wiring is between 22 and 26 American Wire Gauge (AWG); 24 AWG is the *de facto* standard. (AWG is a measurement of a copper wire's thickness. As the numbers increase, the cable's thickness increases.)

STP is most often used in IBM and Token Ring shops. Its bandwidth and maximum distances are appropriate for horizontal subsystems, but it is not usually used for the vertical subsystems. The STP specified by the IBM Cabling System can carry data longer distances and support more nodes than UTP. Because of its shielding, STP is more immune to signal disturbances than UTP; however, STP is more expensive and cannot support voice traffic.

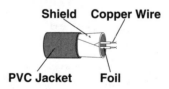

*Figure 5.4.* *Shielded twisted-pair wiring.*

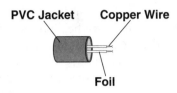

**Figure 5.5.** *Unshielded twisted-pair wiring.*

As a general rule of thumb, you should use UTP on the horizontal wiring subsystem. UTP is ubiquitous; many buildings have unused telephone wire in the wall. If your company has purchased a PBX or key system in the last 10 years, chances are good that you have high-grade telephone wire that can also transmit data.

Like STP, UTP's bandwidth and maximum distances are suitable for the horizontal, but not vertical, subsystem. UTP has broader applicability than STP or coax, however, because it can carry both voice and data traffic. UTP supports LocalTalk, EtherNet, Token Ring, ARCnet, and FDDI data transmissions. UTP is less expensive to purchase and install because of its use in the telephone world. As a point of comparison, running UTP on the horizontal plant will cost you $80 to $150 per termination. Installation costs are lower because both telecom and data communications technicians are familiar with pulling and putting connectors on the cable. Installation and troubleshooting tools are inexpensive and plentiful.

UTP has been exploding as the preferred horizontal wiring medium. In 1991, the number of installed UTP nodes surpassed the number of coax nodes. After the IEEE standardized the 802.3 10BaseT specification for EtherNet transmission over unshielded twisted-pair, products flooded the market. By specifying UTP, you can capitalize on the intense product and price competition as well as on the expertise of the many people who know how to install and troubleshoot telephone wire.

Although the popularity of UTP in a LAN environment has been growing steadily, you should proceed with caution before you use the existing wire in the your buildings' wall. Check out existing wiring very carefully. In many instances, the quality of the existing telephone wire is too low—either because of its specifications or because of normal wear and tear—to be successfully used for data transmission. Purchase a cable scanner or time-domain reflectometer to test the existing wiring, or ask your integrator to check the wiring's quality before you definitely decide to use the existing cable.

Four-pair, twisted-pair wire is the industry standard. If the horizontal subsystem contains only UTP, each application should have one four-pair sheath of UTP dedicated to it. That means you should have one four-pair cable for each workstation at the desktop, a second cable for voice, and a third for terminal traffic. Although this approach is more costly than installing a single 8- or 12-pair sheath, using one four-pair wire helps reduce the problem of crosstalk between the different cable pairs carrying different signals. The telephone's ring and off-hook signals are high voltages that can interfere with digital signals. Additionally, the Integrated Services Digital Network (ISDN) standard specifies a four-pair wiring configuration, so by using multiple four-pair wires, your cable plant has a better chance staying technologically viable.

Most Token Ring and EtherNet LANs use the two outside wires, leaving the inside pair free for use with an analog phone system. To take advantage of mixed services, however, you need to put a custom device on the cable to split out the wire at the termination end and the wiring closet. Using custom connectors is not wise. Connectors are commodities, and you should use standard connectors and pin-outs so that you don't back yourself into an incompatibility corner. It's better to use separate wires, rather than run different signal types in the same cable sheath.

You may want to purchase a composite twisted-pair cable that contains both UTP and STP, cased either in a common outer sheath or as individual sheathed Siamese cables. This enables the data and voice cable to be pulled simultaneously, therefore reducing costs.

## Coaxial Cable

Until 1991, most network nodes were wired with coax. After the IEEE standardized the 10BaseT EtherNet specification in 1990, UTP was installed in unprecedented numbers. Coax, however, is still a viable option for the horizontal subsystem, especially when electromagnetic interference prevents the use of UTP.

The coaxial cable itself has four parts. The inner conductor is a solid wire surrounded by insulation, which is wrapped in a thin piece of metal screen. Its axis of curvature coincides with the inner conductors, hence the name *coaxial*. An outer plastic cover surrounds the cable (see Figure 5.6).

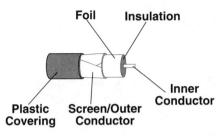

*Figure 5.6.* *Coaxial cable.*

Coax comes in many varieties, but you'll most often encounter RG-58, RG-59, and RG-62. RG-58 is used with thin or thick EtherNet; RG-59 cables are designed for use with cable television or broadband LANs; and RG-62 is ARCnet coax. Coax is also used with broadband cable televison networks.

Thick EtherNet, installed virtually everywhere, has a greater bandwidth, is more resilient to damage, and transmits data over longer distances than thin coax; however, it's more difficult to tap and less flexible. Thick coax is generally too difficult to work with to warrant usage on the horizontal wiring subsystem. It is, however, appropriate for backbones if fiber is not an appropriate option.

Thin EtherNet cable, also called *thinnet* or *cheapernet*, is the black cable that was supposed to solve the problems of thick coax. Until 10BaseT, thin EtherNet was the wiring medium of choice for the departmental network. Thin EtherNet is much easier to work with than thick coax. Because workstations are daisy-chained together, networks can be constructed rapidly.

Maintaining a thin EtherNet network is difficult. The cable has to be terminated, and the terminator often works its way loose. When it does, it brings down the entire network. Disconnecting one device from the thin EtherNet disables the entire network. Thin EtherNet is also difficult to troubleshoot. To isolate a problem, technicians frequently have to detach the BNC connector on a device, test the cable segment, then move to the next device and repeat the process until they discover and correct the problem. Maintaining a thin or thick coax network can be quite costly.

# Fiber-Optic Cable

Fiber-optic cable is primarily used for vertical and campus subsystems; however, if your application requires high security, a large bandwidth, or immunity to electrical disturbances, consider running fiber to the desktop. You can use fiber with AppleTalk, ARCnet, EtherNet, FDDI, and Token Ring.

Electrical voltages are used transmit data or voice as signals over copper media, such as UTP or coax. With fiber, however, the signals are pulses of light, created by LEDs or lasers. The fiber cable itself is lightweight and has a small diameter, making it suitable for small spaces. The cable is composed of an outer protective sheath, cladding, and the optical glass fiber (see Figure 5.7). However, it must be handled quite carefully and technicians must take care that they don't pull or stretch the cable too hard.

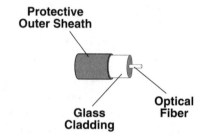

*Figure 5.7.   Fiber-optic cable.*

Networks that run fiber from the central wiring closet all the way to the desktop are expensive to install. Fiber network interface cards are $5,000 to $6,000, plus the cost of terminating fiber at user outlets is high. Regardless of manufacturers' claims, it takes about 45 minutes—not 10 minutes—to do the set-up to polish a fiber termination. When terminating fiber in the vertical runs, you can achieve some economies of scale because you can set up once, then put the connectors on each fiber. When you are connectorizing fiber on horizontal runs, however, you have to set up at each termination, where there are just two fibers. So whereas it costs about $80 per termination on the vertical wiring, it costs about $200 per termination when running fiber on the horizontal. Until the cost of terminating fiber decreases, running fiber to the desktop is not cost-effective unless your application has a real need.

## Wireless Networks

Wireless transmission recently has become a viable option for LAN transmissions. Instead of transmitting signals over a cable, wireless LANs transmit their signals over the air. Wireless networks can be used where you cannot run wire. For example, sometimes there simply is no room in the cable raceways to run any more cable. The building may have been built with insufficient room to run wiring. The walls may be marble (or some other impenetrable material) and not have cable raceways at all. Wireless transmission is also appropriate for temporary or mobile networks.

Most manufacturers of wireless LANs position their products as a cable replacement; however, it is unrealistic to expect wire to disappear. In reality, a wireless LAN complements a wired LAN. Wireless LANs are best used in the department, with the vertical subsystem wired with copper or fiber.

Wireless LANs either use *radio* or *infrared* signals to transmit data. Radio wireless LANs are either *spread-spectrum*, which generally offers limited bandwidth, and 18GHz radio, which must be licensed by the Federal Communications Commission. Because spread-spectrum LANs share the 900MHz bandwidth with many other types of transmissions, interference with other wireless transmissions is possible. Commercially available spread-spectrum LANs generally transmit data at under 1Mbps, which is not appropriate for networks with even average traffic. 18GHz radio wireless LANs can transmit data at up to 16Mbps Token Ring speeds, and are better suited to today's networking. Be forewarned, however, that the throughput of a radio-based EtherNet LAN is lower than with a hard-wired EtherNet LAN, simply because of the physical differences of transmitting through the air versus through a solid medium. Spread-spectrum LANs can cover a greater distance than radio LANs, at the price of speed.

Infrared LANs work much the same way that your TV remote control does. Data is transmitted over a beam of infrared light fixed between two points (see Figure 5.8, which shows the wireless transmitters, which are attached to PCs, talking directly to each other). Some implementations use a diffused infrared approach, where the infrared light is bounced off the ceiling and disperses over a certain area. This approach increases the coverage but usually reduces the bandwidth. Infrared LANs require line-of-sight and their distances are often limited, making them most suitable for workgroups that use open-office environments where there are no walls blocking the transmission. Commercially available infrared LANs operate up to 16Mbps Token Ring speeds.

**Figure 5.8.** *Wireless LAN transmissions.*

Wireless LANs are an emerging technology, and problems must be resolved before they can gain widespread acceptance. For instance, bandwidth and distances covered are often limited. Data should be encrypted for security reasons. Troubleshooting tools and protocol analyzers are virtually nonexistent. The psychological element—that wireless transmissions are inherently unsafe—is unfounded, as far as today's evidence shows, but nevertheless must be overcome. Although wireless transmission is an intriguing technology, you should test carefully before you design wireless products into your enterprise-wide networks.

# Choosing the Vertical Subsystem Wire Type

The cable used on the vertical, or backbone, subsystem must transmit data over long distances and support larger volumes of traffic than the horizontal wiring. In the past, copper has been used as the vertical medium; however, you should specify fiber to ensure a long life for the cable plant. Using copper will require more cable bundles; fiber requires fewer bundles of cables and provides a path for growth.

- *Fiber*—Excellent bandwidth, distances, and security. Immune to electromagnetic interference. Can carry voice, video, and data. Costly. Medium of choice for a vertical subsystem.

- *Thick coax*—Good bandwidth, distances, and security. Can carry data. Difficult to work with. Large base of experienced installers.

- *CATV broadband*—Good bandwidth and good distances. Can carry voice, video, and data. Very difficult to work with and very costly to maintain.

# Fiber-Optic Cable

Fiber offers multiple benefits for the vertical wiring system. It carries data tremendously long distances without having to regenerate the signal. It has a physically smaller core than copper wire, so it can fit into smaller spaces. Because its signals are light, not electricity, fiber is immune to the electromagnetic emissions and radio frequency interference that plague copper cable. This makes fiber ideal for factory networks or for running next to elevator shafts, for example. Fiber is immune to lightning strikes, which makes it appropriate for usage outdoors. It is more secure than copper cable, because taps can be more easily detected than with copper. (When tapped, the light's intensity decreases; a technician can detect the decreased intensity with an oscilloscope or optical time-domain reflectometer.)

Fiber has its drawbacks. It is more expensive to purchase and install than copper wire. Fewer people are familiar with designing and installing fiber systems, and therefore, its cost is higher. Because a fiber cable has a smaller bend radius than copper, it's more easily broken when pulled too hard or too tightly around a corner. Installation and testing tools are expensive and difficult to use. Putting connectors on the fiber ends requires epoxy, polishing, talent, and time, which translates into high cost.

Fiber comes in single-mode and multimode types. *Single-mode fiber* is primarily used in the telecommunications industry; *multimode* is more common in data communications (see Table 5.3).[3] Single-mode fiber has a higher bandwidth and can carry data over great distances because it uses laser diodes to send signals; however, the laser diodes make single-mode fiber more expensive. Multimode has a lower bandwidth, but one that is more than sufficient for data communications. It uses low-cost, highly reliable light emitting diodes (LEDs) to send signals and is therefore less expensive.

Although there are many different types of fiber available and used in networking, the industry standard is 62.5/125 micron multimode fiber. 62.5/125's small core diameter provides high bandwidth, but is still large enough that attaching connectors is relatively simple. It is the cable specified by the American National Standards Institute FDDI, the 100Mbps Fiber Distributed Data Interface network. (The first figure, 62.5, measures the core in microns; the second number, 125, measures the cladding.) Less frequently used fiber sizes include 100/140, 100/125, and 85/125.

---

[3]Tony Nuciforo, "Winning By Design." *LAN Magazine*, November 1989.

**Table 5.3.   Physical and electrical characteristics of UTP and optical fiber in a vertical subsystem.**

### *Unshielded Twisted-Pair*

| | |
|---|---|
| *Physical characteristics:* | 24 AWG solid, thermoplastic insulated conductors, formed into groups of 25, 50, or 100 individually twisted pairs. Overall cable sizes from 25 to 1,800 pairs. Enclosed in a thermoplastic outer jacket. Maximum outside diameter of 0.25 inches. Minimum bend radius of 1.0 inches. |
| *Electrical characteristics:* | Maximum DC resistance is 28.6 ohms/1,000 feet. Mutual capacitance is 17 nf/1,000 feet maximum. |

### *Attenuation and Characteristic Impedance:*

| Frequency (MHz) | Maximum Attenuation (dB/1,000 ft.) | Characteristic Impedance (ohms) |
|---|---|---|
| 4,000 | 15.4 | 100 +/− 15% |
| 10,000 | 25 | 100 +/− 15% |
| 16,000 | 32 | 100 +/− 15% |

### *Optical Fiber*

| | |
|---|---|
| *Physical characteristics:* | Class is multimode, grade index optical fiber wave guide. Nominal 62.5/125 micrometer core/cladding diameters. |

*Performance characteristics:*

| Wavelength (nanometers) Characteristics | Maximum Attenuation | Minimum Information Transmission |
|---|---|---|
| 850 | 4 dB/km | 160MHz-km |
| 1,300 | 1.5 dB/km | 500MHz-km |

# Coaxial Cable

Thick coax can also be used on the backbone; however, it is wiser to use fiber if you are pulling a new cable plant, because fiber will have a longer life cycle and can provide the migration path to tomorrow's high-bandwidth and multimedia applications. Nevertheless, thick coax was the *de facto* backbone cable for many years. Many EtherNet LANs use a thick coax backbone because of its good bandwidth, good transmission distances, good immunity to electromagnetic interference, and low radio frequency emissions.

Although thick coax is less expensive than fiber, it can be quite costly to manage. Coax is especially susceptible to differences in electrical grounding levels that often manifest themselves from floor to floor. These so-called "voodoo" grounding problems are transient and therefore more difficult to resolve. Using coax on the vertical subsystem runs the risk of electrical mismatches. Using fiber avoids this problem.

# Broadband

Another vertical subsystem wiring option is *broadband*. Cable television (CATV) broadband is quite common in older systems, government installations, or installations that require multiple services, such as data, voice, video, and closed-circuit television. Until fiber came of age, CATV broadband was the only option for wiring a network that required different types of services.

Broadband networks mimic the design of CATV networks. Like a cable TV network, a broadband network uses different channels running on the same cable. Each channel has its own frequency, usually 6MHz wide. Using different frequencies enables the broadband network to accommodate multiple services.

Data sent over a broadband network is transmitted in analog, rather than digital, format. Each device must have special RF modems to translate between the computer's digital orientation and the network's analog bent. (This translation necessarily slows transmission.) Once the signals are converted to analog form, they traverse the network until they reach the headend, which is the "master" of the network. The headend translates the transmission frequency into the outgoing frequency and sends the transmission to its destination.

The network itself is designed as a hierarchical tree, with the headend as the root, the cables as the branches, and the user devices as the leaves (see Figure 5.9). Some broadband networks, called dual-cable systems, use two physically separate cables for transmission and reception. A single-cable broadband system uses one cable, but divides the bandwidth into transmitting and receiving frequencies. Broadband networks tend to be inflexible, costly, and difficult to maintain.

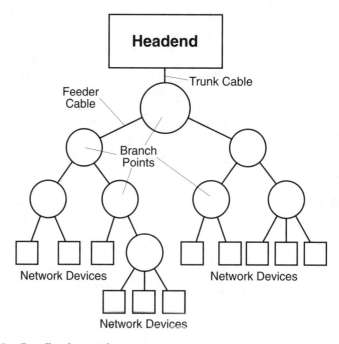

*Figure 5.9.* *Broadband networks.*

Broadband is not a wise choice for today's and tomorrow's cable plants. Broadband, even broadband EtherNet, is expensive, hard to install, and very difficult to maintain. To maintain the network, technicians periodically have to tune the components to make sure they stay within their assigned frequencies. This tuning requires significant expertise in radio frequency engineering. Generally, you should not install broadband for a new cable plant. If you need high bandwidth and immunity to electromagnetic or radio frequency interference, install fiber.

# Choosing the Campus Subsystem Wire

Fiber is again the medium of choice for the campus wiring system, for essentially the same reasons as for the vertical wiring system. However, thick coax and CATV broadband may be used.

When designing the campus wiring system, keep in mind that these cables are used outdoors. Because the cable is more exposed to lightning, use nonmetallic fiber cable to avoid electrical grounding issues. Outdoor cables are susceptible to physical abuses, including animals and vandals. For some reason, rodents like to chew the high density polyethylene cable jackets. The cable is also exposed to the natural elements of wind and rain. If the cable is underground, you may need to specify waterproofing (for rain) and a steel sheath (for protection from rodents and vandals). Waterproofed cable has an inert gel in the spaces between the dielectric, shield, and outer cover. If the cable is aerial, you probably won't need these defenses.

Outdoor cables generally are not appropriate for indoor use because they generate large volumes of smoke when burned. Where an outside cable plant runs into a building, it must be run in a conduit to its termination point, or it must be spliced or cross-connected to a proper indoor cable within 50 feet of entering the building.

The campus wiring subsystem feeds into the corporation's main distribution facility, where internetworking devices and wide-area connections are made. It is from here that the network is connected to remote networks.

■ *Fiber*—Excellent bandwidth, excellent distances. Excellent security. Immune to electromagnetic interference. Can carry voice, video, and data. Costly. Medium of choice for vertical subsystem.

- *Thick coax*—Good bandwidth, good distances. Good security. Can carry data. Difficult to work with. Large base of experienced installers.

- *CATV broadband*—Good bandwidth, good distances. Can carry voice, video, and data. Very difficult to work with and very costly to maintain.

# Migrating from Older Wiring

Most enterprise-wide networks aren't built from scratch. Instead, departmental LANs are interconnected to create an internetwork that spans a corporation's every location. Because of this growth pattern, designers must decide whether to accommodate or replace existing networks. Whether designers should replace the existing cable plant or network or let it remain depends on several elements: the application, the condition of the cabling plant, the network access method, and your budget.

First consider the application. Can the existing network achieve the business purpose of the network. For example, can the existing network support the required number of users? Can it be upgraded cost-effectively? Can the existing network support the traffic loads? Can it support the devices that are needed on the enterprise-wide network?

Evaluate the condition of the cable plant. How old is the cable plant? What is the quality of the cable? What cable is used? How much cable is installed? A ten-year-old cabling system probably bears replacement. A five-year-old plant may accommodate today's and tomorrow's needs, and a cabling system only a few years old will probably meet the needs.

Next, consider the access method of the network. Does the network's speed accommodate the application? For example, LocalTalk and ARCnet won't accommodate bandwidth-intensive applications without being segmented into very small workgroups. Also consider your MIS budget and the depreciation schedule of the cable plant. If it's a new cable plant and not fully depreciated, the cost of replacing the system may be too great.

A network should be designed modularly, so that designers can easily accommodate different types of cables and networks. You can change cable types easily by adding a transceiver to the cable. The transceiver is the device that enables the workstation to transmit and receive on the network. It is usually integrated into the adapter card, but is also available as an external box. With a different transceiver, the old network can make a connection to the new network or device. For example, you can attach a workstation with a thin EtherNet adapter card to a 10BaseT network without replacing the adapter card. Simply purchase an external 10BaseT transceiver. External transceivers pose drawbacks. First, because the device is connected by an AUI port or other such interface, the connection can work itself loose, causing network problems. Secondly, because the connection is external and not in silicon, the connection will be slower.

To connect two dissimilar networks, rather than single workstations, you can often use a repeater, a bridge, or a router. A repeater will change the wiring types but not provide any traffic filtering. Repeaters can be used to extend networks of a similar type. For example, you can interconnect a coax EtherNet and a twisted-pair EtherNet with a repeater, but you cannot use a repeater to connect fundamentally dissimilar networks, such as EtherNet and Token Ring. Bridges and routers both filter traffic. Bridges can connect networks of the same type, such as two EtherNets using a different cabling system. Unlike a repeater, however, a bridge can filter traffic, reducing the amount of traffic that traverses the entire network. Routers can connect networks that are dissimilar, such as EtherNet and Token Ring or EtherNet and AppleTalk. Repeaters, bridges, and routers are discussed in depth later in this chapter.

# Network Access Methods for the Enterprise

Thanks to the OSI model and the separation of the data-link layer into the medium access control and logical link control sublayers, the physical media of the network is not tied to how the devices negotiate access. For example, the access method of EtherNet—carrier sense multiple access with collision detection (CSMA/CD)—is unrelated to the type of physical wire. EtherNet works with twisted-pair, coax, fiber, and wireless. Similarly, the access method of Token Ring—token passing—is independent of the physical layer, and Token Ring can be used with twisted-pair, fiber, and wireless. Change the transceiver and you can change the wiring type. Change the network adapter card and the driver and you can change the network access method. This independence brings freedom to network designers, enabling them to specify the best type of wiring plant as well as the best network access method. Table 5.4 shows the different combinations of wiring and access methods.

**Table 5.4. Network access methods and cable types.**

| | Access Method | | | | |
| Cable Type | AppleTalk | ARCnet | EtherNet | Token Ring | FDDI |
|---|---|---|---|---|---|
| Coax | – | • | • | – | – |
| Fiber | • | • | • | • | • |
| UTP | • | • | • | • | • |
| STP | – | – | • | • | • |
| Wireless | • | – | • | • | – |

Not all medium-access methods are suitable for the enterprise. EtherNet, Token Ring, and FDDI are appropriate for the enterprise-wide network as well as the departmental LAN. LocalTalk, ARCnet, 1Mbps Starlan, and any network that is not an industry standard should be used only on the departmental LAN.

EtherNet, Token Ring, and FDDI are IEEE or ANSI standards. Ranging from 10Mbps to 100Mbps, they have sufficient transmission speeds to accommodate the users' growing hunger for bandwidth. Manufacturers are actively improving their products based on these three technologies. LocalTalk, ARCnet, and Starlan lack the transmission speed and market force that would make them viable in the enterprise. LocalTalk, at 230.4Kbps, is simply too slow for today's bandwidth-hungry applications. ARCnet, at 2.5Mbps, is too slow to serve as a backbone technology. Despite the best efforts of the ARCnet manufacturers, the token-passing technology has not been endorsed by the IEEE. 10BaseT has extinguished all interest and development in 1Mbps Starlan. These three older or slower technologies should be bridged or routed to the backbone network.

# Choosing Among Token Ring, EtherNet, and FDDI

People debate the merits of Token Ring versus EtherNet with near-religious fervor. Token Ring's supporters point to the technology's superior deterministic, token-passing architecture, while dismissing EtherNet as unpredictable and prone to collisions.

As any computer scientist will tell you, token-passing networks excel at handling large packets on heavily loaded networks. Because a token-passing access method is deterministic, you can mathematically determine the worst-case scenario. Collision-detection networks, such as EtherNet and LocalTalk, are best at handling lots of bursts of small packets, which matches normal terminal traffic. (EtherNet can handle packets up to 1,500 bytes long.) In reality, few users will see the difference between the access methods.

Arguments aside, each deserves a place in the enterprise. Most enterprise-wide networks will include pockets of each, and integration is essential. Both are widely used as departmental and backbone networks. Typically, "Big Blue" mainframe-centric shops and other IBM zealots install Token Ring. Universities and engineers generally install EtherNet.

The optimal solution is EtherNet and Token Ring on the departmental network and FDDI on the backbone. EtherNet and Token Ring provide sufficient bandwidth for departmental applications. In many instances, they both provide sufficient bandwidth for backbone networks, as long as the network is properly segmented using bridges or routers. FDDI is appropriate as a backbone in very large networks. Because of its high speeds, it can safely be used to combine the smaller departmental networks into one superhighway.

## EtherNet

EtherNet is one of the earliest local area networks, designed in the 1970s by Bob Metcalfe et. al. at Xerox Palo Alto Research Center (PARC). In 1980, Digital, Intel, and Xerox published the reference specification known as DIX (for Digital, Intel, and Xerox), which is also known as the Blue Book spec. Several years later, the IEEE modified the EtherNet specification and accepted it as an IEEE standard, renaming it 802.3. (Note that there are differences between 802.3 and EtherNet, most notably the usage of a signal quality indicator or a heartbeat.)

EtherNet transmits data at 10MHz, which means that the theoretical maximum speed of data transmission is 10Mbps. When transmitting, a device has control over the entire 10Mbps bandwidth. When a device attached to the EtherNet network wants to transmit information, it simply sends the packet onto the network without regard to what else is currently on the network. If two or more nodes happen to transmit at the same time, the packets will "collide" or the signals will become garbled. Each station "backs off" and waits a random amount of time before it tries to retransmit. The sending station will try to retransmit until the receiving device acknowledges that it has successfully received the transmission. This access control method is referred to as *carrier sense multiple access with collision detection* (CSMA/CD).

Enterprise-Wide Networking

To understand CSMA/CD in more relative terms, think of a room filled with people. When a person has something to say, he or she begins to speak without regard to whether anyone else is already speaking. If someone else is already speaking, the two voices will cross and their messages will be garbled. Then both speakers must stop and try to talk again at a later time. Everyone in the room can all start talking at the same time, but only one person can be heard at a time.

As with the imaginary room filled with people, EtherNet works best when the devices on the network have little to say. EtherNet works best if the traffic demands are low. Also, EtherNet was designed to carry terminal traffic, which tends toward small packets. So EtherNet is best suited to low traffic loads and small packets.

Up to 1,024 devices may reside on an EtherNet. The length of the network depends on the cable type used, but you can achieve the greatest distance with thick EtherNet (1.5 kilometers) and the shortest distance with 10BaseT (100 meters). EtherNet can be physically configured as either a bus or a star, but logically (or electronically) it must be a bus network. Thick coax EtherNet (802.5 10Base5) and broadband EtherNet (10Base36) are physically configured as buses (see Figure 5.10). Thin coax EtherNet (10Base2) is daisy-chained, yet it is still a bus (see Figure 5.11). Twisted-pair EtherNet or 10BaseT is physically configured as a star. Logically it is still a bus network, as each segment is an individual EtherNet (see Figure 5.12). Fiber EtherNet (10BaseF) is a point-to-point connection.

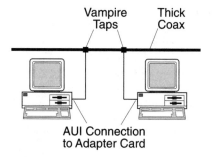

*Figure 5.10.* *Thick EtherNet.*

164

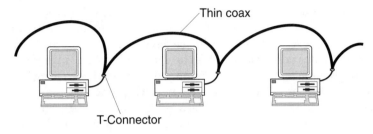

Thin coax

T-Connector

**Figure 5.11.** *Thin EtherNet.*

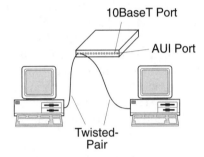

10BaseT Port

AUI Port

Twisted-
Pair

**Figure 5.12.** *10BaseT EtherNet.*

# Token Ring

Token Ring takes a more orderly approach to regulating access to the network than EtherNet does. Instead of allowing devices to talk whenever they want and interrupt as they please, Token Ring's token-passing access method requires that a device possess an electronic "token" before it is permitted to transmit frames. This strategy is like the talking stick used in some Native American cultures, or the conch shell used in *Lord of the Flies*.

The token, which is a predefined pattern of bits, circulates on the Token Ring network. If a device needs to transmit, it requests the token as it passes by. After a station possesses the token (thereby removing the token from the ring), the station transmits frames until it completes the transmission or until the transmission of another frame cannot be completed before a timer expires. The station issues a new token after it completes its transmission. The token continues to circulate on the network.

Token passing is a *deterministic* access method, whereas EtherNet's collision detection is *nondeterministic*. In a deterministic access method, you can calculate the worst-case scenario for how long a device will have to wait to transmit. With EtherNet, it is random and inherently unpredictable. Token Ring is also designed to handle larger packet sizes than EtherNet. Token Ring can transmit data at 4Mbps or 16Mbps. (On most new adapter cards, you can change the speed by flipping a DIP switch.) Between the deterministic access method and the larger frame sizes, Token Ring is suited to heavily loaded networks with medium to large frames. Token Ring also gains much of its popularity from IBM's endorsement as its preferred network.

Token Ring is logically configured as a ring but physically configured as a star, with multistation access units (MAUs) acting as hubs (see Figure 5.13). Each station is attached to a MAU port via two twisted-pairs, one for transmitting signals and the other for receiving them. The MAU itself is a self-contained electronic ring; each port is connected to its neighboring ports. Additionally, a MAU has Ring In and Ring Out ports for connecting the MAUs to its upstream and downstream MAUs to form a larger ring. Each ring can support up to 72 devices. A MAU usually has 8 or 16 ports.

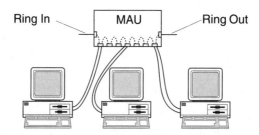

*Figure 5.13.  A Token Ring configuration.*

Both the 4Mbps and 16Mbps Token Ring run over shielded, twisted-pair, unshielded twisted-pair, and fiber. With STP, a device can be up to 200 meters from the MAU. With UTP, a device can be up to 100 meters from the MAU. As of yet, fiber is a nonstandard implementation, so distances vary greatly with the manufacturer.

More management is built into the Token Ring than into EtherNet. For example, if a MAU detects a failure on one of its ports, it will automatically remove that port and its attached station from the ring by bypassing it electronically. In this way, failures can be localized.

Token Ring's chip set provides a wealth of management information via the *ring error monitor*, the *ring parameter server*, and the *configuration parameter server*. The ring error monitor counts soft errors, which are errors that cause a frame to be retransmitted but do not cause the network to fail. The configuration report server collects the MAC frames that list the stations' addresses, so that the network administration package can build a list of network devices, enabling managers to know when devices have been added, removed, or reinserted to the ring. The ring parameter server is used to download information into new network devices. These three elements are included in every Token Ring chip set, but it is up to the card or hub manufacturer to take advantage of them.

Several token-passing access methods were available when IBM endorsed Token Ring, including the MIT Ring and the Cambridge Ring. The IEEE standardized IBM's Token Ring (with a few differences) as 802.5. Olof Soderblom holds the patent for Token Ring.

# FDDI

10Mbps of bandwidth is suddenly paltry when you try to interconnect 10 EtherNet subnetworks. It's like trying to flow the Colorado River through a garden hose. A kilometer or two of distance is measly when you're trying to internetwork an entire campus. It's like trying to use a foot of string to wrap a box that's two feet square. Although today's applications can be adequately handled by Token Ring's 16Mbps and EtherNet's 10Mbps of bandwidth, tomorrow's applications will not be. Imaging and video applications, with their enormous file sizes and intolerance of delay, will become commonplace. Token Ring and EtherNet might be able to meet the bandwidth demands if only one user is allowed per segment, as is done today in some engineering environments. As multimedia becomes common, however, FDDI will become necessary.

FDDI, or Fiber Distributed Data Interface, is ANSI's standard for a 100Mbps fiber-optic network. Like 802.5 Token Ring, FDDI uses a token-passing access method, thereby delivering deterministic performance. Unlike Token Ring or EtherNet, however, FDDI is built to scale to support very large networks. Packets can be up to 4,500 bytes, which is greater than EtherNet's 1,500 maximum. FDDI can support up to 200 devices per ring, with a maximum of two kilometers of separation between nodes. The entire ring may span 200 kilometers. The dual ring configuration delivers a level of fault tolerance not provided by EtherNet or Token Ring.

FDDI's initial application is as a backbone, connecting primarily departmental EtherNet and Token Ring LANs. FDDI has more than enough bandwidth to handle today's departmental LAN load. Most often, designers specify routers with FDDI interfaces to make point-to-point connections between the slower LANs. The routers are configured in a ring. As FDDI becomes more widely used, more companies are buying FDDI concentrators and wiring the network in a star topology. As departmental users demand more bandwidth, FDDI will become more common to the desktop. Today, FDDI to the desktop is most appropriate in engineering environments, where computer-aided design, simulation, and imaging applications spew vast amounts of data across the network.

ANSI specifies that FDDI is configured as dual, counter-rotating rings (see Figure 5.14). This means that an FDDI network is actually two rings, each with traffic traveling in the opposite direction. A station may be attached to both rings; these are called *dual-attach stations* (DASs), or a station may be attached to only one ring; these are called *single-attach stations* (SASs). Using DAS delivers a higher level of fault tolerance, because the secondary ring is essentially a hot standby.

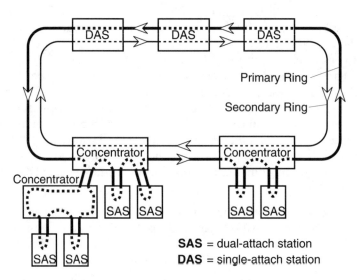

**Figure 5.14.** *FDDI architecture.*

Under ordinary operations, traffic travels on the primary 100Mbps ring. If a cable is severed, the FDDI will detect the failure and switch the traffic to the secondary ring, which is also a 100Mbps network (see Figure 5.15). If a device attached to a single ring fails or its cable is cut, FDDI will simply bypass that station, thereby isolating the problem from the rest of the network (see Figure 5.16).

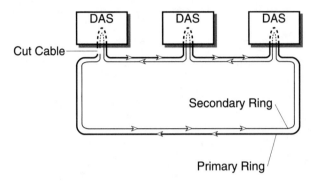

**Figure 5.15.** *Fault tolerance in a dual-attach station.*

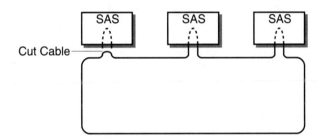

**Figure 5.16.** *Fault tolerance in a single-attach station.*

FDDI is a Physical and MAC layer standard, so an FDDI network can be seamlessly integrated into existing 802-compliant networks. Like EtherNet and Token Ring, FDDI operates with the 802.2 local link control specification. This means FDDI can work with any network operating system that supports 802.2.

FDDI works with both fiber cabling and copper cabling. The ANSI spec recommends 62.5/100 micron fiber, although it accommodates other sizes of fibers. Most FDDIs are installed using fiber, although there is quite a bit of interest in running 100Mbps over twisted-pair. Note there is no IEEE standard for FDDI over copper wire, although there is a working group. Each vendor implements copper FDDI differently, and the implementations may differ from unshielded twisted-pair to twisted-pair. Even when a standard is issued, it is likely that only certain types of high-grade UTP will be suitable.

Like Token Ring, FDDI has built-in network management, called Station Management (SMT). As of 1992, parts of SMT were still in draft form. SMT is designed to deliver configuration information, download new firmware, set parameters in the FDDI adapter, and display controller, usage, and state statistics. Figure 5.17 shows the relationship among the FDDI standards.

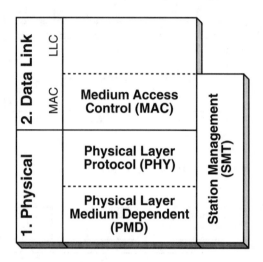

*Figure 5.17.* *The FDDI standards.*

The specification commonly referred to as FDDI is technically FDDI-I. FDDI-II, which is yet to be finalized, will specify a network that can carry voice, video, and data on the network.

The new class of multimedia applications will drain the bandwidth of low-speed LANs, making high-speed networks on the departmental level essential. The catch? The cost of running FDDI and fiber to the desktop is quite high. The adapters alone cost $5,000 or $6,000, plus the cost of installing fiber.

Network strategists are looking to twisted-pair as the solution. Companies are installing 10BaseT as the departmental wire in record numbers, pulling new UTP as well as using existing wire. If the current UTP plant could be used to transmit high-speed data, so much the better, and MIS could subtract the price of pulling fiber to the desktop from the cost of building a high-speed LAN.

Is twisted-pair a viable medium for FDDI? It depends on what type of twisted-pair. For STP, the answer is yes, although most companies are not installing new STP. FDDI over UTP has the greatest applicability, but also poses the greatest engineering challenges.

Running 100Mbps of data over copper means designers have to contend with distance and EMI/RFI. The biggest sacrifice is distance. When using STP, a device transmitting at 100Mbps may be no more than 100 meters from a concentrator (which is also the limit of 10BaseT). However, when run over UTP, that distance drops to approximately 50 meters. Emissions must also be considered, and FDDI over UTP has not yet met FCC requirements.

To make TP FDDI viable, ANSI has specified a new encoding scheme that forces manufacturers to use a new chip and redesign their hardware. Customers must purchase new hardware. The new encoding scheme ensures that UTP and STP implementations are consistent.

FDDI uses the NRZI (Non-Return to Zero, Invert on Ones) encoding scheme. NRZI lowers the transmission frequency without lowering the data rate. But NRZI has too much signal loss to reach a minimum distance from the desktop without generating excessive electrical interference when run over twisted-pair. In 1992, ANSI ratified a scheme called PR-4, which is a partial response signaling technique. Developed by Crescendo Communications, PR-4 can be used on the UTP and STP, thereby ensuring a consistent encoding scheme. Others are advocating one encoding scheme for UTP and another for STP. Copper FDDI manufacturers will implement their products using this chip.

Although STP FDDI is viable, the most practical application would be over UTP. FDDI over UTP will become more viable through the use of data-grade UTP. Formerly, UTP was designed with only voice requirements in mind; however, Belden and AT&T have both developed a UTP around the requirements of carrying data. At 16Mbps and lower, data-grade UTP's electrical characteristics are very similar to shielded cable. At higher frequencies, there are still some difficulties. Nevertheless, data-grade UTP cable, also called Level 4 and Level 5 UTP, will undoubtedly play an instrumental role in copper FDDI.

# Building Subnetworks into the Enterprise-Wide Network

An enterprise-wide network's goal is to provide users with access to resources at all times. But not all users need access to all resources. Mostly, users will access resources on their departmental LANs, with occasional access to remote resources. An enterprise-wide network is implemented as a series of subnetworks. This is a natural follow-on from structured wiring. In fact, premises-distributed wiring provides easy demarcation between departmental and campus networks. Most networks are designed with a backbone that has subnetworks attached via bridges and routers. The subnetworks serve the individual departments. Subnetworks may be further subdivided to serve workgroups.

Subdividing the network reduces overall network traffic, improves flexibility, increases security, and eases management.

- *Segments reduce overall network traffic.* When the traffic load reaches 30 to 40 percent of the EtherNet's bandwidth, users will notice degraded performance due to frequent collisions. When traffic reaches about 20 to 30 percent of a Token Ring's bandwidth, competition for the token will result in decreased performance; users will notice a delay. By reducing overall network traffic, you can improve performance.

  Users communicate primarily with users in their department, and they mostly use local services. The 80/20 rule applies; 80 percent of LAN traffic is local, and 20 percent is destined for a remote segment. By segmenting networks into departmental units, you can reduce the amount of traffic that must traverse the entire network, thereby improving the performance of the overall network.

- *Subnetworks increase a network's flexibility.* By designing a network as a series of subnetworks, each subnet can be tailored to the workgroup's or department's particular needs. For example, the marketing department and the engineering department each can have the workstations, network, and software that best meet their needs, but the two departments may use a completely different setup. Through the use of subnetworks, they can still communicate.

- *Subnetworks increase security.* Segmented networks are more secure. By placing users on physically different networks, you can prevent them from accessing resources that they aren't authorized to access. This reduces the rate of user error as well as intentional corruption. With subnetworks, you can ensure that network traffic from the finance department stays local, for example. By setting packet filters on bridges and via other means of security, bridges enable a minimum of access control; routers ensure a higher level.

- *Subnetworks make network management easier.* As a by-product of lower traffic levels and increased security, segmented networks are easier to manage. Problems are localized to their segment. As with structured wiring, a problem on one network will not affect users on other networks. Subnetworks also ease the *process* of network management. Subnetworks also provide a point of demarcation that separates one department's network from another's, thereby setting up logical management domains.

The building blocks of networks and subnetworks are repeaters, wiring hubs, bridges, routers, and gateways. Each has a unique application, although there is often overlap. Repeaters, which operate at OSI layer 1, strengthen the electrical signal. Wiring hubs are used as a central connection point for different subnetworks and often incorporate repeating functionality. Bridges should be used to segment departmental networks or as connection to the backbone, if both the departmental and the backbone network employ the same medium-access method. Bridges operate at OSI layer 2, and add slightly more overhead than repeaters and require greater management. Routers should be used to connect dissimilar networks to the backbone or to set up impenetrable "fire walls" between segments. Routers operate on OSI layer 3, and they add more overhead to the network operation than bridges do. As is the case as you go higher in the OSI model, routers require more management and administrative overhead. The difference among repeaters, bridges, and routers is shown in Figure 5.18. Gateways connect dissimilar computer systems, such as a PC LAN and a mainframe. Gateways typically operate over OSI layers 4 through 7, and they add the greatest overhead of the internetworking devices. Bridges, routers, and gateways come in remote and local varieties.

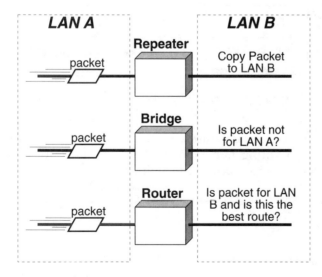

*Figure 5.18.   Repeaters, bridges, and routers*

# Repeaters: The Simplest of Devices

Repeaters strengthen the electrical signal so that the network can be extended. For example, you can use repeaters to extend an EtherNet's maximum distance from 1,000 to 5,000 feet. Repeaters, the most basic unit of connection, operate at the physical layer (see Figure 5.19). Repeaters have no intelligence of their own. They simply take every frame, regenerate the signal, and send it along. The simplest repeaters have one incoming port and one outgoing port. More sophisticated ones have multiple ports; these are referred to as *multiport repeaters*.

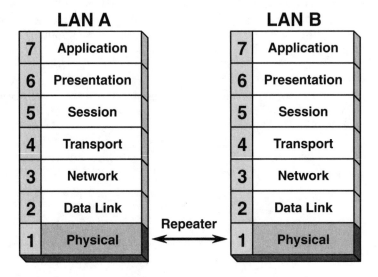

*Figure 5.19.*   *Repeaters operate at OSI layer 1.*

Today, repeaters are rarely used as stand-alone devices. Rather, they are integrated into wiring hubs and bridges. Repeaters are not suitable as subnetworking devices, because they indiscriminately pass all frames that come to them.

# Wiring Hubs: Concentrating the Network

In adopting a structured wiring approach from the telecommunications discipline, the computer communications people also adopted wiring hubs or concentrators. A wiring concentrator centralizes, or concentrates, the individual LAN segments into a single device. It is the "center" of the star-wired network for EtherNet, Token Ring, FDDI, LocalTalk, and ARCnet.

Physically, a wiring concentrator is a chassis or "card cage" with multiple slots that can accept different types of adapter cards, from network interface to bridging. A hub also includes repeater logic to strengthen the electrical signal. The very simplest concentrators are multiport repeaters.

Most hubs accommodate only one medium-access method, such as EtherNet or Token Ring, but not both. For example, Token Ring MAUs connect 8 or 16 devices to a Token Ring. EtherNet hubs can connect nodes usually in multiples of 12 using coax, twisted-pair, or fiber cable, depending on the module. These hubs are most suitable for departmental networks. The larger single-function hubs are appropriate for networks that use only a single medium.

The concentrator most suitable for the enterprise-wide network supports multimedia, integrated internetworking, has a high speed backplane, supports network management, and is fault-tolerant.

Because an enterprise-wide network encompasses more than one type of network, the campus and enterprise hubs should support multiple media-access methods. Multifunction concentrators can support FDDI, Token Ring, and EtherNet LAN segments by plugging different interface cards into the same chassis. These interface cards can support various wire types, including twisted-pair, coax, and fiber. Support for multiple media increases the flexibility of the wiring hub, because it can connect all LAN types. It also reduces the number of chassis needed, because many devices can be connected to one box, all sharing the same power supply and management card.

Without a bridge or router, the hub does nothing to restrict the traffic flow of the network. The network will not become significantly more efficient; it will simply reduce the number of redundant components. For this reason, concentrators can accommodate cards with bridge or routing cards. Again, this increases the network's flexibility while decreasing its cost. Also, integrating internetworking into the wiring hub increases the overall network performance, because packets travel over a backplane or bus, rather than a slower cable. Note that even if a hub accommodates an EtherNet and Token Ring, for example, the two networks cannot communicate directly without the aid of a bridge or router.

A growing number of enterprise concentrators also support wide-area connection services, such as T-1 and frame relay, directly in the hub. Tighter integration of LAN and WAN services delivers better overall performance and eliminates redundant equipment. LAN/WAN concentrators are often used at the point where the LAN "jumps off" to the WAN, such as at each campus' main distribution facility.

To increase performance, many sophisticated hubs implement high-speed backplanes as well as RISC processors. Many departmental hubs use an EtherNet or Token Ring bus as the backplane of the concentrator; either way, the speed is measured in tens of megabytes. Instead of adding multiple low-speed buses to improve performance, an alternative is to design a new backplane, one that implements a high-speed bus. Backplane speed is measured in hundreds of megabytes rather than in tens.

A processor is needed to take full advantage of the high-speed backplane. Add the power of a RISC processor to the backplane, and functions such as packet filtering can occur directly on the backplane rather than in a separate bridge module. This will increase the network's performance, because packets do not have to travel over the bus to the bridge card and back to the bus to their final destination.

As the hub receives more and more functionality, management becomes essential. Technicians must be able to monitor devices and control functions within the hub. This information should be available via a management console, dial-in, and on the hub card itself. Technicians must be able to manage from a console, so that they can stay in one location to manage the network. If the administrator is remote or if the network has failed, the ability to dial into the hub with a modem is essential. When technicians are working in the wiring closet, they need to see LEDs displaying the status of various ports and links.

Some hubs' management cards include a RISC processor so that the hub can do protocol processing on the network, thereby delivering network management and analysis without increasing traffic over the network. Some management cards can fully decode protocols without sending them to a remote analyzer.

Several standards are available for managing the physical layer. For example, many hubs support the IEEE 802.1 Hub Management specification for jointly managing Token Ring and EtherNet hubs. FDDI includes Station Management for physical layer management. In addition, a hub often supports the Simple Network Management Protocol.

As the concentrator becomes an integral part of the enterprise-wide network, its ability to tolerate faults must increase. The hub is the heart of the wiring and internetwork system on which the applications run. Downtime must be minimized. Enterprise concentrators must contain redundant power supplies to guard against power failures. The two power supplies may both be active simultaneously and share the load between them, or one supply may be active while the second one is a hot standby. Repeater logic should be distributed across multiple cards rather than concentrated in a single card, so if one card fails, the network will continue. Also look for a hub that performs switching and bypass functions in silicon, rather than mechanical relays, because mechanical devices are more prone to wear and tear and eventual breakage.

# The Essentials of a Wiring Concentrator

A wiring concentrator appropriate for the enterprise-wide network should

- Support multiple media, such as fiber, twisted-pair, and coax
- Support multiple LAN types, such as EtherNet, Token Ring, and FDDI
- Support integrated bridging and routing
- Have a high-speed backplane, rather than using a low-speed LAN bus
- Support full management of all cards in the chassis
- Deliver fault-tolerant performance by supporting redundant power supplies, distributing repeater logic across multiple cards, and so on

# Building Internetworks with Bridges

A bridge is the simplest device you can use to build an internetwork. A bridge subdivides a network to localize traffic. By restricting the amount of traffic that flows over the entire network, you can achieve a better overall network performance. Bridges are most appropriately deployed when building small networks of the same type. For instance, if you have an all-EtherNet network or an all-Token Ring network, bridges are ideal. Bridges are also appropriate in small networks with fewer than 15 to 20 segments. Bridges are also used on the departmental level in conjunction with routers on the campus level.

Bridges operate at the second level of the OSI model, the data-link layer (see Figure 5.20). More specifically, bridges operate at the medium access control (MAC) sublayer of the data-link layer. As such, bridges connect networks of the same MAC type, so for example, you can bridge one EtherNet to another EtherNet or one Token Ring to another Token Ring. (In the strictest definition, you cannot bridge an EtherNet to a Token Ring, because their MAC-layer frames use different formats. Because LocalTalk or ARCnet lack a MAC layer, you cannot "bridge" them to like networks or to any 802 network. You must use a router to pass traffic from one network to another.)

A MAC-layer bridge's advantage is its independence of the upper-layer protocols. One bridge can connect two EtherNet segments, even if one subnetwork runs TCP/IP and the other runs IPX. That's not to imply that the bridge understands these upper-layer protocols (that's a router's job), but in its ignorance, it is indifferent to their existence. This flexibility makes bridges easy to deploy, because the same bridge can pass multiple upper-layer protocols.

Bridges come in two varieties: transparent and source-routing. EtherNet networks most often use transparent bridges; IBM or Token Ring networks most often employ source-routing bridges.

## How Transparent Bridging Works

In *transparent* bridging, a bridge decides which traffic to forward by comparing a frame's destination address against an internally maintained table of local addresses.

Say one bridge connects LAN A to LAN B, and another connects LAN B to LAN C. The bridge takes the frame off LAN A and compares the frame's source and destination addresses to its internal address table. This comparison is called *filtering.* If the address is not local (for LAN A), the bridge *forwards* the frame to LAN B. The bridge does not know that the frame is addressed for LAN B; it simply knows that it is not for LAN A. The packet could be for LAN C, which lies beyond LAN B. In the forwarding process, the bridge copies the frame to its outbound port and transmits it on the network (see Figure 5.21).

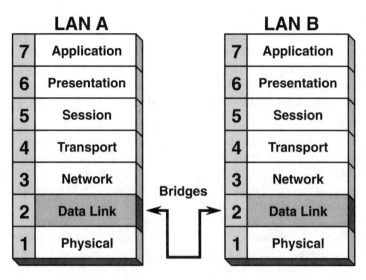

*Figure 5.20.* *Bridges operate at OSI layer 2.*

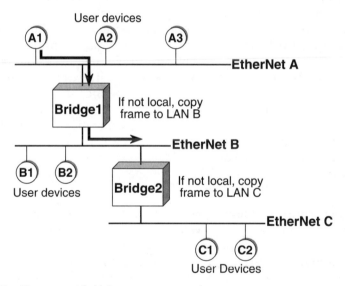

*Figure 5.21.* *Transparent bridging.*

A bridge builds and maintains a table of local MAC-layer addresses. When powered on, a bridge sends out broadcast messages, asking stations to identify themselves. From the acknowledgment frames, the bridge learns the addresses of its locally attached network devices. Because of this process, they are sometimes called *learning* bridges. (In days past, bridges were static, and the network manager had to build the address table manually; however, a static bridge is a rare find today.)

The most basic bridge filters on destination address, and most bridges filter on source and destination addresses. They can also be designed to filter on multicast frames, broadcast frames, protocol type, frame size, or other parameters. This is called *custom filtering*. Custom filtering has its advantages. You may want to ensure that the traffic from a certain department—for instance, finance—stays isolated. You can configure the bridge so that it will not pass to the backbone any frame with a MAC-layer address that belongs to a device in the finance department. As the filtering methods become more complex, bridge manufacturers tend to call the devices *brouters*, for bridge/router. These features cross the line into router functionality.

Although custom filtering has its benefits, it has disadvantages, too. The administrator must manually set up and maintain these filters. Setting many filters reduces bridge performance, and too many filters will choke the network. Also, be forewarned that the IEEE 802.1D bridging standard does not specify how to implement custom filtering. In custom filtering, a bridge looks into the network-layer packet, but it does not use a standard protocol, as a router does. It uses a vendor-specific method. One vendor's method of implementing filtering on anything beyond filtering on source and destination addresses is not necessarily compatible with another vendor's implementation. So, although you may be able to set up the same filter on two different manufacturers' bridges, they probably won't be able to recognize the other's filters. This forces you to choose a single vendor's bridges.

An alternate form of bridging uses a switch at the core, much like a telephone PBX. A switch bridge offers lower delays and higher throughput than a traditional store-and-copy bridge. Instead of examining the frame header and copying it from an incoming port to an outgoing port, as a traditional bridge does, a switch bridge examines only a small portion of the packet header to determine its destination. Then it switches into place a temporary link between the two ports. The packet does not have to be copied, only sent forward. This strategy enables several connections to be made simultaneously, thereby improving the overall performance of the switch bridge. A switch bridge can achieve full wire speeds of EtherNet and Token Ring. Because the packet is switched rather than copied, the end-to-end latency is lower. The drawback of such a device is that it is not scalable to include network-layer routing. With the capability of bridging only, such a device is appropriate more for the departmental network than for the enterprise-wide network.

# Using Spanning Tree with Transparent Bridging

When bridges are a critical link, it's often worth the cost of installing redundant bridges. Without parallel bridges, if one of the remote bridge "halves" fails, the network is partitioned and the users are unable to communicate. With parallel bridges, if the primary bridge fails, the secondary bridge will jump into action and the users can continue without interruption.

The IEEE 802.1D standard specifies the spanning tree protocol to manage this redundancy. Configuring parallel transparent bridges creates a closed loop in the EtherNet topology, which the specification forbids. With a closed loop, when a device transmits a frame, both bridges pass it and the destination device receives two copies. Each bridge receives the other's transmission of the frame and updates its address database accordingly and incorrectly. Once the bridges' address tables have conflicting information, neither will be able to transmit frames to that destination address, because they each assume the other bridge is on the correct path.

Resolving the closed-loop problem requires that the bridges exchange sufficient information to derive a spanning tree. Under the 802.1D specification, each bridge is assigned a unique identifying number and each port is assigned a cost. If the network manager sets all port costs as equal, the optimal path is the one with the fewest number of hops. The administrator could alternately assign lower costs to ports with higher speed lines, which would make the optimal path the one with the fastest lines. The bridges then exchange messages to discover the minimum-cost spanning tree. Traffic then flows over this route. When the network topology changes, the bridges recalculate the cost (see Figure 5.22).

# How Source Routing Works

Nothing in the transparent bridging and spanning tree algorithm precludes its use on Token Ring networks; however, because of the way the politics of networking have shaken out—IBM specifies source-routing—spanning tree and transparent bridging are used almost exclusively with EtherNet networks. IBM and most Token Ring networks use source routing. The politics of FDDI are not resolved; as many networks use transparent bridging as use source routing.

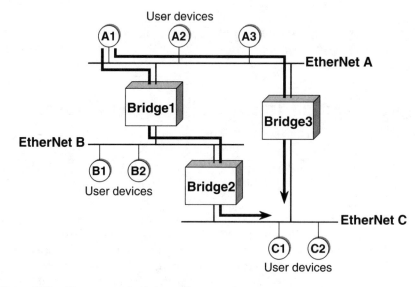

***Figure 5.22.*** *Transparent bridging with a spanning tree.*

With transparent bridging, the frame does not know what path it will take; that path is determined by the bridges it passes through. With source routing, the frame contains information on its route through the network. The sending, or source, device places this information in the MAC-layer header, hence the name *source routing*.

Sending stations learn the layout of the network in a process called *route discovery*. While route discovery is similar in principle to a transparent bridge's building an address, the mechanics differ. During route discovery, each station sends a single-route's broadcast frames around the ring. (Under Token Ring rules, a single-route broadcast circulates on the ring only once.) As each bridge receives the broadcast, it adds the unique numbers of the two LANs it connects plus its bridge number. A bridge number is required because parallel bridges may be configured, and the frame has to know which bridge on the LAN segment it traversed. Bridge numbers do not have to be unique because they are required only to distinguish parallel bridges. For this to work, only certain bridges, arranged in a spanning tree topology, are configured to pass single-routes packets (see Figure 5.23).

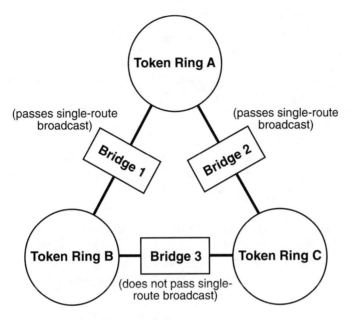

*Figure 5.23.* *Source routing bridging.*

The sending station receives one frame in return. The frame's routing information field contains the path to the destination. The routing information field contains a list of the LAN segment numbers, in the reverse order in which they were traversed.

Then the destination device sends out an all-routes broadcast. (All-routes broadcasts are passed by all bridges and can make seven hops.) The source device receives one or more copies of this frame. If the source receives more than one frame, multiple paths to the destination exist, and it selects the "best" path according to some criteria. One criteria may be the fewest number of hops. The optimal path is chosen during route discovery, and this path will be used for the duration of the communication session.

## Resolving the Bridging Conflict

Transparent bridging and source routing each have their advantages and disadvantages. With transparent bridging, the underlying LANs appear as one large network, and devices are unaware of the bridges' existence. Transparent bridging is not as efficient as source routing, but it is faster. The disadvantage is that the bridges must build the address tables themselves, which requires the bridges to have greater intelligence and processing power. Also, because the bridge determines the optimal path with every transmission, load leveling is more difficult.

Source routing, on the other hand, produces shorter routes and better load leveling. Source-routing bridges can be faster than transparent bridges because they do not have to look up each frame. The tradeoff is that the dynamic route discovery process is far more resource-intensive than the transparent bridging process. The route-discovery process adds network overhead. Also, source routing is not completely transparent. The source device is responsible for route discovery, route selection, and insertion of the routing information in the MAC frame. These additional bits increase the network traffic. With source routing, you get a better end result, but you pay more for it.

In general, however, if you are bridging EtherNet networks, you use transparent bridging; if you are connecting Token Ring networks in an IBM environment, you use source routing. Add a Token Ring-to-EtherNet bridge to the network, and you can connect the two types of bridging.

## Connecting Token Ring and EtherNet

The Token Ring versus EtherNet debate has largely died down, but neither side has won. Instead, EtherNet and Token Ring networks are connected, enabling users to access resources on either network without having to engage in a near-religious debate. Token Rings and EtherNets can be connected using a "bridge" or a router.

More precisely, a Token Ring-to-EtherNet "bridge" is actually a gateway, because the two access methods differ on the MAC layer, and those differences must be translated. The "bridge" mediates the differences between the two access methods, including length of MAC-layer address, type of bridging used (source-routing versus transparent bridging), and speed (16/4Mbps versus 10Mbps). Bridging in this manner will be faster than routing, but because of the translation involved, throughput will be relatively low.

Routers can also be used to connect the two access methods. By moving up the OSI stack and settling on a common network-layer protocol, you can avoid the differences at the MAC layer. For example, you can use an IPX or TCP/IP router to connect Token Rings to EtherNet. This solution is suitable only if both networks use that particular network-layer protocol (or are willing to run the protocol to gain the benefits of connectivity). Routing will be slower than bridging and require greater administrative overhead.

# Building Internetworks with Routers

Routers operate on the third, or network, layer of the OSI model (see Figure 5.24). Because they offer sophisticated path control and management, they can be used to construct more complex networks than bridges can. However, they require an experienced network technician to configure, operate, and manage them.

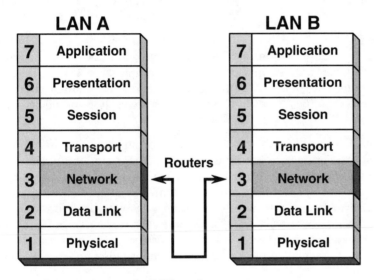

*Figure 5.24.* *Routers operate at the OSI layer 3.*

Routers are network-layer protocol-dependent; bridges are network-layer protocol-independent. Routers are designed for specific protocols. For example, a router must be designed specifically for IP or for DECnet. Not all protocols can be routed. TCP/IP, DECnet, IPX, XNS, and OSI can be routed because they extend to the network layer; LAT and NetBIOS cannot.

In strict Internet terminology, a gateway is a router, whereas in the OSI model, a gateway connects completely dissimilar networks. Fortunately, the Internet meaning of gateway is falling by the wayside, thereby clearing one point of confusion. Also in Internet- and OSI-speak, an *end system* is a host computer and an *intermediate system* is a router.

Whereas bridges cannot easily figure out the optimal path to a destination if two paths exist, a router has the native intelligence to determine the best path.

A bridge merely knows that a frame is not local; a router knows where the packet's final destination is located. A router learns this information and controls the flow of traffic through a *routing protocol*.

Hosts send discovery packets to determine the best path between two end points. The routing protocol, which is sometimes referred to as an *internal gateway protocol*, helps the router discover this information, and shares it with the other routers and hosts every 30 seconds or so. For TCP/IP networks, RIP, or Routing Information Protocol, is most commonly used, but OSPF, or *open shortest path first*, is a newer, more efficient, and standard protocol that's increasing in popularity.

During normal operation, a router takes a packet off the queue, examines its network-layer address, and consults the routing table. If the routing table contains more than one path to the destination address, the router chooses the "best" one. "Best" may be the route with fewest hops or the fastest wide-area link.

Because they use a sophisticated routing scheme, routers offer better path control than bridges. A router can be used to set up "fire-walls" between subnetworks. Broadcast storms are often cited as a reason to use routers. In a broadcast storm, a device malfunctions and repeatedly replicates a frame, which a bridge blindly forwards. Eventually, the network bandwidth is used up by useless broadcast frames. Curing a broadcast storm in a bridged network requires the administrator to turn off each bridge. A router does not propagate these malfunctions because it is not required to copy broadcasts.

A router also performs flow control and packet fragmentation. A router controls the progress of data through the network in a process called *flow control*. The router makes sure that data is not coming in too quickly for it to be processed and retransmitted on the network. Essentially, flow control enables the router to buffer data. (Because bridges cannot perform flow control, they must operate more quickly than routers.)

Depending on the protocol and how the network is configured, some networks can't handle large packet sizes. The router must *fragment* these packets. For example, if the destination has different-sized buffers than the sending network, the packets must be fragmented then reassembled. Or, if the line has many errors, the router can transmit smaller frames.

Routers dynamically configure the routing table, once the network administrator has calculated the "costs" of each path. Under RIP and IGRP, routers send out "keep alive" packets every 10 seconds that notify its nearest neighbor that it is up. If its neighbor fails to receive a "keep alive" packet, it queries the router twice. If it gets no response, it decides the router is down, and recalculates the path. This process, called *convergence*, may take two to five minutes. This notification process adds network overhead.

The tradeoff for tight path control, flow control, and packet fragmentation is speed. Routers are slower than bridges. A good local bridge can forward at the speed of the medium-access method. The average local EtherNet bridge can forward 10,000 to 15,000 packets per second, but the average router forwards 2,000 to 5,000 packets per second. Of course, when you are dealing with remote bridges or routers, the speed point is moot because the limited bandwidth of the wide-area link is the system bottleneck.

A router's slow performance may cause problems for protocols that are very sensitive to delays, including an SNA. This problem is becoming more critical as IBM customers are increasingly using multiprotocol networks in their SNA networks. In this case, TCP/IP routers are generally being used to encapsulate the non-routable SNA traffic and forward it over the SNA network. This requires SNA network administrators to add TCP/IP to their networks.

To solve the performance aspects of multiprotocol routing in an SNA environment, IBM and cisco Systems are having the routers perform "local acknowledgments," where the router sends the packet to its destination. Then the router sends a "fake" acknowledgment to the sending device, so that it thinks that the packet was properly delivered. The router then intercepts the "real" acknowledgment from the receiving device when it comes. If the packet transmission fails, the router will take care of retransmitting. This can be a risky endeavor, because the router manufacturer has to be very adept at handling the *poll spoofing*. Also, it is risky for third-party manufacturers to undertake poll spoofing because IBM controls the SNA code. To date, this is an unproven technology.

An alternative is for administrators to reconfigure their applications' timers, which is very labor-intensive and undesirable. Another solution is a method of routing that is fast enough that SNA applications do not run the risk of timing out.

As mentioned, routers must be built for specific protocols. *Multiprotocol routers*, however, solve the expense and real estate problem of having physically separate boxes to route multiple protocols. As its name suggests, a multiprotocol router can route more than one protocol. For example, it may be able to simultaneously route IP, DECnet, and IPX. Multiprotocol routing is a great boon; however, no standard for implementation exists. For example, a multiprotocol router from Proteon will not work with cisco System's multiprotocol router. The Point-to-Point protocol enables routers from different manufacturers to communicate when talking over a T-1 line, but no similar standard exists for LAN connections. When buying multiprotocol routers, choose your product and vendor carefully because you are buying proprietary technology.

Transparent or source-routing bridging is often coupled with routing because some protocols cannot be bridged. If a protocol lacks a network layer or a routing protocol, it cannot be routed. A combination MAC-layer bridge/network-layer router first tries to route a protocol, then "falls back" to bridging. Such a product enables you to build a multiprotocol network more easily, because the same box can handle all types of network traffic. For example, one internetworking device can handle TCP/IP, DECnet, and LAT traffic. Technicians and managers have to learn only one product; purchasing agents have to buy only one.

One note on server-based routers: Novell and Banyan both use server-based routing. Server-based routers are inefficient for enterprise-wide networks. (Although the process is actually routing, the term *bridging* is frequently and incorrectly used.) In VINES, routing takes place inside the file server, which eats up CPU cycles that should be used to deliver local services to the users. With NetWare, you can set up bridges separately from servers, although the routing can be slow. Dedicated MAC-layer bridges or network-layer routers are best used for enterprise-wide networks, because they provide higher performance and the ability to support multiple network types.

# Choosing Bridges or Routers

Bridges and routers, like trains and airplanes, achieve the same goal, but they transport you differently. Bridges, built around their "plug and play" features, now offer improved frame filtering methods. Routers, renowned for their path control, are now easier to use. To further complicate matters, bridge/routers offer both features. Arguing the benefits of one over the other smacks of the once-heated Token Ring versus EtherNet debate.

If you want to reduce the overall network traffic but retain one large transparent network, use bridges. Bridges are virtually plug and play. They are easy to deploy and inexpensive. A bridge is basically a commodity product; you can buy a good local bridge for $2,000. If you are connecting a few EtherNet networks or a couple of Token Ring networks, bridges are simpler and make sense. The downside of bridges is that they offer limited control. Broadcast storms can and do happen. Custom filters aren't always the answer, because too many filters will bog down the bridge. When you want simplicity, use bridges.

Routers are essential in large, complex networks. They offer excellent control of the traffic loads and routing path. They can easily adjust to link failures and congested paths, automatically routing traffic to another path. If one router is bottlenecked, it can let the other routers know. The downside of routers is that they are more expensive than bridges, slower, more difficult to manage and configure, and require an experienced administrator. Routers definitely are not plug and play.

It is relatively easy to decide to use bridges for an all-EtherNet or an all-Token Ring network. When the network contains a mixture of EtherNet, Token Ring, and FDDI, plus a variety of upper-layer protocols such as TCP/IP, DECnet, and IPX, multiprotocol bridge/routers are your clear choice. Most networks, however, fall somewhere between the very simple and the very complex.

The best enterprise-wide network design is a combination of bridges and routers (see Figure 5.25). This configuration is sometimes referred to as building "clouds" of bridges interconnected by routers. In large enterprise-wide networks, routers should used to connect the building's local network to the backbone LAN or as the connection point from the backbone to the WAN. Routers should be used anywhere you do not want traffic to cross. For example, with a WAN connection, you don't want to clog up the already small bandwidth with excess traffic. A router can ensure that excess packets, or at worst a broadcast storm, does not propagate across the WAN.

Bridges should be used to connect departmental networks to the horizontal network. They should also be used in heavily loaded departmental networks to further subdivide the traffic. Here, the extra security and control of a router is not worth the trouble. Bridges excel on the local network, but when you are paying for packets on a WAN, a router's path control makes more sense.

Building clouds of local bridges interconnected by routers enables you to gain the benefits of both types of internetwork devices while minimizing their disadvantages. Less experienced departmental LAN administrators can easily manage the local bridges. Also, their high performance ensures that users will get response quickly. Time-out issues will not arise, because the distances are short. Security issues are not as critical because the users are from the same department.

On the enterprise backbone, the routers provide the tight flow control that is necessary to localize and secure traffic. Here, a bridge's transparency is a hindrance. Routers require more expertise from your support team, but not at an unreasonable level.

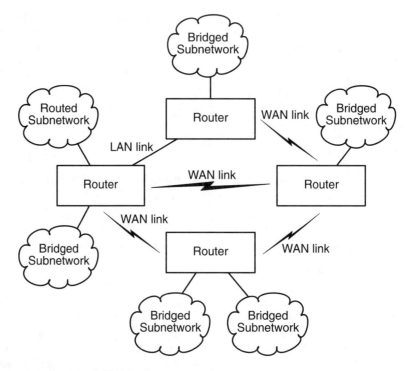

**Figure 5.25.** *Using bridges and routers together.*

## Choosing a Bridge Versus a Router

Here are some guidelines for choosing bridges and routers:

- A bridge is most appropriate when:

  A network is made up of only one LAN type; for example, if the network is all EtherNet or all Token Ring.

  You have fewer than 15 subnetworks.

  A protocol cannot be routed, such as LAT or NetBIOS.

  You want high performance rather than control.

  You want plug-and-play connectivity with minimal management demands.

■ A router is most appropriate when:

A network is made up of multiple LAN types running different network protocols; for example, if the network consists of FDDI and EtherNet running TCP/IP, IPX, and AppleTalk.

A network has 15 or more subnetworks.

You want tight path control and security over where packets can travel.

Speed is not an issue.

You want to balance the load over multiple links that travel to the same destination.

You have the management expertise to configure and operate a router.

# Building with Gateways

More than an internetworking device, a gateway connects two dissimilar computer systems and translates between them. An X.25 gateway, for example, connects a LAN to an X.25 packet-switched network. An SNA mainframe gateway connects a LAN to an IBM SNA network. Gateways operate at the fourth through seventh layers of the OSI model (see Figure 5.26). In data communications terminology, gateways are known as *protocol converters*.

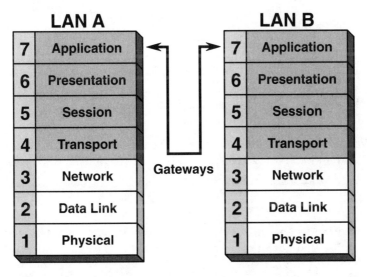

*Figure 5.26.* *A gateway operates at OSI layers 4 through 7.*

One computer is designated as the gateway. It can be either a dedicated PC or a file server. This gateway computer runs the software that performs the protocol conversion between the two systems. The gateway PC emulates the native device that connects the end-user devices to the host computer. In the case of a LAN-to-SNA mainframe gateway, the gateway PC acts as a cluster controller. The gateway PC manages the host sessions and otherwise allocates resources. The individual workstations must run gateway and terminal emulation software so that they can communicate, through the gateway PC, to the host computer.

IBM SNA mainframe gateways come in several types: DFT coax, SDLC, and Token Ring. A Distributed Function Terminal (DFT) coax gateway provides a local connection by distributing many of the cluster controller's functions to the display station. A DFT gateway emulates the functions of a DFT terminal, not of the 3174 cluster controller. With support for at most 40 sessions, a DFT gateway has limited applicability in an enterprise-wide network. If connecting to a local mainframe, the smartest strategy is a Token Ring Interface Coupler (TIC), which provides a direct LAN connection for the mainframe. A TIC is essentially a Token Ring adapter card for the mainframe. An SDLC gateway connects a remote LAN to a mainframe via an SDLC wide-area link. In this configuration, the gateway PC emulates a 3174 or 3274 cluster controller. When local connections are not an option, SDLC gateways are practical.

Most mainframe gateways are DOS-based, and connect NetBIOS or NetWare LANs to the IBM mainframe. They generally offer 128 or 256 sessions on one gateway PC, although in all practicality the gateway cannot support that many sessions. These sessions can be allocated to users statically or dynamically. In static assignment, each user is hard-coded to a particular session number. This approach is superior when security is an issue. For flexibility, you'll want dynamic allocation, where users are served on a first-come, first-served basis from a pool of sessions. Gateway software enables users to have multiple sessions, although most people—even power users—won't use more than three sessions simultaneously.

Gateways are also available to connect IBM midrange systems, including the System/3x and AS/400, as well as a variety of Hewlett-Packard and Digital Equipment Corp. host computers. They work according to the same principles as LAN-to-SNA gateways, although the specifics differ.

Gateways are also available to connect LANs to X.25 packet switched clouds; however, in most new networks, the X.25 functionality is integrated into a router, rather than into a stand-alone gateway. In this way, traffic is filtered before it is sent onto the X.25 network, directly reducing the number of packets sent and the per-packet charges.

# Building the Infrastructure for Tomorrow

The success of design of the network infrastructure—the cabling, the access methods, and the internetworking devices—determines the longevity of your enterprise-wide network. A network designed with yesterday's technology may only last a year until the performance and reliability are too low. A network designed with tomorrow's technology will be riskier—more difficult to design, build, and troubleshoot—yet it will have a longer lifetime, perhaps four years. You must decide the balance between tried-and-true technology and leading-edge technology.

A structured wiring system, although costly at installation time, will prove itself over time in terms of greater flexibility and lower maintenance costs. Don't just cable a few areas, with the assumption that the network won't grow. It will grow. Consider the use of existing cable; most buildings have a surfeit of unshielded twisted-pair that can easily be used for Token Ring or EtherNet transmission. Fiber is typically the medium of choice for all backbones, or the interconnects between departmental LANs. Only fiber delivers the necessary bandwidth and longevity.

The choice of Token Ring versus EtherNet has become less important—don't become bogged down in a religious argument. Both will perform well. Token Ring will always be a more expensive option, but one that you should consider especially if you are an IBM shop. You should, however, avoid standardizing on older, nonstandard technologies such as ARCnet and LocalTalk, because they lack the bandwidth to satisfy the needs of tomorrow's users. Although FDDI is an emerging technology with a small installed base, it is a good access method for a backbone network and it can deliver good performance. Once quite pricey, the cost of FDDI as a backbone medium is dropping rapidly. With the advent of copper FDDI, it may become feasible to run to the desktop.

The enterprise-wide network should be segmented using bridges and routers. As with EtherNet and Token Ring, the debate over using bridges versus routers approaches a religious argument. Routers are best used to form large subnetworks; bridges can then be used to segment routed networks. Routers will provide better control in an enterprise network and are essential at wide area network connections.

Many of the decisions about the campus portions of an enterprise network are often debated. You should make your decisions based on your company's business goals, the company's corporate standards, the availability of today's and tomorrow's networking and wide-area technologies, and the available MIS budget.

# Building the Wide Area Network

**Objectives:**

1. To delve into the wide area service options for interconnecting multiple LANs into an enterprise's wide area network.

2. To examine the issues of building a private network versus using a public network, determining the proper amount of bandwidth, and discussing the spectrum of WAN services, both immediately available and emerging.

# WAN Services: The Lifeblood of the Enterprise-Wide Network

If the local area network—the EtherNet, Token Ring, and FDDI—is the enterprise-wide network's skeleton, giving structure to its form and supporting its data flow, then the wide area network—the WAN services—is the circulatory system, the transport that moves the data from the heart of the network out to its extremities and back again. As there are different types of blood, there are different types of WAN services. Choosing the right combination is essential to the life of your enterprise-wide network.

If you choose too little wide area network bandwidth or the wrong type of service, the network's traffic flow will clot, its arteries thick with packets. The applications in the extremities will wither for lack of bandwidth, and their users will sit frustrated by a lack of responsiveness. If you choose too much wide area network bandwidth, the pipes will remain clear and open and the users will be happy; however, you will waste money paying for services that the users don't need, thereby making upper management unhappy.

Choosing the right amount of WAN bandwidth requires you to carefully measure the traffic, weigh the pros and cons of building a private wide area network rather than using public services, and then finally, choose the particular WAN services. The decision is complicated by the array of emerging wide area network services, plus the plethora of existing ones.

When choosing WAN services for the enterprise-wide network, consider the network's logical and physical designs. For example, if your enterprise-wide network is contained on a single campus, you may use only fiber or short-haul microwave to connect the buildings. If, however, your enterprise-wide network spans the entire country, you will need to decide what types of WAN services are most appropriate. You will also need to decide whether you want to build your own network or lease services from a telephone company.

A revolution is occurring in LAN-WAN connections. Instead of building one network to carry voice, a second to carry terminal data, and a third to carry LAN traffic—and using the public networks to carry fax—multiple services, such as LAN, PBX, host, and fax, are being carried on a single network (see Figure 6.1). As distributed networking becomes more prevalent and featured, high-bandwidth applications such as video will be added to the network.

Another change is happening. In the past, data services were piggy-backed onto the voice network, whether that network was privately or publicly owned. Wide area network services were designed to accommodate voice, and data was tacked on as an afterthought. As the importance of data traffic increases, however, the tables are turning. Data is becoming the primary reason for building an enterprise-wide network, and voice is piggy-backed onto the existing network. Data that is not time-sensitive could be sent over unused portions of a private T-1 network, for example, when voice traffic is not using the bandwidth, which may be at night. By adding bandwidth and sharing the pool of resources, the data and voice traffic can be carried together.

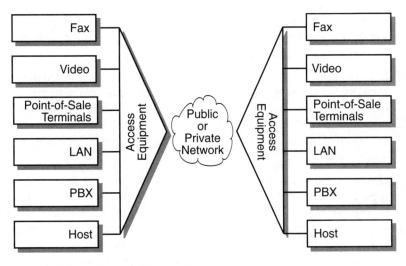

**Figure 6.1.**   *One backbone, multiple services.*

# Measuring the Enterprise-Wide Network's Traffic Flow

Determining the exact amount of bandwidth needed requires a mathematician's skill and a surgeon's precision. When estimating the needed bandwidth, be sure to include only WAN traffic, not LAN traffic. LAN traffic flow from the individual campus networks can be segmented and restricted by bridges or routers so that unnecessary traffic does not traverse the WAN. This will significantly reduce the cost of WAN services. Whereas LAN people typically are unconcerned with the exact volume of traffic traveling across the local network (because it is essentially free), with WAN traffic you have to pay for every packet sent.

To ensure that you strike the right balance between available and needed bandwidth, start by measuring these parameters:

■ *Determine what level of response time is required for users on the network.* Is the current level of response time sufficient or does it need to be improved? Interview key users and department managers to determine this. How dependent are users on the system's response time? Do users need a half-second or a 30-second response time? For example, a customer service department requires a higher response time than users who are retrieving mail.

■ *Determine the average amount of data to be transferred.* How much data does each department typically transfer across the wide area network to each destination point? What are the typical packet sizes and volumes? At what times do the users transfer the data? Is the data time-sensitive, or can some of the data be transferred at night when the telephone rates are low?

■ *Determine the average projected link usage.* Determine what the users' typical loading of the wide area network links will be. This figure may be higher than the current level of usage, because when multiple departmental or campus networks are interconnected, the communications possibilities increase. How will additional services affect the link usage? Users will discover new ways to use the network.

■ *Determine the performance of bridges, routers, and gateways.* Benchmark your existing bridges, routers, and gateways to calculate the average, minimum, and maximum number of packets transferred per second. Is the performance bottleneck the internetworking device or the WAN link? You can use this data to calculate how the internetworking devices will load the wide area network links (see *Measuring Bridge and Router Performance* later in this chapter).

■ *Determine the bandwidth consumed by the attached equipment and services.* Using protocol analyzers, measure the bandwidth consumed by the existing equipment. Then, project the bandwidth that will be consumed when the network is expanded. Place protocol analyzers on various segments to measure the current traffic. Then, using a protocol analyzer's ability to inject traffic into the network, gradually add packets to the network, measuring the reactions of the various internetworking and WAN devices. Determine the worst-case scenario. You may want to use simulation software to project this off-line (see Chapter 4, "High-Level Issues of Enterprise-Wide Network Design").

To calculate the enterprise-wide network's bandwidth, multiply the average packet arrival rate by the average packet size. Then multiply that figure by 2 or 3 to minimize queuing delays.

# Characterizing the Type of Network Traffic

Next, characterize the types of traffic that will traverse the enterprise-wide network. LAN usage can be divided into four categories, each with increasing bandwidth demands: terminal server traffic, remote electronic mail, shared files, and graphic or workstation file transfers (see Figure 6.2).

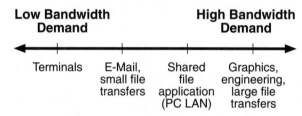

*Figure 6.2.* *The impact of traffic types on WAN bandwidth requirements.*

Terminal server traffic is typified by small packets sent in bursty intervals. Dumb terminals send small numbers of characters back to the host, and each character must be "echoed" back to the terminal to be displayed. Echoing requires that each character sent to the host must traverse the LAN twice. Terminals place a low demand on the network's bandwidth, but responsiveness is critical so that the application does not timeout.

Remote electronic mail traffic behaves like small file transfer applications. In E-mail and small file transfers, the files transferred are small and usage is occasional. These actions place a fairly low demand on the wide area network bandwidth. Responsiveness is less important than connectivity. In this type of network, designers typically place 50 workstations per segment.

In a shared file application, large quantities of data are transferred across the link between the file servers and the users. This is the "traditional" PC LAN model. Transfer times have a direct impact on users' productivity. If the users have diskless workstations or do not store any applications locally, the load on the network will be heavier, because they must also download application programs from the servers. The users' proximity to the file server will directly affect their performance. Medium to high bandwidth is required and response time is important. Designers typically place fewer than 30 workstations per LAN segment.

In a graphic or engineering workstation network, the files tend to be very large. This traffic model best fits UNIX workstations. The large size of the files greatly affects the transmission speed. Users will become frustrated if they have to wait for their screens to update with the new graphic file image. Bandwidth demands are heaviest, and as a result, network designers typically place five or fewer engineering workstations on a segment.

Imaging and video will place very heavy demands on the network. With the advent of imaging and video-conferencing, demand for LAN and WAN bandwidth will be unprecedented. If your company is moving toward these applications, be aware that you will need high-speed networks such as FDDI and beyond.

Table 6.1 and Figure 6.3 give you an idea of the time it takes to load a 64KB file over various wide area network links. The figures are calculated assuming a 100 percent link and protocol efficiency, which is ideal. Although T-1, at 1.544Mbps, is a fast service by telecom standards, LAN users are accustomed to the speedy response times of 10Mbps EtherNet and 16Mbps Token Ring. They demand the same response time from the WAN link as from the LAN link.

**Table 6.1.  Typical response times.**

| Raw Data Rate | Load Time |
| --- | --- |
| 9.6 Kbps | 9.1 minutes |
| 38.4 Kbps | 2.3 minutes |
| 56.0 Kbps | 1.6 minutes |
| 112.0 Kbps | 47.0 seconds |
| 1.544 Mbps | 3.5 seconds |
| 6.312 Mbps | .8 seconds |
| 10.0 Mbps | .3 seconds |

As link utilization increases, contention occurs and queuing delays begin. When the average link utilization exceeds 50 percent, system response time slows considerably. On a 95 percent loaded link, the delay is about 20 times that of a lightly loaded link.

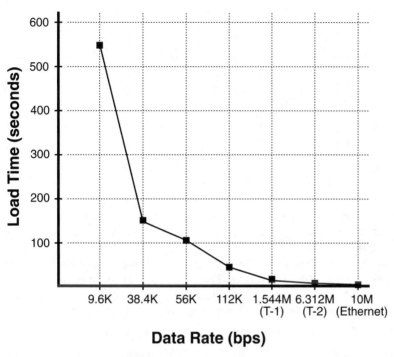

*Figure 6.3.* *Response times and bandwidth.*

# Measuring Bridge and Router Performance

Bridge and router manufacturers typically tout how many packets per second their products can forward. This metric can be misleading, however, because the size of wide area network pipe—not the performance of the bridge or router—is generally the bottleneck. Also, the size packet used to measure this performance statistic often varies from manufacturer to manufacturer.

When a link is full, a traffic jam will occur, leaving the bridge or router to buffer the traffic. No more data can be put on the link until the traffic clears up. With the small size of wide area network bandwidths, congestion occurs often. Table 6.2 gives you a feel for the speed of bridging EtherNet over various WAN services. (The calculations were made assuming a minimum EtherNet packet size of 64 bits.)

**Table 6.2.  Typical WAN bridged EtherNet speeds.**

| Raw Link Speed | Packets per Second |
| --- | --- |
| 9.6 Kbps | 18 |
| 19.2 Kbps | 36 |
| 56.0 Kbps | 106 |
| 1.536 Mbps | 2,909 |
| 10.0 Mbps | 14,880 |

The performance of internetworking devices is typically measured according to their filtering and forwarding rates. The *filtering rate* measures how many packets per second the bridge can recognize and determine whether to pass to the other LAN. The *forwarding rate* measures how much data the bridge can send from one LAN to another. These metrics can be misleading, because different LAN protocols add different amounts of overhead, which means that the amount of data actually transferred in a certain-sized packet varies with protocol.

Also, bridge and router performance can be measured using different-sized packets. Ask the device manufacturer what size packet is used to measure performance. Also, some vendors add the number of packets forwarded on each port but neglect to mention that the figure is aggregate performance. For example, if each port of a four-port bridge forwards 3,000 packets per second, the manufacturer says the bridge forwards 12,000 packets per second, which would be good performance for a single port, but not for all four ports.

The real measure of performance should not be the bridge's packet forwarding rate, but should be a combination of link efficiency and the link's bit rate performance. This figure better measures how efficiently the bridge places packets on the WAN link. The bottom line is that if the link can be kept entirely full in both directions, the bridge is 100 percent efficient. Today, the wide area network link is almost always the gating factor in WAN performance; as speedier wide area network services become available, however, this may change.

# When Data Compression Is Appropriate

Bridges and routers filter traffic to maximize the available wide area network bandwidth. By filtering packets, local packets remain local and remote packets are sent to their destinations. Another option to better utilize WAN bandwidth is *compression*. You can use compression to avoid moving to higher-speed lines or to connect more services and devices to your existing lines. A 2:1 compression ratio is standard, although you can buy commercially available devices that will compress at 6:1 and 7:1 rates.

Compression is most effective with medium-sized packets and lower bandwidths with applications that have not already been compressed. If your network traffic is characterized by lots of small frames, compression won't be much help. Compression is generally used with 56Kbps and slower lines.

Many large files, such as those created by graphics programs, may already have been compressed by their application. Many others are not, however, and can benefit from compression techniques. For example, database files can be reduced to between 13 and 20 percent of their original size. ASCII text and word processing files can be compressed to 25 percent or 20 percent of their original size. Executable files and other object modules can be compressed to about half their original size. Previously compressed files cannot be further compressed, and doing so may actually make a file larger than the original.

Compression has a tradeoff: latency. It takes time for the bridge or compression device to decide the best compression ratio and then compress the file. Generally, the higher the compression ratio, the longer it takes to compress the file.

Bridges generally support compression, but be warned: compression algorithms are proprietary to their manufacturer. A file compressed by one manufacturer's bridge cannot be decompressed by another vendor's algorithm and bridge. Also, compression should be performed in hardware rather than software, because hardware-based compression is much faster and you want to minimize latency as much as possible.

# Using Public or Private WAN Services

When building an enterprise-wide network, you can use a public network, build a private network, or use a combination of public and private services. The majority of companies use public wide area networking services to transport data among their privately owned local area networks. Companies build private WANs where they run mission-critical applications or when adequate public wide area network service is not available.

Data and voice network services are available from a variety of Regional Bell Operating Companies (RBOCs) and Interexchange Carriers (IXC or IEC). The telephone companies and service providers, in their various incarnations, provide services on a local, a national, and an international level. You can purchase services relatively economically. The telephone network, built on a modern digital fiber infrastructure, is reliable (although recent failures have become more frequent and catastrophic).

You should use a public network service if you do not need the control or want the responsibility of building and maintaining a wide area data or voice network. The public carrier you choose will take care of moving the data from one of your sites to another. The intermediate route—and its management and reliability—will not be your concern. You can safely use public services for applications and services that are not mission-critical.

If the enterprise-wide network is mission-critical and you want to control each step, however, consider building a private network or using a combination of public and private services (see the section titled "Dow Jones Moves from Satellite to Frame Relay"). For example, you can build a private T-1 network quite cost-effectively. If you choose to build your own network, you will probably want the network to carry both voice and data traffic. Even if the network is private, companies generally lease the transmission lines from a carrier, because few companies want to go to the expense of pulling their own fiber. Using a private network requires you to build an in-house staff of telecommunications experts who will specify, install, and maintain the tele-com links.

If you choose to build a private network, you must purchase and manage much of the equipment that the telephone companies would ordinarily own. For example, in a private network the end user assumes responsibility for the network access and transmission equipment, whereas in a public network the end user owns only the network access, but not the transmission equipment.

In a public network, the customer owns the equipment needed to connect its computing and voice equipment to the public network. The local carrier and interexchange carrier assume responsibility for reliably and speedily delivering the data from its origin to its destination. Using public network services offloads these responsibilities from the end users. In a private network, the end-user customer assumes responsibility for reliably and speedily delivering voice and data traffic to its destination. The customer owns both the network access equipment and the T-1 multiplexer equipment. The customer may own the physical fiber lines between the multiple sites, although it often leases them from a local or interexchange carrier. The differences in equipment between a publicly owned network and a privately owned network are shown in Figures 6.4 and 6.5.

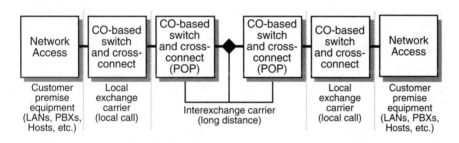

CO = Central Office
POP = Point of Presence

*Source: Telco Systems*

**Figure 6.4.** *Who owns what in public WANs.*

# Dow Jones Moves from Satellite to Frame Relay[1]

Information is the lifeblood of Dow Jones. From the reporting and production of the *Wall Street Journal* to Dow Jones' variety of consumer information products, cost-effective and widespread communication is synonymous with the survival of the company. The flow of information is truly mission-critical.

---

[1]Richard Rothwell, Dow Jones & Company. "How to Implement Frame Relay." Interop, Mountain View, CA. October 1991.

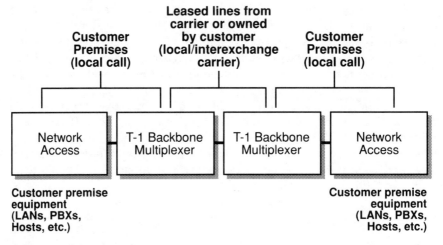

**Figure 6.5.** *Who owns what in private WANs.*

Communication is so important that Dow Jones became the first noncommon carrier to operate its own satellite network in 1974. This network enabled the company to transmit full-page facsimiles of the *Wall Street Journal* pages, which helped the company work closer to the press deadline as well as work more accurately. By 1982, the company had found many more applications for its network than transmitting images of the *Journal* pages, and had to upgrade to a fully meshed 15Mbps satellite network. By 1987, services were expanded to include digital voice, data, and fax services. To accommodate the new services, bandwidth had to be expanded to 60Mbps.

This network enabled the Journal to be printed in 18 locations. From there, Dow Jones continued to improve the quality and breadth of services. For example, an enhanced production system enabled the company to respond more quickly to late-breaking news with regionalized editions delivered nationwide on the same day. Production services supported by the satellite network include advertising distribution, graphic layout, an editorial database, typesetting, full-page facsimile, and pagination.

But as the services increased, the delay inherent in satellite transmission became a problem. The delay—at minimum a half-second—limits Dow Jones' ability to expand into many advanced services, such as multimedia, videotext, and interactive services.

Today, Dow Jones has migrated to a router-based network with connections to its privately owned satellite network. But the company is looking to frame relay as a way to bring its data, voice, and image transmissions back "down to earth." With the installation of public fiber-based networks, it has become more cost-effective to use public fiber services than to build a private satellite network. Still, the company is looking for frame relay services to be available over a satellite transport so that it can maximize its technology investment. But even as it looks to frame relay, Dow Jones knows that frame relay's bandwidth is insufficient to meet the demands of tomorrow's applications, which will include interactive products, multimedia services, and teleconferencing. Its next step may have to be Switched Multimegabit Data Services, or SMDS.

# The Three Service Options

*Bandwidth on demand* is a new concept that calls for the user to be able to call up more bandwidth as the application warrants. It also enables users to pay only for bandwidth that they use, when they use it, instead of paying for bandwidth as a dedicated service whether or not they use it. With fixed-bandwidth services, you must order and pay for a certain amount of bandwidth, regardless of usage. The 1990s will see the emergence of bandwidth-on-demand services, which may be accomplished through circuit- and packet-switched services such as frame relay, ISDN, and switched 56.

Which wide area network services are most appropriate to your company's enterprise-wide network depends on several factors:

■ Your network's architecture. Does the network implement a mesh, point-to-point, or hybrid topology?

■ The types of services needed. Do the users need only voice and data? Do they need fax or video?

■ The bandwidth required. How much bandwidth is required to support the types of services needed?

■ The locations of your data sites. What wide area network services are available in your company's locations? More densely populated locations tend to have more service options.

■ The budget available. How much money can your company afford to spend on wide area network services?

LAN-to-WAN telecommunications services come in three varieties: *circuit-switched*, *leased*, and *packet-switched* (see Figures 6.6 to 6.8). Which services are most appropriate to your company's needs depends on your network's architecture, the types of services needed, the bandwidth required, and the budget available. Some services discussed here are emerging and will become available throughout the 1990s.

*Leased services* are permanent, dedicated private lines that are leased from a carrier. You must have sufficient bandwidth requirements to warrant leasing transmission lines from RBOCs or interexchange carriers (or both), although if you combine voice, fax, and data traffic, private networks and leased lines are often easy to justify. Examples of leased lines include 56Kbps digital lines and T-1 (see Figure 6.6).

**Figure 6.6.** *Three WAN service options.*

With *circuit-switched services*, a temporary dedicated path called a *circuit* is established between two users for the duration of a conversation or transmission. This is accomplished by *time division multiplexing* (TDM), or by assigning each channel a specific portion of the available bandwidth. The users possess this circuit exclusively—they do not share it with any other—until they release the connection. Voice, data, and imaging can be sent via circuit switching, although time-sensitive signals, such as voice and video, are most appropriate for this type of transmission. An example of a commercially available circuit-switched service is ISDN (see Figure 6.7).

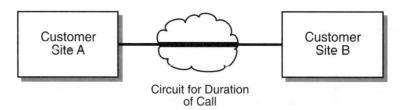

**Figure 6.7.** *Circuit-switched service.*

In *packet switching*, data is segmented into packets and sent across a circuit shared by multiple subscribers. Each packet has a source and destination address, in addition to data and other framing information. As the packet travels over the network, devices such as switches read the addresses and route the packet to its proper destination. Because from the user's point of view, a packet-switched line seems like it exclusively belongs to the user, such a line is often called a *virtual circuit*. Packet-switched services are most akin to LAN traffic, which is asynchronous and bursty. X.25 and frame relay are among the packet-switching options (see Figure 6.8).

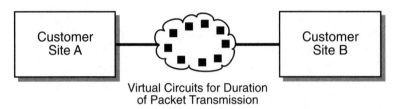

**Figure 6.8.** *Packet-switched service.*

Circuit-switched and leased lines are most suitable for point-to-point connections, whereas packet-switched services are better for mesh networks. You may also build a private backbone using leased lines, to which subnetworks attach. If you have more than four sites and want mesh connectivity, point-to-point connections can be expensive, because the number of connections required is $2^n$, in which $n$ is the number of sites.

# Leased and Private Line Services

Leased or private line services include digital lines, T-1, T-2, and T-3. Digital lines are suitable for networks with low bandwidth demands. T-1 is suitable for moderately loaded networks as well as voice traffic. T-3 is suitable for high-speed voice and data networks. These types of services are most suitable for point-to-point applications.

## Digital Lines

Whereas analog telephone lines are suitable for individual use, the slowest acceptable shared wide area network service is DDS, or Dataphone Digital Service, lines. DDS is a private-line digital service with data rates of 2.4K, 4.8K,

9.6K, 19.2K, and 56Kbps. Of those, 19.2K and 56Kbps are the most commonly used for LAN traffic.

DDS is offered on an inter-LATA basis by AT&T and on an intra-LATA basis by the RBOCs. The benefits of DDS is that it is inexpensive and readily available. Its bandwidth is limited, however, and it is best for networks with terminal traffic or small file transfers.

## T-1 and Fractional T-1

T-1, which delivers 1.544Mbps of bandwidth, is the next increment in leased line services. T-1's bandwidth is divided into 24 channels of 64Kbps each. (Each 64Kbps channel is called *Digital Signal 0* or *DS-0*.) T-1 is available from a number of carriers, or you can build a private T-1 network using T-1 switches and multiplexers. T-1, which is commonly used in large corporate voice and data networks, has enjoyed faster growth than any other telephone company network service. T-1's economies are outstanding, enabling end-user companies to lease a T-1 circuit as a replacement for as few as six analog voice lines. With private systems, the break-even point can be even lower. With the addition of a T-1 multiplexer, T-1 can be used to carry voice, video, and data.

*Fractional T-1* enables you to purchase a portion of the full T-1 bandwidth in increments of 64Kbps, and you pay only for the portion used. When you need additional bandwidth, you call the telephone company and order more, because the T-1 access line was installed when you initially ordered the service. For example, you may initially purchase 64Kbps, but in six months decide that you need 128Kbps, so the service provider can simply "turn on" more bandwidth from its central office. Fractional T-1 places speedy T-1 within the reach of many who do not need or cannot afford the full T-1 bandwidth.

T-1 and fractional T-1's costs are proportional to distance, so the longer the distance, the more it costs. But T-1, even at 1.544Mbps, is not enough bandwidth for today's and tomorrow's LAN applications.

In Europe, the basic carrier is E-1, which operates at 2.048Mbps. In the United States, the basic carrier is T-1, and it multiplexes 24 voice channels onto two twisted-pair wires. The voice signal must be sampled at 8,000 cycles per second using pulse code modulation, and each voice sample is carried as an eight-bit unit. A single frame, which carries a single framing bit plus one sample from each of the 24 channels, contains 193 bits ($24 \times 8 + 1$), and at 8,000 frames per second, the T-1 rate is 1.544Mbps. SONET, an emerging transmission system, will resolve these differences globally.

# T-2 and T-3

T-2 and T-3 are the next increments of raw bandwidth. T-2, which is the equivalent of four T-1s, offers 6.3Mbps of bandwidth. Each T-2 link can carry at least 96 64Kbps circuits. When used with T-1 multiplexers and bridges, T-2 can be used to bulk transport multiple LAN, voice, phone, fax, data, and teleconferencing circuits from one facility to another. T-2 is not offered by the telephone companies except as a part of a T-3 line.

A T-3 circuit carries the equivalent of 28 T-1s in one multiplexed signal stream and provides 672 DS-0 channels. T-3 itself can also be multiplexed into a higher-speed signal (560Mbps or 565Mbps) and sent over fiber. (T-3 itself can be transmitted over microwave or fiber.)

The phone companies are aggressively pricing T-3, and often the cost of a T-3 line is no more than six to eight times that of a single T-1 line, even though you gain many more times the bandwidth. With the addition of a T-3 multiplexer, you can build an efficient, private voice and data network. The down side is that T-3 offerings are often proprietary, which limit their use between the carriers' offices as well as on local loops. If a company chooses T-3 as the WAN infrastructure, it must use equipment from the same T-3 manufacturer at all points. Another drawback of T-3 is its dearth of management features, which is partially due to its newness (see Figure 6.9).

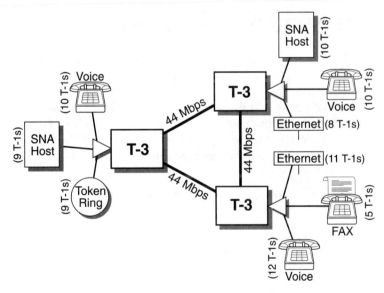

***Figure 6.9.*** *A T-3 network.*

The carriers are considering offering fractional T-3, and it is anticipated that fractional T-3 will work similarly to fractional T-1. Fractional T-2 implementations include Switched Multimegabit Data Service (SMDS).

Table 6.3 is a summary of leased line information.

**Table 6.3.   Leased lines summarized.**

| Type | Speed | Suitable Traffic | Notes |
|------|-------|------------------|-------|
| DDS | 2400 baud to 56Kbps | data, voice | For low-speed needs |
| T-1 | 1.544Mbps | data, voice | For high-speed needs; expensive |
| Fractional T-1 | 64Kbps to 1.544 Mbps | data, voice | Offers greater flexibility than T-1 |
| T-2 | 6.3Mbps | N/A commercially | |
| T-3 | 44Mbps | data, voice, video | Relatively new service |

# Circuit-Switched Services

Circuit-switched services include dial-up lines, switched 56, and ISDN. Circuit-switched services are best suited for *isochronous* (or time-sensitive) traffic such as voice and (given sufficient bandwidth) video, but they can easily accommodate data traffic. These services are typically leased from telephone companies, which frees your company from the responsibility of building and managing these services. These types of services are suitable for mesh-type network topologies, especially where the number of locations makes point-to-point WAN services too costly.

Table 6.4 summarizes circuit-switched services:

**Table 6.4. A summary of circuit-switched services.**

| Type | Speed | Suitable Traffic | Notes |
|------|-------|------------------|-------|
| Dial-up | 9600 baud | data, voice | For low-speed needs |
| Switched 56 | 56Kbps to 1.544 Mbps | data, voice | Offers flexibility |
| ISDN | 1.544Mbps | data, voice | Not widely implemented |

(23 64Kbps channels, 1 16Kbps channel)

## Dial-up Lines

Dial-up lines may be ubiquitous, but they are not suitable for building enterprise-wide networks. With speeds up to 9.6Kbps, dial-up lines are suitable only for the user with low bandwidth or response time needs. Dial-up lines are best used on an individual basis. For example, salespeople on the road can plug their laptops into any telephone jack and dial into the company's inventory database to find out if a part is in stock. Or an executive can dial in to check electronic mail. Compression modems are essential for those who require higher performance.

## Switched 56

Switched 56 lines are dial-up connections that use bandwidth in 56Kbps increments. A maximum of 24 channels can be dialed up, for a maximum bandwidth of 1.5Mbps. With switched 56, a modem or DSU/CSU at the customer site is programmed to dial on demand the telephone number of the destination computer.

## ISDN

ISDN, or Integrated Digital Services Network, has been hyped for years as the solution to integrated voice and data, but it still hasn't arrived. Dubbed "I Still Don't Need it" and "I Still Don't kNow" by cynics, ISDN finally shows signs of arrival.

The ISDN that's nearly here has been renamed *Narrowband ISDN* to distinguish it from the coming *Broadband ISDN* that will offer far greater data rates.

Narrowband ISDN consists of a *Basic Rate* ISDN (BRI) and a *Primary Rate* ISDN (PRI) service. BRI is two *bearer* channels (B) of 64Kbps for bulk data transfer plus a *data link* (D) 16Kbps channel for control and signalling information. PRI is a T-1 pipe that supports 23 B channels plus one D channel, which is normally notated as 23B+D.

ISDN's original intent was to combine the separate voice and data infrastructures into a single network. Customers can attach their host computers, LANs, and telephone services to an ISDN network. The promise of ISDN has yet to be delivered, however (see Figure 6.10).

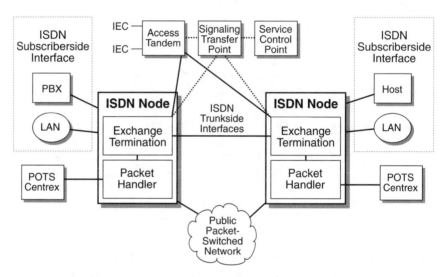

***Figure 6.10.*** *An ISDN network.*

ISDN hasn't arrived in the United States for several reasons. First, the phone companies' central office switches must be replaced or retrofitted to provide ISDN services. With more than 10,000 central office switches in the United States alone, that's a large order. But the logistical problem of upgrading the telephone switches is small in comparison with the technological problem of the many incompatible versions of ISDN. The Consultive Committee for Telephony and Telegraphy (CCITT) standard for ISDN, defined in 1988, allowed for several methods of implementation, and different manufacturers' equipment is incompatible (which is the antithesis of a standard). National ISDN 1, announced in early 1991, is an attempt to finally standardize the different ISDN implementations so that an end-user company can purchase standards-based ISDN services from different service providers.

Another ISDN roadblock is tariffing. The Regional Bell Operating Companies (RBOCs) were slow in providing tariffs for ISDN services, because it meant not only a large investment in hardware upgrades, but also a complete overhaul of the billing systems. The RBOCs wanted to price the variety of ISDN features at different rates. For example, if data and voice were transmitted on the same call to the same destination, they would be priced at different rates, and every call would have to be billed at a different rate.

The telephone companies won't give up easily, however, because they've invested heavily in the service. National ISDN 1 is an agreement among all the major ISDN players that defines plans for a standard implementation and a definite tariff scheduling. The fruits should come by the end of 1992. Also, the RBOCs should have their tariffs ready by the end of 1993. By then, Bell Communications Research (Bellcore) should have finalized an implementation standard that will resolve the incompatibility in the D channel, which each vendor implements differently.

ISDN, once positioned as the way to provide simultaneous voice and data connectivity, is now positioned at the "low end" where it will provide services to residential users, home offices, and small businesses. For example, ISDN can provide videotext, dial-up data services, desktop teleconferencing, and advanced call management to the many users who work at home or out of small business offices.

Besides changing its purpose, another strategy to make ISDN successful is to change its name. Some ISDN providers now shrink from the acronym, preferring *bandwidth on demand* or *switched data network*. Although it's still ISDN equipment and services, vendors talk about the benefits of being able to dial up these services on demand for applications such as disaster recovery and videoconferencing.

ISDN hasn't met with the same fate internationally. Rather, European nations have quite enthusiastically adopted ISDN, and offer it as an alternative to the slower PDN networks. Because wide area services are tightly controlled by each country's PTT, European nations often face fewer incompatibility problems than the United States does. Also, because the European telecommunications infrastructure is not as advanced as the United States', the Europeans were able to leapfrog into the latest technology, whereas in the United States we must retain compatibility with a large installed base.

ISDN is still largely seen as a voice technology that secondarily integrates data. LAN users accustomed to speedy service won't be sated by sharing a single 64Kbps BRI, although a 23B+D interface would suffice. ISDN's strength may indeed lie in connecting the single user to a wider group.

# Packet-Switched Services

Existing packet-switched services include X.25 and frame relay. SMDS and Broadband ISDN are emerging services. Packet-based services are best suited for data, because isochronous traffic such as voice and video may experience delay when packetized. As with circuit-switched services, packet-switched services are typically leased from a service provider (often a value-added network company). They are appropriate for a mesh or cloud network topology, because you can interconnect many locations relatively inexpensively.

Table 6.5 summarizes packet-switched services.

**Table 6.5. Packet-switched services summarized.**

| Type | Speed | Suitable Traffic | Notes |
|------|-------|------------------|-------|
| X.25 | 64Kbps | terminals | High overhead, best for terminal traffic or small files |
| Frame Relay | 64Kbps to 2Mbps | LAN traffic | New service; not widely implemented |
| SMDS | 1.544Mbps to 45Mbps | LAN, image, video | Emerging service; not widely implemented |

## X.25

To date, X.25, a CCITT standard, has been the most popular packet-switched service, primarily because it has also been the only viable one. X.25 was defined to give terminals access to packet-switched services, and as such it is best suited to handle the light traffic of terminals rather than the heavy bandwidth demands of LANs. X.25 is available from many public data networks (PDNs), including BT/Tymnet, Sprint/Telenet, AT&T Accunet, Infonet, and many international sources. X.25 is often the only option for building an international wide area network, because nearly every country offers an X.25 service. Companies may also build private X.25 networks by purchasing X.25 switches and leasing lines.

With X.25, users obtain access to a public or private X.25 "cloud" or network. These connections are usually at 9.6Kbps or 56Kbps, and the maximum speed (including the overhead) is 64Kbps. Any number of logical connections, called *virtual circuits*, can share the same physical network. For example, 10 or 20 LAN users can share the same X.25 access line, and their workstations' traffic will be multiplexed over the single line.

X.25 provides any-to-any connectivity. Once a user connects to an X.25 cloud, he can access any other host attached to that X.25 cloud (given the right permissions and access rights). X.25 also provides protocol translation. It enables users to communicate, even if they do not use the same host type.

X.25 is most popular as a way to connect networks internationally. Nearly every country's PTT offers an X.25 network. Whereas in the United States obtaining leased lines is a simple and cost-effective proposition, obtaining leased lines abroad is an arduous task. Obtaining these lines is time-consuming, and in some countries reliable circuits may not even be available. Because X.25 is reliable, although slow, it is popular abroad.

X.25 is a slow service for LANs. LAN traffic is queued with unrelated traffic from other users, and LAN users often experience heavy delays. Its three-layer protocol is rife with overhead. Because X.25 was designed to operate over the unreliable analog phone system, it carries a high overhead for error correction and detection. X.25 uses a full three-layer OSI stack, and uses up to two-thirds of its "energy" for error policing. Also, X.25 is a packet-switching service, which means that the receiving device must wait to receive the packets, which arrive over many different circuits, before reassembling them and forwarding them along to the destination device.

PDN connections are easy to obtain and save you from dealing with the phone companies, but they can be expensive. PDNs generally charge per packet transmitted plus the connect time. X.25 is the WAN connection service of choice if you have low terminal traffic, but it is too slow for most LANs.

# Frame Relay

Frame relay is an emerging LAN-WAN interconnection method that is better suited to a LAN's traffic patterns than X.25 is. Additionally, frame relay is garnering a great deal of interest because it is priced on a distance- and usage-insensitive basis. T-1, for example, is priced based on distance; the greater the distance, the more expensive the T-1 line. X.25 is priced based on usage; the higher the volume of traffic, the more you pay.

Frame relay's benefits include low overhead, high capacity with low delay, and reliable data transfer over existing public networks. It is designed to be a public service for interconnecting private local area networks. Frame relay provides service at speeds up to 2Mbps, and today carriers are rolling out frame relay services in the increments of 56Kbps, fractional T-1, and full T-1. Frame relay services were just becoming available in the fall of 1991, and services will come from the RBOCs, interexchange carriers, and value-added networks (VANs), including Pacific Bell, CompuServe, Wiltel, and Infonet.

Frame relay achieves its high throughput with low delay by eliminating the overhead of error correction. In the past, transmission techniques included extensive error detection and correction capabilities because analog copper telephone lines are unreliable. With the high reliability of today's digital and fiber lines, however, such extensive error correction is often unnecessary. Frame relay detects errors at only the first two layers of the OSI model, leaving the upper layers to handle the retransmissions. Contrast this with X.25, which is a three-stack protocol that provides extensive error detection and correction (see Figure 6.11). Also, because frame relay operates on OSI layers 1 and 2, it is independent of the upper protocol layers, making it an easy fit into networks.

Frame relay assumes that the end user's equipment will detect and correct errors. This requires that the terminal equipment be sufficiently intelligent, which in today's networked computing environments is a fairly safe assumption.

Frame relay offers independent packet addressing, and thereby reduces the fixed circuit requirements, which have made the traditional hierarchical networks overhead-intensive. Frame relay enables private virtual circuits to be set up between LANs without adding delay between the nodes. The 11-bit address field, called the *Data Link Connection Identifier*, supplies the virtual circuit number corresponding to a particular port on a network's bridge or router. A sending device places an address framed onto the network to where it is directed to the receiving device.

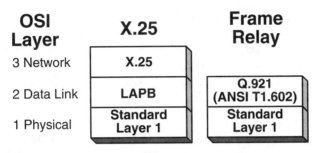

*Figure 6.11.* *X.25 and frame relay stacks.*

Frame relay specifies how the data is placed on the wide area network backbone. From there, you have a choice of circuit-switched, packet-switched, or FastPacket services. FastPacket makes the most sense, because it most closely matches the LAN interconnect method. FastPacket strips most of the error correcting and most of the retransmission capacities out of X.25 and provides a shortened header to deliver low overhead. Data integrity is ensured only through a cyclic redundancy check, and it will discard any packet that it finds to be corrupted. The end nodes must retransmit the data.

FastPacket is neither a product or interface specification, but rather a technique for asynchronously transferring data across the network. FastPacket, a service from Stratacom, provides fixed packets that are given access to the entire T-1 bandwidth rather than the 24 channels as in traditional TDM switches. The proprietary FastPacket is different than the generic fast packet. The generic term refers to various streamlined packet technologies including frame relay, Broadband ISDN, cell relay, and ATM. Each of these methods combines the low delay and high throughput of circuit switching with the packet-level dynamic routing used by packet switching.

Frame relay was developed as a by-product of ISDN. Whereas ISDN allocates time slots, frame relay provides multiplexing across individually addressed units at layer 2. Frame Relay was developed under the aegis of the CCITT I.122 and the corresponding American National Standards Institute (ANSI) committee 1.606. Frame relay comes in two versions: Frame relay 1 sets up a permanent virtual circuit in which the end user has no control over the connection. Frame relay 2 will offer switched virtual circuit service, but it has not yet been implemented.

Additional standards dealing with congestion control and addressing have been proposed by ANSI and forwarded to the CCITT. Because network traffic is bursty, it is quite possible to overload the receiving device's buffer. As a result, the frame relay specification must include congestion control. Explicit congestion notification offers the ability to communicate traffic overload problems downstream and upstream. The basic frame relay specification, however, does not allow packets to be sent upstream (to minimize overhead), so the receiving node does not have a way to inform the sending node that it is congested. As a result, the consolidated link layer management function reserves a DLCI address for the network to send congestion alerts to the network user.

Frame relay makes sense if your enterprise-wide network interconnects more than four sites and network traffic is fairly heavy. If your network traffic is primarily from terminals, X.25 is a better service option; however, if your network traffic is from workstations and PCs, frame relay is probably your best bet (see Figure 6.12).

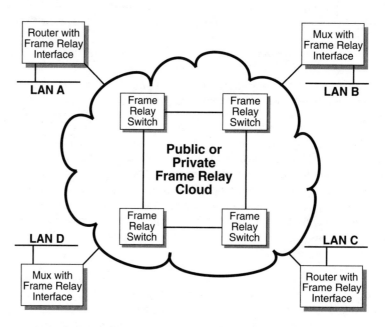

*Figure 6.12.* *A frame relay network.*

Although frame relay provides a cost-effective and network-efficient method of LAN-WAN interconnection, a drawback is its newness. Frame relay services and equipment only recently became available. The service is not mature enough for the glitches and quirks to have been worked out. Also, because few service providers actually offer the service, the area of coverage will be limited until frame relay hits critical mass, which should occur in 1992 or 1993. Nevertheless, frame relay is an exciting new wide area network service and can be used as a significant competitive advantage.

# Switched Multimegabit Data Service

Switched Multimegabit Data Service, or SMDS, is a high-speed metropolitan area network service that is being introduced by carriers for T-1 and T-3 services. Whereas frame relay is positioned as a public service to interconnect private networks, SMDS is positioned as a private network replacement. That means companies will be able to purchase SMDS service from various telephone companies and service providers.

SMDS is specifically targeted for high-speed LAN-WAN interconnection, image transfers, and bulk file transfers. Instead of building your own private WAN, you could use an SMDS service provided by the various RBOCs and interexchange carriers. SMDS is aimed at companies that have multiple geographically dispersed locations, each with its own LAN or host computer that must communicate with all of the other locations. It is also targeted at companies that need a high-speed backbone with greater capacity than currently available. It is targeted also at companies that want to use a public network instead of building a private network (see Figure 6.13).

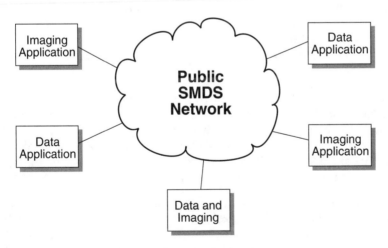

*Figure 6.13.* *SMDS, an emerging high-speed WAN service.*

Even more so than frame relay, SMDS is a fledgling service. RBOCs are either in the trial stage or offering pretariffed, prestandard services. SMDS services within a single LATA won't become fully operational until the end of 1992, and trials with RBOCs and interexchange carriers will occur in 1993 at the earliest. However, all of the RBOCs and interexchange carriers have pledged support for SMDS. Many have conducted trials, including Pacific Bell, Bell Atlantic, Nynex, and BellSouth.

At time of this writing, Bell Atlantic is the only RBOC offering an SMDS service. It is a prestandard, pretariffed service that provides service in Philadelphia and Pittsburgh. Despite these limitations, the price of the service provides the first evidence of how SMDS will be tariffed. Previously, both flat-rate and usage-sensitive schemes were discussed, and the most likely scenario was that the SMDS fee schedule would be a combination of the two. However, Bell Atlantic priced its service at $500 per interface with no additional charges for usage. At this price, SMDS is likely to take off quickly.

SMDS provides features similar to those found in LANs, which makes it ideal as a LAN interconnection method, and indeed, it will be used to interconnect FDDI networks. In particular, SMDS is a connectionless service that provides high throughput and low delay. In addition, SMDS will coexist with current services and equipment and provide an evolutionary path.

Access to the public SMDS network will be made from a dedicated link, typically at the customer premise. SMDS is a connection-oriented service and has to specifically support network-layer protocols. Access will be across a DS-1 (1.544Mbps) or DS-3 (44.7Mbps) line, with service classes defined to sustain a transfer rate of 4M, 10M, 16M, 25M, and 34Mbps. A SONET interface is expected to be defined.

Fundamental to SMDS are its security features. Because the network switching systems can screen frames to see if they can be legally transmitted, a subscriber can build a virtual private network within the public SMDS network, much like companies can with X.25. Closed user groups make SMDS attractive and useful to those companies that do not want the hassle and expense of building their own private wide area networks.

SMDS operates over an underlying distributed-queue, dual-bus (DQDB) network, which is a cell relay network that switches and transmits 53-octet cells. These cells have the same frame format as those defined in Broadband ISDN. SMDS data frames are similar to the DQDB frames so that DQDB provides a compatible format to carry SMDS frames as well as the coming ATM. (DQDB is defined in the IEEE 802.6 standard.)

# The Coming Revolution of High-Speed Networks

Even SMDS, at 44Mbps of bandwidth, isn't enough to sate the bandwidth demands of tomorrow's applications. Over the coming decade, the disjointed forms of communication—voice, image, and data—will be reintegrated in the form of multimedia applications. Just as powerful RISC-based workstations and color printers place increasing demands on the departmental LAN, their users will naturally want to share this information and access these services over the wide area network. Huge files will be shipped long distances as a matter of course. Full-motion video will be transmitted over the network every day, as desktop videoconferencing becomes commonplace. As more and more data is transmitted, the wide area network services must be able to handle the demand.

Because of this coming revolution, the digital infrastructure is being rebuilt from the ground up. Key to the construction are SONET and Broadband ISDN. This underlying network and its accompanying services will be able to meet the demands of tomorrow's applications.

## Broadband ISDN

*Broadband ISDN* (B-ISDN) is defined by the CCITT as a packet-switching service that requires transmission channels capable of supporting rates greater than 2Mbps. Broadband ISDN is a form of packet switching. B-ISDN comes in two types: *interactive* (for a two-way exchange of information) and *distribution* (where information is primarily one way, from the service provider to the subscriber).

Asynchronous transfer mode (ATM), which is also called *cell relay*, is the method that will be used to transmit data over a B-ISDN network. ATM is a form of packet transmission that uses fixed packets called *cells*, where each cell is 53 eight-bit bytes long.

ATM is a packet-based network. Although it will support circuit-mode operations (for isochronous services for voice), it will be done over a packet-based transport mechanism. As with frame relay, ATM allows multiple logical connections to be multiplexed over a single physical interface. It is even more streamlined than frame relay; like frame relay, however, it provides no link-by-link error control or flow control.

The ATM layer consists of virtual channel and virtual path levels. In the language of ATM, logical connections are called *virtual channels*, and they are analogous to virtual paths in X.25 or frame relay. A virtual channel is the basic unit of switching. A virtual path is set up between the two users, and the fixed-size cells travel over this full-duplex path at a variable rate. Virtual channels are also used for control signaling, management, and routing.

The virtual path is a second sublayer added by the CCITT. A virtual path is a bundle of virtual circuits that all have the same end point. This way, the cells flowing over all of the virtual channels in a single virtual path can be switched together. Virtual paths provide for a simplified network architecture by separating the functions of a virtual channel and a virtual path. Also, virtual paths increase network performance because the network deals with fewer entities. The virtual path also reduces the processing and connection setup time. Also, it enhances network services, because the virtual path is used within the network scheme but is invisible to the user. This way, users can define closed user groups, as they can with SMDS.

Many of the details of ATM have yet to be worked out. The CCITT issued a 1990 draft of recommendations on B-ISDN which provided the first detailed and specific master plan for broadband services. However, the majority of the details will come in future CCITT documents.

# Synchronous Optical Network

Synchronous Optical Network (SONET) is the next generation of transmission service, one that will blur the distinction between long-distance carriers and the local loop. On the enterprise-wide networking front, SONET will deliver the services necessary to blur the distinction between the WAN and the LAN. SONET has several important characteristics. First, it will enable a single digital hierarchy that spans the globe. Second, it will deliver a high-speed transmission infrastructure suitable for time-sensitive as well as time-insensitive transmissions. SONET will also deliver the connectivity necessary to carry companies into the next century, while retaining backward compatibility with existing equipment. Plus, SONET can be managed.

- *A single digital hierarchy.* SONET will establish a high-speed digital hierarchy throughout the world that will enable you to send data anywhere and be guaranteed that the message will be carried over a consistent transport scheme. Today, that is not possible, because Japan, Europe, and North America use different digital hierarchies. SONET is also a way for local telephone companies and long-distance carriers to connect various types of fiber transmission systems. Additionally, it will heavily impact Metropolitan Area Networks (MANs).

SONET is not a communications network in the same sense as a LAN. Rather, it is an underlying transport network, and FDDI, DQDB, and SMDS can operate over SONET. Because these transmission methods will be used to interconnect LANs, SONET will play a key role in data networking.

■ *High-speed transmission.* As bandwidth-hungry applications—such as imaging, video, and even graphical user interfaces—become the norm, wide area network bandwidth will become a precious commodity. Even T-3 won't be able to satisfy the demands of the next generation of applications. Consider, for example, transmitting an X-ray over a wide area network. A single X-ray typically takes up 12MB of storage, and when using a 64Kbps line, it would take three minutes to transmit. When sent over a T-1 line, it would take eight seconds, which is better, but not fast, especially if the patient is in critical condition and you are transmitting several X-rays to the hospital. SONET is a high-speed WAN transmission medium. It offers 51.84Mbsp to 2.488Gbps of band-width, and is expandable to 13Gbps.

■ *Synchronous transmission.* Because SONET is synchronous, it enables add/drop time slot interchange multiplexing without bringing all of the signals down to the DS-1 level. This enables it to be more efficient and eliminates midlevel network equipment. This in turn reduces the cost.

■ *Connectivity.* SONET is the future backbone technology for the carriers, while retaining backward compatibility with the T-1 standard. Its importance goes beyond the metropolitan area network, because MANs will eventually provide the infrastructure for B-ISDN. B-ISDN will eventually operate at speeds of 150Mbps to 600Mbps, speeds achievable only over optical fiber. Thus, the optical fiber SONET will play a key role in enabling Broadband ISDN. Furthermore, B-ISDN will use the ATM transport, which can be accommodated over SONET.

■ *Network management.* With SONET, bandwidth can be managed to the DS-0 level. Management is high-level, enabling fault analysis and self-diagnostics to be performed in real time. Plus, the management charac-teristics will be implemented in a standards-based way, ideally enabling products from different SONET manufacturers to interoperate. This is not possible today with T-3.

In 1991, the CCITT approved the first phase of SONET, which defines transmission rates, formats, and optical interfaces. The second phase is concerned with the operation and maintenance aspects. When it is introduced in the mid-90s, SONET will provide reliable, survivable, flexible, and standards-based services.

SONET supports transmission rates that start at 51.8Mbps and reach 2.488 Gbps, in its first phase. The basic increment rate—51.8Mbps—was chosen because it can accommodate either a T-3 or E-3 carrier signal. The transmission rate may be divided into DS-0 (64Kbps) increments, which are multiplexed to make up the 51.8Mbps rate. This rate is called the *Synchronous Transport Signal level 1 (STS-1)* or *Optical Carrier level 1 (OC-1)*. The OC*n* rate is the optical equivalent of the STS electrical signal. In 1991, standards exist defining the frame format for rates from 51.8Mbps (STS-1) to 2.488Gbps (STS-48). Eventually, the standard will specify rates up to 13.2192Gbps (STS-225). SONET line rates are shown in Table 6.6.

**Table 6.6. SONET line rates.**

| Electrical Signal | Optical Equivalent | Line Rate |
| --- | --- | --- |
| STS-1 | OC-1 | 51.840Mbps |
| STS-2 | OC-3 | 155.520Mbps |
| | OC-9 | 466.560Mbps |
| | OC-12 | 622.080Mbps |
| | OC-18 | 933.120Mbps |
| | OC-24 | 1.244Gbps |
| | OC-36 | 1.866Gbps |
| | OC-48 | 2.488Gbps |

As SONET is deployed, beginning about 1994 or 1995, it will not replace existing technology. Instead, SONET will coexist with current networks. SONET will be initially installed in areas with high demand—in metropolitan areas that house corporations and universities with high bandwidth requirements. Eventually, SONET will filter to the less-populated areas.

SONET can be implemented using several topologies: point-to-point, point-to-multipoint, hub, and ring.

The simplest topology is point-to-point. In this configuration, a basic multiplexer concentrates the DS-1 channels as well as the other SONET channels. The customer simply attaches multiplexers to either end of a fiber (see Figure 6.14). But because SONET will be offered by the telephone company, a far more frequently occurring scenario is this: the customer connects two sites via a public SONET network. In this instance, the multiplexer terminates at the telephone company's central office switch (see Figure 6.15). In addition, a company may choose to connect multiple sites in this way. As more SONET is deployed, the more flexible hub and ring topologies will come into play.

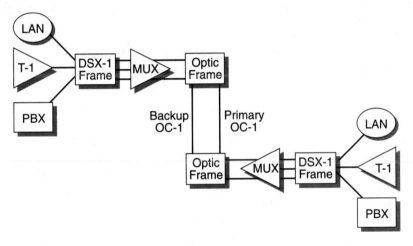

**Figure 6.14.** *Private point-to-point SONET.*

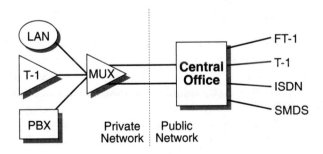

**Figure 6.15.** *Public and private SONET.*

# Putting the Wide Area View into Perspective

Applications are undergoing a fundamental revolution. Office-automation applications are no longer character-based; they are graphical, using Microsoft Windows and X Window. Spreadsheets, word processing, and E-mail will require more and more bandwidth. Now consider multimedia. The coming multimedia applications, with their embedded video, images, and sound, will redefine how people use computers. This graphical and image revolution must be supported by bandwidth on both the LAN and the WAN. LAN speeds are relatively high. With compression, even an EtherNet can support a low level of multimedia traffic. The dropping price of FDDI will encourage its growth. Consider the limited speeds of the wide-area network. Costly T-1 provides only 10 percent of EtherNet's bandwidth. New services are needed.

Most of the existing WAN services were designed to handle voice traffic over analog lines rather than digital data over digital lines. X.25, switched 56, and T-1 are WAN services that can be—and are being—effectively used to interconnect LANs. As the landscape changes, wide area network services are being designed specifically to accommodate data. Frame relay and SMDS are two examples. Fractional T-1, and to a lesser extent ISDN, bridge the gap between the new and existing services. New services over the next five to 10 years will include switched T-3 and SONET.

You must evaluate which of the existing and emerging services is appropriate for your enterprise-wide network. The choices may be dizzying, and the only thing you can be sure of is that your enterprise network will need more bandwidth (see Figure 6.16).

SMDS and frame relay seem to be more promising than ISDN. Frame relay and SMDS are offered in a limited geographic area, but the coverage will increase. From current projections, frame relay and SMDS won't suffer from the same lack of interest, compatibility, and poor tariff structures. Frame relay is available, although there were few commercial, production users in 1992. SMDS will become available starting in 1993. Several years beyond SMDS are the B-ISDN services, which include ATM, that will carry data into the next two decades.

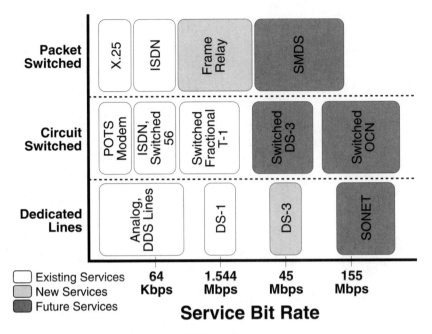

*Figure 6.16.* *Existing and emerging WAN services.*

As T-1 proliferated, many companies built private telecommunications networks. The carriers are looking to return these companies to the "fold." Most carriers are trying to offer services so that companies lease services rather than building a private network. The reliability of these new services, including frame relay and SMDS, is untested. Do you wait for the new services to mature and become widely available, or do you go with the tried-and-true services? By going with emerging services that are cost-efficient and network-efficient, you may be able to achieve a cost savings or an edge over your competition.

# Implementing and Testing the Enterprise-Wide Network

## CHAPTER 7

*Objectives:*

1. To examine the process of implementing, testing, and deploying an enterprise-wide network.

2. To discuss models of implementation, the system integrator's role, finding a qualified integrator, and performing installation and acceptance testing.

3. To explore the option of outsourcing, discuss maintenance service contracts, and cover ways to train end users and network administrators.

# How to Be a Hero Rather than a Scapegoat

You've analyzed, planned, and designed the enterprise-wide network. You've decided you're going to use FDDI to interconnect the myriad Token Ring, EtherNet, and LocalTalk networks on your company's many campuses. Routers and bridges will segment the local traffic. You've specified frame relay and T-1 as wide area network services. Now that you have established all your design criteria, the real test is actually implementing the network. It's your opportunity to be the hero, the scapegoat, or something between the two.

Here are some questions to consider:

- Should you use in-house expertise or hire independent installers?

- How involved should the integrator be?

- What test procedures should be performed to ensure that the network operates successfully?

- What types of service contracts and service level agreements need to be established?

- Does an education and training strategy exist for MIS, applications developers, and end users so that they can learn more effectively about using the network resources to achieve business objectives?

# Models for Implementing the Enterprise-Wide Network

As with designing the enterprise-wide network, you can subcontract the installation to an integrator, implement the network solely using in-house expertise, or use a combination of in-house and contracted expertise.

To determine which strategy is right for you, honestly assess your MIS personnel's experience and quality. What is the MIS department capable of and incapable of? What are their strengths and weaknesses? Do you have enough qualified and experienced MIS technicians to quickly and efficiently deploy an enterprise-wide network without outside help?

Consultants can augment or second-guess your design installation skills. They can act as a "reality check" on whether MIS has designed a network that it can build and manage. An integrator can provide an independent viewpoint that can balance the needs and desires of the multiple groups involved in deploying and using the network.

The best combination is often a team of in-house experts and contracted integrators. You benefit from the experience of independent designers and integrators, plus your in-house personnel are intimately familiar with the network, so they can manage and maintain the system.

You can contract for some or all phases of network deployment, including design, purchasing, installation, application development, management and support, and training. Most integrators no longer sell these services as packages, but have "unbundled" them and sell whatever part of their expertise you wish to contract for. This mix-and-match approach best fits today's MIS departments, enabling them to fill their gaps with hired expertise. Whether you contract some or all of the network deployment, the goal should be to maximize your company's use of its MIS budget. Most companies are reluctant to contract the strategic planning—and wisely so—because the people building the network must have a keen understanding of the business and technology goals.

# Enter the System Integrator

Finding the right integrator for an enterprise-wide network requires research and patience. It's easy enough to find a talented integrator to assemble a 40-node NetWare LAN for a single location; however, relatively few integrators have experience building mission-critical networks that span the country. Few integrators have experience "gluing" together multiple networks into a transparent internetwork. Newness of network technology and a lack of experience are just two reasons for the difficulty in finding integrators who are highly experienced in designing, implementing, and managing enterprise-wide networks (see Figure 7.1).

Integrators hail from many backgrounds, and each claims it is best able to assemble a company's many LANs into an internetwork. They may have mainframe backgrounds or be rooted in PC LANs. You can hire an integrator from the PC LAN VAR channel or a high-level general computer consultant. They can all build networks. But which group builds the best network? You must understand each group's inherent biases to properly weigh the integrators' strengths and weaknesses.

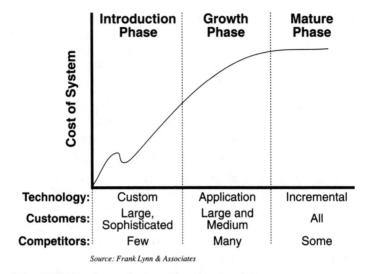

*Source: Frank Lynn & Associates*

**Figure 7.1.** *The three phases of enterprise-wide networks.*

Installers go by many names, and their label's varying prestige is often a matter of marketing. For example, a systems integrator is often considered to be "better" than a value-added reseller, whereas in practice the individual company's experience makes the difference.

You can purchase design and installation services from general computer consultants, systems integrators, network integrators or LAN VARs, vertical market VARs, dealers, independent consultants, and manufacturers' direct sales forces—and many more sources. The following is an overview of the kinds of installers from which you can choose (see also Figure 7.2).

- *General computer consultants*—excel at envisioning your company's long-term, strategic computing goals and architecture, but are weak at the specifics of LANs. They are business specialists, not LAN specialists.

- *Systems integrators*—are accustomed to building very large-scale implementations. They excel at mission-critical applications, usually with a mainframe, rather than network, bias. They are general computer specialists.

- *Minicomputer integrators*—typically build departmental systems, based around UNIX or another minicomputer operating system. They typically lack PC LAN expertise, but can provide invaluable direction on UNIX LANs.

- *Value-added resellers*—are more adept at the specifics of LANs and their installations, but are not as skilled at helping a company define its long-term business and computing strategy. VARs resell manufacturers' products, which causes an inherent bias in the solutions they recommend.

- *Independent consultants*—sell only their expertise, not any products, which makes their vendor-independence their strength. Their expertise must be evaluated on a case-by-case basis.

- *Manufacturers*—direct sales forces have recommended proprietary solutions to customers in the past; however, most have realized that customers will no longer accept this mode of sales. If you are primarily a single-vendor shop, a direct sales force can be effective.

- *Dealers*—are more adept at moving hardware than providing system solutions, although many also offer consulting services. Like VARs, dealers sell manufacturers' products, causing a bias.

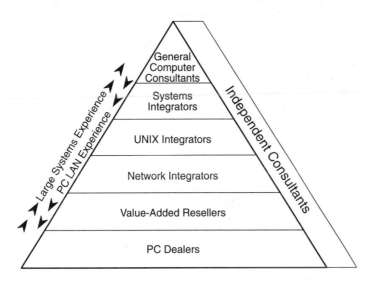

*Figure 7.2.*    *Sources of integration.*

Each source of network integration has an inherent bias, whether it's toward mainframes, minicomputers, PCs LANs, or accounting. Often, the best strategy is to work with several types of integrators. Integrators must have experience building networks that are similar to yours and understand your company's directional pursuits. Here are the pros and cons of each:

## General Computer Consulting Firms

You can hire general computer consultants to design and deploy your enterprise-wide network. Many of the "Big 6" accounting/consulting firms provide such services. Many of these consultants, including Arthur Andersen, KPMG Peat Marwick, or Ernst & Young, have roots in management or accounting consulting.

General computer consultants excel at envisioning your long-term computing goals and architecture. They are accustomed to building very large-scale systems, usually oriented toward transaction processing. Their bias is toward large-scale mainframe systems, and PC LANs are new to them. They are systems generalists rather than LAN specialists.

## Systems Integrators

Like general computer consultants, the traditional systems integrators are accustomed to very large-scale implementations, usually with a mainframe bias. Electronic Data Systems is the quintessential systems integrator. Systems integrators are excellent at envisioning the "big picture." They tend to take a business-oriented view of the network, not a technology approach. Because their background is building nonstop manufacturing and transaction-processing systems, they are very good at building mission-critical systems. Systems integrators, however, may not be as adept at some of the finer points of networking. Large systems integrators include EDS, Perot Systems, and Computer Sciences Corp. IBM, Digital, and AT&T/NCR also offer integration services.

## Minicomputer Integrators

Many traditional UNIX and minicomputer VARs can successfully install your enterprise-wide network. They are accustomed to building departmental minicomputer-based systems, usually for purposes such as inventory control or accounting. However, they lack the nuts-and-bolts experience of a LAN installer. If minicomputers are an integral part of your enterprise-wide network, mini-integrators can deliver valuable expertise.

# Network Integrators or Value-Added Resellers

Network integrators or value-added resellers are members of the "traditional" VAR channel: VARs resell manufacturers' products, adding value by installing or customizing the system. At the high end they are called *network integrators*; in the medium range and at the low end they are called *value-added resellers*. A few are national, but most are regional, which may present a difficulty if your enterprise-wide network encompasses many cities.

LAN VARs tend to excel at the finer points of building networks. They know how to make the many pieces of the network work together. Their PC LAN focus can be a drawback, because some may have a good base in UNIX or minicomputers, but most lack mainframe experience. Experience across the breadth of systems is even more unusual. VARs sometimes lack the complete vision of what can be achieved from total computer systems integration.

Because they resell manufacturers' product lines, VARs have an inherent bias in the products that they recommend or specify. Sometimes they carry their lines because they believe them to be the best products to install and support, but it could also mean that they haven't had the time to research new ones.

To reduce this bias, you can contract with network VARs for their consulting services but not allow them to bid on supplying the products so that they will not recommend specific products. Be aware that this is a more expensive option, because a VAR prices its consulting services lower if it knows that it has a chance of supplying the hardware and software, which are high-margin items.

A variation on a network VAR is one specialized in a vertical market, such as banking or insurance. *Vertical-market VARs* can offer services to satisfy your specific industry's business. The drawback of such specialization is that they are very narrowly focused.

VARs include Network Management, Inc., Evernet, US Connect, The Asset Group, LANSystems, Data Systems Network, and American Communications.

## Independent Consultants

An independent consultant sells network expertise and does not resell any hardware or software products. The independent consultant's strong point is objectivity, because independent consultants gain nothing from recommending a specific design or product, unlike resellers.

Although these firms may be made up of only a few individuals, don't eliminate them on the basis of small size. Independent consultants often gain their experience in a network integration or general consulting firm, and their knowledge is often first-rate. The generalists employed in larger consulting firms may not have experience to get you over the many network hurdles.

## Manufacturers' Direct Sales Forces

Many computer and networking companies employ direct sales forces that will design and build your network. Although direct sales forces traditionally push their employers' products, most have recognized the industry's move to open systems and vendor-independence, and no longer do so as overtly. Still, their offerings are often spread across a wide variety of divisions and may be difficult to coordinate. Using a direct sales force may be the best option, however, if your data center is filled with a single vendor's equipment. Examples of manufacturers that also provide consulting include IBM, Digital Equipment Corp., and Hewlett-Packard.

## Dealers

Computer and PC dealers such as ComputerLand, MicroAge, and JWP/ Businessland offer consulting and installation services to their corporate clients. Although dealerships are often good places to get low prices on hardware, they often do not provide the high-level support and service required to build an enterprise-wide network. Although they understand PCs and PC LANs, they lack minicomputer and mainframe expertise. If your company has sufficient in-house expertise, a dealer can be a cost-effective channel through which to procure equipment at a low cost.

Table 7.1 lists a few of the sources of network integration.

**Table 7.1. Sources of network integration.**

| | |
|---|---|
| General Consultants | Arthur Andersen |
| | KPMG Peat Marwick |
| | Deloitte Touche |
| | Arthur D. Little |
| Systems Integrators | Wang |
| | Perot Systems |
| | Computer Sciences |
| Minicomputer Integrators | Digital Equipment |
| | Hewlett-Packard |
| | Electronic Data Systems |
| Manufacturers Direct Sales | IBM |
| | AT&T/NCR |
| | Digital Equipment |
| | Hewlett-Packard |
| LAN VARs | US Connect |
| | Network Management Inc. |
| | Evernet |
| | LANSystems |
| | Allied Data |
| | American Communications |
| Dealers | Computerland |
| | JWP/Businessland |
| | MicroAge |

# Who to Choose?

Finding expertise to help you design or install your enterprise-wide network is no mean feat. Networks are still relatively new, and no clear-cut source exists. Each network integration source is quite capable of gluing together disparate systems into an enterprise-wide network, but each is biased in some way, whether it's toward mainframes, minicomputers, PCs LANs, or accounting. No certification program carries a weight equivalent to becoming a Certified Public Accountant or a member of the Bar. Certification programs generally are valid only for a single vendor.

Despite the difficulty in finding a qualified integrator, the many sources of integration can enable you to choose a method or methods that best fit your company's operation and needs. Whatever the source, the integrator must have experience in building networks that are similar to yours and must understand your company's directional pursuits.

Installing an enterprise-wide network requires that you make an integrator your business "partner." An enterprise-wide network's uniqueness necessitates that you work closely with multiple integrators, vendors, and consultants. For instance, you may work with a general consultant on the overall architecture and a network integrator to put together the LAN nuts and bolts. You can then maximize the strengths of the consultant and the integrator while minimizing their weaknesses.

Although communication difficulties are directly proportional to the number of parties involved, the end result of working with several integrators is often better because more opinions are offered and each group can gauge the other's skills. Working with multiple integration sources means that you must write your contracts more carefully and force one group to take final responsibility.

One complaint frequently leveled against network integrators and consultants is that they don't understand the company's business, and therefore don't properly design the network. MIS must define the network's business goals before it bids out the system, however, because a properly defined problem is the groundwork of a successful network. Ultimately, the hired gun can't understand your business as intimately as your business-line managers, MIS, and key end users do.

# Selecting Your Network Integrator

When qualifying an integrator, start by asking these questions:

- *What services does the integrator offer?* A network installer does more than install a network. It can design the network, procure the equipment, develop custom applications, train the users, and provide post-installation maintenance and support. It can also provide strategic planning consulting. You can contract with integrators for some or all of these services.

- *What is the integrator's bias?* Does the firm have a mainframe, minicomputer, or PC LAN background? What is its specialty? Does it excel at global issues or the nuts and bolts of systems installation? You may need to contract with several integration sources to gain the full range of expertise needed.

■ *Is the integrator experienced with your types of systems?* Although it may specialize in one type of computer system or operating system, it may have experience in others. You must be sure to choose an installer that is experienced with the systems installed in your company. For example, if you have an SNA network, your integrator should have a basis in SNA; a TCP/IP expert alone won't do.

Where proprietary environments are going to be integrated, verify that the integrator has experience in this area, otherwise you will pay for his or her education. For example, Wang is unlike any other system; to integrate a Wang system into the enterprise-wide LAN, you need someone who already knows Wang, not a PC person or UNIX expert.

■ *Is the integrator experienced in building networks for companies of your computing size?* The integrator should provide evidence that it has built networks of a similar size to yours. Many people want references from companies with equivalent gross sales, but the size of the computing project is more telling. Calculate your company's computing size by counting the number of network nodes, the number of servers, the number of cities, and the number of in-house or externally managed applications.

■ *Does the integrator understand your business type?* Verify that the integrator has experience building networks for your business type. Even if they are not vertical-market VARs, integrators tend to specialize in networks for certain industries, for example, manufacturing or finance.

■ *Does the integrator have wide area networking experience?* LANs use one set of technology, whereas wide area networks use another. If you are installing a network that will span multiple sites, the installer must be experienced with dealing either with issues of installing fiber LANs or with telecommunications issues, including tariffs and telephone companies. This is especially crucial if your network spans multiple countries, because you will have to deal with a different telephone company and sets of regulations in each.

■ *Does the integrator have experience building local, campus, and metropolitan area networks?* Is it familiar with telecom and transmission services from public carriers such as digital lines, T-1, fractional T-1, and T-3? Is it familiar with public packet switching offerings such as X.25 and frame relay? Does the integrator have experience with terrestrial, microwave, and satellite transmission? Does it have experience building international or domestic networks? Is the integrator familiar with bridging versus routing?

- *Does the integrator have diversity of talent?* Does the installer have the depth of talent to see you through the project? Ask to see the resumes of the project leader, designers, and technicians who will work on your project. If the integrator does not have the breadth or depth of staff required to complete the design and installation of your network, it will negatively effect your installation in timeliness and quality.

- *Can the integrator commit sufficient resources in the time window you need?* If you need five technicians for six months, for example, can the integrator guarantee the same five people for that time? If the integrator changes project members, the project will be slowed as the new members get up to speed on the specifics of your installation.

Examine the integrator's ability to manage a project. Has the integrator demonstrated cost-effective and successful large-scale project management in previous installations? Often, it is not the lack of technology experience that negatively impacts a project, but ineffective project management. Evaluate the integrator's ability to manage a project, including its coordination and communication skills.

- *Does the integrator have a lab environment to perform the necessary interoperability and performance testing?* The integrator should test all components of your network before actually installing them in your offices. The integrator should first test that the components actually work, and then it should set up a small pilot network to test that the components work with each other.

- *Does the integrator have offices in each of your locations?* If not, how will it install and support your network in those sites? VARs tend to be regional or national, but even national VARs don't necessarily have offices in every city in which you need them. If the integrator will subcontract with a regional VAR, will it take primary responsibility for the relationship? If your contract is large enough, the integrator may open an office for you.

Check the installer's certification. What systems and products is the integrator certified to install, sell, or train people to use? Does the installer belong to any professional organizations? For example, many VARs belong to the Local Area Network Dealers Association (LANDA), which began offering a certification program in 1992. Does the integrator belong to a national consortium of dealers such as The Asset Group or US Connect? Manufacturers also offer certification programs of their own. For example, Novell, Banyan, and Microsoft offer certification programs for their resellers and field engineers.

■ *What is the integrator's corporate background?* Find out how long the company has been in business, what its gross revenues were for the past several years, and how many networks and nodes it has installed overall and last year. If it is a small firm, who are the principles of the company?

■ *How many employees does the integrator have?* What is the ratio of technicians to salespeople? What is the revenue per employee? What is the staff turnover rate?

# Implementing the Pilot Network

Phased installation and careful testing are essential to your successful deployment of an enterprise-wide network. Because of an enterprise-wide network's scope and budgetary cycles, installation is usually performed in phases, and the total project often lasts several years. For example, a law firm might first upgrade all of its employees' workstations in a single site so that they can be connected to the network. In the second phase, the firm will connect the secretaries', paralegals', and word processors' computers to the network. In the third phase, the firm will connect the lawyers' computers to the LAN. In subsequent phases, the firm may install local networks in other locations, and connect each back to the central headquarters. Breaking the project into phases makes it more manageable and easier to complete. You should adopt a divide-and-conquer strategy.

Before deploying an enterprise-wide network, you should build a pilot network to verify that the individual pieces work separately and together—at least on a small scale. This gives you an opportunity to test the network, judging its ability to meet the technology and business criteria set out in the company's network requirements analysis phase. Then once you begin to install the production network, use installation and acceptance tests to ensure that the network works and meets its business goals. The following are reasons to build a pilot network:

■ A pilot network ensures that the network will work in the production environment.

■ The pilot network shields the users from the details of integration.

- Such a network introduces a feedback cycle from the users.

- The pilot network gives MIS an opportunity to work out problems before they affect users.

A *pilot network* is a small but representative version of the total production network that is usually set up in a lab or with an adventurous department. A pilot network has several purposes beyond verifying the network's operation. Building a pilot network shields the users from the integration issues and therefore lessens disruption from their work. If you install the system and it doesn't work—even temporarily—the users are going to think the network is a failure. With a pilot network, you've ironed out most of the difficulties ahead of time, and you don't have to explain to each user and the manager of the department why the system failed. By verifying a network's working condition, users don't have to stand by while MIS fixes any initial glitches.

A pilot network gives you feedback on menu systems, application grouping, security, and other issues that directly address the needs of the users' environment. Having this feedback dramatically reduces rework costs. Lastly, the pilot network tests the acceptance criteria specified in the RFP or contract to provide a measuring stick of the network's success.

After the pilot network is assembled, test every aspect from the cabling to the print queues to mainframe connectivity. On the departmental level, test to see that the workstation's operating systems work with the applications and that the applications work with the network shells. Check that the network shells work with the network's protocol stacks. After you've established basic operation, verify with at least three people that they can simultaneously use each feature of the system before you put it into production.

After you verify that the departmental aspects of the pilot work as planned, test the internetwork portion of the pilot LAN. Test the traffic loads and routing paths to determine the performance of the wide area network. Use a protocol analyzer to inject traffic into the network to see how much additional load the bridges or routers can handle. Simulate the network's busiest hours, such as when the business day begins and every employee logs into E-mail simultaneously. Also test events that are known to consume bandwidth, such as workstation-based backup and large file transfers. Calculate the effects of this traffic on the WAN links. Check that the TCP/IP, DECnet, and SNA configurations work and that the host environments have been adapted to the new configuration. Verify that modem connections can be made—even during times of heavy network usage—and are reliable.

# Installing the Enterprise-Wide Network

When you've determined that the pilot network is operational, it's time to deploy the system into the production environment. Preinstall whatever you can. Install the network operating system onto the server before you get to the user site. Even with pre-COMPSURFed drives, installing NetWare is time-consuming. LAN Manager has improved installation routines, but it too takes a long time. Although VINES isn't as difficult to install, planning the StreetTalk naming scheme requires a great deal of up-front planning. At installation time, you'll have to customize printer control, user directories, security, default system files, and backups so that multiple file systems can be correctly backed up. Work out routing addresses on paper before you install, to minimize the chance of duplicate addresses. Configure routing tables and modems as much as possible beforehand.

# Testing for Success

When the installation is complete, test the system. Functional testing covers more than a basic level of operation; it ensures that the system achieves its business purpose. Use the same tests as with the pilot network, and install the network piece-by-piece, testing after each portion is installed. Then put the network through a battery of functional tests.

Set up benchmark tests to determine if the system is working and to provide a baseline of performance. Measure the mean time between failure and the mean time to repair. Your benchmarks should also measure actions typically performed on the LAN and the WAN. These tests will provide a measuring stick for current and future performance. Define the acceptable increases in response time before the system must be reconfigured or upgraded. If you are contracting with an independent integrator, it should guarantee these performance levels over the life of the network, as long as the volume of processing set out at the design is not exceeded.

For example, if the network is primarily used for word processing, you might set up your benchmarks using a 50-page document in WordPerfect. The test may be performed from a single workstation during certain hours while there is no other activity on the network (see Figure 7.3). The test may include the times to store a file, retrieve a file, save a file to another directory, search for a specific document, and delete the document. Also set up benchmarks for printing functions, such as spooling a file, viewing the print queue, and deleting a document from a print queue. Construct similar tests for other applications, including E-mail, a database, and spreadsheets.

Define in your legal contract with the network integrator or service provider the meaning of terms such as *effectiveness level, operational use time,* and *system failure downtime.* Effectiveness level is the percentage obtained by dividing the operational use time of the system by the sum of the operational use time plus the system failure downtime. The operational use time is the accumulated time during an end-user company's operating hours where the system is operating and available for use by the company. System failure downtime is the period of time during the company's operating hours when the system is inoperable due to, for example, any failure of the file server, more than 10 percent of the workstations, more than five percent of the printers, a disk drive, or an inoperable application. These conditions should be defined for each network.

Also define a standard of performance, which means that the system operates in conformance with the initial network specification at an effectiveness level that is equal to some percentage—for instance, 96 percent—during some defined performance period, and during that period, the system operates at maximum performance. For example, if your service provider—for example, AT&T—guarantees a 99.6 percent uptime of its circuits, it may provide rebates on monthly fees for outages beyond a particular length of time or if the overall uptime falls below that level.

Negotiate into the contract the consequences of the network not meeting the functional testing. For example, if the system does not meet the standard of performance during the first 30 days of the functional test, you may want to continue the use of the system until the standard of performance can be met by the integrator or request that the integrator replace—at its cost—any portion that does not meet the standard of performance.

Each benchmark test will be performed three times and the average will be taken. The complete test will be performed immediately after installation from a single workstation while there is no other activity on the network. The complete test will be performed at acceptance on an active network from a single workstation between the hours of 2:00 and 4:00 p.m. For all testing, a master WordPerfect document will be used through the company at all locations in all phases. The test document is 50 pages long.

Each benchmark test will be performed three times and the average will be taken. The completed test will be performed immediately after the installation from a single workstation while there is no other activity on the network. The complete test will be performed at acceptance on an active network from a single workstation between the hours of 2:00 and 4:00.  For all testing, a master WordPerfect document will be used through the company at all locations in all phases. The test document is 50 pages long.

The percentage increase allowances are:

| LAN Test | | WAN Test | |
|---|---|---|---|
| 0 to 10 seconds | 100 percent | 0 to 10 seconds | 200 percent |
| 11 to 30 seconds | 35 percent | 11 to 30 seconds | 70 percent |
| 31+ seconds | 25 percent | 31+ seconds | 35 percent |

Test 1. WordPerfect Test

| Action | Response Time | Percentage Increase Allowable |
|---|---|---|
| Store 50 page document | _____ | _____ |
| Retrieve 50 page document | _____ | _____ |
| Search for a specific document | _____ | _____ |
| Spool 50 page document | _____ | _____ |
| Delete 50 page document | _____ | _____ |
| View print queue | _____ | _____ |

Test 2. Menus

| Action | Response Time | Percentage Increase Allowable |
|---|---|---|
| From menu, suspend and enter: | | |
| E-mail | _____ | _____ |
| Personal information manager | _____ | _____ |
| Spreadsheet | _____ | _____ |
| Text search and retrieval | _____ | _____ |
| Database | _____ | _____ |
| Word processor | _____ | _____ |

Test 3. E-mail on LAN

| Action | Response Time | Percentage Increase Allowable |
|---|---|---|
| Time required to deliver a single page message within LAN | _____ | _____ |
| Time required to deliver a single page message with a 50 page document attached over a LAN | _____ | _____ |

Test 4. E-mail on WAN

| Action | Response Time | Percentage Increase Allowable |
|---|---|---|
| Time required to deliver a single page message over a WAN | _____ | _____ |
| Time required to deliver a single page message with a 50 page document attached over a WAN | _____ | _____ |

Test 5. File Transfer

| Action | Response Time | Percentage Increase Allowable |
|---|---|---|
| Time required to transfer a 50 page document | _____ | _____ |
| Time required to transfer a 100 page document | _____ | _____ |
| Time required to transfer a 150 page document | _____ | _____ |

*Figure 7.3.*  *Sample benchmark test specifications.*

# Support Options for the Enterprise

As the networking paradigm shifts from terminal-to-host to peer-to-peer, the divisions of responsibilities and definitions of policies and procedures are not quite clear. This is most obvious when it comes to managing networks. Because of a dearth of tools that work effectively in a heterogeneous network, network management is personnel-intensive. It can also be quite political, with no clear lines of responsibility. One way to reduce the MIS head count is to subcontract network management in a process termed *outsourcing*. MIS departments are turning to third-party maintenance organizations to support their computers and networks. Management is often outsourced because there is a great lack of expertise within corporations to effectively manage networks as a business; it is typically driven by technologists and engineers. Often, the cost of keeping up with rapidly evolving technology causes executives to think twice about maintaining networking expertise in-house, and they are subcontracting it to integrators and third-party maintenance organizations. A range of plans can be put into action, from completely outsourcing network maintenance to simply purchasing hardware and software support contracts for critical network components.

Outsourcing enables an MIS department to reduce costs, avoid capital investment, increase the department's flexibility, and improve operational efficiency. If support is even partially subcontracted, MIS staffs can be smaller, thereby saving the overhead of paying salaries and benefits. This money can be applied to fund new product development, or it may be absorbed into the corporation and spent on the company's primary business.

Subcontracting network support increases flexibility, because it supplies technicians on an as-needed basis. You do not need to ramp up or reduce the MIS staff size as projects wax and wane (and staff reductions are bad for morale). For example, if you need to install 200 nodes to an existing network, you can call the integrator, and it will assemble enough technicians and project managers to complete the installation within your required time frame. Network installation is manpower-intensive; maintenance and day-to-day operations are not. In this case, outsourcing the installation enables you to be more flexible and efficient. Although installation can be easily subcontracted, outsourcing day-to-day support can be more tricky.

# Should You Outsource Network Support?

By outsourcing network operation and support, your company can

- Reduce MIS costs
- Make effective use of the technology without having to keep up with the technology boom
- Avoid capital investment
- Increase the department's flexibility
- Improve operational efficiency

The risks of outsourcing include:

- Performance problems
- Lack of responsiveness from the company to whom you outsourced
- Technology overkill
- Organizational and political conflicts
- Lack of information to make strategic decisions

To determine if your company can safely outsource support for the enterprise-wide network, you must disassociate the network applications from the network resources. The network applications are strategic; however, their underlying resources are not necessarily strategic. For example, a customer service center relies on toll-free 800 numbers to solve its customers' problems, but it does not need to own those physical telephone lines. Similarly, an airline reservations department uses a mission-critical application, but the underlying resource—the Token Ring or EtherNet LAN—may not need to be owned by the company. Similarly, it does not have to own the management facilities for that network.

Outsourcing has many risks, and horror stories abound. The rewards of success, however, are great. Risks include performance, lack of responsiveness, technology overkill, and organizational conflicts. Although all of these conflicts exist whether the network is supported in-house or contracted out, the importance is magnified when the expertise to deal with these problems is no longer maintained in-house. Again, the benefits are reduced cost, increased productivity, and greater flexibility.

Sufficiently analyzing the costs, benefits, and risks of outsourcing may be thwarted by a lack of available information. Experience with outsourcing is limited, and information is scarce. Gauging how much money your company spends on network management can be difficult, because the responsibility is divided among so many groups: MIS, LAN, network management personnel, telecommunications, and end users themselves.

For most networks, at least part of the network can be successfully sub-contracted. Support is often the simplest task to outsource. As technical so-phistication increases, the appropriateness of outsourcing decreases (see Figure 7.4). Support for business-line functions can be outsourced, but you should proceed very carefully. If the mission-critical application has unique requirements—for example in the areas of technology or geography—outsourcing may not be a wise decision. However, if the mission-critical application is generic, outsourcing can be very cost-effective. For example, Chevron has outsourced its point-of-sale network to Hughes and United, and other airlines use Covia's system.

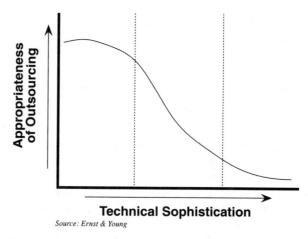

*Source: Ernst & Young*

**Figure 7.4.**  *Should you outsource?*

Successful outsourcing requires you to clearly define the responsibilities and outline the expectations of the parties involved: MIS, telecom, business units (and their end users), and the service provider. For example, if users are accustomed to being supported from an on-site help-desk, and MIS outsources end-user support, users' expectations of response time may have to change. Can users live with longer response times and not having support personnel on-site? Outline the expectations and responsibilities for all of the involved parties. For instance, define who at the client site should call the service provider, the hours of support, what the charges cover, and what devices and applications are covered. Also define an escalation policy and a final point of responsibility.

Although you can contract the installation and day-to-day operation and user support, you should not subcontract the technology planning portion. Keeping this expertise in-house is crucial, because you will have the best insight to deal with the business issues. Building a successful enterprise-wide network requires vision, strategy, planning, implementation, and management. Implementation and management, because they can be dissociated from the business, are the most easily outsourced. High-level consultants can help with the strategy and planning, but the long-term vision should come from within the company itself (see Figure 7.5).

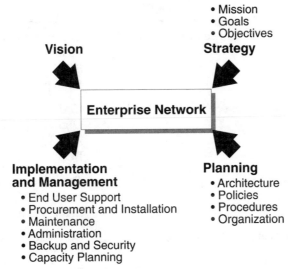

*Figure 7.5.* *Building an enterprise-wide network.*

# Sources for Network Support

Traditional computer service vendors, computer manufacturers, and network integrators can support your network. Choosing the right service provider depends on many factors, including the geographic extent of the coverage, support escalation procedures, on-site service capabilities, technical experience and expertise, packaging, and breadth of services.

The traditional third-party maintenance organizations (TMOs) may lack the necessary level of network experience, because they are usually oriented toward supporting mainframes or PCs. Network integrators, although they possess the skill to support a multivendor network, often lack the geographic coverage. Large computer vendors may be uniquely positioned to maintain your network. Among the traditional TMOs are TRW, Eastman Kodak, Sorbus, and BancTec. Large computer vendors that offer support of multivendor networks include Hewlett-Packard, IBM, and Digital Equipment Corporation. If you're considering buying support from a network integrator, consider a national firm. Choose a service provider that can deliver the plan that best meets your needs, which translates into a need for flexibility (see Table 7.2).

**Table 7.2. Sources of network support.**

| | |
|---|---|
| Third-party maintenance organizations | Computerland/TRW<br>Eastman Kodak<br>Sorbus<br>Bantec |
| Integrators/support services | IBM<br>Digital Equipment<br>AT&T/NCR<br>EDS |
| LAN VARs | The Asset Group<br>Network Management<br>LANSystems |
| Disaster recovery | Comdisco Disaster Recovery<br>Sun Guard Systems<br>Chi/Cor |

Support is sold on a *fixed rate* or *time-and-materials* basis. With a time-and-materials or pay-as-you-go plan, you pay for support on an hourly basis. (Be careful: hourly charges ring up quickly.) Some maintenance contractors allow you to purchase a block or bulk rate of hours that you debit through telephone or on-site support. Others offer pricing based on a number of prepurchased support requests, and a single support request encompasses as many telephone calls and site visits as are required to resolve the problem.

With a fixed-rate plan, you negotiate the price of support per month or per piece of equipment. Annual fees may be based on a percentage of the equipment's purchase price (somewhere between 10 and 20 percent) or calculated per file server (about $3,000 to $5,000 per server). Budgeting for a fixed-rate support contract is simpler because you negotiate the price ahead of time. If your equipment needs to be repaired, it's covered by the contract.

Support vendors offer a variety of plans for different response times, designed to meet the network's uptime requirement. Support packages generally offer a four- or eight-hour response time. The service provider should carefully define what it means by "response time," because it can mean the time to answer the telephone, deliver a patch or replacement part, or the time it takes to go to a facility.

You can purchase software and hardware support separately. Consider purchasing hardware support contracts on all essential network components—not only file servers, but bridges, routers, and wiring hubs. For particularly critical components, you may want to consider keeping spares on-site so that you can swap out the failed device and swap in the backup. You or the TMO can provide these spares.

# Questions for the Third-Party Maintenance Organization

Ask potential third-party maintenance organizations the following questions:

- What functions will the service provider perform? For example, will it provide ongoing maintenance, help-desk support, or install new segments and services?

- Are networks the service provider's primary business? What percentage of its revenue is derived from service?

- Can the service provider support your network in every city in which you need support?

- How will it divide your company's support tasks between in-house and contracted expertise?

- How are services priced—pay-as-you-go or fixed-rate?

- What response time do you need? How does the service provider define response time?

- Do you need coverage eight hours a day, five days a week, or 24 hours a day, seven days a week? Can the service provider deliver that service?

- What spare parts does the service provider keep in stock on your site? If the provider doesn't keep spares on-site, how fast can it get parts?

- Will the service provider make a replacement unit available to you while yours is being repaired?

- Does the service provider use remote-access software to dial into your network?

- Does the contract include a document of understanding, a scope of work document, a problem escalation policy, and a no-excuses clause?

- How many technicians work for the service provider, and are they certified to work on the products that make up your network?

- What is the ratio of salespeople to technicians?

- What is the ratio of service contracts to engineers? (It should be 10:1 or better.)

- What is the service provider's reputation?

# How to Best Train MIS and End Users

Training is arguably the most important and overlooked aspect of business computing. The enterprise-wide network's metric of success—whether it is reduced inventory turns or improved communications—is predicated on the end users' ability to use the system and MIS's ability to operate it. Companies typically do not, however, dedicate sufficient resources to training their people. End users and MIS alike are consistently undertrained and ill-prepared to deal with new and existing applications and systems. If end users and MIS personnel are not sufficiently educated on the best methods for using applications and systems components, innovative new applications, services, and ad hoc uses for the network will never be created.

You should select a training program that is not only customized to the topics, but also to your users' experience levels. Users shouldn't be forced to sit through classes that teach them what they already know, nor should they take classes that cover advanced topics when they need instruction on the basics.

You might want to set up one training series for advanced users and another for beginners. Similarly, "old school" MIS personnel will have to be trained on the "new ways" of an enterprise-wide network. They may be very experienced with mainframes, but require training on LANs. Training courses should be tailored as closely as possible to your company's individual needs.

The courses should emphasize hands-on experience. Although end users and MIS can be lectured on how to use and manage the system, nothing replaces experience. Otherwise, it's all theoretical and academic. Although hands-on experience may be the single most important aspect of training, it may also be the most difficult to fulfill. Make sure your source of training guarantees that each person sent for training has a computer to use during the training session.

Training can be done on-site at your premises or off-site at the trainer's facilities. Either way, training is typically performed in two or three days, depending on the course material covered. On-site training is more convenient, because the trainees have to leave their "real" work for a limited amount of time. However, sufficient computer facilities may not be available for training and the daily concerns of their jobs may encroach on training time. Off-site training is advantageous because it frees people from the day-to-day concerns of their jobs. The trainer has the facilities to enable each trainee to gain hands-on experience with the systems in a classroom setting. Users feel more free to discuss problems without their bosses around. On-site training is slightly more expensive than off-site training; not only do you pay the price of the courses, but you have to pay the travel expenses of the trainers.

# Where to Get Network Training

Training is available from many sources, including independent training organizations, resellers, manufacturers, independent consultants, self-paced study, videos, in-house training, and universities. You can also conduct training in-house. You should choose the source that is flexible enough to meet your needs and falls within your education budgets. Here is an evaluation of training sources:

■ *Manufacturers*—Network and application software manufacturers train users on their products, although most of their classes are directed toward resellers and consultants, who in turn train end users. For example, Banyan, Microsoft, and Novell have procedures to become certified to install their networks and procedures to become certified to train others to use their networks. Of the three NOS companies, only

Microsoft trains users directly, through its Microsoft University seminars. You may want to send several MIS people to manufacturers' training classes so that they can come back and train your users.

- *Resellers and integrators*—Your reseller or integrator offers training courses on a wide variety of topics. Using your integrator as your trainer has one very important advantage: the integrator is intimately familiar with your network, because it designed and implemented it. It can offer customized, personalized training. In addition to "standard" course offerings, your integrator can tailor coursework to your specific environment. Being trained by your integrator, however, is not without liabilities. Although resellers offer more diversity of courses than manufacturers, they generally offer training only on products they resell. Ask your local reseller if it also performs training or can recommend someone. LANDA, an association of resellers, also offers a certification program called NETWERC that guarantees installers have a baseline of network expertise.

- *Independent training organizations*—One trend in the network industry is toward the establishment of third-party, independent companies whose primary purpose is training end users and administrators. Independent trainers generally offer the broadest range of training classes. For instance, they may offer training on more than one network operating system. Also, they tend to fill in the "gaps" in manufacturers' or integrators' training offering. For example, many training companies conduct training on internetworking.

  The advantage of a training company is its independence; its revenue does not depend on selling certain vendors' products. However, independent training centers often have less access to vendor resources and they may not be certified by the manufacturer.

  Major independent training organizations include Wave Training, Data Tech Institute, and Digital Consulting. These companies offer seminars, usually lasting from one day to a week, that educate people on various aspects of networking, from the hands-on to the theoretical.

- *Self-paced study*—Computer-based training is an alternative. You can purchase training materials that enable users and MIS to do "independent study" when they have the time, which may be after business hours or on weekends. The flexibility is the key benefit here. Computer-based training has several drawbacks: it cannot deliver hands-on experience, it isn't the most scintillating way to learn, and it's not customized to your environment. However, for those with a shoestring budget who are training the occasional user, computer-based training is an option.

■ *Video training*—You can purchase videos that train users on various aspects of managing networks and using network applications. Like self-paced training, people can watch the videos at their convenience, whether that's on the lunch hour or on the weekend. Video training also has the advantage of actually showing the training it is talking about, whereas paper-based training can only describe it with words. With computers, seeing what is being done is critical to a quicker understanding.

■ *In-house training*—You should set up ongoing training as an internal function. In-house training will enable you to build expertise within a company; it should be done through internal training programs, on-the-job training, and employee mentor programs. In-house training works well if you consistently have a large number of users coming on-board that will need to be trained on the system, and it is not cost-effective to send them to a hired training source as an ongoing endeavor. As with network installations, many people will work independently.

■ *Universities and colleges*—The traditional places of learning are also sources of training on network administration and application usage. Depending on the institution of higher learning, this method can be very cost-effective. Training will take a longer time, because it is paced over a semester rather than packed into a three-day seminar. Whereas courses taught in universities and colleges will have more of an academic flavor, courses taught in community colleges may be more practical. In addition, community college courses are generally taught by those who have full-time jobs as network administrators or installers. Check your local colleges for courses.

Integrators and third-party training companies tend to have broad course offerings and can customize the training to your needs. If you are not pressed for time, self-paced study, videos, and colleges are good places for training. Whatever the source, end users and MIS should take training courses customized to their individual needs. Hands-on experience is absolutely critical.

# Moving from Planning to Production

The installation and testing phase of your enterprise networking plan is the true test. Here you will prove if the network that you've designed actually meets the business needs of the users. You can minimize your risk and improve your odds of success by considering the following suggestions:

Don't hesitate to hire an integrator or consultant; it isn't an admission of ignorance. Experienced integrators and consultants can provide invaluable advice and can prevent you from falling into common pitfalls. Even after you hire an integrator, don't be afraid to second-guess his or her opinion. Each integrator has a unique perspective—from PCs to mainframe to business—but you have the best understanding of your company's desires and needs. An enterprise-wide network requires the melding of MIS, LAN, telecommunications technologies and business needs, so you may want to hire consultants with expertise in these areas. Few consultants can handle all such technologies.

Carefully design a pilot network to work out the kinks of your network and install it first in the lab and then in a business department that's willing to take a few risks. When you are sure the enterprise-wide network works, deploy it on a production basis—but do so department by department and site by site. By using a divide-and-conquer implementation strategy, you will be able to work out the kinks on an individual basis rather than company-wide.

Service and maintenance is a critical aspect of network management. Never subcontract the network's strategic planning to a third party, because planning is intricately linked to your business. You can subcontract the day-to-day maintenance of the network, however, which is done for both political and practical reasons. Outsourcing forces you to give up some control over the network; you must rely on and trust your service provider to supply competent administrators and react quickly to the network's problems. Outsourcing may make your department more flexible and more lean, because you simply "order" more support from the service provider as you need it.

Many companies overlook training. If the MIS managers and end users don't understand how to use the network, they won't use it. MIS personnel should be cross-trained on the different technologies of computers and telecommunications. Train users about what it means to work on a LAN rather than a mainframe; teach them what it means to work on an enterprise-wide network rather than a departmental LAN. Don't just bring out the benefits; explain the downsides as well. You can obtain training from third-party companies or perform it yourself.

# Standards and Interoperability

## CHAPTER 8

*Objectives:*

1. To explore interoperability among dissimilar types of standard networks.

2. To explain why standards are crucial and to distinguish between de facto and de jure standards.

3. To discuss strategies for interoperability among the different protocols existing in a heterogeneous network.

4. To discuss the specifics of the TCP/IP, OSI, DECnet, and SAA protocols.

5. To explore the remote-procedure call tool's role in interoperability.

## What Is Interoperability?

Consider the electrical plug. You don't normally think about an electrical plug; you simply plug it into an electrical outlet, and whatever is attached to the other end of the cord—the lamp, the food processor, the microwave, the personal computer—is turned on. But when you travel abroad, suddenly you must think about electricity, outlets, and plugs. When you go to Germany, for example, you can't plug in your blow dryer or electric shaver to any outlet. The electrical voltage, outlets, and plugs are different, or *incompatible*. Even if you manage to fit the American electrical plug into a

German outlet, your blow dryer won't work—and the DC voltage might make it begin to smoke. Now consider that electrical outlets are different in nearly every country. You need different plugs for England, France, Australia, and Japan. So when you travel abroad, you must buy a voltage adapter and plug adapters. It's not an earth-shattering problem, but it's inconvenient. *Compatibility* is the challenge of getting dissimilar products to coexist without "blowing up" or not working at all.

Just as there is no one standard for electrical plugs, there is no one standard for computer connections and communications. After you have handled the problem of compatibility, there remains the problem of bridging the gap among the protocols that various computer systems use to communicate. A variety of protocols exist that enable multiple computers to talk to each other, and a variety of methods can physically connect them. The protocols used for a given system usually depend on that system's native format. For example, if your company has UNIX computers, it probably uses TCP/IP and EtherNet to connect them. If you're using IBM host computers, you're probably using SNA protocols and/or Token Ring. Using DEC VAXs often means you're using DECnet and EtherNet. PC LANs use Novell's NetWare, Banyan's VINES, IBM's LAN Server, or Microsoft's LAN Manager with EtherNet, Token Ring, or ARCnet hardware.

The existence of many different protocols poses no problem until, for example, you want the NetWare LAN to talk to the IBM host, or you need UNIX workstations connected to a VAX. When you want to internetwork multiple LANs, the babel of protocols becomes incomprehensible. Situations like these present problems because the protocols are incompatible. For instance, computers speaking TCP/IP simply don't understand the language of SNA.

Most enterprise-wide networks today use more than one protocol—they aren't exclusively SAA/SNA, DECnet, or NetWare. Simultaneously supporting multiple protocols becomes even more important and complicated as networks grow in size and number. Over the next four years, the number of computers running multiple network protocols will grow by nearly six times.[1] By 1994, 14 percent of all networked systems in the United States will run multiple protocols. Getting different protocols to understand each other so that end users can exchange meaningful information is the challenge of *interoperability*.

---

[1]Forrester Research, Cambridge, MA.

# Strategies for Interoperability

The existence of many different protocols isn't a problem when the different networks are kept separate. Most large companies maintain multiple redundant networks (see Figure 8.1). For example, a company may have an SNA network for its IBM mainframes, a DECnet network for its VAXs, a TCP/IP network for its Hewlett-Packard or other UNIX computers, a PC LAN for its PC users, a Mac network for its Macintosh users, and a voice network for its telephone and fax traffic. Each of these networks requires its own equipment, spare parts, maintenance staff, technical support staff, and experts. Rarely does the expertise for any one network overlap into another network, so companies are faced with the expensive prospect of employing experts in many areas.

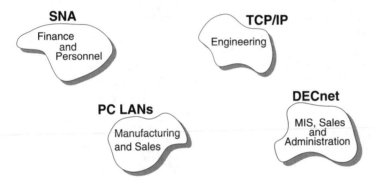

*Figure 8.1.* *One company, many networks.*

As a way to eliminate this wasteful practice, companies are looking to combine their multiple, parallel networks into a single network that carries multiple services and spans the company (see Figure 8.2). By combining these networks, the company can benefit from a cost savings by reducing redundant spare parts stores, maintenance personnel, and expertise.

There are two main strategies for achieving interoperability on an enterprise-wide network. The first method consists of maintaining existing networks in parallel and placing gateways at strategic locations so that users of dissimilar systems can communicate. In the second method, you can establish a common transport, where one or two protocols are chosen as backbone protocols, and all other protocols are accommodated to be compatible with the backbone.

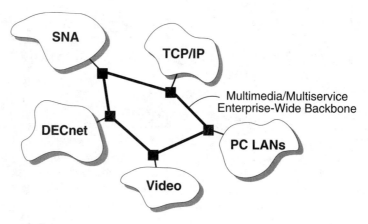

*Figure 8.2.   One company, one network.*

A number of network protocols are available and widely used, but no single protocol is currently the hands-down choice for distributed, client/server networks. You should choose the enterprise backbone protocols carefully, because each is optimized to a particular environment and won't necessarily scale into another. For example, SNA was designed principally for terminal and mainframe networks. TCP/IP is optimized for use in wide area networks (but not local area networks). NetBIOS and NetWare's IPX/SPX are optimized for local area networks. OSI's TP4 is one option for local and wide area networks, but it's not as efficient as TCP/IP.

# Interoperability Through Gateways

*Pros:*

- Keeps host systems pure and free from non-native software, which increases performance and reduces the possibilities of problems.

- When problems arise, they are typically localized.

- MIS maintains its domain of expertise, which does not change the status quo.

*Cons:*

- Gateways are slow; users will see a performance degradation.

- Gateways are not transparent to end users; they must master a new command set.

■ MIS must continue to operate dissimilar networks in parallel.

■ MIS must retain expertise in each of the different protocols in use.

You can achieve interoperability while maintaining discrete, dissimilar networks, but you'll need gateways to translate between two dissimilar systems (see Figure 8.3). For example, using gateways to translate between the dissimilar systems on an as-needed basis, you could maintain an SNA network for the terminal and mainframe users, a TCP/IP network for the minicomputer and high-end workstation users, and a NetWare, VINES, or LAN Server network for the PC users. To connect the UNIX users to the mainframe, for example, you would use a UNIX-to-SNA gateway. To connect the NetWare users to the UNIX users and to the mainframe, you need a NetWare-to-UNIX link plus a NetWare-to-SNA gateway.

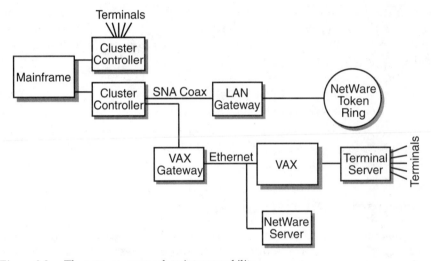

**Figure 8.3.** *The gateway approach to interoperability.*

IBM-oriented shops traditionally favor the gateway approach, where each network or computer system uses its native protocols, and a device translates and masks the differences. A gateway is typically a combination of hardware and software residing in a machine dedicated to its purpose. Using gateways carries the advantage of leaving the native systems "pure." Because native protocols are optimized for their respective environments, introducing foreign protocols may corrupt or slow the system for its native users.

The gateway approach can be expensive, because you need separate experts, technicians, and equipment for each network type. Because network experts are rarely cross-trained, you'll probably have to hire a completely different set of people for each network. Connecting VAX users, SNA users, and NetWare users, for example, requires not only a VAX-to-SAA gateway, a LAN-to-SAA gateway, and a VAX-to-NetWare gateway, but also the human expertise to install and manage this complex system.

Gateways are a single point of failure on the network. All traffic from one system must pass through the gateway on its way to the other system. This poses threats to the network's reliability and performance. Gateways are a performance bottleneck. Because they operate at the upper layers of the OSI stack, gateways are subject to far more overhead than devices such as bridges and routers. By their nature, gateways will be slower than bridges and routers.

Users may see other drawbacks to the gateway approach. Gateways are slow and lack transparency. Users may be frustrated by the slow system response. Accessing remote systems through gateways requires using foreign and possibly counterintuitive commands. Mastering a different command sequence for each gateway is a challenge in itself. For example, Macintosh users, accustomed to their computer's friendly interface, may balk at the nonintuitive 3270 interface.

Most companies are using the simpler gateway approach to build interoperability; however, this approach provides less flexibility than enabling interoperability through a common platform.

## Interoperability Through a Common Platform

A second approach to building an interoperable enterprise-wide network is to establish a common platform that all the computers and networks can "plug" into. This approach is more difficult and a newer strategy than using gateways. In a platform or transport approach, one or two protocols are selected to be the protocols used on the enterprise backbone, and other protocols not "suitable" for enterprise-wide networks are encapsulated or translated before being transmitted onto the backbone (see Figure 8.4).

*Pros:*

- Reduces the number of protocols and parallel networks in use, which simplifies the network in general.

- Simplified networking eases management responsibilities and reduces possibilities for problems.

■ Simplified networks reduce the cost of maintenance.

*Cons:*

■ No clear-cut common language has been universally accepted.

■ This is the cutting edge of technology, and is therefore riskier than maintaining the status quo.

■ Users may be disrupted by transition.

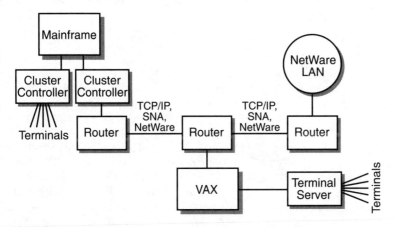

***Figure 8.4.*** *The platform approach to interoperability.*

Using a single network with a reduced number of protocols lays a common groundwork to which you can add applications and services. This approach simplifies network management and reduces the system's costs in the long run, because you are supporting fewer technologies. However, migrating existing discrete networks to a single-protocol enterprise-wide network is challenging. You may have to disrupt existing networks and users, and sometimes the disruptions do not warrant the benefits.

You must strike a balance between the number of protocols on the backbone and the network's flexibility and speed. The fewer the protocols, the easier the network is to manage; performance, however, may suffer. A multiprotocol network is more difficult to manage than a single protocol network, but encapsulating one protocol into another's format is even slower—in fact much slower—than using multiprotocol routers to route several protocols.

Protocols suitable for the enterprise backbone include TCP/IP, DECnet, SAA/SNA, and OSI. Protocols such as NetWare's IPX, NetBIOS, and Apple's

AppleTalk are not currently suited for wide area network communications, and should be encapsulated or translated into other protocols for wide area network transmission. IPX/SPX was designed to be a local protocol and is not efficient on a WAN because of its routing update procedures. NetBIOS is intended to be a local protocol, and does not include routing functionality at all; it must be encapsulated or translated into a WAN protocol. AppleTalk, although it requires a facility for routing, requires a great deal of overhead because of the frequency its routers dynamically update their address tables. Such frequent updating can quickly clog a WAN pipe that has narrow bandwidth.

Protocols such as TCP/IP, DECnet, SNA, and OSI are better suited to a wide area network, because their routing schemes are tuned to that environment. A suitable protocol must accommodate the bursty nature of PC LAN traffic as well as the time-sensitive nature of terminal traffic. This is no mean feat; LAT, TCP/IP, DECnet, and SNA were designed for terminals, but some can be used more easily for LAN traffic, including TCP/IP and OSI.

Often, neither the gateway nor the platform approach makes sense as an immediate strategy for interoperability. As is often the case with enterprise-wide networks, a hybrid solution is more logical in the interim or as a long-term solution. In this case, you can build a network that uses both gateways and a common platform, with pockets of interoperability. For example, in Figure 8.5, the network uses a LAN-to-mainframe gateway, and the PC LAN runs TCP/IP, which is a combination of the two methods.

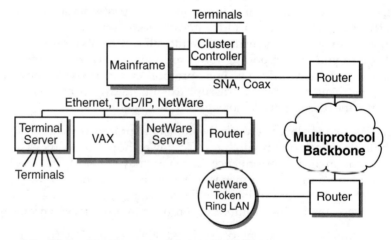

**Figure 8.5.** *The combination approach to interoperability.*

MIS can give users access to different types of computer systems either by setting up gateways to translate between the dissimilar systems or by laying a common protocol platform.

# Multiprotocol Routing and Interoperability

Routers and bridges are integral devices in the construction of homogeneous and heterogeneous networks. Without multiprotocol routers and MAC-layer bridging, a network could not easily support multiple, dissimilar protocols.

A multiprotocol bridge/router combines the functionality that used to require several distinct devices—a router for each protocol plus a MAC-layer bridge to handle protocols that can't be routed. Today, products from companies such as cisco Systems and Wellfleet Communications support a plethora of protocols as well as transparent bridging through an architecture that supports high-speed or RISC processors, and high-speed backplanes. In addition, these routers are employing increasingly sophisticated routing protocols and have useful management systems.

The crux of multiprotocol routers is the fact that some protocols can be routed and others cannot. An OSI network-layer protocol with a routing protocol can be routed; a non-network layer protocol cannot be routed. The network-layer subprotocol enables the protocol's routers to talk to each other, calculate the most efficient path between two points, and relay status and traffic information. Protocols such as TCP/IP, IPX/SPX, and OSI can be routed because they all have a routing protocol; protocols such as NetBIOS and LAT cannot be routed because they are not implemented at the network layer. Protocols that lack a routing layer must be bridged transparently. SNA can be routed, although it does not implement an industry-standard routing protocol.

A router's job is to determine the best path from the sending station to the destination station, and then to forward the packets appropriately. If the destination station resides on a different network, the router must decide what is the best path to that destination. Unfortunately, "best" can have several meanings. For example, is the best path the one with the fewest hops? The least congestion? The fastest link? What if the path with the fewest hops is also the slowest? The different routing protocols implement the "best" path differently (see Figure 8.6).

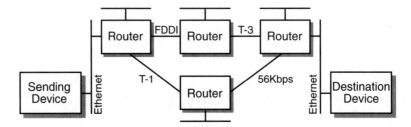

*Figure 8.6.*  *Which is the best path?*

Several industry-standard routing protocols are available, including Routing Information Protocol (RIP), open shortest path first (OSPF), and Intermediate System-Intermediate System (IS-IS). RIP is the most widely implemented, yet it offers the least functionality. TCP/IP, NetWare, and XNS all use RIP. OSPF is a newer protocol that is starting to be used in TCP/IP networks; OSPF offers a more efficient method of routing than RIP. IS-IS is an OSI protocol that offers greater functionality than RIP.

RIP is a simple routing protocol; it calculates the best path based on the fewest hops. (If a destination station and source stations are on different networks, a hop is the number of links the packet must traverse. For example, if one router sits between a sending station and the destination station, the hop count is 2.) RIP is relatively unsophisticated. When calculating the best path, it doesn't allow for faster links; it assumes all links are the same speed.

A newer Internet protocol, OSPF, is the answer to RIP's unsophistication. OSPF, or open shortest path first, enables the network administrator to assign priorities to network links, thereby accommodating not only the number of hops but also the speed of the links. OSPF was developed by Proteon and is now an Internet standard. A number of router manufacturers support OSPF.

IS-IS has the advantage of being the ISO routing protocol. IS-IS is a link-state algorithm, which is more responsive and robust than distance-vector algorithms. Unlike other routing protocols, IS-IS's packet encoding is flexible, so it can support multiple protocol suites. IS-IS is supported by a number of vendors, including Digital Equipment Corp., cisco Systems, Proteon, Retix, Vitalink, Wellfleet, and 3Com. A public domain implementation is available from the University of Wisconsin.

Multiprotocol routers also support MAC-layer bridging. Typically, a router will first attempt to route a packet, but if it discovers the protocol can't be routed, it will "fall back" to transparent bridging. In transparent bridging, the bridge does not know the whereabouts of the destination station or even how to find it (as a router does). Instead, the bridge simply recognizes that the packet is not local. If it is not local, the bridge copies the frame from its incoming port to its outgoing port, where it is sent to the devices on the other segment. This process is repeated until the packet reaches its destination.

Although multiprotocol routers are critical when you build interoperable networks, the routers themselves are not interoperable. A cisco router will not work with a Wellfleet router; a Wellfleet router will not work with a Proteon router. Although the router manufacturers may even use the same routing protocol, each has implemented its products in a fundamentally different and incompatible manner. End users are essentially locked into a single-vendor solution.

The only area of compatibility among router vendors is over T-1 links when the router manufacturers implement the Point-to-Point (PPP) protocol. In this case, different manufacturers' routers can communicate over the WAN.

# Standards Are the Way to Interoperability

Standards are key to building interoperable networks. In the past, computer vendors have locked end users into their solutions by selling equipment that would work only with other equipment from the same manufacturer. Imagine if stereo manufacturers owned record companies, and would allow people to play only music recorded on their labels on their stereos. Although such business practices are completely unacceptable in other areas of business, this is commonplace in computing. But things are changing.

By using standards-based products, you won't be locked into a particular vendor's network strategy, development schedule, or business priorities. You can build your network according to your company's business strategy, schedule, and priorities. If a certain manufacturer does not make a product that you need, you are free to purchase it from another company, and the product will work in your existing network.

When selecting products for your corporate standards, whenever possible choose from standards-based products. A modular network enables your network to more easily accommodate existing technologies as well as developing ones. By designing your network to be modular and relying on standards-based products, you can reduce the speed at which your network becomes technologically obsolete.

By using standard network components, network designers can build a modular network, mixing and matching components. For example, just as a designer can swap out one vendor's MAC-layer bridge for another vendor's with relative ease, with a standards-based, modular networking approach, designers can achieve equivalent functionality by using various technological approaches to a problem. For example, a network running NetWare can run using EtherNet, Token Ring, FDDI, ARCnet, or LocalTalk hardware.

Choosing standards-based products helps ensure the network's long-term viability. Standards also invite competition, which drives down the prices of products, which ultimately benefits the network buyer. With de facto standards, there may be only a single source, but a variety of third-party manufacturers. In the case of official standards, the specifications are in the public domain, and competition to manufacture these products is often fierce.

Using open systems ensures that you can choose among a variety of products that solve the problem. Although the variety is confusing, having the choice is critical. The days of single-source networks are over. Few, if any, all-IBM shops are left.

There are two types of standards: *de jure* and *de facto*. De jure standards are endorsed by official standards organizations. De facto standards are widely used and implemented, but controlled by a single vendor or group. Examples of de facto standards include Novell's NetWare, the Internet's TCP/IP, and IBM's SNA. De jure standards are endorsed by standards bodies such as the Institute of Electrical and Electronic Engineers (IEEE), American National Standards Institute (ANSI), and the Consultive Committee for International Telephony and Telegraphy (CCITT). Examples are FDDI (an ANSI standard), EtherNet and Token Ring (IEEE standards), and frame relay (an emerging CCITT standard). For more on choosing standards, see Chapter 4, "High-Level Issues of Enterprise-Wide Network Design."

The following sections explore the viability of the primary enterprise networking protocols—TCP/IP, DECnet, SNA, and OSI.

# The TCP/IP Stack

TCP/IP has taken the networking industry by storm. Once an academic networking protocol popular only among people who knew UNIX (such as researchers in universities and labs), TCP/IP has caught the fancy of corporate network designers—and for good reason. Corporate network designers now face the same interoperability problems that university network designers faced years ago.

Universities typically have a diverse set of computing equipment because various academic departments tend to buy systems independently. Additionally, manufacturers commonly give universities computer equipment or use them as testing sites. This adds up to one thing—heterogeneous networking.

A similar set of circumstances and the same resulting problems present themselves to corporate network designers. In the 1970s, minicomputers were brought in as a cheaper alternative to mainframes, and in the 1980s, PCs were introduced to free people from the constraints of MIS. Business units with enough cash bought their own computer systems, whether they were minis or PC LANs. Mergers throughout the 1980s resulted in multiple computer systems within a company. MIS now faces the task of quelling the cacophony of dissimilar computer systems.

TCP/IP was developed in the early 1970s for the Department of Defense so that users of the ARPANET could connect their computers, which were located in government and military facilities, at contractors' sites, and in universities. Since then, TCP/IP has become the protocol used on the Internet, a packet-switched network made up of more than 2,000 individual networks in the United States and around the world. Because TCP/IP was required to connect to the Internet, many universities adopted TCP/IP for their campus-wide networks.

TCP/IP is popular because it is mature, available, and effectively provides interoperability. Despite its many incarnations and implementations, the core of TCP/IP remains consistent and interoperable. Even though it is not an IEEE or ANSI standard, the TCP/IP protocol suite is stable. The Internet Activities Board, the coordinating committee for the design, engineering, and management of the Internet, controls the TCP/IP's development and engineering.

TCP/IP is widely available. Literally hundreds of TCP/IP vendors have implementations for just about every computer type, starting with the IBM PC and ranging up to Cray supercomputers. You name it—you can probably find a version of TCP/IP to connect it. TCP/IP is also vendor-independent. Plus, in many cases, TCP/IP is free. For example, TCP/IP has been bundled with Berkeley UNIX since as early as 1982.

TCP/IP also gets the job done. It enables users to transfer files, exchange E-mail, and log on remotely and run applications. It provides a facility for managing networks. OSI, the official standard for achieving interoperability on a heterogeneous network, is not yet completely defined, and it offers many of these services but not as widely or as efficiently. TCP/IP exists now, and it is being used to solve problems today.

TCP/IP's biggest problem is that it was viewed largely as UNIX was viewed: academic and indecipherable by the average user. Like UNIX, TCP/IP can be difficult to use. For the inexperienced user, TCP/IP isn't exactly transparent. Many TCP/IP products are available, however, to help overcome some of the difficulties. For example, some products convert obscure TCP/IP commands into items on a menu. Administrative tasks, such as configuring and managing IP routers and administering the addressing, are also complex and demand a tremendous amount of administrative overhead.

However, like UNIX, which is finding favor among corporate MIS departments, TCP/IP is quickly becoming the preferred method of internetworking, at least for UNIX and PC LAN networking. TCP/IP can solve the problems of computers that won't talk to each other, and corporate MIS departments are getting up to speed quickly.

# What Is TCP/IP?

TCP/IP is a packet-oriented, layered protocol. Like other packet-oriented protocols—SNA, DECnet, and OSI among them—the different layers communicate only with the layers directly above or below them, enabling a certain amount of independence and freedom for the different layers and applications.

- *Services*—Uses LLC services on the lower layers. Routing through IP and routing protocols RIP or OSPF. Network services through TCP or UDP protocols. Applications include file transfer (FTP), mail (SMTP), remote terminal access (Telnet), management (SNMP), and more.

- *Pros*—TCP/IP is popular, mature, available, and effectively provides interoperability among dissimilar systems. With hundreds of implementations, TCP/IP is the most widely used protocol for heterogeneous networks.

- *Cons*—TCP/IP is based on 1970s technology. It is designed largely for minicomputer, rather than personal computer, connectivity.

TCP/IP is a four-layer protocol suite that roughly follows the lower four layers of the OSI protocol stack (see Figure 8.7). (TCP/IP is not an OSI protocol, however.) TCP/IP, commonly uttered as one word, is actually two protocols: the Transmission Control Protocol (TCP) and the Internet Protocol (IP). The term TCP/IP is also used generically to refer to the TCP/IP protocol suite, which includes file transfer, remote host login, and mail.

## OSI

| 7 | Application |
|---|---|
| 6 | Presentation |
| 5 | Session |
| 4 | Transport |
| 3 | Network |
| 2 | Data Link |
| 1 | Physical |

## TCP/IP

| 5 | Operating System and Applications |
|---|---|
| 4 | Transmission Control Protocol (TCP) |
| 3 | Internet Protocol (IP) |
| 2 | Logical Link Control / Media Access Control |
| 1 | Physical |

*Figure 8.7.* *The OSI and TCP/IP stacks.*

IP is roughly equivalent in function to an OSI network layer protocol, which means that its job is to provide packet routing over different subnets of a TCP/IP network. IP enables applications to be independent of the media, because it hides the physical addressing details by using its own 32-bit addressing scheme. IP is a datagram protocol that knows how to discover the source and destination addresses for nodes on different networks. Also, IP puts information into packets. If an application tries to send a packet that is too large for TCP, IP breaks it into smaller chunks, sends it out over the network, and puts it back together at the receiving end. IP does not ensure that a packet will be received intact or in order; however, it resolves the differences between subnetworks.

TCP is akin to an OSI transport layer protocol, which means that its job is to provide a reliable connection between two nodes. Providing a reliable end-to-end connection poses several problems. First, when an application on one network node wants to communicate with another application on another node, that other node may or may not be located on the same network. This may lead to confusion in addressing. Second, because no two networks use the same addressing scheme, the protocol must be smart enough to learn where its data is destined to go. To solve these problems, TCP uses a three-level addressing scheme. The first level is the application or program (called a *process*) plus a unique address. The process address is combined with the address of the originating node, which forms a *port address*. Finally, the port address is combined with a network address to form a *socket*. Each socket is unique.

TCP prepares data for IP to send in packets. A TCP packet contains the application data plus a TCP header, which consists of addressing and other information. After TCP has completed forming the packet, it passes it to IP. IP then repackages the TCP packet into the IP packet format. The IP packet, which envelops the TCP packet, is placed inside a logical link control (LLC) packet, which has an address and control header. The whole packet is placed inside a MAC transmission frame, for transmission out of the node and onto the network. Then the packet is sent out on the network. On its journey, the packet may encounter several IP routers, or its destination may be on a local subnetwork. When it reaches the destination address, the packet is disassembled. As it passes through each layer, that layer strips off its own information, and finally, the data is passed to the computer.

Providing a reliable end-to-end transport requires a great deal of overhead. TCP must manage the sockets it creates and ensure delivery of the data. When the overhead is too great, UDP, or the User Datagram Protocol, is often used. UDP is an unreliable data transport and a connectionless-oriented protocol. Because UDP is packet-oriented rather than socket- or connection-oriented, it demands far less overhead. However, using UDP means that the recipient is not guaranteed to get the data. UDP is useful for simple query-response transactions, such as are used in network management. The Simple Network Management Protocol (SNMP) uses UDP, for example. UDP and TCP may be run on the same network at the same time.

The term *TCP/IP* is often meant to refer to other proprietary applications, including File Transfer Protocol (FTP) for file transfer; Trivial File Transfer Protocol (TFTP), a simpler file transfer application; Simple Mail Transfer Protocol (SMTP) for E-mail; Telnet for remote log in and terminal emulation; and ping and SNMP for network management. Figure 8.8 shows the complete TCP/IP suite.

TCP/IP provides file transfer rather than remote file access. It provides a simple mail facility rather than a full-featured one. In short, its applications provide only the basics, unlike the ISO suite of protocols. ISO provides applications for services running from terminal emulation to electronic document interchange to electronic funds transfer. Other vendors have enhanced the TCP/IP application services, making them more functional or easier to use. Note that implementations of TCP/IP and its applications from different vendors *should*, but won't necessarily, interoperate. Table 8.1 lists some TCP/IP products.

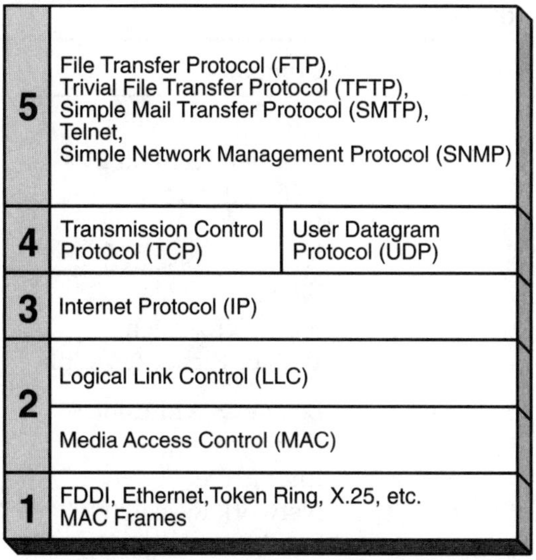

| 5 | File Transfer Protocol (FTP), Trivial File Transfer Protocol (TFTP), Simple Mail Transfer Protocol (SMTP), Telnet, Simple Network Management Protocol (SNMP) | |
|---|---|---|
| 4 | Transmission Control Protocol (TCP) | User Datagram Protocol (UDP) |
| 3 | Internet Protocol (IP) | |
| 2 | Logical Link Control (LLC) | |
| | Media Access Control (MAC) | |
| 1 | FDDI, Ethernet, Token Ring, X.25, etc. MAC Frames | |

*Figure 8.8.* *The TCP/IP stack.*

**Table 8.1. Some TCP/IP products.**

| Operating System | Company |
|---|---|
| Macintosh | Apple Computer |
| | Banyan |
| | Intercon Systems |
| | NCSA |
| | Novell |
| | Wollongong Group |
| DOS | Beame & Whiteside |
| | Banyan |
| | Frontier Technologies |
| | FTP Software |
| | Hughes LAN Systems |
| | Network Research |
| | Novell |
| | Walker Richer & Quinn |
| | Wollongong Group |

*continues*

**Table 8.1. continued**

| Operating System | Company |
|---|---|
| OS/2 | Banyan |
| | Frontier Technologies |
| | FTP Software |
| | IBM |
| | Network Research |
| | Novell |
| | Sun Microsystems |
| | Walker Richer & Quinn |
| UNIX | Beame & Whiteside |
| | FTP Software |
| | Interactive |
| | Network Research |
| | Sun Microsystems |
| VMS | Network Research |
| | TGV |
| VM/MVS | Fibronics |
| | IBM |
| | In-Net |
| | Interconnections |

Sun Microsystems (Mountain View, CA) has the most widely used TCP/IP applications. Sun's architecture, called Open Network Computing (ONC), solves many problems of using "raw" TCP/IP. On the physical layer, ONC includes support for EtherNet, Token Ring, and FDDI. On the transport layer, it uses UDP or TCP. On the network layer, it uses IP. At the presentation layer Sun uses remote procedure call (RPC) tools, and at the session layer it uses Extended Data Representation (XDR). Application-layer services include Network Filing System (NFS) for remote file access, remote program execution, and Yellow Pages for directory services, in addition to the usual array of TCP/IP applications, such as TELNET and SMTP.

# The Open Systems Interconnection Standards

OSI is a grail for the computer industry, as the idea of all computers speaking the same language is computing nirvana. But like nirvana, OSI requires a long arduous journey, one that most people don't achieve. Although Open System Interconnection (OSI) has far from taken the computer industry by storm, its acceptance is mandated by the United States government, in the form of the Government OSI Profile (GOSIP), which requires that government networks built after 1990 provide a migration path to OSI or directly support OSI. OSI is more popular in Europe than it is in the United States, presumably because European companies have a smaller installed base of equipment, all speaking their own protocols. Europe also has more countries needing to communicate.

- *Services*—At the lower layers, OSI supports EtherNet, Token Ring, FDDI and others as well as LLC, X.25, and ISDN. Network, transport, and session layer services are provided but not widely implemented. Application layer services include file transfer, terminal emulation, directory services, and mail. Directory services and mail show the most promise.

- *Pros*—OSI is an international, vendor-independent standard. If fully implemented, it would facilitate intercommunication among companies, partners, and suppliers. Such interconnection is hampered by addressing, naming, and security issues—which OSI can partially resolve. It provides a full suite of more sophisticated services than TCP/IP.

- *Cons*—To date, OSI has not been widely implemented, although the application services show the most promise. OSI protocols are generally CPU-intensive, making OSI less than suitable for PC LANs, but acceptable for host systems.

The OSI suite includes specifications for the seven-layer model. The lower layer standards are fairly widely implemented and often correspond to ANSI and IEEE standards. OSI implementations at the network, transport, and session layers, however, are less widely used. In recent years, ISO has been focusing most of its efforts on developing the application-layer services, and it is here that OSI appears to have the greatest promise (see Figure 8.9).

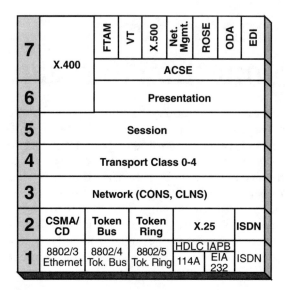

| 7 | X.400 | FTAM | VT | X.500 | Net. Mgmt. | ROSE | ODA | EDI |
|---|---|---|---|---|---|---|---|---|
| | | ACSE | | | | | | |
| 6 | Presentation | | | | | | | |
| 5 | Session | | | | | | | |
| 4 | Transport Class 0-4 | | | | | | | |
| 3 | Network (CONS, CLNS) | | | | | | | |
| 2 | CSMA/ CD | Token Bus | Token Ring | X.25 | | | ISDN | |
| 1 | 8802/3 Ethernet | 8802/4 Tok. Bus | 8802/5 Tok. Ring | HDLC LAPB 114A | EIA 232 | ISDN | | |

*Figure 8.9.* *The OSI protocol stack.*

Most organizations are still planning their OSI migration strategies, and a few are working on pilot programs. For example, the Navy is working on a GOSIP pilot program, and NFSNET is working on a pilot connectionless transport network. Widespread OSI implementations won't occur for several years, except where mandated by the United States government.

Unlike TCP/IP, OSI tends to be driven by vendors. End users or MIS tend to drive the migration to TCP/IP, because it provides an immediate benefit: a deliverable service. On the other hand, vendors are driving the migration to OSI. For example, AT&T has based its Stargroup system entirely on OSI protocols, making the AT&T users the largest installed base of OSI in the world.

GOSIP-compliant products emerged in 1991 and will continue to ship throughout 1992 and beyond, but a critical mass of products won't occur until at least 1993. In this time frame, you can expect to see OSI begin to provide a cost savings and productivity increase. Applications such as electronic data interchange won't become possible until 1994 to 1996, or after enough corporations adopt OSI to build the common infrastructure making such OSI-enabled applications possible. (Note that EDI does exist and is used today; however, it is not the OSI-compliant specification.) Third-generation products providing useful distributed applications won't be realized until around 1995.

# What's All the GOSIP About?

End users and vendors are not adopting OSI without a reason. For some, the impetus to move to GOSIP is the desire for standards-based, interoperable networks and products, and more specifically, the vendor-independence and lower costs that result. At least within the United States, most of the fire comes from the government and its GOSIP Federal Information Processing Standard (FIPS).

GOSIP version 1 mandates that "GOSIP shall be used by Federal government agencies when acquiring computer network products and services and communications systems or services that provide equivalent functionality to the protocols defined in the GOSIP documents."[2] The key words here are *equivalent functionality*. The FIPS document continues: "For the indefinite future, agencies will be permitted to buy network products in addition to those specified in GOSIP. Such products may include other nonproprietary protocols, proprietary protocols, and features and options of OSI protocols that are not included in GOSIP." These issues indicate that GOSIP is required to become every government agency's "second language" in the 1990s, and most agencies will evolve to make GOSIP their first language.

GOSIP version 1, which has been in effect since August 1990, does not mandate complete OSI computing or compatibility. For a complete OSI stack, the industry must wait for GOSIP versions 2, 3, and beyond (see Figure 8.10). A larger number of protocols exists at the lower layers of the GOSIP specification, primarily because different protocols are needed to handle the different communications requirements, such as local and wide area networks. As the specification evolves, more protocols will be added to the upper layers. Currently, the major higher-layer protocols are FTAM and X.400.

GOSIP is one flavor of the OSI, and other countries are specifying other, often incompatible flavors. However, GOSIP is the version that will be used in the United States. Most of the interest in OSI comes from the government sector. Many large government agencies have developed plans to migrate to OSI-based networks, and many government suppliers, defense contractors, and systems integrators have started using OSI.

---

[2]Uyless Black. *OSI: A Model for Computer Communications Standards.* Englewood Cliffs, NJ: Prentice Hall, 1991.

| Layer | GOSIP 1 August 1990 | GOSIP 2 February 1991 | GOSIP 3 February 1992 | GOSIP 4 February 1993 |
|---|---|---|---|---|
| 7 | • ISO 8650 (ACSE), • FTAM subset, • MHS/X.400 1984 | • ISO 8613 (ODA) • ISO 9041 (VTP) | • ISO 8571 (FTAM defined by NBS III), • CCITT X.400 1988 (MHS/X.400), • ISO 9041 (VTP w/ page & scroll forms), • Interim network mgmt., • CCITT X.500, ISO 9504 (X.400 dir. services) | • Network mgmt., • ANSI X.12 (EDI), • ISO 9072 (ROSE), • ISO 9066 (RTSE) |
| 6 | • ISO 8923 Presentation | | | |
| 5 | • ISO 8923 Session | | | |
| 4 | • ISO 8073 (TP0, TP4) (TP0 for X.400 messaging domains only) | • ISO 8602 (CNLS) | | |
| 3 | • ISO 8208 (X.25) • ISO 8473 (CNLS) | • ISO 9542 (ES-IS) • ISO 8348 (CONS) | • CCITT Q.931 (ISDN) | |
| 2 | • ISO 8802/3 (Ethernet) • ISO 8802/4 (Token Bus) • ISO 8802/5 (Token Ring) • ISO 7776 (HDLC LAPB) | | • CCITT Q.921 (ISDN) • CCITT I.430 (ISDN) | |
| 1 | • ISO 8802/3 (Ethernet) • ISO 8802/4 (Token Bus) • ISO 8802/5 (Token Ring) • ISO 7776 (HDLC LAPB) | | • CCITT Q.921 (ISDN) • CCITT I.430 (ISDN) | |

*Figure 8.10.  GOSIP schedule.*

One of the roadblocks to OSI acceptance is users' concern that OSI products will not be completely compatible with each other, despite the efforts of conformance testing organizations such as the Corporation for Open Systems (COS) and the United States government. OSInet is an organization of American users who are trying to solve the problem of testing for OSI interoperability. Similar organizations are working on the problem in other countries.

# ISO Network and Transport Protocols

Although ISO specifications certainly include physical and data-link layer specifications, the following sections concentrate on the higher layer specifications, including those for the network, transport, session, and application layers, because the lower layer specifications have been covered elsewhere in this book.

## Connection-Oriented or Connectionless

ISO offers two basic methods of network layer communications: *connection-oriented* and *connectionless*. The Connectionless-Mode Network Service (CNLS) does not require a connection to be established between two end users before the conversation is begun. In connectionless service, data is transmitted as independent and separate entities, and the service does not maintain a relationship between successive data transfers.

The Connection-Oriented Node Service (CONS) is ISO's specification for connection-oriented services. Such a service sets up a logical connection before data transfer is begun. Usually, the service maintains a relationship between the data units being transferred through the connection. Connection-oriented services require a three-way agreement among the two end users and the service providers, and it also enables the parties to negotiate certain parameters and quality of service functions. When the data transfer begins, the data units do not need to carry this overhead; they just carry a short identifier to allow the end users to look up the full address.

A connectionless network is more robust than a connection-oriented network, because each data unit is handled separately and independently. This way, data units can take separate routes to avoid failed nodes or congestion. The drawback is that connectionless networks require more overhead.

## Providing a Class of Service

The OSI transport layer mediates the differences between connection-oriented and connectionless network services, so that users get a consistent quality of service regardless of the underlying network layer. To do so, the transport layer requires the user to define a quality of service, which specifies the error tolerance and recovery requirements.

The ISO and CCITT specification provides five classes of transport service, Classes 0 through 4. TP0 and TP4 are most common in OSI networks.

- *Class 0—Simple Class* provides very simple transport connection to support a network that needs an acceptable residual error rate and acceptable quality of service, where the transport layer does not have to provide recovery or resequencing services. Class 0 provides for connection-oriented support during the network connection and release phases. Class 0 was developed for telex.

- *Class 1—Basic Error Recovery Class* is associated with X.25 networks. The protocol data units, or packets, are numbered, unlike with Class 0. Class 1 service can segment data and retain all data and packets, if necessary.

- *Class 2—Multiplexing Class* enhances Class 0 service by allowing for the multiplexing of several transport connections into a single network session. It also provides for explicit flow control to prevent congestion; however, it provides neither error detection nor recovery.

- *Class 3—Error Recovery Class* provides for the services in Class 2, and also can recover from network failure without having to notify the user. The user data is retained until the receiving transport layer sends back a positive acknowledgment of the message.

- *Class 4—Error Detection and Recovery Class* provides Class 2 and 3 level flow control, but assumes that nearly anything can go wrong in a network. Like Class 3, it permits expedited data and sequences the acknowledgment messages. When a connection is released, a TP4 link cannot be reused, because the protocol assumes that some data may arrive late. TP4 is designed for a network connection that provides a residual error rate that is not acceptable to the user. In this class of service, the transport layer must recover from failures and resequence packets. Such a class of service is necessary for local area networks, mobile networks, and datagram networks.

# Application Services

Most of the interest and activity surrounding OSI is occurring at the application layer. ISO has standardized four application layer recommendations: Message Handling Systems (MHS, CCITT X.400 through X.420), Virtual Terminal (VT, ISO 9040 and 9041), File Transfer, Access, and Management (FTAM, ISO 8571), and Job Transfer and Manipulation (JTM, ISO 8831 and 8832). Directory services, still under development, will also play an important role.

## OSI Application Services

- *Message Handling Systems (MHS, X.400)*—Provides a store-and-forward messaging facility. X.400 will be widely implemented as companies build E-mail systems that communicate with dissimilar end-user mail systems.

- *Directory services (X.500)*—Still under development, X.500 will play an important role in building a worldwide directory system of computing users.

- *Network Management (Common Management Information Protocol, CMIP)*—CMIP is the facility to monitor and manage OSI devices. Still under development, its deployment has been stalled by the popularity of SNMP. On paper, CMIP provides much more functionality, robustness, and flexibility.

- *Virtual Terminal (VT)*—Provides a remote login facility for terminal users.

- *File Transfer, Access, and Management (FTAM)*—Provides the ability to transfer files among OSI-compliant computers.

- *Job Transfer and Manipulation (JTM)*—Provides the ability to remotely execute batch jobs on host computers.

## X.400 Message Handling System

The X.400 Message Handling System (MHS) provides an internationally recognized standard for store-and-forward electronic messaging. X.400 mail systems are often the starting point when corporations and governments migrate to OSI networks, because X.400 solves a problem that is not solved by any existing system. No other E-mail protocol or system works on so many different systems and is independent of a vendor.

E-mail is an essential and widespread application, regardless of the computer platform—mainframe, minicomputer, or PC. Many different E-mail systems are used on each of these platforms (see Table 8.2). As corporations build enterprise-wide networks, these dissimilar E-mail systems need to be connected through a common transport. Very often, that platform is X.400. A gateway is configured between an X.400 backbone and E-mail system, providing complete E-mail connectivity. It was once commonly accepted that end users would adopt X.400-based E-mail packages, but to date, this hasn't occurred. (For more on electronic mail, see Chapter 9, "Network Applications.")

Table 8.2.   E-mail systems commonly used today.

| Host or LAN Type | E-Mail Product |
| --- | --- |
| IBM | PROFS |
| | SNADS |
| DEC | VAXmail |
| | All-In-1 |
| Hewlett-Packard | HPOffice |
| UNIX hosts | SMTP |
| | UUCP |
| Sun | LifeLine |
| | SMTP |
| | UUCP |
| Wang | WangOffice |
| PC LANs | Lotus cc:Mail |
| | Microsoft Mail |
| | DaVinci eMail |
| Mac LANs | Microsoft Mail for Mac |
| | CE Software QuickMail |

X.400 will allow multivendor, multiplatform mail applications to intercommunicate directly, without the use of today's gateway products. Today, you often find different mail gateways implemented in a network, creating management and administration headaches. In addition, these gateways are expensive. In many other cases, corporations have no E-mail standard, with each group or department using their favor and with no interconnectivity. X.400 can help solve these problems.

MHS defines an electronic mail system into a *User Agent* (UA) and *Message Transfer Agent* (MTA) component. Figure 8.11 shows a diagram of the components of an X.400 Message Handling System. As the "mail box," the UA interfaces directly with the end user. The UA is responsible for message preparation, submission, and reception for the user. It also provides text editing, presentation services, security, message priority, and delivery notification. The UA is an interface rather than an end-user application, so it does not define the specifics of how it interacts with the user. That is left to the E-mail product developer.

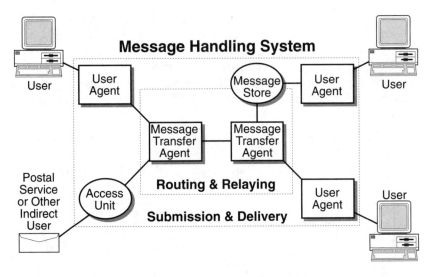

*Figure 8.11.* *The X.400 message handling system.*

The MTA routes and relays the electronic message. Its responsibilities include the store-and-forward path, channel security, and actual routing of the message through the communications media. An MTA's operation is straightforward. The UA sends its message to the local MTA. The MTA checks the message for syntax errors and then delivers the message to a local UA. If the message is not local, the MTA forwards it to the next MTA. The next MTA repeats the process until the message is successfully delivered.

A collection of MTAs is known as a Message Transfer System (MTS). The MTS is usually specialized to a particular vendor's product, although standardization work is under way here. The Message Store (MS) provides message storage, submission, and retrieval functions, and works in conjunction with the UA for devices that are not always available, such as PCs or terminals. The Access Units (AUs) provide connections to other types of communications systems, such as telex services and postal services.

Following the post office metaphor of local, regional, and main post offices, messages follow the metaphor of the letter. The term *envelope* describes the control information used to deliver the *content*. An MHS envelope contains all the information the MTA needs to invoke the many service elements. MHS also uses *distribution lists,* which are similar to the routing lists commonly used in offices.

A *management domain* is a collection of at least one MTA and zero or more UAs that is administered by a single organization. Management domains may be *private* (PDMD) or *administrative* (ADMD). An ADMD is managed by an administration such as a PTT or telephone company, and a PDMD is managed by any other type of organization. This hierarchy of management domains allows the configuration of a worldwide MHS system with unique addressing (see Figure 8.12).

Commercially available X.400 mail products are sold by WorldTalk, Isocorp, SoftSwitch, and Retix. Wollongong Group, Interactive Systems, Novell, IBM, Frontier Technologies, and Digital Equipment also sell X.400 products.

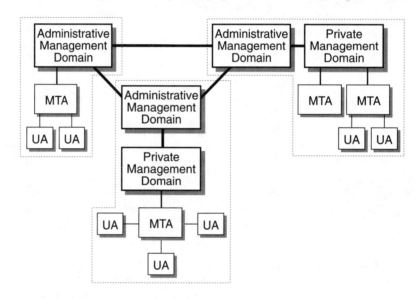

*Figure 8.12.* X.400 *management domains.*

# Virtual Terminal

Virtual Terminal (VT) is an ISO protocol that has not received as much attention as X.400, but its functionality is quite necessary. Say a user on a PC wants to dial into a VAX and run a job. The user simply buys the necessary software to emulate a VT-100 terminal, loads it, dials in, logs on, and runs the job. Now imagine that the user needs access not only to a VAX, but to an IBM 3090 and an HP 9000. The number of terminal emulation packages grows rapidly. If each host system ran the ISO terminal emulation protocol software, however, users dialing in would need only one terminal emulation protocol: VT. The PC users could use the same software to dial into multiple dissimilar hosts, changing only the access parameters and passwords for entry to each.

A virtual terminal isolates the terminals and the applications from one another, enabling different terminals to access different applications running on different systems. A virtual terminal defines a terminal's behavior in terms of its characteristics and sessions in a flexible manner so that the terminal user can readily change the terminal's behavior as well as provide a means for a terminal or user to access a variety of different applications. The ISO incorporated this widespread function into its standards as the Virtual Terminal (VT) specification.

## File Transfer, Access, and Management

File transfer is the most basic of computer system services. Access to files, either locally or remotely, is necessary regardless of whether the higher-level application is word processing, E-mail, databases, or remote program execution. ISO provides this data management function through File Transfer, Access, and Management (FTAM). Along with X.400, FTAM has enjoyed the widest implementation success among the ISO protocols.

A basic model of data management is virtual file storage, where the physical location of the files may differ from their logical mappings. For example, in DOS, this mapping is accomplished via the File Access Table (FAT), and in OS/2 it is accomplished through the High Performance File System (HPFS). In OSI, the definition is FTAM, which is a much more complex and functional implementation. FTAM describes the characteristics of the virtual file store, not the actual file, which permits different file formats to be mixed together.

FTAM provides the facilities to locate and reach a file's contents and includes verbs for inserting, replacing, extending, and erasing a file's contents. FTAM also provides the facilities to manipulate an entire file, including file create, delete, read, open, close, and select attributes.

Vendors of FTAM software include: Banyan Systems, Digital Equipment, Frontier Technologies, IBM, Interactive Systems, Novell, Retix, Sun, World-Talk, and Wollongong Group.

## Job Transfer and Manipulation

JTM, or Job Transfer and Manipulation, enables users and programmers to submit jobs to be processed by a host computer. A job control language, which enables jobs to be submitted, directs the computer's actions by identifying the programs and files that must participate in the job. The ISO's JTM allows jobs submitted on any JTM host to run on any other JTM host. To use JTM, a user must know the specifics of the job to be submitted, for example, the job control language, and the facilities of the remote system. ISO's JTM supports traditional batch jobs, transaction processing, remote job entry, and distributed database access.

# X.500 Directory Services

Imagine a worldwide network, connecting computers not only within a single corporate enterprise, but also between different companies. Now imagine a user in New York trying to send E-mail to a user on the Paris subnetwork. Users will have a difficult time remembering names and naming conventions on a single-site network. Now compound that with a global addressing scheme. The names probably will be long and cumbersome—and difficult to remember and type. How does a user look up names and resources quickly and efficiently? How does the user maintain a list of local users without having to call up the entire directory listing, while maintaining these local users in the main database? *Directory services* can help reduce the complexity of finding a user or resource on an enterprise-wide or global network.

Now consider the problem of managing a large enterprise-wide or global network. Accurately tracking the devices and resources, whether hardware, software, or people, would demand several people's full attention. Keeping track of resources and devices on a 40-node NetWare LAN is difficult enough. Directory services are expected to significantly aid network management, or at least in locating, tracking, and accessing resources.

As networks grow larger, directory services become essential. Unfortunately, most directory services lack the required capability for enterprise-wide networking. Few network operating systems, whether PC LAN or minicomputer-based, offer directory services. Banyan Systems has distinguished itself by offering StreetTalk, a superior distributed global naming service for its VINES network operating system. StreetTalk has continued to win Banyan ardent supporters among those who build and manage the very largest networks. Digital Equipment Corp. has a distributed global naming service for its DECnet. Beyond these two, however, few complete services are offered.

ISO's answer is the X.500 Directory service standard. Although the specification is not yet complete, pilot projects are under way, most notably Performance System International's White Pages and the North American Direc-tory Access Forum.

Systems can use the X.500 directory service to exchange information about objects such as data, applications, hardware, users, files, and nearly anything that can be defined as an object. The X.500 directory facilitates the communication of this information between different systems, which can be OSI applications, layer entities, management entities, and communications networks.

The X.500 structure is somewhat similar to the X.400 structure, in that it enables a hierarchical structure designed to scale to the very largest networks (see Figure 8.13). In an X.500 system, directory information is stored in a *Directory Information Base* (DIB). *Directory User Agents* (DUAs) access the information stored in the DIB. The DUA is an applications process rather than an end-user product. A DIB is hierarchically ordered and made up of *entries* and *objects*. Each entry is a collection of information about one object, such as a user, hardware, or an application. The DIB permits the use of aliases, so an object name can have alternative names. The use of aliases is important, for example, for logical and physical addressing, which simplifies resource identification.

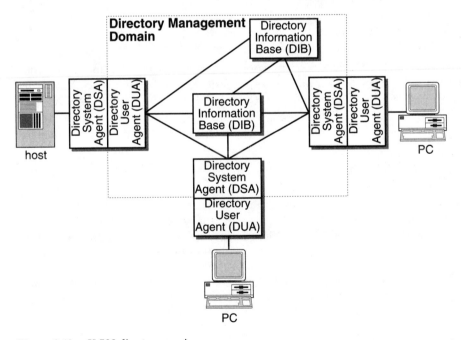

*Figure 8.13.* *X.500 directory services.*

X.500 is designed to be a distributed directory service. To ensure that a directory can be distributed, the Directory System Agent (DSA) provides access to the DIB from or to other DSAs. To satisfy a request, the DSA can work with other DSAs. A Directory Management Domain (DMD) administers the directory, and it is a set of one or more DSAs and zero or more DUAs. The DMD may be a country, PTT, or anything designed to manage the DIB.

# Putting OSI in Perspective

For most corporations, migration to OSI will come at the government's bequest. Migrating from an existing system—whether TCP/IP, DECnet, or SNA—is disrupting, and few IS managers like disruption.

OSI is likely to be explored in the context of an existing system. Nearly every large computer and network manufacturer is supporting OSI in some way. In many cases, the existing transport can remain untouched, and OSI applications can be loaded on top. Note, however, that this gateway approach may be slow and reduce OSI's interoperability benefits. Nevertheless, running OSI applications on top of a TCP/IP, DECnet, or SNA infrastructure is a good way to become acquainted with the next-generation protocols.

Although X.400 and X.500 solve problems that existing solutions can't solve, their widespread acceptance will be slowed by their grand scale, their complexity, and their expense. Although only anecdotal evidence is available about the cost of X.400 systems, this evidence points to high costs. X.400 and X.500 are computer-intensive applications; whereas a minicomputer or mainframe can handle the load, an ordinary PC cannot. So in the PC LAN environment, X.400 and X.500 services are likely to require a separate, high-powered server.

It is unlikely that the market can deliver a single OSI application that is so desirable and so powerful that it will compel users to migrate to an OSI network. Most likely, a few OSI applications will be installed, such as those built on E-mail and directory services, in the context of an existing protocol.

# Digital Equipment Corporation's DECnet

Digital Equipment Corp. has a master plan, called Digital Network Architecture (DNA), for specifying how its computers communicate at each layer. Whereas DNA is the overarching specification on paper, *DECnet* is the physical implementation. Digital has delivered five *phases,* or iterations, of DECnet, but Phase IV and Phase V are the most relevant to enterprise-wide networks.

- *Services*—Services include physical through application layer services. Advantage: Networks (DECnet Phase V) give end users the choice of using DECnet, TCP/IP, and OSI services.

- *Pros*—Provides good connectivity for users of DECnet computers.

- *Cons*—Although other types of computers are supported, DECnet is primarily for VMS hosts. It provides support for TCP/IP and OSI, but DECnet is still controlled by Digital.

When Digital introduced DNA Phase IV in 1982, it defined a 16-bit network address that enabled users to build networks of up to 64,000 devices. Phase IV also included support for EtherNet and offered a routing capability that enabled designers to build hierarchical networks. Phase IV was not based on the OSI model, but on Digital's similar, but slightly different, layered approach (see Figure 8.14). But more importantly, whereas Phase IV wholeheartedly supported DECnet protocols, including EtherNet and proprietary routing algorithms, it had only marginal support for the ISO protocols.

Digital announced Phase V in 1987 and began shipping Phase V-compatible products in 1991. When it announced Phase V, which Digital now calls Advantage-Networks, it stressed its commitment to helping customers build and manage multiprotocol networks. With Phase V, Digital networks now simultaneously support DECnet, TCP/IP, and OSI protocols. Digital also moved outside its traditional realm of EtherNet and X.25, and now supports Token Ring and FDDI. DECnet runs primarily on computers running the VMS or Ultrix operating systems, although DECnet implementations exist for Windows, DOS, and Macintosh. For PC LANs, Digital supports Macintoshes under its Pathworks and PCs under LAN Manager for UNIX. Pathworks supports also Novell NetWare and Banyan VINES. Phase V isn't just a rework of Phase IV, which supported only DECnet. It is rewritten from the ground up, conforming to the ISO model, so the protocols operate modularly.

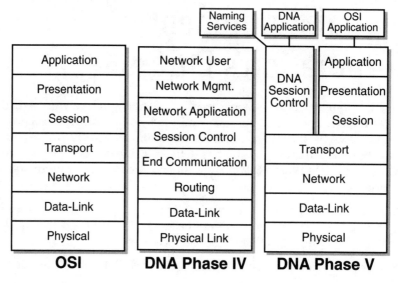

*Figure 8.14.* *DNA Phase IV and Phase V functional layers.*

Digital has realized that it cannot sell proprietary networking systems, locking end users into its vision of computing. Advantage-Networks provides TCP/IP and OSI services in addition to DECnet. It also provides some of the advanced services that are absolutely critical in an enterprise-wide, heterogeneous network, including distributed naming and distributed management.

# The Principles of DNA

DECnet is designed to conform to the architectural design principles in Digital's network architecture. These principles include self-stabilization, no single point of failure, locality, minimal dependence on network management, determinism, scalability, interoperability, and configurable redundancy.

DECnet networks should self-stabilize so that when a failure occurs, the system can attain a stable state when the failure is corrected or the failing component is removed from the network. For example, the Phase V routing algorithm stabilizes to "good routers," providing that no continuous topology changes occur. Similarly, a DNA network should contain no single point of failure, so that a failure of one component will not disable the entire network. Even if continuous failures occur, DNA provides for locality of failure, where individual parts of the system will self-stabilize.

Wherever possible, DNA calls for a network that depends as little as possible on human network management. With a largely self-managing system, the human managers can concentrate on policy management rather than day-to-day management.

DNA also calls for determinism, scalability, and interoperability. For example, the state of the system should not be determined only by the system's characteristics. For example, in routing, the routes calculated must be a function of the network topology as well as past events, making it possible to predict the network's operation. Also, algorithms and protocols are designed to scale into the very largest networks as well as to facilitate the connection with a variety of different types of equipment.

Another design principle is configurable redundancy, where it is possible to configure several network topologies to make trade-offs among cost, performance, and availability. In this way, a critical application on a DECnet network can continue to run even if a node or link has failed.

# The Specifics of DECnet

DNA Phase V supports far more than the EtherNet, X.25, and Digital proprietary protocols of Phase IV. For example, DNA networks now simultaneously support DECnet, TCP/IP, and OSI protocols (see Figure 8.15).

Here's a run-down of the protocols Digital supports at the different DECnet layers:

- *Physical layer*—At the physical layer, DNA provides support for modems; EtherNet (both Version 2 of the EtherNet specification and IEEE 802.2/802.3), Token Ring, and FDDI.

- *Data-link layer*—At the data-link layer, DNA Phase V supports the High Level Data Link Control (HDLC), an ISO standard; LΛPB, a subset of HDLC for X.25 networks, and the 802.2 specifications for EtherNet, Token Ring, and FDDI; as well as DDCMP, a DECnet specification for the data link layer.

- *Network layer*—The network layer in Phase V is similar to the routing layer in Phase IV, and it provides ISO connectionless mode service

(CLNS) as well as connection-mode service (CONS). Using ISO network layer standards and supporting ISO network addressing enables designers to use globally unique addresses. The network layer also provides support for the connection-mode service required for Phase V nodes to communicate directly with other nodes on an X.25 network.

■ *Transport layer*—The transport layer of Phase V is similar to the end communication layer of Phase IV, and it provides support for Digital's and the OSI's transport services, the Network Services Protocol, and Transport Class 0, 2, and 4, respectively.

■ *Session layer and above*—Two separate protocol stacks exist above the transport layer, each providing support for a different class of applications. The dual stack approach is a migration from the old DECnet to the new Advantage-Networks. This division enables Digital to support its own applications, ISO's applications, as well as future ones. This dual stack allows network applications to take advantage of the application programming interfaces for FTAM and X.400. The DNA Session Control layer provides the platform for DNA applications. OSI applications communicate with other OSI applications using the OSI session, presentation, and application layers.

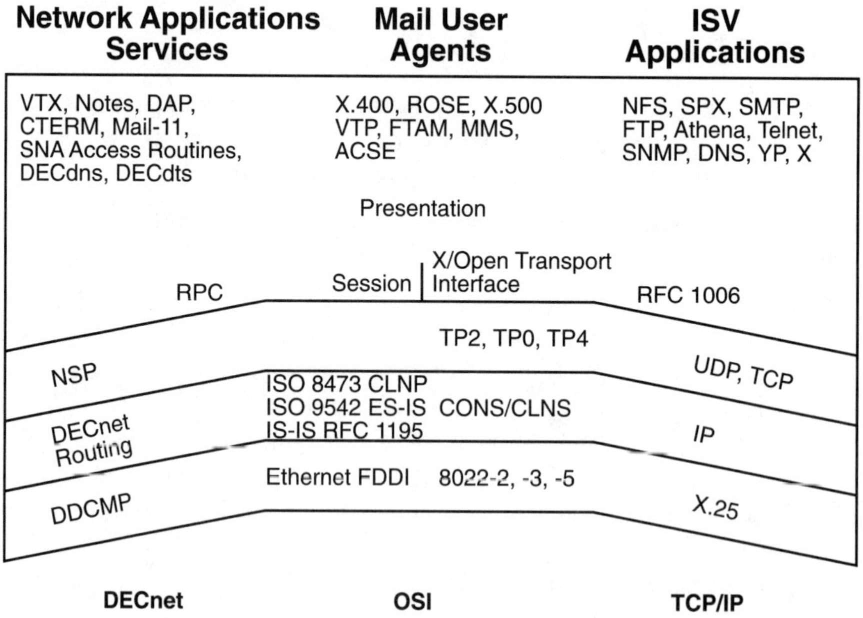

| Network Applications Services | Mail User Agents | ISV Applications |
|---|---|---|
| VTX, Notes, DAP, CTERM, Mail-11, SNA Access Routines, DECdns, DECdts | X.400, ROSE, X.500 VTP, FTAM, MMS, ACSE | NFS, SPX, SMTP, FTP, Athena, Telnet, SNMP, DNS, YP, X |

Presentation

RPC | Session | X/Open Transport Interface | RFC 1006

TP2, TP0, TP4 — UDP, TCP

NSP

ISO 8473 CLNP
ISO 9542 ES-IS   CONS/CLNS
DECnet Routing   IS-IS RFC 1195   IP

Ethernet FDDI   8022-2, -3, -5

DDCMP   X.25

**DECnet**          **OSI**          **TCP/IP**

*Figure 8.15.* *Digital's Advantage-Networks.*

Advantage-Networks works with VMS and Ultrix. Extensions for DECnet-VAX V5.4 provide OSI end-node and DECnet capabilities for VMS. DECnet/OSI for Ultrix V5.0 implements OSI and DECnet on Ultrix. (TCP/IP was already packaged with Ultrix.) Digital plans to ship DECnet/OSI for VMS, which will offer VMS users the full capabilities of OSI and DECnet. The company will enhance its TCP/IP Services for VMS to provide mail, remote terminal, remote printing, SNMP support, and access to Ultrix, TCP/IP, and NFS file systems to VMS users. Digital will support the 1988 X.400 and X.500 across its range of operating systems. In addition, the Pathworks product will deliver OSI services to DOS and OS/2 computers.

Advantage-Networks also includes a global naming service and a network-wide time stamp. In a naming service, the user provides the naming service with a name, and the naming service passes back a set of attributes associated with that name. For example, a user can give the directory service the name of a user or printer, and the naming service can return the address of that resource. The Digital Distributed Name Service (DECdns) enables administrators to establish one naming scheme that can be used throughout a global network, significantly easing management.

The Digital Distributed Time Service (DECdts) establishes a "Greenwich Mean Time" for networks, enabling all servers to maintain the same time stamp, which also eases network management by accomplishing the seemingly simple task of ensuring all devices have the same time stamp.

DNA also provides network management facilities as part of Digital's Enterprise Management Architecture (EMA). EMA is specifically designed to manage distributed networks, and DNA Advantage-Networks network management is part of the family of EMA management solutions. Each major component of DNA Advantage-Networks provides facilities for network management so that managers can monitor network operation and change its operating parameters. DEC is also working with third-party developers so that DECmcc can more effectively manage multivendor networks. For example, Cabletron's wiring products can be managed from a DECmcc console. DECmcc can also speak various management protocols, including DEC's NICE, SNMP, and CMIP. (For more on network management, see Chapter 10, "Network Management: Organizational and Practical.")

Digital has also taken an important step in licensing its DECnet software to third parties, enabling these companies to develop versions of DECnet to run on non-Digital platforms. For example, Bell Atlantic Software Systems sells DECnet for SCO UNIX, a Phase IV end-node implementation for 386 and 486 PCs.

# IBM's System Application Architecture

IBM's System Application Architecture (SAA), announced in 1987, is the company's blueprint for uniting its many different system architectures. SAA is a set of standards, development approaches, and software interfaces that define a strategy for system design and development. It is IBM's grand plan for creating software that retains essential common elements regardless of the hardware platform or the specific functions. More specifically, SAA is also IBM's plan for standardizing the interface between the users and the applications, between the programmers and computers, and among the programs that communicate with each other.

- *Services*—SAA provides a complete suite of services from data link to applications.

- *Pros*—SAA provides a new paradigm of peer-to-peer computing in an IBM environment. IBM has recently begun to adopt industry standards, such as UNIX, TCP/IP, and EtherNet.

- *Cons*—SAA (as APPC) is not widely implemented, and 3270 still dominates. Despite IBM's acceptance of industry standards, SAA is still controlled by Big Blue.

SAA is more than a new computing architecture. It represents a significant change in the way IBM thinks. System Network Architecture (SNA), IBM's computing plan that it introduced in the 1970s, follows a strict hierarchy: an intelligent mainframe and dumb terminals. The terminals talk to the cluster controllers, and the cluster controllers talk to the mainframes. Conversations are terminal to mainframe. The PC and other intelligent end stations threw a monkey wrench into this architecture. PCs, with local processing power, are capable of holding conversations with each other independent of the mainframe. Their applications are also capable of communicating directly with mainframe applications. These more complex communications were prevented by the SNA master/slave mind-set.

In contrast, the newer SAA is a peer-to-peer architecture. SAA recognizes that other intelligent devices exist beyond mainframes. In SAA, applications can communicate directly with each other, without the intervention of a network control device.

Another important difference is SAA's acceptance of industry standards. IBM suffers less and less from the Not-Invented-Here syndrome, and its product line includes FDDI, EtherNet, UNIX, SNMP, OSI, and other industry standard protocols, in addition to the usual array of 3270 coax, SDLC, Token Ring, VMS, MVS, OS/2, and NetView.

SAA, however, was defined while proprietary network systems were accepted by end users. Today, that is no longer true. SAA, even for its acceptance of industry standards, is controlled by IBM. Advanced Peer-to-Peer Networking (APPN), IBM's architecture for peer-to-peer networks, has not been widely implemented; SNA still dominates. In order to play in the multiprotocol enterprise-wide network of today, the IBM architecture must fundamentally change. Whether IBM can reinvent the way it does business, as its new organization is supposed to enable it to do, remains to be seen.

# Multiprotocol Routers in an SNA Network

Many companies are restructuring their SNA networks to accommodate PC and UNIX LAN traffic. With more than just 3270 terminal traffic traveling across its network roads, the once-hierarchical, single-vendor SNA networks must change. The challenge: How does an SNA network support non-SNA traffic? The architecture, philosophy, and protocols of an SNA and a multiprotocol network are fundamentally different. An SNA network is constructed hierarchically, using a set of IBM protocols, and is fundamentally static. A multiprotocol network, such as a TCP/IP internetwork, is peer-to-peer, uses industry-standard protocols, and always grows and changes.

Whether the SNA network must accommodate the LAN protocols or the LAN protocols must accommodate SNA is largely a matter of perspective, to date. IBM devices are accommodating multiprotocol networks. Similarly, multiprotocol routers are becoming an integral part of an SNA network, routing TCP/IP, SNA, and other LAN traffic across an enterprise backbone. In some instances, companies are even using multiprotocol routers in place of their 3745 Communications Controllers. Multiprotocol routers offer greater flexibility and lower cost than communications controllers.

Enterprise-Wide Networking

The leading router manufacturer, cisco Systems, has made significant inroads into the SNA community with its routers. The number 2 company in the router market, Wellfleet Communications, also supports SNA. In 1992, IBM announced its own multiprotocol router, the 6611, which is based on its RS/6000 RISC machine. Although cisco's router offers greater functionality in an SNA environment, IBM's entrance into this market is a significant event.

IBM's 37XX communications controllers function as SNA Type 4 Nodes or routers. Type 4 Nodes use static routing tables that must be manually configured before the SNA network is activated. Such a static routing method is inflexible in a constantly changing multiprotocol network. IBM's Advanced Peer-to-Peer Networking (APPN) supports dynamic routing among its Network Node routers. Although it uses dynamic routing, APPN does not use an industry-standard routing protocol, such as Routing Information Protocol (RIP) or open shortest path first (OSPF); rather it uses a proprietary IBM protocol. So although APPN Network Nodes support TCP/IP, IPX, and DECnet, APPN routers cannot be used instead of an industry-standard multiprotocol router.

In order to accommodate non-SNA protocols in an SNA backbone, software can be added to Type 4 Communications Controllers. IBM calls this *protocol enveloping,* but the more common industry term is *tunneling* or *encapsulating.* Although this is not "real" routing, it provides the necessary functionality today.

Multiprotocol routers can carry SNA traffic across multiprotocol networks. Like the cluster controllers, the multiprotocol routers technically do not route; they support SDLC tunneling. SNA devices connect with the new multiprotocol routers via SDLC data links. The routers add IP headers to SDLC frames, thereby creating IP datagrams; they then route the IP datagrams over the internetwork.

Tunneling has the advantage of transparency; the physical SDLC link is simply replaced with a logical data link that traverses a TCP/IP network. Tunneling's biggest drawback is timing. If all SDLC frames are simply passed through the TCP/IP network, the LAN introduces variable delays into the SDLC data link, resulting in NCP data link time-outs. One stopgap solution is to manually increase the time-out thresholds during NCP generation, although this process is both time-consuming and not guaranteed to eliminate time-outs.

The solution? The routers themselves must become smarter, handling the local SDLC polling and acknowledgment of frames. In this scenario, routers acting as SDLC secondary link stations would then respond locally to NCP polls. Routers attached to peripheral nodes function as SDLC primary link stations and locally poll the downstream nodes. This approach solves the time-out problem, but requires the router manufacturers to produce new software (which many are doing, including cisco Systems).

As mentioned, the tunneling approach is not real SNA Type 4 routing. To have "real" routing, NCP functionality has to be embedded into multiprotocol routers, although NCP software—controlled by IBM—is not easy for a third-party vendor to replicate.

# The SAA Communications Protocols

SAA has four parts: the *user interface*, the *developer tools*, *communications support*, and the *applications* that include the SAA components. Common User Access (CUA) is a set of standards for designing what users see and how they interface with systems. For example, CUA defines the user interface, how users get help, how they choose items from a list, and so on. The Common Programming Interface (CPI) defines the languages and systems interfaces that programmers use. Common Communications Support (CCS) describes the pieces of a communications model for developing distributed and cooperative applications running on different hardware platforms. Applications that follow the SAA standards and use the SAA interfaces are called *SAA applications*. Although a common user interface and a common programming interface are certainly important, the Common Communications Support is particularly pertinent here.

Figure 8.16 compares the OSI, SNA, and SAA architectures. An eight-layer model, SNA was defined several years before the seven-layer OSI model, but the two architectures are similar at the lower layers. The six-layer SAA specification is most similar to OSI at the lower layers and provides facilities for SNA and OSI networks.

SAA is a six-layer architecture that spans IBM's entire range of hardware and software products. The protocols supported at each layer are described in Table 8.3.

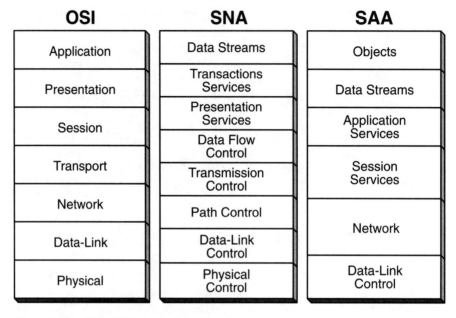

**Figure 8.16.** *OSI, SNA, and SAA architectures.*

**Table 8.3.  SAA communications protocols.**

| Protocol Type | Common Communication Service Component |
| --- | --- |
| Objects | Presentation Text Object<br>Image Object<br>Graphics Object<br>Font Object<br>Formatted Field Object |
| Data Streams | Mixed Object: DCA<br>Revisable Form Text: DCA<br>3270 Data Stream<br>Intelligent Printer Data Stream<br>Character Data Representation Architecture |
| Application Services | Document Interchange Architecture<br>SNA Distribution Services<br>SNA Management Services<br>Distributed Data Management<br>Distributed Relational Data Architecture |

| Protocol Type | Common Communication Service Component |
| --- | --- |
| | File Transfer, Access, and Management |
| | Association Control Service Elements |
| Session Services | LU6.2 |
| | OSI Session Layer |
| Network | Node Type 2.1 |
| | OSI Connectionless Network Service |
| | OSI Connection-Oriented Network Service |
| Data Link Control | Token Ring |
| | EtherNet |
| | FDDI |
| | Synchronous Data Link Control |
| | X.25 |
| | ISDN |

- *Data-link layer*—On the data-link layer, SAA supports Token Ring, EtherNet, and FDDI as well as Synchronous Data Link Control (SDLC) and X.25. SDLC is a subset of ISO's High Level Data Link Control (HDLC). IBM also supports ISDN terminal adapters. Recently, IBM has been making a concerted effort to support the industry specifications and ship products for EtherNet and FDDI as well as Token Ring.

- *Network layer*—At the routing layer, SAA calls for Node Type 2.1 (NT2.1) for SNA networks and the two ISO protocols for OSI networks. NT2.1 provides low-level networking for direct connectivity between two SAA systems on a peer-to-peer basis, meaning either end can initiate a session. NT2.1 is the only one of the four IBM Node Types that is available across all of the SAA operating environments. NT2.1 defines "peripheral" nodes that give the end user access to the network, rather than acting as network routing or control points. NT2.1 nodes support direct connections, without going through a network control point. This is particularly useful in application-to-application communications. NT2.1 is supported on all SAA platforms, via OS/400, OS/2 EE, and NCP/VTAM on S/370s.

Additionally, SAA supports OSI's connection-oriented (CONS) and connectionless (CLNS) network services for use in OSI networks.

- *Session services*—SAA's session service layer encompasses the functionality of OSI's transport, session, and presentation layers. They establish communication, support data transfer, and allow termination of communication between application programs on a network. This is referred to as *program-to-program communication*. As with the network layer, here SAA accepts both SNA and OSI protocols. Logical Unit 6.2 (LU6.2) and its Advanced Program-to-Program Communications (APPC) interface are the SAA protocol.

APPC and LU6.2 have received vast amounts of attention. They were heralded as the one path to distributed computing in an IBM environment. In reality, the move to APPC has been very slow. Both the mainframe and the PC application have to be written from the ground up to take advantage of APPC. Quite simply, few MIS departments want to rewrite their existing applications. If they do, building an application that takes advantage of APPC requires the expertise of a mainframe person, a LAN person, a communications programmer, and an applications programmer. APPC is being used sparingly in new applications, but most of the applications are developed using IBM's HLLAPI, a programming interface that runs with existing mainframe applications. If and when APPC takes off, it will be a powerful tool for building distributed applications.

OSI session services are provided via the standard ISO protocols, including TP0, TP2, and TP4. CCS also supports the ISO session layer protocols. The ISO presentation layer establishes connections, transfers data, and terminates the presentation services. Abstract Syntax Notation One (ASN.1) defines a variety of ISO data types and data structures.

- *Application Services*—In SAA parlance, applications services provide commonly used management and communications functions, such as document transfer, message transfer, and network management. Different applications are used in SNA and OSI networks.

The Document Imaging Architecture (DIA) provides services to applications that pass complex documents to each other. Services include distribution, library storage, and file transfer. DIA calls the SNA Distribution Service (SNA/DS) for distribution of documents across the network. SNA/DS specifies how files, documents, and messages are routed and delivered in an SNA network.

SNA Management Services (SNA/MS) defines what messages the network computer and devices can send. SNA/MS allows IBM and non-IBM products to manage the network consistently. NetView and other products initiate and control these messages.

Distributed Data Management (DDM) is IBM's architecture for implementing distributed data applications. Its data connectivity language makes it easier to exchange data across different system architectures. Level 3 of DDM supports Distributed Relational Data Architecture (DRDA), which specifies the commands and data needed to implement a SQL interface over a distributed interface. DRDA is built on an LU6.2 foundation.

OSI application services include FTAM, X.400, and ACSE for defining how applications transfer information.

■ *Objects*—To transfer a document to other SAA systems, the document must be structured within the specified boundaries. The Object Content Architecture (OCA) eases the difficulties inherent in such transactions by defining the structure and content of the document. Object architectures in OCAs include presentation text, images, graphics, fonts, and formatted data.

■ *Data Streams*—When applications communicate directly with each other, they often need to exchange streams of data, rather than manipulate individual records or files. To facilitate this type of communication, SAA/CCS provides four data streams—Mixed Objects: Document Content Architecture for application-to-application communication; Revisable Form Text: Document Control, also for application-to-application communication; 3270 Data Stream, for transmitting a formatted data stream between an application and a terminal or printer; and Intelligent Printer Data Stream for a system-to-printer data stream for all-points-addressable printing.

# OSI and TCP/IP

IBM seems committed to open systems. Although SAA is the major architecture for IBM-to-IBM networking, IBM intends for SNA and OSI to coexist. IBM and third-party vendors offer TCP/IP for MVS, VM, OS/2, and AIX. IBM is growing this TCP/IP base beyond the UNIX-RISC architecture to extend into the more "traditional" IBM environments. Support for TCP/IP also extends to NFS and X Window. Importantly, IBM is also supporting SNMP on a range of systems, enabling NetView to manage TCP/IP networks as well as SNA.

Eventually, NetView will be able to manage and control OSI, SNA, TCP/IP, and asynchronous networks. The area of network management is one area where IBM plans to distinguish itself from the pure open systems vendors.

With its NetView and SystemView management applications, IBM's plan—as is Digital's—is to be able to manage all of the devices connected on the network, whether those devices have data, voice, or communications capabilities.

# Remote Procedure Call Technology

Software developers are in a bind. Software developers have to choose which network protocols they will write their applications to run on. Most developers can't write for NetBIOS, TCP/IP, APPC, IPX/SPX, VINES IP, AppleTalk, and Named Pipes protocols; they must choose one or two, and in doing so should choose wisely. If they choose a network protocol that falls into disuse, their application may fall by the wayside as well. But writing to several network protocols is a time- and resource-consuming process. The developer must gain expertise with many different network protocols and must maintain code for each. Software developers have more than just the network issues to consider; they also must decide which graphical user interface to use, whether to use object-oriented technology, which operating system to write to, and the function of the application itself.

To encourage developers to write networked applications, the process must be made easier. Remote procedure calls (RPCs) are one way. With RPCs, choosing network protocols no longer carries the risk of choosing the wrong protocol or the great commitment to resources. RPCs liberate the developer from the details of each network protocol.

When using an RPC tool, a program is split into a *client* module and a *server* module, which run on different machines. The RPC tool hides this split from the application. If a client wants to send a message to the server asking it to perform a particular task, the difficulty is how to get the message across the divide between the client and the server. If the client and the server were parts of a single program running on the same machine, getting the message across would be simple: the client makes a function call to the server (see Figure 8.17). However, if the client and server are not running on the same machine, the client can't pass a variable to another software module. Passing that message requires an intermediary. The RPC tool enables the client to call the server module just as if it were located in the same code (see Figure 8.18).

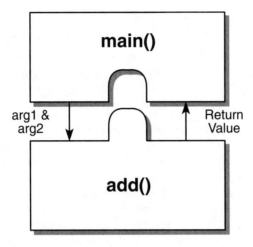

**Figure 8.17.** *A local procedure call.*

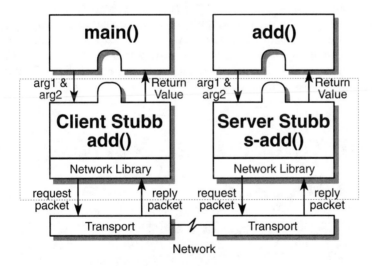

**Figure 8.18.** *A remote procedure call.*

To use an RPC tool, the programmer writes an application, either as a whole program or as a client-server program. The programmer then writes the RPC specification containing the declarations for all server functions that will be called by the client and for all external variables, as well as for information on how the client locates the server. Then using the RPC compiler, the specification is processed twice, once to generate the source code for the client and a second time to generate the source code for the server. Finally, the programmer links and executes the client and the server code to build executable files.

At the server side, the RPC tool generates server *stubs* for each remote function. These stubs are linked with the remote procedures and a *dispatcher* procedure to create a server module. On the client side, the RPC tool generates a client stub that acts as a surrogate for the procedure.

When the client calls the remote procedure, the client stub gets the call, packs up the request, and sends it to the server module using whatever network protocol—TCP/IP, IPX, or AppleTalk, for example—was linked during compilation. When the dispatcher at the server receives the remote procedure call, it hands the request to the proper server stub. The server stub unpacks the packet, executes the request, and returns the answer to the dispatcher, which returns it to the client. The result is that when the client calls the stub function, it executes as if it were local. This way, the existence of the network becomes transparent to the application.

RPCs are important for software developers because they hide the details of the network protocols from the programmers. This aids programmers by reducing the amount of expertise they need, enabling the programmer to concentrate on the application rather than the details of networking. This way, there are more applications that run on a variety of network protocols for the end user to choose from.

# Reengineer Your Network to Interoperate

An enterprise-wide network must be an interoperable one. In building an enterprise-wide network, you must enable communication among different types of computers, from mainframes to PCs, as well as among different sites. If you are like most companies, you have a vast number of different types of computers, some of which date back 10 or more years. In addition, there seems to be a PC and PC LAN every time you turn around. How do you make them all talk? Is interoperability the boondoggle it seems to be?

Before you can build an interoperable network, you must decide which systems and applications are strategic. As part of your requirements analysis, evaluate which systems have strategic value, which have a reasonably long technology and business life left in them, which perform to the satisfaction of the users and MIS, and which you can't afford to be without. Get rid of the rest.

Establish corporate standards for everything that is attached to the enterprise-wide network and publish this list to the MIS and end user employees. Although enforcing standards may seem futile, at least the attempt reduces the number of systems used. This reduction makes the enterprise-wide network more stable. Establishing corporate standards will help MIS support the users better, because MIS will have to learn fewer applications and figure out fewer interactions between networks and applications. Never ram standards down users' throats. Select which systems and applications are most useful in conjunction with the users and business managers. They have to actually use the network—MIS doesn't. Provide the users with a choice, or they'll find a solution on their own.

When building an interoperable network, you should establish a common network platform, which most companies do at the OSI network and transport layers. Wherever possible, settle on a few network protocols, such as TCP/IP, NetWare, and AFP, and standardize on one or two operating systems, such as NetWare and UNIX. Simplifying the network helps reduce the complexity and provides a solid framework on which users can use many different applications and workstations. Such a network will be easier to control and manage because there are fewer "ingredients."

When defining corporate standards, select from the products, solutions, and protocols that have a large installed base, are based on industry standards, are built from relatively new technology, and have the wholehearted backing of their manufacturers.

# Network
# Applications

*Objectives:*

1. To understand that a company's network architecture is in direct response to the requirements set forth by that company's application architecture.

2. To explore the client/server model as well as applications that take advantage of a network's architecture, including databases, electronic mail, mail-enabled applications, workflow automation, and desktop videoconferencing.

## The Network's Raison D'Etre

Without system software, a network is a collection of hardware incapable of doing anything. The disk driver software makes the disk drives store and retrieve data; the server software makes the file servers deliver data to users' fingertips; the network operating software makes the many individual computers act together as a network; and routing software makes the routers transport the packets to the correct location.

Without application software, a network is nothing—it is a technology looking for a purpose. Applications exist only to help people get their jobs done better, faster, and more efficiently. Pure and simple, the network exists to help a company's employees get their jobs done. The tools of the trade are many: word processors, spreadsheets, databases, electronic mail, project management, inventory control, accounting, workflow automation, and image processing.

Each tool helps the business units of the company achieve their goals. The network architecture is determined by the applications used on the network (see Figure 9.1). Some applications may span several departments. E-mail, for example, is best implemented across an entire corporation. Other applications, such as accounting, may be localized to a department, with some crossover to other departments. For example, salespeople need access to accounting information so that they don't continue to extend credit to a client who is untimely in paying bills. Other applications are even more specialized, such as a marketing department using presentation software to design slides. The difficulty of integrating these applications varies according to the types of applications used, the age of the applications, the types of machines used, and the locations in which they are used.

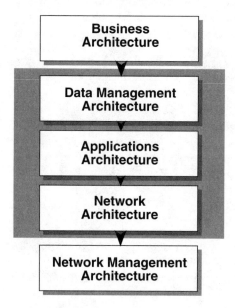

**Figure 9.1.** *Enterprise-wide network architecture.*

A vast number of applications can run on enterprise-wide networks, ranging from mission-critical production, point-of-sale, or accounting programs to the productivity tools people typically associate with PCs. Many off-the-shelf network applications are no different from stand-alone PC applications in terms of functionality. Network applications in the true sense of the word, however, exploit the opportunities that running on a network offers. To take advantage of these opportunities, applications must take into account the "environmental hazards" of networked computing. The following sections detail special characteristics of network applications, features that continue to make the PC-based network computing platform robust.

Some applications run on a network, some run better on a network, and some can run only on a network. Applications can be network-ignorant, network-aware, or network-intrinsic.

■ A *network-ignorant program* cannot run on a network without "blowing up," hanging, or corrupting data. Today, most off-the-shelf, commercially available programs support at least the basic DOS file-locking feature, although some custom-developed programs may still be network-ignorant.

Without file or record locking, each of two users can open the same file at the same time and make changes, and the first person's changes will be overwritten when the second person saves his changes. This leads to data corruption.

■ A *network-aware program* "knows" that it is running on a network and takes the necessary precautions, including file and record locking, to ensure data integrity. Today, the majority of applications are network-aware. An application that supports file locking "locks" a file that one user has open so that no other user can write changes to the file, although other users can read the file's contents. Record locking is the same action carried out on a smaller scale: only a record, or small portion, of a file is locked. Record locking is particularly appropriate with databases. Word processors typically use file locking. This architecture is called *server-based* also.

■ A *network-intrinsic program* also knows that it is running on a network, but it takes advantage of the network's unique architecture. For example, it may take advantage of the server's processing power as well as the client's CPU. A client/server database is an example of such an application. Or the program may need multiple computers to exist, such as a distributed processing application. A network-intrinsic application exploits the network's architecture.

# Understanding the Client/Server Model

Client/server applications are uniquely designed to take advantage of a network's distributed intelligence and processing power. Client/server applications, although several years in the making and slow in arriving, are essential for networks to achieve their full potential. Client/server applications have a number of benefits. First, they distribute the load of the application between the hosts and the PCs while reducing the overall network load. A client/server application enables processing to be concentrated at the front end and the back end. Multiple front ends can access back-end data, and multiple back ends can communicate with each other. Let's take a closer look at the client/server model.

Under the client/server model, an application is divided into two parts: the *front end* and the *back end*. The back-end portion, or engine, handles the "heavy duty" work. The back-end application runs on a server and is responsible for data processing, concurrency control, and ensuring data integrity. The front end, which runs on the client computers, is responsible for displaying data and interfacing with the user (see Figure 9.2).

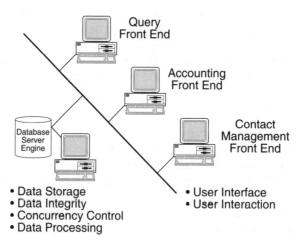

*Figure 9.2.* *The client/server model.*

Contrast the client/server model with the traditional file server model (see Figure 9.3). In the file server-based model, an application resides on a shared file server but does not actually run there. Instead, the file server is little more than a disk server, doling out files to users. For instance, when a user running a database application requests information, the entire database program and data files are downloaded from the server—across the network—and to the user's workstation. When the user requests the records for all of the company's customers located in New Jersey, the user's workstation must search through the entire data file, looking for the records that meet the criteria (see Figure 9.4). Examples of file server-based databases include Borland's (formerly Ashton-Tate's) dBASE and Paradox, and Revelation Technology's Advanced Revelation.

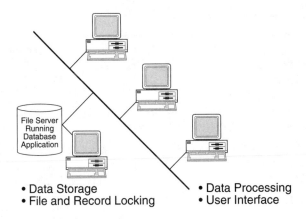

*Figure 9.3.* *Traditional file server model.*

The file server model has its advantages. Developers can create relatively simple applications in a short time. Prototyping is fast and simple because these environments have fairly friendly interfaces. Also, a large number of applications are developed around these database environments, which means that there is a large pool of talented and experienced programmers that further reduces the application development time.

The server-based model has several drawbacks:

■ It does not scale well into an enterprise-wide network. The program and data files are downloaded from the network, thereby drastically increasing network traffic. Even if the user needs only one record, the entire database may need to be downloaded as the application searches for the record. Although additional traffic bogs down a 10Mbps or 16Mbps local area network, such traffic loads make sharing databases over a wide area network nearly impossible. You simply cannot share dBASE on NetWare over a 56Kbps link.

■ Users' machines typically are much less powerful than the server. Users must either sit around and wait while their slow machines churn through data, or the MIS department must purchase more powerful client machines for the users. Either way, it means more money.

■ The file server model causes large portions of the database to be locked, thereby preventing many users from efficiently and elegantly accessing the data.

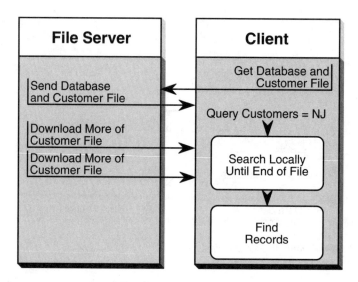

*Figure 9.4.* *The file server-based query.*

The client/server model is a much more efficient way to use a network. If the same user makes the same request—find all customers located in New Jersey—the request is sent from the front-end portion of the client to the server. The back-end application searches through the data file (which remains on the database server), looking for all of the New Jersey customers, and the back end returns over the network only the answer to the user (see Figure 9.5).

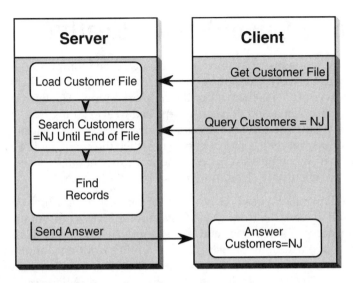

*Figure 9.5.* *The client/server-based query.*

The client/server model reduces network traffic—only the request and the answer, not the program and data files, are transmitted over the network. Again, reduced traffic is particularly important in implementing a shared database in a wide area enterprise-wide network. Also, client/server databases can support many more users than a server-based database can. Another advantage is that the processing power can be concentrated at the server; users may have less powerful workstations, while the server has a powerful processor (or processors), large amounts of RAM, and a gargantuan amount of disk space. Examples of client/server databases include Microsoft/Sybase SQL Server, Novell's NetWare SQL, Oracle's OracleServer, and Gupta Technologies' SQLBase.

The client/server model isn't without its drawbacks, however. Discussed for about five years, the architecture is just beginning to appear in significant numbers within production environments. IS managers, LAN administrators, program designers, and programmers need to learn the details of working in this new paradigm. It isn't easy, and it takes time—more time than the manufacturers of the back-end engines initially predicted.

# What Is Client/Server, Really?

The computer industry is abuzz over client/server computing, distributed computing, network computing, or enterprise computing, when really the client/server model is the fruit of the network model. The term *client/server* has been sorely misused. It has been applied to everything from a powerful multiprocessing file server to network operating systems to applications. In reality, client/server is an architecture in which the client neither knows nor cares who or what the server is, and the server neither knows nor cares who or what the clients are. This anonymity provides freedom.

This freedom makes possible a new type of application, in which the back end is uncoupled from the front end. Many different types of front-end applications can access a single back end. For example, if the back end is a customer database, one user may be using an accounting front end, another may be using a contact-management application, and a third may be printing mailing labels. The front ends individually may use Microsoft Windows, X Window System, Presentation Manager, or the Mac interface. They may be running DOS, Windows NT (when it arrives in 1993), or UNIX. The back-end engine may be running UNIX, NetWare, LAN Manager, VM, or some other powerful operating system. In each case, the many front ends are accessing the same database of back-end information, and the users are unaware. The identities of the front ends don't matter to the back ends, as long as they have a common method of communication.

This division of labor enables the client and the server to be dedicated to a specific purpose, each doing what it does best. By employing the client/server model, MIS can keep corporate information in a single location, where it can be protected by MIS's policies and procedures. This data might be stored on huge mainframes or powerful LAN servers, or across a combination of host computers. On the other side, personal computers, which are best suited to data manipulation and displaying information, rather than protecting information, can be used as front ends to the data servers. This combination enables users to retain the flexibility and power of having personal access to this corporate, shared information. Users can run whatever front-end application they need, if the front end is capable of accessing the database back-end application.

The client/server model, in the end, can save application developers' time and labor. For example, if a developer wants to write a contact-management system, she can use an off-the-shelf database engine, and write her application around an existing core application that already provides record handling, record locking, and other tools. She can concentrate on writing the user interface. Or, by using an existing file-management engine, a developer can write a document-management system and concentrate on creating a better document manager rather than hassle with network issues. Using off-the-shelf database engines to develop applications saves work, and therefore time. However, the process of learning to use the application development environments and understanding how to divide an application into a client portion and a server portion is no mean feat. If your company is building its own client/server applications, allow plenty of time for design and development.

# Windows' Role in Client/Server Computing

Microsoft Windows 3.x no doubt has taken the computer industry by storm. In the first 12 months since its introduction, Microsoft shipped 14 million copies of Windows. Windows has experienced explosive growth, and has outstripped even Microsoft's best-case expectations.

One reason Windows has sold extremely well is that it is easy to try. You can buy the graphical user interface for a low price, load it on your desktop computer (even on a 286 PC, although Windows doesn't run very well on these machines), and try it. If you don't like Windows, it's easy enough to stop using it. And, if you want to use the GUI only occasionally, that's easy too.

Windows stands to make a greater impact than just becoming the desktop GUI of choice. It will become the front end of choice for client/server computing.

Windows is based on the client/server model—it sends a request and gets an answer in return. If you can swap the request out for a network function, you have a networked application. This same request-answer sequence can be extended across the network, and even across the wide area network, if both of the applications understand the communications protocols.

In addition to application-to-application communications, Windows provides device independence. Device independence is crucial in trying to deploy large-scale networks, because myriad disk drivers, network drivers, video drivers, and printer drivers must be accommodated. Windows provides a mechanism for setting up a single configuration file and deploying it network-wide. Because Windows provides memory management also, MIS isn't left trying to deal with DOS's limited memory capabilities. Users can load all the TSRs they want, and let Windows arbitrate among them.

Critical to Windows' success in the network environment is DDE and its successor, OLE. DDE (*dynamic data exchange*) enables applications to communicate with each other without human intervention. DDE has existed for several years, but many developers find it difficult to work with. OLE (*object linking and embedding*), is the newer, more powerful DDE that essentially provides a more standard way of providing DDE. OLE requires much less programming than DDE. With OLE, you can link information created in one package into the display and presentation of another package. When one source of information changes, it updates all the dependent applications. Microsoft usually uses the example of being able to import graphics into a word-processing document, but the implications are much greater than can be realized on a stand-alone computer. Again, replace the inner communications with a network link, and OLE just might be the way to provide networked application-to-application communication in the DOS environment. When OLE was released with Windows 3.1, it did not support networks, but Microsoft says such support is coming.

# Client/Server Databases

The first application to take advantage of the client/server model is the database. A database is the warehouse of information that is vital on not only a corporate level, but also a personal level. By employing the client/server model, MIS can protect the corporate data as well as deliver access to this information to users.

The client/server database is a key piece of technology in *downsizing*, the process of moving applications from a mainframe down to a PC LAN (see Figure 9.6). As MIS's resources become more scarce and as the cost of PCs and PC LAN systems continues to drop in comparison with expensive mainframe and minicomputer systems, downsizing becomes an attractive option. In *upsizing*, a related trend, new mission-critical applications are being designed to run on a PC LAN, whereas in a nonnetworked computing model, they would have been developed to run on a minicomputer or mainframe. You can save your company significant money by reducing its reliance on expensive systems; however, you must carefully weigh the advantages, risks, and costs of moving to a new system.

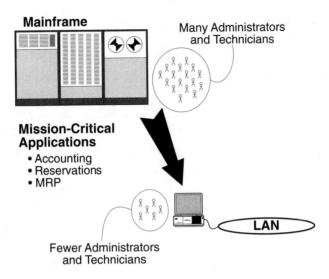

*Figure 9.6.*  *Downsizing.*

Although in some cases entire applications are moved from minicomputer to PC LANs and the minis are discarded, the more common form of downsizing is using the mainframe and mini in conjunction with the PC LAN. By creating a hierarchy of corporate and departmental databases using mainframe and PC servers, respectively, users get better performance and accessibility and the load on the mainframe is reduced. Developers benefit as well, because UNIX and PC-based databases offer a shorter development time for custom applications than do mainframe databases.

Not all database applications are suitable for the client/server model or downsizing (see Table 9.1). When the response-time requirements are real-time or near-real-time, such as in factory automation or financial arbitrage, a custom-designed or very finely tuned database is more appropriate. The client/server model is suitable for applications that require high-speed transactions such as airline ticketing or credit card verification, as well as for applications that need high-speed lookups and batch updates, such as point-of-sale systems and computer-aided design database systems. Client/server is appropriate also for applications that require moderate lookups and concurrent updates, such as order processing, inventory tracking, and telemarketing. It is critical that you choose the database architecture that best fits the needs of your business application. Do not install a client/server application simply because it is client/server. Install it only if it provides the best benefits for your business organization.

**Table 9.1.  When is client/server appropriate?**

| Application Type | Characteristics | Example |
|---|---|---|
| Custom-designed | Real-time or near-real-time response | Financial arbitrage<br>Factory automation |
| Client/server | High-speed transactions | Airline ticketing<br>Credit card verification |
|  | High-speed lookups or batch updates | Point-of-sale<br>Computer-aided design |
|  | Moderate lookups | Order processing<br>Inventory tracking<br>Telemarketing |
| File server | Slow to moderate lookups | Departmental or workgroup databases |

# Inside the Database Engine

A relational database engine may run on myriad platforms, ranging from the PC and DOS to the mainframe and VM. Regardless of the operating system and hardware the database may require, the basic principles remain the same. A back-end database, or database engine, protects the data and gives access to authorized users by way of the front-end application. The front end and back end communicate through a common language, usually SQL. The database engine must also maintain data integrity through concurrency control and disaster recovery techniques such as roll forward and roll back.

The easiest way to classify the various database engines is through the operating systems they require. Of the database engines based on multitasking, multiuser operating systems such as UNIX are best, although OS/2, as a multitasking operating system, provides a good second choice. Additionally, database applications that run as NetWare loadable modules are fast also because they run as part of the NetWare operating system. Table 9.2 lists some client/server database engines.

**Table 9.2. Database engines.**

| Operating System | Product |
| --- | --- |
| DOS | Gupta SQLBase<br>XDB Systems XDB Server |
| NetWare<br>(running as NetWare<br>loadable modules) | Novell NetWare SQL<br>OracleServer for NetWare<br>Gupta SQLBase<br>Informix Informix Online<br>XDB Systems XDB Server |
| OS/2 | IBM OS/2 Database Manager<br>OracleServer for OS/2<br>Microsoft SQL Server<br>Gupta SQLBase |
| UNIX | OracleServer for UNIX<br>Informix Informix Online<br>Sybase SQL Server<br>Ingres |

The following sections discuss the commonalities and principles involved in database engines, regardless of their core operating systems.

# SQL, the Structured Query Language

Essential to the client/server model is the Structured Query Language, or SQL (pronounced *sequel*). SQL is the common method of communication between the back end and the front end of a relational database. IBM invented SQL in the 1970s, and it has become the *de facto* standard for extracting information from relational databases. It has gained momentum among the PC LAN databases since 1987. Support for SQL is nearly a prerequisite for multiplatform relational database access.

SQL is nothing more than a query language. It governs the procedures of how to request information from a database. This English-like query language enables you to perform queries such as:

SELECT customers FROM customerdatabase WHERE state = NJ

SQL is a query language, not a procedural programming language, such as C. It cannot be used alone; it must be used in conjunction with a programming language.

SQL's power comes from its broad support within the database industry. Nearly every relational database manufacturer supports at least some form of SQL, providing at least the basis of a common platform from which users can access information and developers can write code. SQL is available for nearly every relational database platform, including those for the Macintosh, DOS, OS/2, UNIX, VM, MVS, VMS, and many more. The difficulty of using SQL is that it is not completely standard.

Database vendors use the basics of SQL, and then write extensions to make the language more powerful. Or, they implement only a portion of SQL. Both the American National Standards Institute and IBM have slightly different versions of SQL, although the SQL Access Group, a consortium of relational database vendors, is standardizing a single version of SQL.

In the world of Macintosh applications, SQL is not king; Apple's Data Access Language (DAL) reigns. DAL is based on SQL, but it provides far greater functionality. DAL is essential for client/server applications involving Macintoshes.

Whether the query language is SQL or DAL, the end user should be insulated from it. The front end should hide the operation and quirks of the query language. The user should see only the graphical interface, not the intricacies of the query. The query language is the facilitator between the front-end and the back-end database, and therefore should be the concern of the programmer. Unless the users are power users, they won't want to learn SQL. For the programmer and program designer, SQL offers a common way to access databases from different vendors.

# Ensuring Concurrency Control and Data Integrity

Controlling concurrent access to the data files is the database engine's first function. This is done through record locks, both exclusive and shared. In an *exclusive* lock, only one user can modify the record at hand. This is necessary for inserts, updates, and deletes. *Shared*, or *read-only*, locks are employed when a user wants just to read the data, not modify it in any way.

*Roll forward* is the capability to recover from major disasters such as disk head crashes or power failures. During roll forward, the administrator tells the database to read the entire transaction log and reexecute all the readable and complete transactions. The *transaction log*, or transaction *journal*, is a file that contains an audit trail of all transactions requested and written, thereby saving an image of the new and old states of the database. Transactions are written to this log before they are committed to the data file.

With roll forward, users do not have to reenter data in case of a system failure; however, the database can recover only as many transactions as were recorded in the previous backup. To minimize lost work, you may want to explore a higher level of fault tolerance, such as disk duplexing or disk arrays. The trade-off is that maintaining the transaction log is additional overhead on the system, but one that is necessary if the database will be used for a mission-critical or business-line function.

*Roll back* is the capability to abort a transaction before it has been committed. For example, if a user realizes that he is entering a stack of incorrect invoices, he may choose to abort or roll back the update, if the transaction has not yet been committed. Again, the roll back procedure uses the transaction log. Roll back and roll forward are essential features for a mission-critical database application. Many of the low-end database servers lack these capabilities.

The *two-phase commit protocol* is crucial in distributed databases. A *distributed database* is one in which there are not only many clients, but also many servers. (In the strict definition, a client/server database has many clients but only one server.) The multiple back ends must communicate with each other, mediating access to information and ensuring that their information remains up-to-date and synchronized. The two-phase commit protocol must be used because a transaction may involve updating more than one database table. In this case, record locking does not ensure the referential integrity of the multiple files.

In a two-phase commit protocol, a "coordinator" in the database sends out a request to all the nodes involved in a particular transaction. The coordinator says, "I am ready to commit the transaction I previously sent." If all the nodes respond, the transaction is committed. If some nodes don't respond, the transaction may not be committed, depending on the vendor's implementation of the protocol. Some databases won't commit a transaction if even one client does not respond; others will commit it if a majority of the nodes respond. Oracle 7.0 will include two-phase commit (see Figure 9.7). Two-phase commit is critical in ensuring the data integrity of multiple database servers on the same network. Evaluate how the database vendor has implemented this feature.

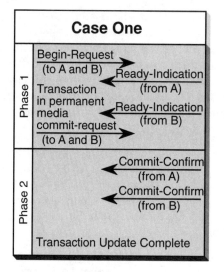
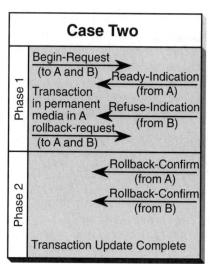

*Figure 9.7.  The two-phase commit protocol.*

When PC LAN database servers emerged in force in 1987, much ado was made about stored procedures and triggers. A *stored procedure* is a group of compiled SQL statements stored on the database server. Using precompiled SQL statements is faster because the server doesn't have to compile them on the fly. Other applications or a user can call a stored procedure. *Triggers*, on the other hand, are invoked automatically, and are akin to rules. They can be used to verify that a user's input matches the criteria set for that particular record. In reality, stored procedures and triggers are not widely used today.

Database engines may or may not physically reside on the same server as the file server. With powerful superservers such as Compaq's SystemPro and NetFrame's NetFrame, configuring the database server and the file server in separate machines may not be necessary, because the NOS and database applications can run on separate CPUs within the same box. Also, as database engines are being written to run as processes within the network operating system rather than as applications on top of the NOS, it becomes more efficient to run the database server application in the file server. Several database engines, including Oracle and XDB, are being written as NetWare loadable modules so that they run inside the NetWare operating system.

More important than where the database engine runs is the CPU power of the machine on which it runs. Consider fast 486 and 586 or RISC-based servers. Buy a server that is optimized for I/O. To provide users with fast performance, the server must also be rich in RAM. RAM is used for LAN communications buffers, the system kernel, the network operating system processes, and caching. The server must have also a large disk and the fastest network interface card you can afford.

# Database Routers

In addition to SQL, another key to communication between the front end and the back end is a database router. Departmental networks have the luxury of running a single network protocol and using a limited number of applications. In an enterprise-wide network, however, users are just as likely to need access to local resources as they are to need remote resources, the latter often running on a variety of hardware types.

If the database application runs across dissimilar platforms, a common transport foundation must be laid, and a database router often provides this foundation. For example, if users on a UNIX network want to access a DB2 database on an IBM mainframe with the same ease and simplicity they enjoy while accessing the Oracle database running on a UNIX host, the network will require software that bridges the differences in the database formats.

These database routers provide a common transport layer interface, in addition to the hooks to connect the database to the particular transport mechanism. For large-scale databases, common transports are TCP/IP and Advanced Peer-to-Peer Networking (APPN), IBM's protocol for peer-to-peer access in SNA, ranging from mainframes to PCs. Although these products facilitate the connection, they often are very slow and are tied to a single transport protocol.

A number of database vendors and third-party developers offer these routers. IBM's OS/2 CICS, Oracle's SQL*Net, Gupta's SQLNetwork, and Micro Decisionware's Database Gateway support mainframe peer-to-peer communication for OS/2 Database Manager, SQLBase, and SQL Server, respectively.

# Database Front-End Applications

Because the client/server model dictates that clients do not know or care who the server is, and vice versa, front-end applications can be divorced from the back end. For example, a spreadsheet may act as a front end to a database engine, as Excel can do with SQL Server. Or, a front end may be a mail application that interfaces with a database of mailing and directory information.

Database front ends come in three varieties—query and reporting tools, data-access and -manipulation tools, and application development environments. Table 9.3 lists some popular database front ends.

**Table 9.3.  Some database front ends.**

*Decision Support Tools*

| | |
|---|---|
| Borland | Paradox SQL Link |
| Concentric Data Systems | R&R Report Writer |
| DataWiz | Capture |
| Gupta Technologies | Quest |
| Pioneer Software | Q+E |
| Channel Computing | Forest & Trees |
| Microsoft | Excel |
| Oracle | OracleCard |

*Development Environments*

| | |
|---|---|
| Advanced Business Microsystems | Platinum Toolkit |
| Blyth Software | Omnis |
| DataEase | DataEase SQL |
| Datawiz | DBSQL |
| Datawiz | SQL Server Toolkits |
| Gupta Technologies | SQLWindows |
| Information Builders | PC Focus |
| JYACC | JAM |
| JYACC | JAM/DBI |
| Matesys | ObjectView |
| Novell | Xtrieve Plus |
| Oracle | OracleTools |
| Progress Software | LAN Progress |
| Software Publishing | InfoAlliance |
| Vinzant | SQLFile |

# Query and Reporting Tools

Query tools provide the simplest (and most limited) access to SQL databases. Designed to be used by typical business users, query tools require no programming skills and minimal database expertise. These applications act essentially as an intermediary between the user and the database so that the user doesn't have to understand SQL or the ways of the particular database engine.

Such query tools are not suitable for building business-line applications such as inventory control; however, they are acceptable for enabling users to query databases and extract reports and information on the fly. Using an off-the-shelf query tool relieves the user from the task of creating many database reports. Using a query tool, users can simply point and click with a mouse to find information or generate reports. Behind the scenes, the query tool translates the point-and-click query into SQL, manages the communication with the database back end, returns the answer, and displays the results for the user.

Critics say that it is unwise to give end users such tools, because they could make nonsensical queries or, in the worst case, corrupt data; however, query tools are one way to open up the access to database servers and enable users to start experimenting. Unless users are able to try client/server technology, it will remain a technology and never become a solution.

Users may use a query tool to get the information from a database and then set up DDE links or use the clipboard to cut and paste information into a Windows or OS/2 application. Generally, users can use query tools to browse, insert, update, and delete records in different SQL databases without having to understand or master the syntax of SQL. For example, users can use the same query tool to access OracleServer, SQL Server, and DB2. The degree to which these products insulate the users from SQL varies with each tool. For example, Pioneer Software's Q+E is designed for simpler queries than is Gupta Technologies' Quest; unlike Quest, however, Q+E offers real-time access to both SQL and non-SQL databases. Often, these tools help you to expand your queries beyond SQL by enabling you to import data from ASCII or flat-file database formats. When purchasing query tools, consider their flexibility and ease of use, as well as their support for multiple back ends. Generally, unsophisticated users will use these query tools.

# Decision Support Tools

The personal computer has always excelled at helping people with decision support. Empowered with a spreadsheet, you can calculate the variances of a particular equation. Armed with a graphics program, you can view statistics in a graphical manner, making numbers easier to digest. In its role as a front end to a database engine, the personal computer remains a powerful decision support tool.

Decision support applications enable users to pull data from various sources, perhaps running on dissimilar computers in distant locations (see Figure 9.8). Users import data into a decision support application and then analyze the information using their familiar applications. Whereas a query tool is designed to report and display data, a decision support front end is designed to enable you to manipulate it.

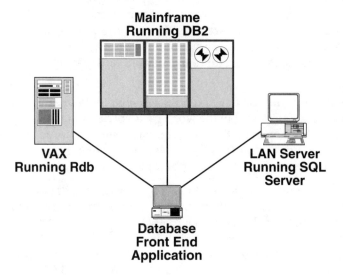

**Figure 9.8.** *One front end, many engines.*

For example, an engineer at an oil refinery may use Windows, SQL, and a small "glue" application to gain information from process control equipment, gauging the current levels of oil pumped and processed. The same engineer may also use Windows and an SQL application to extract from UNIX-based database servers historical information about oil pumped and processed.

A decision support application enables users to extract useful information from the vast amounts of data available without having to understand the details of retrieving it.

# Application Development Environments

The traditional flat-file database providers are changing their applications to fit the client/server model. These non-SQL databases can be used as front ends to database engines, including Borland's Paradox, DataEase International's DataEase, and Revelation Technology's Advanced Revelation. These applications are designed for the traditional insert-modify-delete database operation, and they can be used to create powerful programs for business functions, including inventory, personnel, and accounting. Unlike the query- or data-manipulation tools, these environments are intended to accomplish a business function rather than to help an executive or sales manager better understand the data at hand.

The newest crop of application development environments are easier to use, facilitating the growth of client/server and removing one of the stumbling blocks to the advent of client/server applications. Generally, these tools manage the interface for you, but you still do the database programming and create the relations among the tables. These tools provide screen-painting facilities, making it easier to create user screens that include GUI elements, such as dialog boxes, radio buttons, and icons—without having to write the screen handling or GUI code yourself. These applications' second job is to react to user input. When a user clicks an icon, the tools provide high-level commands and interfaces to 3GLs so that some action can be taken. A single high-level command can substitute for many lines of standard 3GL code.

# What's Stopping Client/Server's Progress?

The computer industry has been discussing the PC LAN client/server model since at least 1987, yet the architecture has not come to fruition. If client/server is truly the model for networked computing, why has it been so slow in coming? One by one, the roadblocks that have slowed the progress of client/server are being removed. New difficulties may manifest themselves, or existing ones may not be cleared within the time frame that MIS professionals will consider client/server a relevant architecture. Today, the database engine tools are available, but the applications—inventory, accounting, and personnel management—are only beginning to take advantage of them.

The first problem was underestimating the job. When database vendors first announced database engines, they promised that porting applications from the file server-based model would be simple and easy, requiring only a few months' labor. That statement turned out to be untrue. When products finally were shipped, they didn't always work properly. For example, the first version of dBASE that supported SQL returned different answers when using the same query. Implementing the client/server model required developers to completely rearchitect their applications. The last thing developers want to do is throw out their existing code base and start over. Even if developers are forced to rebuild their applications from the ground up, it takes time—several years, in fact—to learn and implement the new architecture.

For a long time, the lack of tools thwarted client/server's progress. Beyond programming in a 3GL such as C or COBOL, few tools existed to help developers port their applications more easily. Remote procedure call (RPC) tools helped to a degree, but they are useful primarily for operating system-level products rather than for applications. RPC tools enable developers to write a common core of code and then compile it to work with different network protocols. In this way, a developer can use the same code for an inventory-control system that runs on VMS, UNIX, and DOS, each time recompiling it for the appropriate network protocols: DECnet, TCP/IP, and NetWare's IPX. (For more information about RPCs, see Chapter 8, "Standards and Interoperability.") Today, more application development environments are available that deliver what programmers need and want: more power, less programming, support for more databases, and support for Windows.

Another problem is that complex business applications must be customized. Every business is unique, and its applications reflect its own approach to business. Although every company must maintain inventory, track accounting data, and provide an executive information system, each does so in its own way. Consequently, a company's applications must be customized, and customized applications are more expensive to create and deploy. As these business-line applications, which typically have run on UNIX or mainframe hosts, are being downsized, many are moving to a client/server architecture.

Another impediment is a lack of expertise, which is closely tied to the need to customize applications. In addition to having to understand the client/server architecture as well as SQL, a 3GL, and a graphical user interface, the programmer or systems integrator must understand also the company's business. It's a tall order, indeed, to expect a few individuals to be able to accomplish this expertise across a wide range of platforms. In building your team of developers, you will need to include applications and communications programmers, as well as LAN and mainframe experts. And don't forget the business managers.

Slowly these roadblocks are being removed, but a lack of integration expertise still hampers client/server's progress. Value-added resellers and even some systems integrators don't really integrate systems; they resell hardware, adding little value to the applications. Minimal expertise exists to integrate the various hardware platforms, software environments, and business functions into a seamless enterprise-wide network. This should come from the integration channel, but, to date, it has not.

# Electronic Mail

Electronic mail is the most widely used network application. VenCom, a San Francisco venture capital firm specializing in communications, estimated that by 1992, 35 percent—or 95 million—of all LAN users would be using LAN E-mail. As more users migrate to LAN-based and enterprise-wide E-mail, host-based messaging systems will decline (see Figure 9.9). LAN-based E-mail will become more powerful, providing the infrastructure for the next decade of applications. Consider E-mail's role in your enterprise-wide network.

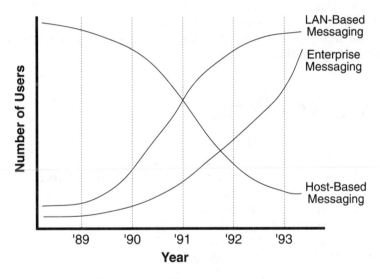

*Figure 9.9.* *Trends in electronic messaging.*

Even in its simplest incarnation, E-mail speeds communication, acting as the transport for quickly and efficiently disseminating information. By using E-mail, users find it faster and easier to file status reports, send and read memos, calculate and retrieve daily sales figures, and toss around ideas among coworkers. E-mail enables users to think about and compose their messages "off-line" and respond to others in the same way. Companies often install a network just to reap the benefits of E-mail.

Still, E-mail is not a cure-all. It has not created the paperless office, nor has it eliminated those boring memos your boss sends. Also, it creates work. Users must manage their mailboxes, by deleting, forwarding, and archiving messages. In a large company, the daily inrush of E-mail can approximate your home mailbox at Christmas—filled with junk mail and items for sale. Or, imagine taking a two-week vacation to Hawaii: When you return, your E-mail in-box is overflowing with old messages. Your tan could begin to fade while you're still sorting through the messages. Without E-mail housekeeping help, workers soon find that E-mail's immediate productivity gain becomes a loss.

E-mail remains a critical application, serving as the foundation for many other applications to come. Today, E-mail is changing. Vendors are rewriting their E-mail applications to fit within the client/server model, and are preparing the way for enterprise-wide communication as well as the next generation of mail-enabled applications.

## LAN-Based E-mail

Users see and interact with the user agents, or the portions of the E-mail that sit on their desktop computers. The user agent is the central E-mail command. From their desktops, users manage their E-mail: sending, receiving, and forwarding messages; building personal mailing lists; and accessing public mailing lists. An E-mail package suitable for an enterprise-wide network should cover the entire range of desktop systems, including DOS, Windows, OS/2, Mac, and UNIX. In this way, users have an interface they are familiar with, and the help desk has a single feature set to support.

E-mail deals best with text messages, but it also enables users to enclose text files and graphics files within a message. Because some E-mail packages include fax capabilities (or work with another vendor's fax server), users can send and receive faxes from their desks. Another key feature of the user agent is security; many packages encrypt messages, and nearly all support passwords. In the future, user agents will be better equipped to handle images and sound files.

In the PC LAN world, most E-mail systems use the MHS E-mail protocol; in the international or heterogeneous computing world, E-mail systems generally employ OSI's *X.400 store-and-forward messaging protocol*. MHS, or the Message Handling Service, was developed by Action Technologies and is used by Novell in its message-handling system. In early 1991, Novell purchased MHS outright, making it the core of its messaging engine, which will run as a NetWare loadable module within the network operating system. Banyan already includes StreetTalk and VINESmail as part of its network operating system. X.400 is the OSI standard for directory services, and will be the platform of choice for heterogeneous or global computer networks.

# E-mail for the Enterprise-Wide Network

Enterprise E-mail can be divided into user agents, mail services, gateways, and directory services.

- *User agents* provide message preparation, reception, and submission facilities. Users interact with this component.

- *Mail services* include reliable message transmission and message storage.

- *Gateways* provide connectivity between dissimilar E-mail systems, such as the Mac and a mainframe.

- *Directory services* provide a global "white pages" or address book of users' mail addresses and locations.

E-mail confined to a single office is inherently restricting. Users need to communicate with coworkers in other offices and even with people in other companies. A single-location E-mail cannot meet this challenge, but enterprise E-mail can. Gateways, directory services, and X.400 support are important in building an enterprise messaging system.

Although enterprise E-mail packages should support a wide range of desktop operating systems, not all E-mail systems do. Minicomputer and mainframe users have been using messaging for more than 10 years, and their users are firmly entrenched. Many different E-mail systems exist, and few are clear leaders. Most companies use a variety of E-mail systems, and the challenge lies in determining how to integrate them into one system, or in deciding whether integrating them is even the wisest choice. To build an enterprise messaging system, host-based messaging systems must be connected to PC LAN messaging systems, and the public messaging services also must be tied together in such a way that individual users are unaware that they are communicating with users of a different system.

*E-mail gateways* have the onerous and thankless task of tying together the many E-mail systems in use. This job isn't a trivial one, considering the large number of different E-mail applications used on different host and PC systems (see Table 9.4).

**Table 9.4.   Popular E-mail systems in use.**

| Host System | Messaging System |
| --- | --- |
| Mainframe | IBM SNADS |
| | IBM PROFS |
| | IBM DISOSS |
| Minicomputer | DEC VMSmail |
| | DEC All-in-One |
| | TCP/IP SMTP |
| | UNIX UUCP |
| | Wang WangOffice |
| | Hewlett-Packard HP Desk |
| PC LAN | Lotus cc:Mail |
| | Microsoft Mail |
| | Da Vinci eMail |
| | AT&T PMX Starmail |
| | Hewlett-Packard OpenMail |
| | CE Software QuickMail |
| | Banyan VINESmail |
| Public services | MCI Mail |
| | GEnie |
| | AT&T Mail |
| | CompuServe |

# Auditing Mail Systems and Planning System Requirements

Before you decide which type of messaging and gateway architecture best fits your company's structure, you must perform a mail audit, requirements analysis, and benefits study, just as you did in building the hardware infrastructure of the enterprise-wide network (see Chapter 2). Build a business model of the E-mail system, then a technology model, and then a physical model. Here are some steps you must take:

## Audit the Existing Mail Systems

First, you must audit the existing mail systems.

- What systems and protocols are being used? For instance, what do the VAX, HP, IBM mainframe, and PC LAN users use?

- To what locations is E-mail sent, both local and remote?

- What is the current volume of E-mail sent and received?

- What types of messages are sent? For instance, do messages consist of text, graphics, enclosed files, images, fax, or telex?

- What security procedures are in place or should be implemented? What is the password scheme? Do you need encryption?

- What are the uptime requirements?

- How will E-mail be charged out to the users? Will it be charged per message or on a flat-fee basis?

- What are the requirements and limitations of the E-mail administration staff?

- What are the shortcomings of the existing systems? For instance, in a PC LAN, is there Mac support? Is the functionality limited? Is the user interface difficult to learn?

## Plan the Systems Requirements

Next, you plan the requirements of the system.

1. Form a committee of business managers, key end users, departmental LAN managers, and MIS managers to identify the requirements for the E-mail system.

2. Evaluate the status of the existing E-mail systems and consider how they can be improved.

3. Determine your system requirements to assess the complexity of the E-mail system.

4. Determine which departments and users need to communicate with each other and whether they are using compatible E-mail systems.

5. Calculate how much you expect the use of the E-mail system to increase with the new network.

6. Determine what new types of file enclosures you expect users to want.

7. Decide whether your E-mail system can be constructed from off-the-shelf products or whether system integration is required.

# Enterprise E-mail Architectures

If your enterprise-wide network, like most other ones, contains a startling variety of E-mail systems, gateways are necessary to link the dissimilar systems. There are three types of gateways: point-to-point, backbone, and X.400. Which gateway is most effective changes as the number of users, the complexity, and the geographic dispersion increases. Point-to-point is suitable in the simplest networks, and X.400 is best for the most complex networks.

■ *Point-to-point* systems are effective when the network is relatively simple, even if it has a large number of users. In a point-to-point E-mail system, you "connect the dots" of your company's locations (see Figure 9.10).

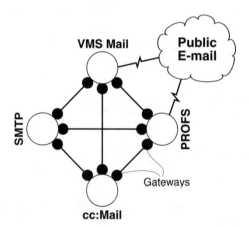

*Figure 9.10.* *Point-to-point E-mail architecture.*

The drawback of point-to-point gateways is that they do not scale effectively into the enterprise. As in building a mesh enterprise-wide network, the cost of connection is $2^n$. For example, connecting three systems requires three links, and connecting four systems requires six links. A point-to-point solution becomes expensive as the number of sites increases, not only in terms of communications and equipment costs, but also in administrative costs.

■ If your company's needs outstrip the benefits offered by a point-to-point solution, consider a backbone architecture. A *backbone* solution, such as that offered by SoftSwitch's SoftSwitch Central or OSI's X.400, provides a networked backbone message switch in a mainframe host environment. Here, a centralized mainframe E-mail server delivers connectivity among the host-based, LAN-based, and public E-mail services (see Figure 9.11). This type of gateway can deliver fax, telex, and X.400 services. Essentially, the backbone acts as a central post office, in much the same way as the United States Postal Service has regionalized its sorting and routing centers.

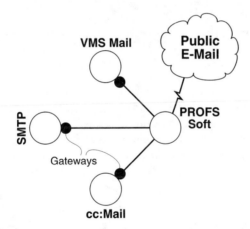

*Figure 9.11.* *Backbone architecture.*

With the backbone switch approach, you still need a gateway to each location; however, the centralized server provides a single point of communication, creating a star-based E-mail network. For example, if you have four locations, you need four SoftSwitch Central gateways in addition to the SoftSwitch Central switch. As the E-mail network grows, the backbone approach requires fewer connections and less equipment than the point-to-point approach, but it makes sense only if you already have a VM or MVS mainframe.

- *X.400* is another option, primarily for companies with tens of thousands of users, a variety of mail platforms, multiple large campuses, and multinational business. As with the SoftSwitch Central architecture, there is a central post office, but the remote sites either use native X.400 or have gateways into the system (see Figure 9.12).

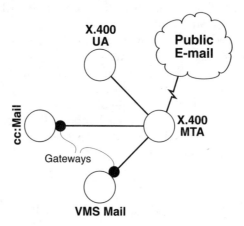

*Figure 9.12.* *X.400 architecture.*

X.400 is OSI's standard for store-and-forward electronic messaging. It has international recognition, making it the mail protocol of choice to connect multinational businesses. (For more information on the specifics of the X.400 protocol, see Chapter 8, "Standards and Interoperability," which discusses the OSI protocols.)

Whatever the architecture, the goal is to provide the same level of service on either side of the gateway—a lofty goal. Gateways that offer high performance tend to offer less-than-transparent services, and gateways that offer nearly transparent services often require tremendous amounts of processing power.

## X.400, the International Messaging Standard

No single mail system can run over every platform in existence. Even if it did, taking away users' familiar E-mail systems would decrease productivity as users learned a new package. One solution to the myriad E-mail systems and protocols is an international truce—X.400. ISO's solution for store-and-forward messaging is the X.400 Message Handling System (MHS). X.400 also has the distinction of being the most widely accepted OSI protocol, largely because it's the only one that delivers an immediate and unique solution to a wide-ranging problem.

X.400 can be used to build a bridge of sorts between users' dissimilar mail systems. For example, All-In-One users can continue with their familiar messaging system, Mac users can use their favorite package, and NetWare users can use their packages. With X.400, however, these groups of users also can exchange mail with each other. X.400 is emerging largely as a gateway technology. Few E-mail packages used in the United States are implemented as native X.400. In Europe, however, X.400 end-user applications are far more prevalent.

X.400 defines a user agent (UA) and a message transfer agent (MTA) (see Figure 9.13). The user interacts with the UA, or "mailbox." The UA handles for the user the chores of message preparation, submission, and reception. It also provides text editing, presentation services, security, message prioritizing, and delivery notification. Because the UA is an interface rather than an end-user application, it does not define the specifics of how it interacts with the user. That is left to the E-mail product developer.

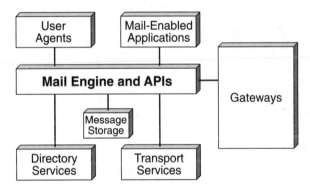

*Figure 9.13.*   *The client/server E-mail architecture.*

The MTA routes and relays the electronic message. Its responsibilities include the store-and-forward path, channel security, and routing the message through the communications media. The message store (MS) provides message storage, submission, and retrieval functions, and supplements the UA for devices that are not always available, such as PCs or terminals. The access units (AUs) provide connections to other types of communications systems, such as telex services and postal services.

# Directory Services

If you need a telephone number and it isn't in your personal address book, you can dial the area code plus 555-1212, and the telephone company will provide the number, if the person you want to call is listed in the phone book. The telephone company has made it easy to get the numbers of its subscribers. There's no equivalent service for computer networks. Learning a person's E-mail address requires a telephone call to that person or reading the address from previous E-mail. Compound this inconvenience with the fact that typical users have several addresses, including phone, fax, telex, local E-mail, public mail, UNIX mail, and perhaps X.400 mail.

Finding mail addresses is comparatively simple if the people are in your same location; it's a little more difficult if they're located in another of your company's offices. The problem intensifies when people work for another company or are located abroad.

Network-wide directory services can resolve the E-mail addressing problem; however, much development work needs to occur. Directory services will be solved on a national and international level, but any project of this magnitude progresses slowly. On the global level, messaging directories will be built around X.500, the OSI standard for directory services. The OSI is still developing the X.500 standard, however.

X.500 directory service enables applications and other objects to exchange information. The X.500 structure is similar to the X.400 structure in that it is hierarchical and capable of scaling to the very largest networks. Its greatest benefit—its scale—also makes developing the system a long, slow, and complex process.

In an X.500 system, directory information is stored in a directory information base (DIB). Directory user agents (DUAs) access the information stored in the DIB. The DUA is an applications process rather than an end-user product. A DIB is hierarchical and made up of entries and objects. Each *entry* is a collection of information about one *object*, such as a user, hardware, or an application. Because the DIB permits *aliasing*, an object name can have alternative names. Aliasing is important, for example, for logical and physical addressing, which simplifies resource identification.

X.500 is designed to be a distributed directory service. To ensure that a directory can be distributed, the directory system agent (DSA) provides access to the DIB from or to other DSAs. To satisfy a request, the DSA may work with other DSAs. A directory management domain (DMD) administers the directory, and it is a set of one or more DSAs and zero or more DUAs. The DMD may be a country, PTT, or anything designed to manage the DIB.

One challenge is that the multiple copies of a directory must remain synchronized. In a centralized mail server, synchronization is done by keeping "shadow" copies of a particular E-mail directory on the host. After changes are uploaded from the local E-mail to the copy of the directory on the host, the host disseminates the changes to the other local E-mail directory systems.

If you must assemble a multivendor, enterprise-wide directory service today, you likely will end up patching together your own. The X.500 specification is still under development, and few commercial solutions exist today. Your most viable solution is to manually propagate the changes to the address database. Expect to see great strides made in directory services in the next two years.

# Mail-Enabled Applications

E-mail, despite its many advantages, is inherently limiting. Although it can enable communication in an entire company, it is restricted in the types of information it can handle. Although E-mail handles text messages well, and can even handle graphics files, it does nothing for video frames or sound. E-mail does little, if anything, to help users *manage* the flow of their messages or automate their work. Additional functionality is needed, and is coming.

E-mail provides the foundation for the next generation of network applications. Networks provide the physical infrastructure for information sharing; databases provide the warehouse of information; and E-mail provides the distribution of this information.

To better distribute this information in an enterprise-wide network, E-mail is being rearchitected according to the client/server model. Instead of existing as one chunk of code, E-mail is being modularized into portions, including end-user interfaces, mail handling, directory services, and so on, thereby enabling mail to become the platform of many new applications (see Figure 9.14). Developing these mail-enabled applications may take five more years, just as it took three to five years to move from the stand-alone, network-ignorant application to the networked, client/server database application. The rewards will be great, however.

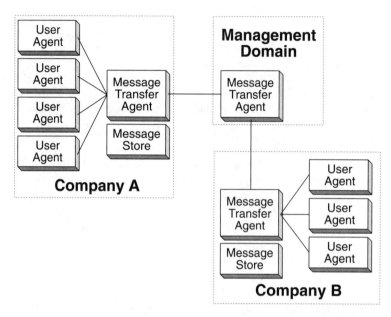

**Figure 9.14.** *X.400 messaging.*

As with client/server databases, separating the front end from the back end enables developers to concentrate on what they do best: the back-end engine or the front-end interface. After developers get up to speed on the intricacies of client/server E-mail, this division of labor will produce better applications in less time. Front-end developers can concentrate on writing their front ends, whether they are scheduling, mail management, workflow management, or others. The companies developing the mail engines can concentrate their efforts on better directory services, transport services, and X.400 support, for example.

Users will benefit because they will be able to mix and match their E-mail systems and applications. For example, users may be able to mix and match their directory services, user agents, message transports, and mail engines from different vendors. Then they can add applications, such as workflow management, on top. In the future, an end-user company may purchase an MHS E-mail engine and Mac, UNIX, and Windows user interfaces from Vendor A, buy a gateway to X.400 and PROFS from Vendor B, and purchase workflow applications from Vendors C and D. This mix-and-match service will become available only when mail vendors move to the client/server architecture and then publish their engines' APIs so that third-party developers can write these applications.

Such a utopian E-mail world is still in the future. Engine providers must deliver better services. Standards must be established. Most important, however, programmers must gain experience with the client/server model, E-mail, and graphical user interfaces. Developing client/server mail applications is even more troublesome than developing client/server databases. It requires everything the database application requires, in addition to mail-specific features and also communications.

Engines are based around either Novell's MHS or OSI's X.400. The mail engine providers are changing the architecture of their E-mail systems. Lotus, with its cc:Mail (formerly cc:Mail, Inc.), and Microsoft, with its Mail (formerly Network Courier from Consumers Software), are redoing their architectures to follow a client/server model. Da Vinci Systems, which runs DaVinci eMail on an MHS engine, has built its latest release from scratch to be client/server.

Application programming interfaces (APIs) enable third-party developers to write add-on applications that take advantage of the E-mail engines. APIs are essential to the development of client/server applications. By writing to different APIs, a provider of E-mail front ends can write applications for the different back ends. For example, Beyond's BeyondMail is a front-end E-mail package that uses an MHS engine. The problem here is a lack of standardization for mail APIs.

# Workflow Automation Software

Workflow software is an exciting area because it promises to bring automation to the white collar "information" worker. Whereas spreadsheets and word processors automate the processes of crunching numbers and words, no application helps users manage their information. Workflow automation, sometimes nebulously called *groupware*, is part of this attempt.

Work is routed in three ways: paper, shared database, and electronic mail. Paper is the most predominant. More and more information is generated electronically, but it still is printed and circulated in its paper incarnation. Many businesses still rely on the hard-copy paper version for the document to be considered authentic or valid.

Work can be routed through a shared database, such as with the so-called groupware products, including AT&T's Rhapsody and NCR's Coordination.

Rather than advance to the next stage of applications, these products are more similar to their integrated host E-mail predecessors, such as All-in-One and HP Desk. In many cases, these groupware applications are several other applications—E-mail, database, calendaring, or scheduling—tied together with more or less elegance, depending on the implementation. Shared databases enable users to congregate their information in a central location, but they do nothing to help users manage or route that information.

Electronic mail is the simplest form of workflow automation. Electronic mail, although very powerful, can handle only text messages and sometimes graphics. It cannot handle forms or compound documents. It can only broadcast a message—it cannot specifically route a message from user to user; users themselves must have the genetic intelligence to figure out how to route the message.

Workflow software doesn't leave it to the user to know how to route a message, and who to route it to, because the application has that intelligence built in. Embody a mail application with intelligence, and it can route objects from one user to another, from an application to a user, and between applications. Objects may be a variety of things, from forms to compound documents. In their travels, objects may be created on one type of end-user workstation and displayed on another.

Such applications will enable forms to be part of the standard E-mail document menu so that purchase orders and invoices can be sent electronically. Although today this sending can be done with expensive electronic data interchange software and costly mainframes, in the future such application-to-application communication will be done with inexpensive, standards-based networking products.

Workflow automation software will enable people to think of projects as units, not as disjointed efforts. All work—such as data files, application programs, and messages—that belong to a certain project will be grouped together. For example, one person's responsibilities in sales and marketing will be grouped together, including E-mail messages, spreadsheet files, and contact-management software. The person's budgeting responsibilities will be contained in another project grouping, or "desktop." In this way, a user calculating sales forecasts no longer will have to know the specifics of loading up the spreadsheet application (the application name and drive location) and finding the data (the files containing the 1992 budget projections), but can simply click an icon for the 1992 sales projections.

Workflow applications include Reach Software's MailMan, Beyond's BeyondMail, and Lotus Notes.

# Desktop Videoconferencing

Today, holding a videoconference from your desktop is something you find only in the pages of science fiction or in the conference rooms of the richest companies. Affordable, standards-based videoconferencing is not yet a reality, but it is coming. With the advent of desktop videoconferencing, executives won't have to get on airplanes to travel to a meeting; they can simply set up a conference over a network, whether public or private. They gain the advantages of a face-to-face meeting, including developing a working relationship with other participants and seeing their body language, but they reduce travel time and increase productive time. With desktop videoconferencing, you can meet without leaving your seat.

Desktop videoconferencing is just one multimedia application. Other applications of video on networks include multimedia mail and documents, course authoring, audio and video editing, surveillance, and television on the screen.

Desktop videoconferencing adds video and audio to a workstation, thereby reintegrating the various forms of communication—word, sound, and picture—that have been disjointed by computers, telephones, and distance. Although desktop videoconferencing exists primarily in the labs, with the emerging video and audio standards, more powerful RISC-based workstations, and high-speed FDDI fiber-optic networks, desktop videoconferencing can move into the conference room (see Figure 9.15).

Building a feasible, affordable desktop videoconferencing application requires product designers to reduce the bandwidth consumed by the video, voice, and data so that it fits within the network's available bandwidth; handle the bursty traffic loads typified by compressed data; and enable conversations among the conference members.

First, to support audio and video, a workstation must easily handle large amounts of data. Video files are huge: An uncompressed 10-minute video clip consumes 22 gigabytes of storage, and voice-grade audio eats another 5 megabytes of storage. Storing such gargantuan files on workstations isn't feasible (and transmitting them over a network is unrealistic). Compression algorithms can reduce the file sizes. Vendors are developing compression chips that use a variety of data-reduction techniques. Three compression algorithms are competing for ANSI standardization: ISO's Joint Photographic Experts Group (JPEG), Motion Picture Experts Group (MPEG), and the CCITT's Px64 standard.

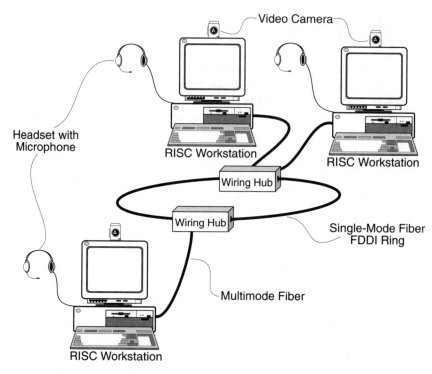

*Figure 9.15.* *Desktop videoconferencing with FDDI.*

But compression chips are not enough. For instance, JPEG-style compression reduces a 10-minute video clip to a file requiring 73 megabytes of storage. At this 30-to-1 compression rate, the video quality is expected to be comparable to the original. Seventy-three megabytes per file is still unwieldy and impractical. Video digital signal processors or programmable compression chips will offer vendors more flexibility to choose quality levels.

A key component in desktop videoconferencing is FDDI, the ANSI standard for a 100Mbps fiber-optic network. FDDI delivers the bandwidth needed for such an application. Filling an entire 1280 × 1024 true-color workstation screen, however, requires data compression, because FDDI's available bandwidth is limited to 100Mbps. FDDI, as a LAN protocol, is particularly well-suited to desktop video conferencing when the size of video frames ranges from 20 to 80 kilobytes.

Remember that because videoconferencing is an *n*-way conversation, the bandwidth requirements increase as the number of participants increases. When conferences increase beyond two people, multicast packets can be used so that bandwidth requirements do not increase linearly. Using multicast addressing, adding a third person to a conference increases the bandwidth required by only 50 percent. In this way, a three-way teleconference at 30 frames per second consumes 28.2Mbps of FDDI bandwidth (using the JPEG algorithm), whereas a two-way conference requires 18.8Mbps of bandwidth.

Videoconferencing isn't going to be cheap. Desktop machines will approximate a 25-MIPS RISC workstation with 32 megabytes of memory, a 1-gigabyte disk drive, an audio capture and playback board, a 1280 × 1024 × 24 graphics frame buffer that also can digitize standard video, an FDDI controller, a 1280 × 1024 resolution color display, and a video camera, microphone, and headset.

Today, standards-based desktop videoconferencing exists only in labs. Even then, it is limited to local area networks rather than wide area networks, because today's wide area network services simply cannot handle the bandwidth requirements. Desktop videoconferencing and other multimedia applications, however, will fully exploit what a network can do for the business and home user.

# The Challenge Ahead

Client/server applications—databases, electronic mail, accounting, project management, workflow—offer a new age of network-enabled applications. These applications will bring automation to the white-collar worker, in much the same way the spreadsheet and word processor brought freedom in the 1980s to those who handle figures and letters.

The path to network-enabled applications isn't clear. Client/server databases are five years in the making, and they are just beginning to bear fruit today. Building client/server electronic-mail systems is even more difficult because they include all of the challenges of creating database engines, and the added complexity of communications.

Network-enabled applications are not screen savers, or word processors, or even departmental E-mail. These applications run the core of your business—inventory, invoicing, and materials requirements planning. Such applications cannot "sort of" work, or sometimes work, as has been the norm with PC LAN applications. They must work completely and perfectly all of the time (or they must work at least as well as mainframe applications work).

Deploying a network-intrinsic application takes expertise. Systems integrators, the traditional outside source of computer expertise, regularly fail when it comes to understanding their clients' businesses. The business-line manager and the MIS department are left to bring that understanding to the systems integrator, but the business manager lacks the technical expertise, and the in-house MIS person often lacks the breadth of experience that the systems integrator possesses. For network-intrinsic applications to become a reality, these groups must work together, and working in a team is never easy.

The rewards of network-intrinsic applications are great, but so are the risks.

# Choosing the Network's Applications

Users don't care whether you bought cisco or Wellfleet routers. They don't want to know if the enterprise-wide network uses frame relay or T-3. They don't want to hear the details of the Simple Network Management Protocol. But let a server fail or allow a T-1 line to go down, and the users care. They call to complain that they can't get to Excel, Oracle, and WordPerfect, and they have a huge presentation due tomorrow.

Network applications are evolving. Sure, users can run networked word processors and spreadsheets, but the true network application will provide a new level of utility and enable a new way of working. When designing and choosing the applications for the enterprise-wide network, consider how the work flows within your company. It's probably designed around routing paper, but imagine how the business could function if the workflow were based around electronic access to and routing of information. Automating an inefficient, paper-based system will result in an inefficient automated system. Client/server can deliver a new way of working.

The client/server architecture affords a greater application flexibility than the earlier master-slave architectures. Within a network context, client/server provides better performance than stand-alone applications run on a server. Data can be protected and stored in back-end applications such as databases. Front-end applications—ranging from electronic mail to query tools to phone books—can access the different back ends. These back ends can reside anywhere on the enterprise-wide network. Carefully approach the integration of client-server applications into your network. Such applications are new and few people are experienced in designing, building, and managing them.

Enter the next generation of applications: workflow, image processing, videoconferencing, and multimedia. IBM, Apple, Microsoft, and Intel are just some of the companies that are pushing multimedia applications. Although the sheer weight of a manufacturer can't force users to purchase products (as OS/2 and ISDN have proven), multimedia applications will become available over the next few years. Such applications will require a great deal more bandwidth than is supplied by Token Ring and Ethernet. Many advances will occur, including compression, that will allow these applications to be run over existing networks. Also consider moving to a higher-speed network such as 100Mbps FDDI.

# Network Management: Organizational and Practical

*Objectives:*

1. To explore the organizational and physical aspects of network management.

2. To discuss the different strategic approaches, including centralized and decentralized approaches, and the tools of network management, including the enterprise-wide network managers and the Simple Network Management Protocol.

3. To discuss disaster recovery.

# Defining Network Management

Network management is in a crisis. Corporations are building expansive networks and connecting every computer in every location, but they can't quite manage the network with the finesse and control required in an enterprise-wide network. A general lack of experience in managing enterprise-wide networks is the first problem. What's the best strategy, companies wonder. Then, the tools are still limited in function. If corporations are going to rely on their networks, the tools and strategies for managing their computing utilities must improve.

Even the definition of network management is not concrete. The term is bandied about quite loosely, and can mean anything from users managing with Norton Utilities the files on their local hard drives to MIS administering multiple mainframes by way of IBM's NetView. In the strictest sense, network management is the job of keeping the network running. It involves the operation and maintenance of the network components, including the physical cable plant, wiring concentrators, bridges, routers, and gateways.

Types of network management as defined by ISO include configuration, fault, performance, security, and accounting.

*Configuration and name management* is the configuration of the network components, such as network operating system parameters, router paths, and bridge address forwarding tables. It is used to identify and control objects so that they can be initialized, operated, and controlled. Configuration management is used also for naming objects.

*Fault management* involves detecting, defining, and resolving network problems, and is necessary to guarantee the operation of the network. This type of management includes tracing problems through the system, performing diagnostics, and correcting errors.

Problem management, a critical function related to fault management, defines such things as help desk functions, problem prioritization, escalation plans and procedures, and logging and reporting problems.

In *performance management*, technicians and administrators track the network's performance, gauging the network's response time and traffic loads, to glean historical and trend information for planning.

*Security management* includes access control and preserving data integrity. It provides authentication procedures, access-control routines, supports encryption keys, and maintains authorization facilities. In addition to the common security standards, you must look at the simpler but critical issues such as password management, host account management, external access, and connections to other networks. Most break-ins are a result of poor password management and control.

*Accounting management* includes resource and device inventory and management. It permits usage, charges, and costs to be identified and assigned.

Network management often is confused with *system management*, which involves ministering to the needs of the host computers, including the operating systems running on these computers. End-user *device* administration (including PCs, Macintoshes, and UNIX workstations) and peripherals (such as printers and plotters) is another type of management.

Dividing computing equipment into domains can become restrictive quickly because their functionality and duties often cross over the artificial boundaries of system management and network management. For example, even in an area seemingly as simple as peripheral support, the PC support group may support the stand-alone PC printers, MIS may support the mainframe and minicomputer printers, and the LAN support group may support the networked printers. This crossover exists on other levels of network management. For example, bridges and routers fall into the domain of the LAN support group; if they are remote bridges and routers, however, the telecommunications group may become involved.

Another way to look at management is to divide it by function. Management can be subdivided into *operations* and *planning* duties (see Figure 10.1). In operations management, the administrators and technicians concern themselves with the day-to-day issues of running the network. These tasks are the reactive ones; the help desk and the technicians react to problems reported by users, MIS personnel, or network management tools. Administrators must address fault, configuration, security, and performance issues. Much of this information is distilled from daily operations data. Planning involves also capacity planning, demand forecasting, network applications planning, and new technology planning.

The planning aspect of network management enables network administrators and MIS personnel to behave proactively toward the network. They can anticipate problems, and upgrade the network at their convenience rather than replace failed hardware while payroll is being run, for example. Duties of network planning include system design, acquisition, and implementation, in addition to training end users and administrators.

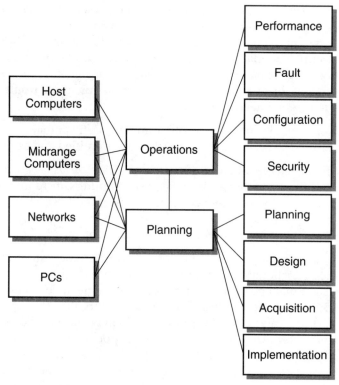

**Figure 10.1.** *The facets of network management.*

# More Challenges of Network Management

One problem of network management is that it is inherently difficult to define. You can divide the responsibilities by function (planning and operations), by equipment type (PC, LAN, and host), or by business group (departmental or MIS). Although such a divide-and-conquer strategy may break the network management problem down into manageable pieces, the efforts of the different groups must be coordinated.

Other significant problems include a shortage of trained people, a lack of management tools, and a lack of defined and documented network policies, procedures, roles, and responsibilities. Trained, experienced network administrators are in high demand by MIS departments but in low supply in the open marketplace. An experienced administrator can cost $60,000 per year in salary alone—that is, if you can find one. Experts cost far more. Finding administrators and technicians who can implement and manage an enterprise-wide network is not an easy task.

There is a lack of truly useful, multivendor, multiprotocol management tools. Most so-called management tools don't manage the network; they merely monitor it. These tools watch the network, but don't take action when a problem or potential problem occurs. MIS managers and network administrators need the tools that enable them to monitor, control, and manage the network, all the while gleaning historical data so that they can plan for upgrades and expansions.

Also, many useful network management tools work with network equipment from only the same vendor that manufactured the management system. Few tools elegantly and efficiently scale from the department up to the enterprise-wide network. A partial solution is the wide-ranging industry support for the Simple Network Management Protocol, but even SNMP is not enough. Tools alone don't manage networks, however. Network management also involves policies, processes, procedures, and plans.

# The Organization of Network Management Departments

Just as networks significantly affected the way that end users deal with information, LANs have affected the way that MIS is organized. Overall, MIS departments are becoming much more LAN-oriented. A few years ago, MIS regarded the LAN group largely as renegades who could be ignored, but many MIS departments have changed their way of thinking and operating. LAN experts are gaining equal footing with the mainframe experts.

Developed outside MIS's domain, LANs now are moving under the MIS umbrella. This trend is borne out by market research. In 1991, Business Research Group conducted telephone interviews with 400 people who have LAN administration responsibilities and work in sites with more than 1,000 employees, and who have an average of 18 LANs and 27 servers.[1] In this survey, an average of eight people administered each company's network.

Of the respondents, 79 percent of the MIS departments supported PC LANs, and only 21 percent of the MIS departments did not provide support for them. An equal number of respondents work for MIS as work autonomously. Fully 57.4 percent of the administrators interviewed report directly to MIS, and 57.3 percent report to non-MIS personnel (see Figure 10.2). Although the majority of LAN managers that BRG interviewed have only one boss, 24 percent report to MIS as well as to another group leader. Of the administrators who report to bosses who are not part of MIS, 28.2 percent report to a department head who does not belong to MIS, 22.7 percent report to a workgroup manager, 5.2 percent report to no one or are decentralized, and 1.2 percent report to another unidentified group. This research shows that as LANs gain a more important role in enterprise computing, their administration and control is falling within MIS's domain.

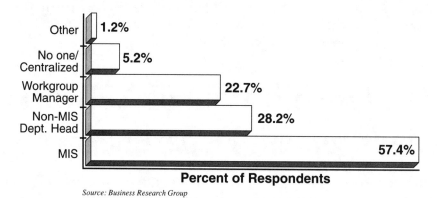

Source: Business Research Group

**Figure 10.2.** *Who manages LAN administrators?*

---

[1]Business Research Group. "PC LAN Integration and Management: User Trends." Newton, MA: Cahners Publishing, 1991.

In pre-LAN days, information technology departments typically had an MIS director or vice president of information systems with three operating groups: host computers, applications and users, and telecommunications and wide area networking (see Figure 10.3). Outside this group were the PC support and LAN people. The host group was the traditional glass-house MIS, responsible for maintaining the mainframes and minicomputers. The applications group, which included representatives from the large business units, was responsible for maintaining mission-critical applications. The telecommunications group was responsible for the PBXs, tie lines, and T-1 lines. Even if these groups reported to a single person, their functions were largely independent.

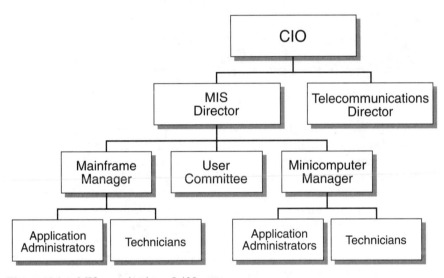

*Figure 10.3.* *MIS organization—LANs autonomous.*

In the newer model, these once-independent groups are being integrated. MIS is being called on to manage PC LANs as they take on a strategic role in the company's business functions. PC LANs are becoming as strategic as a company's mainframe, and it must be treated as such. Because in many instances each department managed its own PC LAN, however, the power and politics are colliding. The MIS director is gaining responsibility over a fourth operating group: LANs, and the LAN group reports on equal footing with the mainstay groups of host, applications, and telecommunications (see Figure 10.4). In some cases, the LAN group has more than equal footing because in the enterprise connectivity model, the network is the medium for connectivity, and access to the corporate databases is delivered through the network.

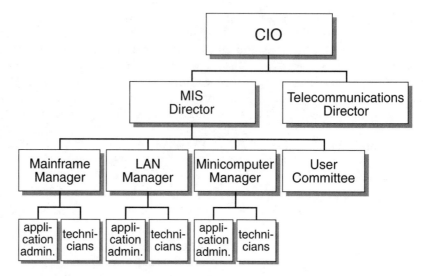

*Figure 10.4.* *MIS organization—LANs integrated.*

The host, LAN, and telecom groups are coming together because an enterprise-wide network is made up of all three functions, in addition to applications and users. As corporate computing evolves from stand-alone PC LANs to an interconnected enterprise-wide network, and as the host resources are distributed over local area networks, the expertise of the three information services groups—host, LAN, and telecom—in addition to the users, must be cross-fertilized. Building an enterprise-wide network requires cooperation among these groups, which often compete for resources and power. Consider how your MIS, LAN and telecommunications departments are structured, and evaluate this against the demands of your enterprise-wide network. It is easier to restructure your information management departments at the same time you install the network, rather than doing it later.

Users want access to information any time and any place, regardless of the host machine. It is MIS's responsibility to deliver that information to end users. Still, you cannot pretend that this integration is occurring completely without conflict. How charged the conflict is depends on the individual company.

The key to power, in DP terms, is where the business applications reside. If the applications are LAN-based, the LAN people are in control; if the applications are mainframe-based, the traditional MIS people are in control. The office automation applications—the spreadsheets and the mail—are already on the LAN, but MIS is largely not interested in such "personal" productivity applications.

The struggle is over control of the on-line transaction processing, inventory systems, accounting applications, and the like. With the advent of client/server computing, however, the huge database applications that are the underpinnings of these applications are moving onto the network, and connectivity is becoming more important. In most cases, it's not a win-or-lose situation, and both the LAN and the host environments are going to exist for a long time.

A partnership or a melding of functions needs to occur. The host and LAN people have to forget their differences. They have to work with each other, as well as with the telecommunications group, systems integration people, and users to build a network of applications suitable to run the company's business. This will take a new awareness and willingness to cooperate, but in the end, the rewards are great for all involved parties.

In the Business Research Group study discussed earlier in this chapter, nearly three-fourths of the people interviewed agreed that department managers should control PC LAN applications, but that MIS should control the other aspects[2] (see Figure 10.5). More specifically, 37 percent strongly agreed, 36 percent somewhat agreed, 16 percent somewhat disagreed, and 10 percent strongly disagreed. Users don't want to give up the freedom and control they gain by installing LANs; however, they generally don't want the responsibility of managing a mission-critical system.

The departments wanted help with the traditional MIS services, including network maintenance, integration, capacity planning, equipment maintenance, and help desks, according to the study. Departmental LAN administrators also want MIS's help with security administration, network cabling and installation, network application administration, server backup, network application development, and PC data backup.

---

[2]*Ibid.*

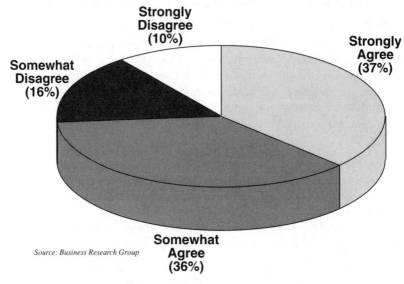

**"Departmental managers should control PC LAN applications, but MIS should control other aspects of PC LANs."**

*Source: Business Research Group*

**Figure 10.5.** *Who should control PC LANs?*

# The Changing Structure of Information Management

PC LANs gave end users the freedom to control their own computing fates; end users traded the mainframe's reliability and uptime for the flexibility of having whatever applications they chose. Those departmental LAN applications are changing from nonessential to mission-critical, and as such their reliability and uptime must be guaranteed. However, this will not happen with the MIS, LAN, and telecommunications structure existent in most companies. For an enterprise-wide network to properly support these mission-critical functions, most companies' MIS, telecommunications, and LAN groups will have to be reorganized.

In most companies, no one group is in complete control of all information systems. MIS manages the mainframes and minicomputers and their applications. In some instances, the minicomputers may be supported locally. Local LAN gurus support the PC LANs, so pockets of LAN expertise exist throughout the corporation. The telecommunications department supports the PBXs, key systems, and T-1 network. In some companies, the telecommunications department may be responsible for the data that travels over the T-1 network.

To build an enterprise network, one group must obtain control of the network. Although this can easily turn into a political battle among the MIS, telecommunications, and LAN groups, in reality, no group can meet all of the needs of the enterprise-wide network, and a new management organization must be formed.

## Centralized MIS Functions

Today, most companies attempt to use a centralized approach to information management. This is the traditional model of MIS (see Figure 10.6). One data center performs all daily operations and planning responsibilities for the networks, minicomputers, and mainframes. This data center administers and maintains the applications, the machines, and access. Backup data centers may exist for redundancy and fault tolerance, but little of the responsibility is distributed. Network management, including design, acquisition, implementation, name management, and training, is performed centrally. Administrators preside over the host computers, managing their configuration, security, performance, problems, and cable systems.

This model has its benefits. This centralization of personnel and material resources delivers faster access and lower costs. For instance, if a technician needs to repair a router, she does not have to travel to a different floor or across campus, because the router is located in the data center rather than out in the departments. This not only allows her to repair the problem faster, because all tools and expertise are at hand, but also it enables her supervisor to track her whereabouts more easily. With the centralized model, you do not have to place an expert in each location, because a few experts can support many users. Also, several administrators are acquainted with each network setup, so the MIS department has backup if one administrator isn't available.

In addition to achieving economies of scale, you will find it easier to enforce corporate standards. Quite simply, if the device isn't on the list of supported equipment, MIS won't support it. And by having a united thrust for equipment on that list, you'll have an easier time enforcing that rule. By instituting corporate standards, you can more easily build a common platform for your enterprise-wide network. Because the departments don't have autonomous network management, you'll find it easier to mediate among the requirements of the different departments.

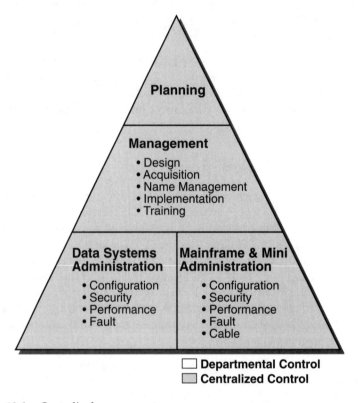

*Figure 10.6.   Centralized management.*

The centralized approach has its disadvantages. For one, the departments lose control over their own computing fate, and must rely on an outside group who may not be as responsive as if the systems were controlled internally. With most of the expertise centralized, users may have a slower response time to problems. No longer do they have a guru on-site who is familiar with them and with their needs. Also, with a centralized approach, the computing systems won't be as customized to the departments' needs, again because no expert is local.

Setting up one or two main locations of support and maintenance leaves you vulnerable to disasters. If a natural disaster destroys your data center, you will be left without any computer support. Most companies build a back-up data center for this reason; however, doing so doubles your costs.

# Decentralized MIS Functions

Although MIS has attempted to institute a centralized approach, this is not the actual structure many companies use. In most companies, the IS functions are distributed or decentralized, but haphazardly and inefficiently. The individual departments plan and administer their networks, and no one group has total responsibility (see Figure 10.7). Departments must design, acquire, wire, install, secure, support, and maintain their own networks. They must find their own administrators and train their own users. Usually, a central MIS department manages the mainframes, but the planning and management for the minicomputers and LANs are performed within the departments and local sites.

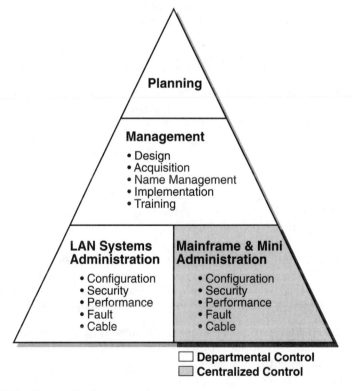

*Figure 10.7.*    *Decentralized management.*

This approach allows each department to control its own resources, enabling it to better customize its system to meet its needs. This approach guarantees a fast response time, because local administrators, intimately familiar with the applications, hardware, and users, may be able to solve a problem more rapidly than an administrator in a data center.

A completely decentralized approach can be costly. For each department or remote location, you'll need an administrator plus tools. Trained, experienced network administrators are in high demand with low supply, and placing experts in the field may not be the best use of their talent—if you can even find them. Because each subnetwork has only one administrator, there's no backup available for him or her.

With the decentralized approach, resources are not coordinated among the departments. Departments may purchase duplicate systems, each using half the capacity, when they could have easily shared a resource. Also, with a decentralized approach, it becomes quite difficult to implement corporate standards, because departments are more likely to purchase whatever they want. This will make it more difficult to build an enterprise network.

## The New Enterprise IS Structure

In an enterprise-wide network, neither a completely centralized nor a totally distributed architecture makes the most sense. Instead, a combination is the most efficient approach. Many MIS departments are currently consolidating their operations, and then distributing some of the responsibilities to the local departments in an effort to forge a new information management structure, the enterprise IS (EIS) department.

MIS departments are consolidating operations. Whereas the responsibilities of information and system management were distributed among many different departments, they are increasingly being handled by a single group. As networks have sprung up in nearly every user department, users have gained flexibility and independence from MIS, but at the price of unreliability, inefficiency, and a lack of strategic planning on the local level. Sources of network implementation and support include traditional IS personnel, full-time departmental LAN managers, and a guru or power users.

Consolidating the many local support organizations enables the business departments to concentrate on their business functions, leaving computer system management to the MIS and telecommunications groups. This is especially important with the guru users, who end up supporting less technically adept coworkers instead of performing the job for which they are directly employed (and budgeted). So instead of having a hundred different groups individually manage their networks, for instance, companies are consolidating so that only a few groups are given the responsibility. This helps reduce overlapping functions and makes the process more streamlined and efficient.

At the same time they are consolidating operations, MIS departments are decentralizing. MIS is beginning to recognize that in order to allow the business units to take advantage of the enterprise-wide network, they must change how they offer services. Users want to be able to "plug into" network service, in the same way that telephone service, electricity, and water are available. A user doesn't want to hear from the network support person that the network is down, but it's the T-1 network and that's the responsibility of the telecommunications department, not the LAN group.

MIS departments are being reorganized to allow for centralized management as well as local autonomy (see Figure 10.8). This is the *enterprise IS* model. Instead of organizing responsibilities around a type of system or technology, support for an enterprise network should be organized around a function. Whatever group can best perform a particular function should be the one that is given the responsibility.

In the enterprise IS model, a centralized IS group is responsible for strategic planning, policies and procedures, and resource management. It is responsible for the enterprise-wide network design, including internetworking issues and telecommunications. The enterprise IS group establishes the network naming conventions and maintains the directory services. It manages the applications that are shared by most or all users. It develops the applications that are used across the corporation. The centralized MIS group must provide sufficient leadership and direction for the local business units.

The business units are responsible for the daily operation and planning for their networks. The departments manage their networks, including local applications, support, and training. Configuration issues, such as adding users and adding applications, are performed locally. Adding, moving, and changing users, servers, and segments is done locally.

Acquisition of network and computer components are centralized so that economies of scale can be achieved. Acquisition can be performed in conjunction with the company's purchasing department. You may also want to consider consolidating help-desk support into one location.

Advantages of the enterprise IS approach include coordinated planning and administration, so that a united information technology strategy exists. The departments continue to retain the control and management of their systems, so they can still have the systems that are best suited to their needs and response times. However, MIS, which is suited to the finer points of computer operations—not the specifics of the business operations—maintains the computer systems. This model enables MIS to consolidate its resources and achieve economies of scale. Also, this approach offers the fruits of cross-training that the centralized model offers.

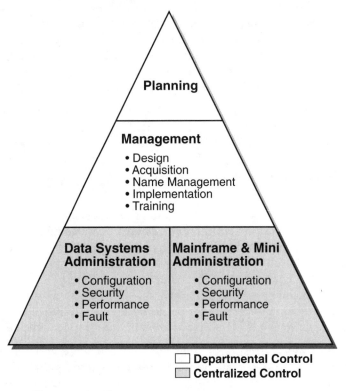

*Figure 10.8.* *The enterprise IS structure.*

For such a division of labor to be successful, the responsibilities of each group must be agreed on and clearly documented. Failure to outline and document responsibilities is a common pitfall of enterprise network management. In a classic case of fingerpointing, one group may think that another was responsible for performing a certain task, and in the end, the job is not a success.

The greatest disadvantage of the enterprise IS model is that you will have to reorganize your MIS, LAN, and telecommunications groups, which is a task not to be taken lightly. This restructuring requires a partnership among the business unit managers, the departmental LAN managers, and the MIS managers. It requires a new way of thinking.

Organizing an enterprise IS structure is likely to be quite political. Each group—traditional MIS, LAN, and telecommunications—will look to gain control, often to the exclusion of the other. A successful enterprise IS structure, however, demands the cooperation, not the competition, of these groups. You must have a rapidly evolving or mature climate of cooperation among the business departments as well as within the MIS, LAN, and telecommunications groups. Without shared goals and a willingness to work together, the enterprise IS structure is doomed to fail.

The enterprise network manager must have an understanding of computer, network, and telecommunications issues, as well as application issues. This is a new breed of information personnel; they may be traditional IS personnel or they may be users. You find these employees in conventional and unconventional places.

When building an enterprise IS department, examine your existing departments, identify the problems, and work to resolve them. The enterprise-wide network exists to support mission-critical business functions, yet few traditional MIS departments have a good understanding of the company's business needs, because IS departments typically focus too intently on technology. Give business needs priority over technical achievement and gain an understanding of the business requirements.

Many traditional IS departments use rigid and time-consuming methodologies that will not be suitable for an enterprise network. An enterprise IS department must be sufficiently flexible in order to meet the business users' constantly changing needs. Long development cycles and complex methodologies are not appropriate, and will cause users to look for another source of support and direction.

Your company must have a good economic reason to decentralize or set up an enterprise IS department. In addition to the hard costs of restructuring IS, consider the hidden costs, such as the time business employees will have to spend on technical issues. Also consider the cost of lost productivity as users and technical personnel ascend the learning curve.

Reorganizing MIS is uncharted territory, but the payoff can be large. Many companies have realized such a payback by consolidating their MIS departments, using an enterprise IS solution, and defining effective and documented standards, policies, and procedures. Reorganizing MIS requires a partnership among the business unit managers, the departmental LAN managers, and the MIS managers.

# The Tools of Network Management

A chasm separates what's needed in network management from what's available. What's needed is a management system that monitors, controls, and manages every element in an enterprise-wide network, from the most rudimentary to the most sophisticated device. This ideal management system watches the network, and when it sees a problem, leaps into action, fixes the problem, and notifies the administrator that a problem arose and was solved.

In addition, the management system should cull historical data from the rush of real-time information so that network designers can plan and anticipate events. In this way, the administrators can proactively upgrade the network, not repair devices after they've broken down. This calls for a database, definitely using relational and perhaps even object-oriented technology.

Because the demarcation of system and network management has blurred, the ideal enterprise management system should provide links to manage the end-user devices and host computers. Factor in the telecommunications links, and the ideal enterprise manager should provide a venue to handle the telecommunications aspects as well (see Figure 10.9).

Of course, this ideal network management system is not proprietary nor does it lock you into a single-vendor solution. It is easy to use, and delivers as much useful information in a meaningful way. Unlike many network management tools, it doesn't offer just a pretty interface, but has the muscle to back it up. Also, it is reasonably priced.

The reality is far different. Yes, you can manage the network wiring system, internetworking devices, host computers, and telecommunications system. You may even be able to control operating parameters remotely. But you can't manage these different systems using a single network management system. Instead, the sophistication of ordinary network operations centers nearly equals the equipment needed to launch the space shuttle. Fifty or sixty network management consoles, stacked and scattered around the network operations center, is not unusual.

Not only do these many different management consoles occupy precious real estate in an already crowded NOC, but the technicians and administrators must learn and master each one, and each one has a different method of operation.

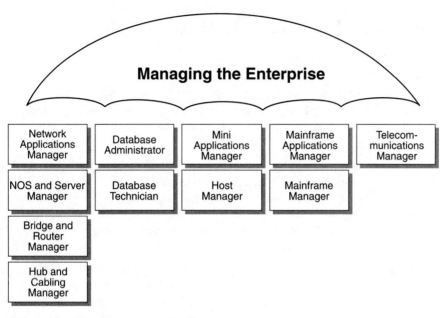

*Figure 10.9.* *The management umbrella.*

A single management system suitable for an enterprise, multivendor network does not exist, and most likely never will. Most management systems are vendor-specific. When you buy a mainframe from IBM, you generally buy its management software, and IBM is uniquely positioned to design this system. The same goes for bridges or wiring concentrators.

Until recently, vendor-specific management systems were the only option because the management interfaces were proprietary. With the advent of the Simple Network Management Protocol (SNMP) and eventually OSI's Common Management Information Protocol (CMIP), this situation has changed. Now with standards-based network management systems, you can buy one system that manages several vendors' devices. You often trade off control and functionality, however, because a general system usually doesn't give you great control over specific devices.

# Stacking Up the Management Architectures

The lack of scalable, usable network management systems isn't lost on manufacturers. The computer and network vendors are spending millions of dollars to develop enterprise-wide network management systems, with varying degrees of success.

Several management architectures are used: the universal interface, the manager of managers, the management mesh network, and the platform approach. Despite their architectural differences, in each of these systems one or more management consoles serves as the linchpin, and the lower-level managers or devices report information to this central location. They are as follows:

- *Universal*. Every computer, network, and peripheral device implements the same management information protocol so that they all can talk directly to an "integrated" manager. It is unrealistic to expect a corporate-wide network to consist of pieces of equipment that all can run the same management protocol. Too many systems are already in existence.

- *Manager-of-manager*. A hierarchy is constructed. Low-level managers deliver information to the next manager in the tree. Because of this hierarchy, existing systems can remain in place—all they need is a piece of software to talk to the integrated manager. The existing managers can continue to perform their specific functions. Low-level managers are abundant, but, to date, no supreme high-level manager has emerged.

- *Mesh*. With many manager-of-manager systems in place, a mesh of network management is possible. The multiple integrated managers also can communicate directly with each other. Element managers communicate with other element managers as peers. Sufficient integrated managers have not emerged to make the mesh possible. Also, a mesh is very complex.

- *Platform*. A multivendor management platform or application programming interface (API) is defined and agreed on by the network and computer vendors, and they write their management applications to a single interface. Developers can concentrate on the specifics of network management applications because the core services are provided in the platform. The platform can be also a vendor-neutral approach.

# The Universal Interface

A universal management standard would solve the problem of having one system to manage a multitude of vendors' equipment. If every computer, network, and peripheral manufacturer, in addition to third-party developers, implemented the same management protocol, one management system could interact directly and control all of them (see Figure 10.10).

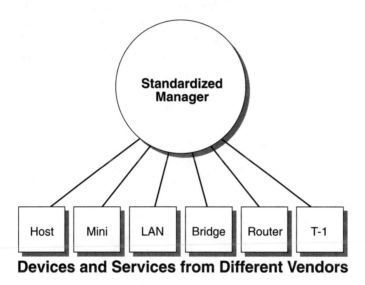

*Figure 10.10.* *Universal interface.*

Although this two-tier approach to network management is valiant, it isn't realistic. It's equivalent to saying, "Let's all use IBM equipment," or "Let's buy DEC." A universal solution doesn't solve the problem. First, the huge base of existing equipment, currently managed by these manufacturers' management systems, doesn't conform to this universal management protocol. Second, the likelihood that the industry will rush to support one protocol is slim. Even the IEEE has two different working groups defining network management standards. Too many divergent approaches exist already for a convergence to occur. Even if the entire computer industry supported a single protocol, it would take a tremendous amount of time for vendors to migrate all of their devices, equipment, and applications to make fullest use of the protocol.

IBM, with its NetView and SystemView, and AT&T, with its Accumaster Integrator, use this approach.

# The Manager-of-Manager Strategy

Another approach to solving the problem is the manager-of-manager interface (see Figure 10.11). Rather than replace the existing network managers, the manager-of-manager strategy implements a management hierarchy. The *integrated manager*, at the root of the tree, gathers information from the lower-level *element managers*, which are "children" of the integrated manager. The element managers, in turn, gather information from their "child" *devices* or *services* from different manufacturers. Communication is up and down the tree only, not across the tree. Because element managers do not communicate directly with each other, they do not have to speak the same management language.

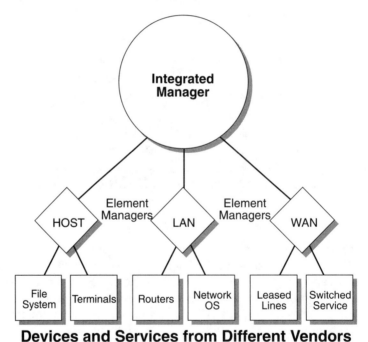

**Devices and Services from Different Vendors**

*Figure 10.11.*  *Manager of managers.*

Because of this hierarchy, existing systems can remain in place—all they need is a piece of software to talk to the integrated manager. The existing managers can continue to perform their specific functions.

SNMP often is positioned as an element manager, with IBM's NetView, AT&T's Accumaster Integrator, or another enterprise manager as the integrated manager.

# The Management Mesh Network

As more manager-of-manager systems are developed, a complete management network is possible. In this system, several integrated managers communicate with one or more element managers. The element managers, in turn, communicate with the vendor-specific agents within the devices.

The management mesh network differs from the manager-of-manager strategy in that the multiple integrated managers can communicate directly with each other also. The element managers may communicate directly with other element managers as peers. These any-to-any conversations create a complex meshed network of managers (see Figure 10.12).

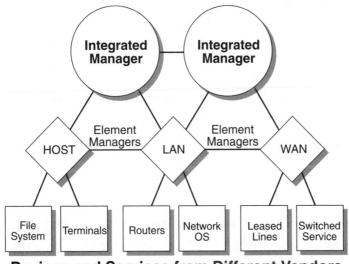

**Devices and Services from Different Vendors**

*Figure 10.12.* *Management mesh network.*

This mesh approach is the goal of the OSI network management effort, among others. It is a very complex and complicated effort, however. As the number of management systems increases, the number of interconnections increases exponentially. Nevertheless, the mesh approach has more utility and practicality than the universal interface or the manager-of-manager approach.

# The Platform Approach

Because the mesh management network is so complex, a simpler way is the platform approach (see Figure 10.13). Here, a multivendor management platform is defined and agreed on by the network and computer vendors, and they write their management applications to a single interface. By writing to an API, the management vendors—whether third-party or managing their own devices—can concentrate on the specifics of management and leave to the platform vendors the core details—management protocols, management data definition, and interface issues. Multiple protocols can continue to exist, as long as they can talk to the common management platform.

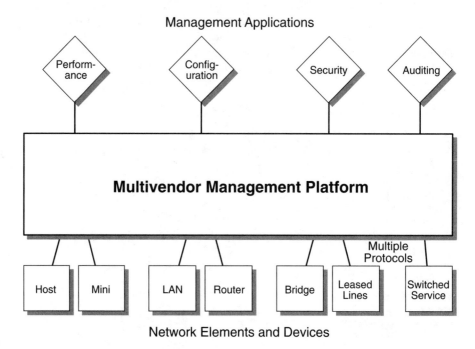

*Figure 10.13.* *Platform approach.*

Using SNMP, Sun Microsystems' SunNet Manager and Hewlett-Packard's OpenView are two systems that take this approach.

Of the four approaches, the platform approach seems to make the most sense. Enterprise-wide networks are made up of equipment from a multitude of vendors, and the complexity will only increase, not decrease. For a management system to be successful, it must artfully manage many different vendors' equipment. The platform approach is the only one that will enable vendors to differentiate their products and still conform to a common platform.

# Enterprise Management Systems

The major players in enterprise-wide network management are IBM, AT&T, Digital Equipment Corporation, and Sun Microsystems. IBM and AT&T implement a traditional hierarchical system, and DEC, management "newcomer" Hewlett-Packard, and Sun Microsystems offer an approach more suitable in a distributed enterprise-wide network.

## IBM's NetView and SystemView

IBM was the first vendor to define an integrated management approach for heterogeneous systems; however, its systems are the least hospitable to multivendor networks today. IBM's NetView and SystemView are its stated direction for the integration and automation of enterprise-wide network and data-center management.

In 1986, IBM laid out the Open Network Management Strategy and Open Network Management Architecture, which defined three components: focal points, entry points, and service points. In IBM's terms, *focal points* are managers, which generally are mainframe-based. *Entry points* are agents embedded in a managed resource, such as an operating system or a multistation access unit. Entry points report management data back to a focal point using an SNA protocol. In a pure SNA network, this protocol is Network Management Vector Transport (NMVT). The *service point* provides a gateway function and translates between the non-SNA management protocols and the NMVT. SNMP and eventually CMIP are supported through service points. As of NetView version 2.0, announced in 1990, both NetView/PC and LU6.2, the peer-to-peer SNA protocol, may serve as the interface.

SystemView is IBM's plan for achieving a more uniform, consistent, and integrated network and system line. (NetView is the platform for SystemView in the S/370 and S/390 environment.) SystemView provides a standard user interface (end-use dimension); a consistent way to model, store, and retrieve systems management data (data dimension); and a modular management application for business, change, configuration, operations, performance, and problem management (application dimension). SystemView's intent is similar to SAA's—it's an attempt to corral the diverse IBM solutions and make it easier for customers. The project is large-scale, however, and will take several years to come to fruition.

In many ways, SystemView and NetView are old technologies applied to a new problem. With the advent of client/server computing, the old world of the hierarchical mainframe structure no longer is applicable. Support for LU6.2 solves the problem of the mainframe hierarchy, but NetView still requires a mainframe, which most—but not all—enterprise-wide networks contain. Having a mainframe should not be a requirement for network management. In NetView, SNMP is not supported natively, but through a gateway function only. In the end, NetView and SystemView are most suitable if yours is largely an IBM shop. A multivendor management architecture must be much more flexible and more adept at accommodating other vendors' products.

## AT&T Accumaster Integrator

AT&T holds the distinction of being the first vendor to produce an enterprise management alternative to challenge IBM. Like IBM, AT&T chose the classic hierarchical approach for managing multivendor networks when it outlined its *Unified Network Management Architecture* (UNMA) in 1987. AT&T knew, however, that to succeed against IBM it had to provide options for multivendor management; it therefore based its efforts on the OSI manager/element interface.

Although AT&T wisely emphasized multivendor management, the OSI management standard is largely incomplete. Because it needed to move faster than ISO, AT&T froze a copy of the January 1988 ISO specifications and began implementing its products based on the interim standard. (Several manufacturers, frustrated with the slow progress of OSI network management, later founded the OSI Network Management Forum to produce interim management parameters and objects. AT&T incorporates elements of this group's definitions.)

AT&T's Accumaster Integrator is the first integrated management system based on the principles of OSI management. It offers color graphics, an integrated relational database, real-time management data links into the AT&T public network, and an expert system for correlating alarms. Accumaster is especially appealing for its links to the public network.

Accumaster's greatest benefit is also its greatest weakness. Even in 1992, the OSI management standard is still far from complete, which limits the number of element managers that can communicate with it. Without a firm standard, network management and computer vendors are not writing to the OSI standard, choosing SNMP instead. AT&T does not publish its specifications for any interfaces beyond the database, thereby preventing third parties from developing Integrator add-ons. Customers are wholly dependent on AT&T's resources for developing the Integrator. Customers cannot customize the Integrator. In the end, Accumaster is still most useful if you have a lot of AT&T equipment.

Another weakness of Accumaster is its centralized approach. The architecture is hierarchical, with only one master Integrator. You cannot configure backup master Integrators as a precaution against disaster, and you cannot perform monitoring regionally. A hierarchical approach is restrictive in an enterprise-wide network, which is much "flatter" and more peer-oriented.

## DEC's DECmcc

IBM has Open Network Management Architecture, AT&T has Unified Network Management Architecture, and Digital has Enterprise Management Architecture (EMA).

DEC was the first vendor to describe a distributed management architecture, EMA, and its incarnation, DECmcc. Like other management systems, EMA defines a manager-agent relationship, which DEC calls a director-entity relationship; however, multiple directors may share the responsibilities of managing a set of entities, and the directors themselves can communicate with each other across the network. This peer-to-peer communication is important in an enterprise-wide network.

The EMA architecture is both distributed and object-oriented. DECmcc uses DEC's distributed name service, its distributed directory service, its distributed time service, and remote procedure calls.

DEC's platform supports *functional, presentation,* and *access management* modules, in addition to a common repository or database for management information. The director kernel is an object-oriented API that employs RPCs. Access modules establish interfaces to other vendors' management systems and elements. The access module makes a remote entity conform to its object specification, and it works with objects as much as possible. Using the access modules enables DEC to support multiple management protocols, proprietary and standard.

DECmcc's functional modules implement the specific management applications, including configuration management and alarm handling. Because the presentation modules implement multiple user interfaces, one DECmcc console may have a plain ASCII interface, another DECmcc application can sport a graphical user interface, and a third interface can link the system to dial-up lines, for instance.

DEC uses an open approach and encourages other vendors to write to the EMA specification. Many network device vendors are using the DEC console application to manage their specific devices, such as bridges and routers. DECmcc runs on VMS and Ultrix.

# Hewlett-Packard's OpenView

OpenView, from Hewlett-Packard, offers a solution that is more open than either IBM's or AT&T's and is similar in intent to Digital's. In 1988, Hewlett-Packard threw the gauntlet into the management ring, stating that many different management protocols will exist, but that end users don't really care what they are. HP's strategy was to publish a set of APIs and get other vendors to build management products on top of OpenView, which provides basic management services. Although the initial DOS version is limited, the UNIX version of OpenView is very sophisticated, and HP is enjoying much success with it. It runs on both HP's own hardware as well as on Sun workstations.

OpenView has the following four components:

- *Presentation services* incorporate the OpenView Windows application and offer the Open Software Foundation's Motif X Window-based interface.

- *Data store management* provides the database and event management services.

- *Communication protocols* implement SNMP and eventually CMIP.

- *Management application programs* access these services by way of a set of APIs implemented in the distributed communication infrastructure.

The distributed API makes it possible for many different applications to access OpenView's services across a network, without knowing the details of where the components are located. The management applications can communicate with each other through the API.

Hewlett-Packard has garnered relatively good support from other vendors, including those making telecommunications equipment as well as the traditional computer and networking companies.

By using the platform architecture, OpenView offers flexible and scalable multivendor management suited to a distributed enterprise-wide network.

## Sun Microsystems' SunNet Manager

Sun Connect, a business unit of Sun Microsystems, offers SunNet Manager, one of the most popular platform-oriented SNMP managers. HP and Sun lead the market in SNMP managers, and many third-party developers have written applications that use either the OpenView or SunNet Manager SNMP framework. In 1992, Sun said there were nearly 120 companies that were writing or have applications for SunNet Manager. HP says 110 applications are available based on OpenView. Many of these developers offer hub, bridge, router, or telecommunications managers; others offer management applications such as trouble-ticketing systems.

The latest version of SunNet Manager, version 2.0, is targeted toward the network administrator, whereas earlier versions were written with the convenience of the developer in mind. SunNet Manager supports tens of thousands of nodes. It is an SNMP console that communicates with SNMP agents and proxy agents. Individual proxy agents can communicate with many nodes. SunNet Manager includes a set of applications that discover and identify network devices. Network managers can set defaults for tools, system operation, and alarms control windows. SunNet Manager runs on the company's SPARC systems, and in the future will run on Solaris 2.0, the RS/6000, and the HP 9000.

# The Simple Network Management Protocol

The SNMP has become something of a darling of the network and computer vendors. Its advocates bless its simplicity; its detractors denigrate it. Hundreds of computer and network manufacturers, from the starting players to the third string, have announced or shipped network management products that incorporate SNMP. SNMP has managed to delay, and possibly even prevent, the acceptance of CMIP, the OSI's solution to network management protocols. What, then, is SNMP? It is the protocol that a great many network management stations, tools, and programs use to communicate with network devices to obtain information about status, performance, and overall characteristics.

# Defining SNMP

For all the hubbub, SNMP is a protocol—a simple protocol, a method of query and response. It is nothing more, nothing less. SNMP's success lies in its simplicity, availability, and vendor-neutrality. By definition, SNMP is simple. It's easy to implement and incorporate into network management products. Its command set is small. It can be used to control nearly anything, from a network interface card to a router to a host computer to a toaster. Because it doesn't require a large amount of overhead, it is feasible in PC LANs, an area in which CMIP falls down.

Also, SNMP is readily available; CMIP is not. SNMP was developed by the University of Tennessee at Knoxville and placed in the public domain. Source code is available from several organizations. Taking its cue from the success of UNIX, TCP/IP, NFS, EtherNet, and other mainstays of the Internet world, SNMP is free and available. SNMP is widely supported by EtherNet, TCP/IP, and router manufacturers; its use in Token-Ring networks is growing, and a number of telecommunications device manufacturers also are supporting it.

SNMP is vendor-neutral. It was developed by engineers in the Internet who needed a solution to a problem. The Internet is largely free of the corporate maneuvering prevalent in formal standards bodies.

But *what is* SNMP? SNMP is a query-response protocol that can be used to control anything. It doesn't aspire to be a network management system; it handles only the communication aspects of device management and control (see Figure 10.14).

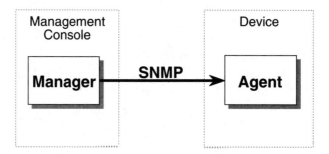

*Figure 10.14.   SNMP managers and agents.*

SNMP places the complexity of the protocol in the network management station, not in the remote agent. In this way, the device being managed is saddled by minimal overhead, enabling it to use its CPU cycles for its intended function—routing, bridging, or processing I/O requests—not for passing management information. If the device lacks the capability to run the SNMP agent or employs another management protocol, it may communicate with a *proxy agent* running in an adjacent device, which endows the device with SNMP functionality (see Figure 10.15).

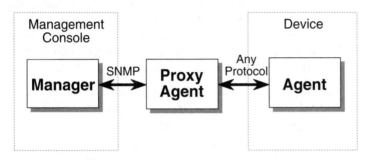

***Figure 10.15.*** *SNMP proxy agents.*

SNMP is a transaction-oriented protocol that can directly query network entities. It models a request/response transaction between a network management station and an agent. The bulk of the work is done in the network management station. Agents rarely initiate management operations, but they do so when a significant event occurs. In SNMP, significant activities are defined as agent initialization, agent restart, link failure, link restart, bad authentication, and a lost neighboring router. If any of these events occur, the agent sets a trap. Vendors may define their own set of significant events.

Network management information is retrieved from a management information base (MIB), which essentially is a database of objects. The MIB lists the network objects, including errors, packets, and routing information. Operations on the MIB are simple: information requests, control instructions, and alarms or traps. MIB 1, the initial specification, allows retrieving and reading information. Altering, or setting, the values of the object is part of MIB 2's specification.

RMON, or the remote network monitoring MIB, is the newest addition to SNMP functionality. Before RMON, SNMP could not be used remotely; it could control devices only locally. The RMON MIB enhances the set of remote monitoring features to include additional packet error counters, more flexible historical trend graphing and statistical analysis, an EtherNet-level traffic matrix, more comprehensive alarms, and more-powerful filtering to capture and analyze individual packets. RMON MIB agents can be located on a variety of devices or consoles, and they are designed to enhance the management information available from typical hubs, bridges, and hosts.

SNMP uses a connectionless transport protocol, which ensures a good response time and enables it to be useful during network failures. SNMP runs on top of the User Datagram Protocol (UDP), which is part of the TCP suite. Connection-oriented protocols, such as TCP, have too much overhead to be efficient for network management. With a connectionless protocol, the network manager can perform its own retries, reset parameters, and other transport-level functions. Also, a connectionless protocol can get through the LAN even if the network is failing—something a connection-oriented protocol can't achieve. You need network management most when the network is failing.

SNMP prepares the way of OSI management, because it uses Abstract Syntax Notation 1 (ASN.1), the style of notation used in OSI management, as well as employes MIBs, used also by OSI management.

Despite its success, SNMP often is seen as a solution to managing only TCP/IP networks. Although SNMP most often runs over UDP, it can run over TCP, OSI Transport Protocol Class 0 and Class 4 (TP0 and TP4), OSI Connectionless Transport Service (CNLS), and link-layer or MAC-layer protocols. Support for SNMP in other transports is growing. For example, Novell supports SNMP management starting with NetWare V3.11.

Although SNMP has enjoyed tremendous support among the bridge, router, and EtherNet wiring concentrator vendors, support must come from the Token-Ring vendors, those selling FDDI wares, and others.

## The SNMP Management Console

SNMP communicates information between agents and a network management station (NMS). What, then, does the NMS do? The network administrators and technicians view and interact with the network from the NMS. The NMS is a powerful computer, typically running UNIX but sometimes running DOS or VMS, that acts as a window into the network. The UNIX and VMS managers are typically aimed at the midrange, and the DOS ones are aimed at the low end. The NMS usually provides a graphical user interface, based on X Window or Microsoft Windows, but sometimes has only an ASCII character interface.

At minimum, the NMS should provide the following functionality: automatic network map configuration, real-time network status display, real-time event trapping, real-time performance monitoring, historical trend analysis, connectivity testing, duplicate IP address testing, EtherNet cable testing, network traffic monitoring, station traffic monitoring, station conversation traffic monitoring, and alarm generation. It should provide a relational database so that the significant aspects of the event and traffic data can be stored for historical and trend analysis. Reporting is an essential ingredient. The console should offer the capability to store and retrieve historical data and generate reports.

Add to this base the functions needed to manage the specific devices. For example, with an SNMP concentrator management system, you should be able to turn ports on and off, disable links, determine what devices are on the network, and discover error counts for the EtherNet, Token Ring, and FDDI concentrator. Bridge, router, and host manufacturers also must create management functions to control the specifics of their products.

A key to SNMP's success is the device vendors' ability to easily extend the standard MIB to include management features for their specific devices. These vendor extensions are read into, or are compiled into, an SNMP NMS. Such extensibility enables vendors to continue to add functionality and still conform to a standard protocol.

The ease with which vendor extensions can be read into NMSs must be drastically improved. It often can be difficult to import these vendor-specific MIBs. When they can be imported, the console application tends to display its own manufacturers' products in an attractive, useful graphical manner, and the MIBs from other vendors tend to be little more than ASCII text. This problem is being solved over time. For example, many manufacturers have placed their specific extensions into the public domain, making it easier for NMS vendors to incorporate the MIB extensions. Also, more featured MIB compilers will become available.

No clear winner has emerged in the struggle for control of the NMS platform. Many network device vendors sell their own consoles, and you can buy a broad-based SNMP NMS console that supports various vendors' MIB extensions. These broad-based NMSs include Sun Microsystems' SunNet Manager, Lexcel's LANCE+, Hughes Network Systems' Monet, and Hewlett-Packard's OpenView. Additionally, there are full-blown management systems that incorporate SNMP, such as Cabletron's Spectrum.

Although SNMP is painted as the solution for network management in a multivendor environment, something more than using the SNMP protocol is required. Vendors must work together to make their products interoperate and exchange information. The only real way to determine the level of interoperability, unfortunately, is to test it.

## The Essentials of a Management Console

A network management console should:

- Be based on a standard management protocol, such as SNMP.

- Enable the administrator to monitor the device's performance remotely.

- Enable the administrator to remotely configure devices, including performance variables, turning ports on and off, and so on.

- Allow the administrator to set performance thresholds that, if violated, create alarms. Performance statistics should be reported regularly to the administrator.

- Store historical information in a relational database. This database should not be proprietary, and administrators should be able to export the information to discern trends.

- Provide a graphical user interface to help the administrator picture the physical layout of the network.

- Provide a mechanism to track problems.

- Work with a variety of manufacturers' equipment.

# The Common Management Information Protocol

Multivendor network management needs a standards-based management information protocol. The two contenders are SNMP and CMIP. Once neck-and-neck competitors, SNMP is now years ahead of CMIP in terms of implementation and industry support.

CMIP takes the long-term view. Unlike SNMP, CMIP was designed to accomplish network management on a grand scale. CMIP is only one fork in ISO's management thrust, which includes defining MIBs and providing network management in the areas of configuration, performance, fault, accounting, and security.

Like SNMP, CMIP is the communications vehicle between the manager and the agents. CMIP provides greater control, however. Whereas SNMP verbs are limited to getting, setting, and trapping information, CMIP verbs include get, set, action, event-report, create, delete, initialize, and terminate. These additional verbs make CMIP far more powerful and functional than SNMP.

Like SNMP's MIBs, OSI MIBs are made up of information ferreted out by CMIP. The network manager can manipulate the objects contained in the MIB. For each managed object, ISO must define and agree on a definition. For each router, each printer, and each host computer, ISO must get myriad vendors to agree on what should be managed—no easy feat. Input is coming from the OSI Network Management Forum, a consortium of computer and network vendors chartered to speed the definition of the MIB objects. The OSI Network Management Forum will define a common network management interface and leave the implementation to the vendors.

Much of the CMIP-SNMP debate has died down. The bulk of support is for SNMP, and the few network management vendors who have been shipping CMIP solutions have deemphasized them. CMIP may be the protocol for the long term, but SNMP is solving the problems at hand. If and when the time comes for migration, SNMP and CMIP share some commonalities, including ASN.1 notation and the use of MIBs (see Figure 10.16).

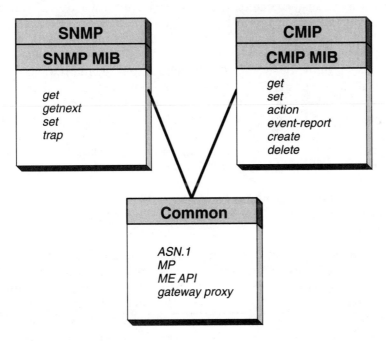

*Figure 10.16.* SNMP and CMIP models.

# Which Way to Go?

IBM, AT&T, Digital, and HP are the "Big Four" of network management; they have positioned their management tools as the solutions that can monitor, manage, and control all aspects of the network. Of the four, HP and Digital have managed the most open approaches, but SNMP is the clear leader in network management protocols.

Network management can't—and won't—come from a single vendor. Each network is unique, and therefore one tool never will suffice. Network management requires cooperation among vendors because a network contains equipment from so many different vendors. In this environment, a network management solution from a single vendor almost always will be less effective than network management tools from several different vendors. What, then, is the solution to the network management crisis?

For network management tools to become truly useful, network manufacturers must open up their product architectures enough that other vendors—most likely those specializing in network management—can write applications to manage those network components. SNMP helps, but it isn't enough. For example, numerous vendors write their management products to work with Sun Microsystems' SunNet Manager console. Digital has an increasing number of vendors who support its DECmcc console. SNMP is supposed to be the solution to the problem of multivendor network management. Configuring and using an SNMP system, however, is very difficult. Different vendors' MIBs are "read into" the SNMP console. That is, the SNMP console must be programmed to recognize the parameters and variables needed to manage each vendor's network device. This process of "reading in" isn't so transparent. If the vendor hasn't done the work for you—including creating a graphical interface—you're left with hexadecimal numbers and obscure variable names.

Network management must become more than device management; it must include tightly integrated network management applications. For example, Cabletron, the maker of the network management system Spectrum, has teamed with several companies that make management applications, in addition to the usual suspects of device management. Two such partners are Remedy Network Systems, a maker of a trouble-ticking application, and Isicad, a maker of facilities management and tracking software. The companies have exposed their product architectures to each other and are writing interfaces so that the products can communicate directly. The users will gain a tightly integrated management environment that can detect problems with network devices (Spectrum), send and manage trouble tickets to technicians (Remedy), and manage device inventory (Isicad).

Better integration at the device level also is required. For the most part, network management is really local area network management. Very little integration with WAN products has been achieved. For true enterprise-wide network management, WAN products, such as T-1 devices, modems, and multiplexers, must be managed in conjunction with their bridges and routers. SNMP will play an important role here. SNMP is becoming popular in the telecommunications world, as it has among the LAN internetworking vendors. More and more telecom vendors are supporting SNMP management, including Micom and Network Equipment Technologies.

One challenge of integrating the management of different devices and building management applications is priorities. When several network management modules detect a problem, which one is really seeing the root of the problem? Which alarm is most serious? For example, if a user can't access a remote file server, and the network management receives alarms from the T-1 mux, a router, a server, and a user device, which one is really seeing the original problem and which ones are reacting to secondary problems? Alarm correlation is a challenge that management vendors are tackling.

# Security Issues in an Enterprise-Wide Network

Keeping the network operational is a key part of management, but far from the only facet. Ensuring data integrity is the role of security management. By building an enterprise-wide network, you are opening up access to data and thereby increasing its risk of intentional or accidental damage. As the economy tightens and competitive global pressure increases, fewer workers make more decisions. Even though users need access to more information, the data must remain protected. The golden rule of security is *need to know*. If users need the information, give them access; otherwise, don't.

Threats to your data come from accidental and intentional acts. People make mistakes. They accidentally delete important files—accounts receivable, perhaps. Machines have glitches, hard disks crash, and tape backups fail. People are malicious—they plant viruses or purposely destroy or corrupt files.

# Assess Your Security Exposure

The first step in securing the enterprise-wide network is to perform a risk/exposure assessment. A *risk/exposure assessment* determines how much you can afford to lose and how likely you are to lose it. Evaluate the types of information stored on the network and how easy it is to get at that information. A server with payroll information needs greater security than does a printer server.

For each department, evaluate how the users are organized. Are there workgroups or do workers frequently cross departmental lines? Can you restrict employees into workgroups, or otherwise limit their access to only the information they need to know? By grouping users based on their requirements, you can contain a problem if it occurs.

Department managers should not have universal access to the network's data. They may be the bosses, but that doesn't give them the right to have complete and free access to information. Similarly, network administrators should not have access to the contents of files. They manage the network, not the business functions.

Next, make a security plan that consists of the following elements:

- *Access levels and definitions.* Access has several aspects: authorization, identification, access control, accountability, and auditability.

- *Workgroups and how they map to the access rules.* Define who is in each workgroup or department, and which workgroups have access to which data, application software, and server volumes.

- *Access rules.* Define your company's password policies and rules for accessing server volumes.

- *Physical installation and access guidelines.* What devices are locked in wiring closets or server rooms?

- *Accountability guidelines.* Which network and business administrators are accountable for which servers and subnetworks?

- *Internetwork requirements and access levels.* What are the routing paths or bridging filters for the various subnetworks? Will you permit access to bulletin boards, asynchronous communication servers, or modems?

- *Periodic auditing policies.* Define how you will audit the security policy. Will you use software or reports? Stick to your stated policy.

■ *Software upgrade, auditing, and installation policies.* Some viruses are introduced through commercially available software, and many are downloaded from bulletin boards.

# Establishing Lines of Defense

You can establish lines of defense against security breaches and intrusions in your enterprise-wide network. As you define, publish, and enforce your security policies and procedures, remember that too much security is as detrimental as no security. If the security policies interfere with the users' ability to do their jobs, they will find ways around them. For example, if users need four different passwords that expire every 30 days to log into the network to access their E-mail, they may not use the E-mail system and won't gain the benefits of networking.

■ *Physical security.* Physical security is the most basic and simplest of the security methods. You can go to the extremes of using biometric devices to read the employees' retinas to make sure they are who they say they are, but locks and keys are effective enough to deter the casual data thief. Lock file servers, wiring hubs, bridges, routers, and telecommunications access equipment in a secure room. Users should not have direct physical access to network devices beyond workstations and printers or other devices where they could inadvertently or purposely alter the network's configuration or parameters.

■ *Authentication.* The next line of defense should be authentication. The network or a security service on the network must verify that the person is who he or she claims to be before allowing access. The security system can do this by requiring the person to deliver something (a password or a security card for example) or by verifying a physical characteristic (a fingerprint).

■ *Passwords.* Users routinely give their passwords to other workers, leave them written on desk blotters, or worse, tape them to their monitors. Users also typically use passwords that are easy to guess, such as their first names or a spouse's name.

■ *Secure access from the outside.* Any outside telecommunications link is a risk. Modem servers, while they make it very easy for employees on the road or at home to dial into the office network, are security risks because any user can dial into your network, impersonating a valid user. Limit access to certain directories or servers. Use modems that will call users back at specified numbers so that it will reduce the chance of intruders gaining access to the network.

- *Secure your remote services.* On UNIX machines, *rlogin* and *rshell* are often used as a mechanism to break into a system, because these commands allow users to move from one machine to another, gaining access rights as they go. Use Kerberos or a similar authentication scheme to prevent this (see the following section about Kerberos).

- *Imitated IP addresses.* Remote TCP/IP protocols identify machines by their network addresses. An intruder can disable the real machine and impersonate it using its IP address.

- *Use fiber-optic cabling.* In addition to the other benefits of fiber—ability to carry signals over long distances, immunity to electromagnetic interference, and vast amounts of bandwidth—fiber cabling is more secure than copper wiring. Whereas it's quite easy to eavesdrop on an electromagnetic conversation that's traversing a copper wire simply by placing a radio frequency receiver nearby, it's much more difficult to listen in on a light-based conversation on a fiber cable, because the intruder has to physically tap into the cable. The resulting dip in light levels can be detected.

- *Encryption.* Ultimately, the only way to truly protect the data going over the wire is encryption. Encryption is the scrambling of data so that it is nonsense to everyone except the authentic users who possess a key to decrypt it. The Data Encryption Standard (DES) is the most commonly implemented type of encryption.

Some network operating systems, including NetWare, permit you to encrypt passwords, but if your application is sensitive, you may want to consider using a third-party package to encrypt every packet that traverses the LAN and WAN. Then the data is nonsense to everyone except the intended receiver. Hardware-based encryption devices are faster and more secure than software-based encryption.

# Kerberos: Security for Multiprotocol Networks

A heterogeneous client/server environment presents a unique set of security problems. Whereas PCs, Macintoshes, UNIX systems, and VMS hosts all have their own security systems, the greatest difficulty is providing a security scheme that works among the different platforms. When you must mix platforms, few security schemes exist. Kerberos is an authentication protocol developed at MIS that's currently implemented for TCP/IP and UNIX networks, but will also be used to help secure UNIX, VMS, OS/2, DOS, and Mac machines.

Kerberos provides authentication, which means Kerberos determines who someone is, not what they can do. The particular Kerberos server must decide what services and files a user is allowed to access. To prove a user's identity, Kerberos uses three things: shared secrets, Data Encryption Standard (DES) encryption, and a system of tickets that allow a user to prove his identity to a server via a Kerberos server.

The shared secrets are keys, which are strings of characters used for encryption. They are so named because the secret is shared between the client and the server. You can decrypt the message only if you also know the same key. In Kerberos, some keys are *persistent*; they stay the same until someone changes them. Persistent keys are usually known only to the device they belong to, and to Kerberos. Session keys are good for only one communications session. Session keys may be known to Kerberos and two other entities, such as the client and the server.

Here's how Kerberos works: Kerberos uses a string of requests and tickets to authenticate a user's identity. The client's password is entered into a database at the Kerberos server, where it is encrypted. That encrypted password is the client's key. A ticket-granting service running on the Kerberos server issues a ticket, and the client uses that ticket to prove its identity to the server that the client wants to access.

When a user types a password to log onto a particular server, the Kerberos client software sends a request to the Kerberos server, asking it to issue a ticket that grants the client another ticket. The Kerberos server responds with a message encrypted in the client's key that contains the ticket-granting-ticket. This ticket-granting-ticket is the shared secret between the client and the Kerberos server.

The client uses this key to decrypt the message from the Kerberos server. At that point, the client has the ticket, and its ability to decrypt the message and obtain the ticket proves to the Kerberos server that the user gave the right password. The user has had to prove his identity without ever sending his password across the network, which is critical if you are trying to prevent users with protocol analyzers from snooping network passwords off the wire.

The client software sends its requests to the Kerberos server, encrypting them in the shared key. The Kerberos server provides tickets for the services that the user wants to use.

The ticket server also demands that the client send another piece of proof that he is who he says he is. This authenticator consists of a time stamp, the user's address, and user's name, which are also encrypted. The time stamps have to be within a certain period of each other, although the time slot varies among the different versions of Kerberos. Requiring a time period reduces the odds that an intruder could steal a password and key and impersonate the rightful user, thus gaining improper access to the network. Once the ticket-getting-ticket is obtained, the client will obtain tickets for services as needed, without user intervention.

Separate tickets are required for each service on each server machine. The requirement for a new ticket for each server breaks the "chain of trust" inherent in remote UNIX protocols. Kerberos keeps track of which servers you're allowed to access and lets you into only those servers. Kerberos is an important security scheme for multiprotocol networks.

# Planning for Disaster

Here are some statistics to think about: The average network is disabled 23.6 times a year for an average of 4.9 hours each time. That's twice a month. An average company loses an average of more than $606,000 in revinue per year because of downtime, yet companies spend only $60,000 per year in LAN maintenance to keep these networks running. The average Fortune 1000 company spends more than $650,000 per year in LAN performance up-grades.[3]

These statistics are taken from a research report from Infonetics. Since 1989, when Infonetics interviewed 100 MIS and network managers at Fortune 1000 companies, the situation has become worse, if anything. At that time, networks were largely departmental; today, they are internetworks and enterprise-wide networks. Problems such as broadcast storms, jabbering or beaconing devices, and configuration errors can disable an entire LAN. Telecommunications failures can halt an entire WAN. As more data is placed on networks and as companies rely more heavily on their networks, the severity of each failure increases like rings in a pond. And, these are just "normal," everyday failures.

[3]Infonetics. "The Cost of LAN Downtime," San Jose, CA: Infonetics Research, Sept. 1989.

What would happen to your network and, subsequently, your business if electrical power were out for a half-hour? Or eight hours? Easy, you say—the uninterruptible power supplies on the file servers would provide battery-backed-up power, and when the batteries ran out of juice, they would gracefully shut down the network. If the servers were running a mission-critical application, you would have spare batteries, charged up and ready to go. But what would happen to your network if a fire broke out in the data center? An earthquake? A tornado? Or any other natural disaster?

While you consider your answer, here's another statistic to keep in mind: 43 percent of all companies that don't prepare and suffer a disaster never recover. Of those who do reopen, 90 percent are out of business within two years.

Mainframes are well-protected. They're housed in air-conditioned, raised-floor rooms. Their data is backed up every day. The tapes are periodically moved off-site, in case a natural disaster strikes. But networks, even enterprise-wide ones, typically are not. What about your network servers? Do you have redundant bridges or routers for mission-critical devices? Do you have redundant telecommunications links between important sites? The cure is costly, but the illness is worse.

Disaster recovery plans range from having UPSs to off-site storage to redundant file servers, hosts, internetworking devices, and communications lines, either leased or owned outright. Of course, overplanning is costly. If users are sending E-mail and sharing printers with their NetWare server, an hour of downtime will be inconvenient but not disastrous. If the users are telemarketers taking orders, however, an hour of downtime will have direct, measurable results in the number of sales.

The balance between too much protection and too little is delicate. A number of companies specialize in disaster recovery, including AT&T, IBM, ChiCor, Comdisco, and Sunguard. Additionally, accounting and computer consulting firms can help you formulate your disaster recovery plan.

# Fault Tolerance and Redundancy

The most insidious problems on a network are far less dramatic than a fire or earthquake. These disasters don't make the newspaper headlines, but they are far more prevalent and possibly just as damaging—users and normal equipment use can be a danger to the network. This section discusses redundancy issues on the LAN and on the enterprise-wide network.

# Fault Tolerance on the LAN

When you are considering fault tolerance on the LAN, consider the network design. Make sure that there are no single points of failure, and, if a network device is critical, you may want to have a hot backup. Also consider issues such as keeping backups on-site so that if a device fails it can be replaced quickly. You may want to have multiple runs of wiring at local sites and configure dual FDDI rings.

Users make mistakes. They delete the wrong files, accidentally restructure databases, or press a combination of keys that suddenly makes the accounts payable file disappear. The AC power can surge, spike, brown out, or black out, potentially causing problems by blowing out circuits, hard disks, and other electronics. The normal operation of writing to and reading from a disk, for example, causes wear and tear that eventually can result in a disk crash or disk controller meltdown. Bridges, routers, gateways, modems, and other LAN equipment can fail.

The front line of fault tolerance is backup. Even if you diligently back up the servers daily and store the weekly backups off-site, however, the day will come when a user accidentally deletes accounts payable, hours before the month is supposed to be closed. Yesterday's backup is worthless because all of today's work must be reentered. Fault tolerance is in order.

The theory of fault tolerance is that two is better than one. If you have two identical components and one fails, you can use the second one. Most often, fault tolerance is applied to server disks. The simplest form of redundant disks is *mirroring*, in which two disks are exact images of each other. Each write is made to both disks so that they stay in sync (see Figure 10.17). If one disk fails, the network administrator can disconnect it and swap in the good disk (or the software can do it automatically), and operation continues virtually without stopping.

The first catch of redundancy is that having two doesn't necessarily double the speed; it often decreases performance. For example, with disk mirroring, one disk controller makes every write twice, doubling network traffic. Mirroring decreases performance, but better guarantees the system's operation.

The next step in redundant disks is *duplexing*. As in mirroring, there are two disks, but also two disk controllers. Duplicating the controller protects against the possibility of the failure of the controller as well as against the failure of the media, which mirroring protects against. Duplexing also allows writes to occur much faster because one disk controller doesn't have to manage two disks. This improves performance (see Figure 10.18).

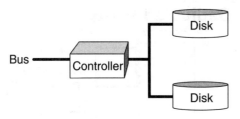

**Figure 10.17.** *Disk mirroring (RAID 1).*

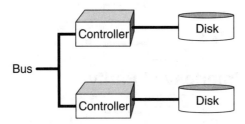

**Figure 10.18.** *Disk duplexing.*

The next step in disk redundancy involves the use of the terms *disk array* and *RAID*, or *r*edundant *a*rray of *i*nexpensive *d*isks. Simply, a disk array consists of multiple disks used in parallel. It uses multiple "ordinary" disks rather than a single disk to store information (see Figure 10.19). Disk array ensures redundancy using *parity*, a mathematical calculation that enables the disk array to reconstruct any information stored on the data disks if a drive fails. RAID, used first with supercomputers, is becoming an intrinsic part of mission-critical networks.

Five levels of RAID are defined:

■ *RAID 1.* In disk mirroring, all data is written to two disks. RAID 1 provides good interactive performance and does not incur a write penalty, but it requires you to buy twice the storage to use only half of it, thereby doubling the cost of storage. The write penalty can be slightly offset by duplexing the disks.

■ *RAID 2.* This level has supercomputer applications, but it is not used for transaction processing and LANs. In RAID 2, bit-interleaved data is transferred across multiple disks, and additional disks perform error detection using the Hamming code algorithm.

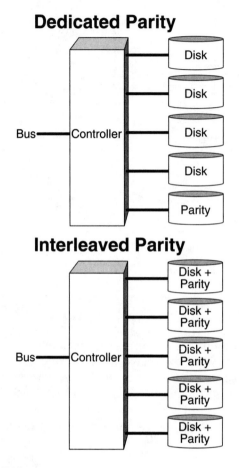

**Figure 10.19.** *Disk array.*

■ *RAID 3.* RAID 3 uses one dedicated parity drive and an even number of drives for storing data. In operation, data is transferred to the data drives one byte at a time, and parity is calculated and stored on the dedicated parity drive. RAID 3 uses a single drive controller, and reads and writes are performed in parallel. RAID 3's sequential performance is very high, but because the multiple drives do not operate independently, its on-line and interactive performance is low (see Figure 10.20).

| 00 | 01 | 02 | 03 | | |
| 04 | 05 | 06 | 07 | parity | RAID 3 |
| 08 | 09 | 10 | 11 | | |
| 12 | 13 | 14 | 15 | | |

| Sector 0 | 00 | 01 | 02 | 03 | | |
| Sector 1 | 04 | 05 | 06 | 07 | parity | RAID 4 |
| Sector 2 | 08 | 09 | 10 | 11 | | |
| Sector 3 | 12 | 13 | 14 | 15 | | |

| Sector 0 | parity | 00 | 01 | 02 | 03 | |
| Sector 1 | 04 | parity | 05 | 06 | 07 | RAID 5 |
| Sector 2 | 08 | 09 | parity | 10 | 11 | |
| Sector 3 | 12 | 13 | 14 | parity | 15 | |

**Figure 10.20.** *RAID levels 3, 4, and 5.*

- *RAID 4.* This RAID level is similar to RAID 3 in that it has one dedicated parity drive; however, it does not write data in parallel. Instead, the controller writes data one sector at a time. Because reads and writes occur on independent drives, reads can be made from any of the drives, thereby improving performance. RAID 4 incurs a write penalty, however, because parity information must be updated for every write (see Figure 10.20).

- *RAID 5.* In the highest defined level of RAID, the controllers write data one segment at a time and interleave parity bits among all the disks. Unlike RAIDs 3 and 4, RAID 5 does not use a dedicated parity disk. RAID 5 offers good read performance, but it incurs a write penalty when parity information is changed. RAID 5 generally writes at a fourth of the speed of a single disk. RAID 5 is better with smaller files (see Figure 10.20).

Which RAID is right? It depends on what's important: cost, bandwidth performance, transaction performance, or data availability. Disk arrays are expensive, and they aren't necessarily faster than using a single disk (as they often are portrayed). Use Table 10.2 to help you find the right level of RAID, and consider these points: This matrix, developed by NCR's peripheral products division, assumes a 10-drive configuration. The cost-per-megabyte column assumes that the controller consumes 16 percent of the drive costs and represents the space available for user—not parity—data.

Table 10.2. Which RAID level is right for you?

| RAID | Cost/MB | Storage Bandwidth | Transaction Data | Level User Data Density Performance | Performance Availability |
|------|---------|-------------------|------------------|-------------------------------------|--------------------------|
| RAID 0 | 1 | 1 | 0.25 | 1 | 0.0005 |
| RAID 1 | 0.5 | 0.5 | 0.25 | 0.6 | 1 |
| RAID 3 | 0.8 | 0.8 | 1 | 0.2 | 0.99 |
| RAID 4 | 0.8 | 0.8 | 0.25 | 0.5 | 0.99 |
| RAID 5 | 0.8 | 0.8 | 0.25 | 0.5 | 0.99 |

The entire server can fail, but mirroring and duplexing really protect only the administrator from disk failure. The next step is server redundancy, and it must be enabled at the level of the operating system. Two servers are set up in parallel, down to the cable. One is the primary server, and the second is a mirror image. Every I/O operation that crosses the bus of one server is duplicated to the second server. Such a high level makes PC LAN NOSs suitable for transaction-processing environments because the completion of each operation is virtually assured. This level of fault tolerance can speed network performance also. Because the two servers are identical, reads can be satisfied by either server. This level of fault tolerance will be provided by NetWare SFT III when it ships.

# Fault Tolerance on the Enterprise-Wide Network

When you are building fault tolerance into an enterprise-wide network, consider the critical points—whose failure can bring down the network. These include internetworking devices such as bridges and routers, and WAN circuits. Configure multiple WAN circuits per site using routers and bridges that can handle multiple paths. Use diverse carrier paths on circuits leaving a site. If the telco circuits return to the same central office switch by way of the same telephone wire, a single outage can take out both circuits. Make sure that you have different carrier paths. Consider contracting with multiple carriers so that if one carrier's network fails, the other one may still be up. If you're making international connections, don't send all your traffic over the same equipment or use the same public data network or satellite network.

When you are building in fault tolerance on an enterprise-wide network, consider duplicating critical internetworking devices, such as bridges and routers, so that you don't have a single point of failure. Routers were designed with the capability to change network paths if they detect a fault. Bridges also can do so; however, because they are simpler, the fault tolerance is not as elegant.

To build fault tolerance into bridged internetworking, you must configure two sets of bridges in parallel. For EtherNet, these MAC-layer bridges must implement the *IEEE 802.1D spanning tree algorithm*. With parallel bridges, if the primary bridge fails, the secondary bridge jumps into action and users can continue without interruption. Without parallel bridges, if one of the remote bridge "halves" fails, the network is partitioned and users are unable to communicate.

IEEE 802.1D manages this redundancy. Configuring parallel transparent bridges creates a closed loop in the EtherNet topology, which the specification forbids because it causes the bridges to update their address tables incorrectly and eventually prevents proper network operation. Resolving the closed-loop problem requires that the bridges exchange sufficient information to derive a spanning tree. Each bridge is assigned a unique identifying number, and each port is assigned a cost. If the network manager sets all port costs as equal, the optimal path is the one with the fewest number of hops or connections between routers. The administrator could assign lower costs to ports with higher speed lines, which would make the optimal path the one with the fastest lines. The bridges then exchange messages to discover the minimum-cost spanning tree. Traffic then flows over this route. When the network topology changes, the bridges recalculate the cost (see Figure 10.21).

You can configure parallel bridges in a Token-Ring network to ensure a level of fault tolerance. With the source routing used in Token Ring, the path is determined at the beginning of the transmission session, not at the time the device is powered on. During route discovery, each station sends a single-routes broadcast frame around the ring. As each bridge receives the broadcast, it adds the unique numbers of the two LANs it connects in addition to its bridge number. A bridge number is required because parallel bridges may be configured, and the frame has to know which bridge on the LAN segment it traversed. Bridge numbers do not have to be unique because they are required to only distinguish parallel bridges. For this to work, only certain bridges, arranged in a spanning tree topology, are configured to pass single-routes packets.

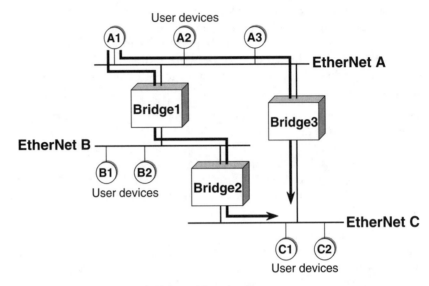

*Figure 10.21.  Transparent bridging with a spanning tree.*

Routers inherently provide fault tolerance. In addition to being able to choose a different path if the primary path fails, routers can perform load balancing, dividing the traffic over several links, according to traffic levels, packet types, addresses, or other criteria. A router also performs flow control and packet fragmentation.

# Redundancy in Network Components

Consider redundancy for critical network components such as server disks, server, and internetworking devices. Redundancy often doubles the initial cost and doesn't necessarily improve performance; if a failure occurs, however, the savings in productivity easily can pay for the cost of having hot spares. The following list summarizes redundancy options for important network equipment.

- *Departmental resources.* For disks, redundancy options include mirroring, duplexing, and RAID 3, 4, and 5. For servers, redundancy options include redundant server disks and spares on the shelf. Options soon will include hot spares, such as those that will be delivered by NetWare SFT III.

- *Local LANs.* For wiring, use multiple runs of cable for critical local sites. For LAN hardware, use dual FDDI rings for critical loops, or configure a secondary Token-Ring or EtherNet network that is used only in the event of an emergency.

- *Internetworking.* For bridges, options include EtherNet bridges configured in parallel using the spanning tree algorithm. Token-Ring bridges using source routing recalculate the path if a link goes down. Routers automatically reroute a transmission if a link failure occurs.

- *Enterprise.* Use multiple WAN circuits per line. Use diverse carrier paths on circuits leaving a site. Use diverse routes for international or long-haul lines.

# Managing Your Enterprise-Wide Network

An enterprise-wide network demands the cooperation of MIS, LAN, and telecommunications technologies, and as such its management requires the melding of those different expertises. Successfully managing your enterprise-wide network demands that you balance the technology aspects and personnel aspects.

Honestly assess the ability of your MIS, LAN, and telecommunications structures to function in the enterprise environment. Evaluate the amount and quality of LAN management that's performed in the local business units. You will probably have to redistribute the management responsibilities among the traditional technical departments and the business departments. A rule of thumb: give the responsibility to whatever group is best able to carry it out.

Don't rely on a single person to run the network. Most companies retain one expert, which leaves the company vulnerable. Nor should you wait for the arrival of a single "super-tool" that will manage every aspect of the network.

Enterprise network management will always require the use of many different tools, often coming from the LAN, internetwork, and telecommunications worlds. The best you can hope for is a consolidation of management systems and better integration and communication among the tools that you do use. Look for management hardware and software that accommodates multivendor network management, is based on standards, is flexible, and provides you with enough information that you can make proactive decisions.

Remember that network management should be proactive rather than reactive. Although most administrators spend their time putting out "fires," the goal of network management is to be able to anticipate problems rather than to react to them. More tools are becoming available for these functions. The daily network management functions provide critical information for strategic planning. In the effort to maintain your network, don't neglect change management, security management, and performance management.

Plan for disaster. Whether nature- or user-inspired, data will be lost, servers will crash, routers will fail, and telecommunications lines will go down. Have a disaster recovery plan written so that you are ready if disaster strikes.

Organize your enterprise IS department to perform three overall functions: administration, operation, and planning. Administrative services include inventory, operations management, and user and device registration. Operational services include problem management, fault management, and application services. Planning includes capacity, new technologies, and environmental issues.

In delivering these services, consider how they will be delivered. Will you implement a centralized or decentralized structure? What will be the roles and responsibilities of the groups involved? How will you handle end user and technician training? How will you define, establish, and publish policies, procedures, and processes for the enterprise-wide network? Then consider the products and tools that are required to implement and automate the enterprise-wide network.

# The Future of Enterprise-Wide Networks

## CHAPTER 11

*Objectives:*

1. To discuss the future of network technology, including network integration, metropolitan area networks, FDDI, ATM, SMDS, SONET, and the shift toward standards.

2. To discuss the future of network management, including network management tools and the consolidation and subsequent distribution of the management structure and responsibilities.

3. To discuss the future of network applications, including the arrival of client/server applications, true distributed applications, multimedia applications, and imaging applications.

4. To discuss the evolution of networks, including personal communications networks, networks to the home, and global internetworking.

# The Future of Network Technology

Industry pundits bemoan every new development as an evolutionary one, when in reality networks are undergoing a revolution unlike any before. Networks have become commonplace; they're accepted. Networks have metamorphosed from a technology that companies used to improve their business to an integral part of a company's structure. Companies rely on their networks to give them a strategic advantage, not just to run their companies a little better. Companies are betting their businesses on their information systems and computer networks.

For instance, American Airlines' Sabre reservation system gives the company a strategic advantage. Travel agents can use Sabre to book passenger reservations on a number of airlines, but because they can use fewer keystrokes to book tickets on American than for other airlines, they tend to do the easier thing. Dow Jones uses its satellite-based network for everything from transmitting editorial and advertising pages of the Wall Street Journal to sending fax and voice traffic. The ability to download information to the printer at the last minute and therefore have a more accurate newspaper is so important to Dow Jones that the company was one of the early investigators into frame relay, an emerging 2Mbps wide-area service offering.

In a global marketplace, immediacy of information can give a company a strategic advantage over its competitors. An enterprise-wide network is the plumbing that can deliver information to any user at any time. An enterprise-wide network will be one key to success in the next decade.

Perhaps the most fundamental and important change is an architectural change. No longer do networks take on hierarchical structures; the days of the mainframe and the SNA/SDLC pyramid are waning. The new architecture is peer-to-peer, and any information server—be it a mainframe, a PC server, or a RISC machine—can directly access resources on any other server. Unlike with the mainframe hierarchy, no one host reigns supreme. Peer-to-peer, enterprise-wide networks are comprised of myriad servers, minicomputers, and mainframes from a wide range of vendors.

This architecture brings a great deal of flexibility, but at the price of complexity. The only sure thing about networks is that the kaleidoscope of technology changes constantly. Networks are constructed individually; each is unique.

This allows a company to tailor its network to its business needs, therefore giving it an advantage over a cookie-cutter solution.

Because of the rapid pace of change, you should consider modifying the typical 3-year to 5-year planning cycle to be an 18-month to 3-year cycle. Although your cable plant may indeed be viable for 5 to 10 years, chances are your computing systems and applications will not have such a long, useful life. Network technology changes too quickly for anyone to have a clear picture of what will happen 5 years from now. Plan to change now and you won't be caught by surprise.

Important areas of change include: network integration, FDDI and fiber LANs, new WAN services, and a shift toward standards.

# Network Integration

The system vendors—IBM, Digital Equipment, and Hewlett-Packard—no longer present a supreme vision of corporate computing, forcing customers to make more decisions about what computing equipment to purchase, and even what vendors to purchase from. No longer is it accepted and common practice for an IS manager to allow the system vendor to dictate the solution. A force-fitted or cookie-cutter solution does not enable a company to build a network to its strategic business advantage.

The absence of one or two vendors leading the way has created confusion in the marketplace. What does an IS manager do? You have several options:

■ Continue to allow your systems vendor to act as your systems integrator and dictate your solutions.

■ Hire a systems integrator that will provide you vendor-independent advice.

■ Gain the expertise in your staff—either by hiring the expertise or training a current employee—so that the role of systems integrator can be played in-house.

■ Wait and do nothing, hoping that a clear solution will present itself.

Waiting and watching could be the most detrimental action, because your competitors may be integrating their own networks in the meantime. You need to define your own vision, either with outside, independent expertise or by gaining that expertise within your staff.

Systems integration, however, is a complex business. Today's computing landscape has SNA, minicomputers, PC LANs of every type, and telecommunications. Products are proprietary and standards-based from many different manufacturers. Even a single-vendor solution now comprises a variety of open systems and proprietary products. For example, you may decide to stay with IBM, and still have to choose among Token Ring, Ethernet, and FDDI as well as between NetWare and LAN Server.

The need for network integration and services is vast, and by market research projections, this segment will explode. Companies specializing in network integration will help companies define a computing strategy and then implement it. Integrators will be large (such as Electronic Data Systems and Arthur Andersen), to medium-sized (such as US Connect and Evernet), to small (such as your LAN reseller on the corner). Each type will be able to provide a unique point of view. For example, EDS or Arthur tend to provide a high-level strategic view, whereas a LAN reseller presents a nuts-and-bolts version. Also new to the integration business are companies that once manufactured hardware, such as Wang, that are reselling other companies' hardware and providing network integration services.

Consider partnering with an integrator as well as developing expertise in-house. Get as intimately involved in the business aspects of the network as the technology aspects. If your network is indeed strategic, you should maintain its planning and control in-house, even if you choose to outsource or subcontract the maintenance to a third party.

# FDDI and Fiber LANs

FDDI, the 100Mbps Fiber Distributed Data Interface fiber-optic LAN, has long been proclaimed as being on the verge of a population explosion. Despite the projections, however, the actual installed base of FDDI is quite small—less than 10 percent in 1991 by several market researchers' estimates. Still FDDI is an important technology. Why?

FDDI is most important as a backbone technology. Its access method is optimized for a large network with thousands of stations, providing fair and equal access to the network services. Fiber enables it to cover a large geographic area and enables a high bandwidth. Companies are internetworking their networks into a single campus network, and FDDI offers both the bandwidth and geographic coverage to deliver adequate service. In addition, an FDDI network can span several hundred kilometers, which provides sufficient coverage for most companies' networks within a single city.

A revolution in network applications will force the use of high-speed LANs to the desktop. Although FDDI is optimized for use as a backbone technology, it will run to the desktop, providing end-users with vast amounts of bandwidth. More than just engineers working on computer-aided design drawings will need this bandwidth, however. In the next decade, multimedia applications will be developed. People will no longer use character-based applications or even Windows-based applications; they will gain the benefit of still four-color images, full-motion video, and interactive video. Books will be published on CD-ROM. Schools are adopting multimedia and FDDI systems for students. If priced properly, copper FDDI will be the medium that brings these applications to workers, students, and other people.

# Metropolitan and Wide Area Networks—ATM, SMDS, and SONET

FDDI will be implemented largely by an end-user company for private use, rather than offered as a service from a network provider company. As with their departmental LANs, corporations will own all of the equipment for their networks. Another option exists: instead of actually owning the equipment, companies can lease network services from a third party, usually a telephone company of some sort. For public service, many companies will lease SMDS and ATM service.

Metropolitan Area Networks (MANs) will enable companies to efficiently and effectively connect their locations within a limited geographical area, usually a city. Companies can build a private MAN or use a public service as offered by a telephone service provider (see Figure 11.1).

LAN standards are largely for campus networks; they offer limited speed and distances. Even FDDI, which offers 100Mbps of bandwidth, is relatively restricted in geographical coverage. MANs are the answer to LANs' limitations. MANs are designed to carry different types of traffic simultaneously over longer distances and at greater speeds than LANs. Whereas LANs—even FDDI—are designed to carry data, MANs accommodate the integration of voice, video, and data over the same network. Such simultaneous service enables a company to integrate its now-discrete communications. In addition to combining voice and data services, MANs enable companies to partake in applications such as videoconferencing.

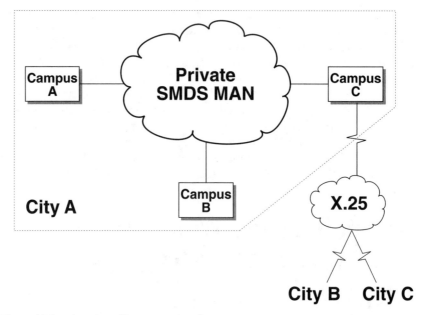

*Figure 11.1.* *A metropolitan area network.*

Characteristically, MANs offer data rates above 100Mbps, cover a geographic area up to several hundred kilometers, support a thousand stations, and have low error rates. Options for the physical layer include fiber, CATV coaxial cable, and wireless transmissions; however, fiber is likely to be the most popular. Switched Multimegabit Data Service (SMDS) is likely to be the MAN service of choice. SMDS provides networking at T-1 (1.5Mbps) or T-3 speeds (44.7Mbps), thereby providing sufficient bandwidth even for multimedia applications shared among many users. For applications requiring even larger bandwidth, the telephone companies will offer a SONET-level service.

MANs may be publicly or privately owned. A company could install its own MAN equipment or lease the service from a provider. A telephone company could install a metropolitan area network and sell its service. For example, Contel, the Florida regional Bell operating company, has installed an FDDI MAN in Tallahassee and offers a pretariffed trial service that the city of Tallahassee uses to connect several of its government offices.

The RBOCs and interexchange carriers are deploying public SMDS service as the technology matures. Over the next five years, end-user companies will be able to buy SMDS service as easily and perhaps as cheaply as they buy T-1 or X.25 today. The telephone companies are lining up heavily behind MANs, hoping to be the public service providers for network interconnections. Buying MAN service from a provider can make good sense and allow an end-user company to concentrate its resources on core business technologies.

Beyond SMDS is ATM, or asynchronous transfer mode. Although ATM will support circuit-mode operations for voice, it will be done over a packet-based transport mechanism. As with frame relay, ATM allows multiple logical connections to be multiplexed over a single interface, which will allow an ATM network to support many different types of services and channels. ATM will be deployed by the telephone companies over the next 5 to 10 years. Many of the details of the specification have yet to be standardized; however, ATM will play an important role in high-speed networks.

FDDI will largely be used as a private, relatively localized service. SMDS will be available before ATM, and that service will generally be leased from the telephone companies. ATM is some 5 to 10 years out. When ATM is available, you will be able to lease it from the phone companies as well.

## The Shift Toward Standards

Technology changes rapidly, but it changes in a world that is increasingly standards-based. Many people criticize standards for stunting creativity, by forcing all engineers to design the same product; however, standards also level the playing field so that a minimum level of service is guaranteed. From there, engineers can design additional features to the products. Standards actually fertilize a product type, allowing for more competitors and ultimately lower prices. You should build your network from standards-based products, because doing so will allow you to choose from a wide base of products and ensure your network's modularity, and therefore its flexibility. Standards can be dictated by the size of the installed base or by an official standards-creating body.

# The Future of Network Management

Companies are building networks that connect every computer in every location, but they are living "on the edge." They can't quite manage the network they've created. Most MIS departments don't even know about all the devices that are connected to their networks. They typically don't know all the types of devices, how many devices there are, and sometimes they don't even know about all the external connections to the network.

More dire than just not knowing about network inventory is the fact that most administrators don't have a good reading on the network's health. Mostly network managers monitor the network, but they can't control it. They react to network catastrophes instead of anticipating problems in a proactive manner.

Network management will continue to change in several areas: more sophisticated tools, a consolidation of management structure, and a decentralization of structure.

# Network Management Tools

Network managers don't want users to call them to tell them that the network has broken. They don't want to have to run down the hall with a Sniffer to attach it to the failed segment so that they can begin the laborious process of decoding protocols. Network administrators want to sit in their chairs, working on a better network design and be notified by a device—not a user—when a problem exists. Network managers want a box that sits in the corner of their offices, collecting dust until it sees something go wrong with the network. Then the box should leap into action; it should diagnose and fix the problem, and then tell the network administrator what it has done to fix the problem.

This scenario is an ideal one, and this box exists only in the imaginations of harried network managers. Today's network management falls hideously short. Network management tools monitor the network; they don't manage it, and they certainly don't control it. Most provide almost nothing in the way of security. At best, a tool watches the MAC-layer traffic and tells the administrator that it has noticed an anomalous packet pattern. Useful information is scarce; information, when given, is usually in overwhelming and ultimately useless detail. Very often, the tools don't even have the courtesy to speak the same language that the administrator speaks, instead giving the information in hexadecimal or some other computer-speak.

Hope for network management lies in better management systems, more tightly integrated applications, and expert system technology. With applications written specifically for network management, such as trend analysis or trouble-ticketing, network managers and technicians can spend their time solving more meaningful problems instead of setting up protocol filters and interpreting hexadecimal addresses.

Expert system and rules-based systems can help turn network management into a proactive art rather than a reactive stance. For example, a management system powered by an expert system can give administrators a useful assessment of the problem, not just a hexadecimal packet dump. It can tell the difference between a station that's quiet because it has failed and one that's quiet because it is not used much. With expert system technology, an administrator doesn't have to go through elaborate machinations to tell the management system what to look for. The system already knows. Add another piece of software and the analyzer could try to solve the problem and notify the administrator of the action. This vision is still a bit futuristic. A preemptive strike on network management is an essential part of a good network design.

In the quest for proactive management, management applications need to communicate with each other, passing along network intelligence. For example, if a device-management application detects a failure, it could trigger an inventory application to get detailed information about the device— exactly what it is, where it's located, who manages it, whether it's under warranty, and who owns it. That management application could then trigger a trouble-ticketing application that tells a network technician that the device is failing. The inventory information is also delivered to the technician. All the while, the device management application could be running diagnostics on the device. This way, when the technician is told about the problem, she has a baseline of information. She didn't discover the problem through an irate user's phone call.

LAN and WAN integration must be tightly integrated, and this is one area that must be vastly improved. Today, LAN managers have one set of tools and telecom managers have another set of tools. Little, if any, overlap exists, even in a common area such as protocol analyzers. Enterprise network management demands the integration of the two tool bases. For example, if there is a traffic flow problem, the source could be a server, a router, a WAN device, or a WAN service. Management applications must differentiate local problems from WAN problems. Applications must be integrated and communicate with each other.

Trouble-ticketing systems will become crucial. Whereas trouble ticketing is common in mainframes, it's rare to nonexistent for PC networks. Technicians and administrators fill out electronic trouble tickets or forms when a problem arises. This maintains a record of all problems and actions. Technicians can also search through the base of existing tickets to see if a similar problem has occurred and how that technician solved it. This system not only preserves the history of learned information, but also it enables less experienced technicians to learn from others.

Security must be improved. In order for network management applications to tightly control the network, security systems must be in place so that the network management doesn't create a security hole. Security must be implemented at the user level as well. Many corporations get hit by a virus but still don't implement security. This lackadaisical attitude is a recipe for disaster. Networks absolutely must be secured, and the importance only increases as departmental networks are connected into an enterprise network. Access to data is broadened, and more important data is kept on the network.

# Management Consolidation and Decentralization

Many companies make the error of relying on a single person to manage the entire network. This person—a guru—is often an engineer who helped design and install the network. Although this person undoubtedly knows the network best, it is very dangerous to have a single source of expertise of network planning and firefighting. What if that person leaves the company? It's too risky. Also, this person would have immense bargaining power and a high salary—something most companies would probably like to avoid.

Companies also often make the error of hoping that the be-all and end-all of management systems will come along. This system, they dream, will be able to manage the entire network, from T-connector to T-3 DSU/CSU. The ultimate in management systems is unlikely to ever appear. Instead, companies must realize that network management tools will never be sufficiently functional. They must also realize the dangers of relying on one guru to manage the network. And they must structure their IS departments accordingly.

The organizational structure of IS departments must change. It is not cost-effective for each department to plan, design, implement, and maintain its own network. For the network to be a strategic asset, the planning and designing must be performed by a central group. This group should be comprised of MIS, LAN, and telecommunications experts. MIS personnel must be cross-trained on the various systems, so that they understand the interactions of the different systems. Furthermore, MIS departments must not rely on the expertise of any one person to ensure the network's operation.

A strict hierarchical structure isn't necessarily the best. If the departmental networks are small, they can be managed remotely for the most part. In many instances, however, you'll want local administrators present to take responsibility for the daily tasks of network maintenance. Keep the planning and design functions centralized, but the daily maintenance, such as backups, can certainly be distributed to the departments. Whatever structure you choose, it's critical to clearly define and document the organizational roles and responsibilities. This will ensure that each department understands the beginning and end of its responsibilities toward the network.

# The Future of Network Applications

Most of what is considered to be a network application is actually quite primitive. Most applications running on networks were not designed from the ground up to take advantage of the distributed intelligence. Most of these applications simply don't "blow up" on a LAN. With the advent of client/server and distributed applications, however, applications will finally begin to take advantage of the LAN, fundamentally changing how people work. Imaging and multimedia applications will become prominent.

## The Advent of Client/Server Applications

Many corporations are downsizing, or reducing their reliance on host systems and increasing their dependence on LANs. This trend will continue, because mainframes are expensive to purchase and maintain, whereas PC and LAN servers are less expensive. Although some corporations dispose of their mainframes in favor of PC LANs, most use a combination. For example, companies may keep the critical inventory and accounting systems on the mainframe, where they are safe, locked away, and air-conditioned. But the data-entry or data-manipulation functions may be moved to the PC LAN, because people are comfortable using their familiar PCs or Macintoshes and MIS can off-load mainframe CPU cycles to a less expensive resource.

A key piece in the downsizing puzzle is client/server technology. With client/server, the server doesn't know who the clients are and the clients don't care who the servers are. You can use the same client—which may be a PC running Windows, for example—to access a database on an IBM mainframe, a Sybase SQL Server database, and a Novell NetWare SQL database. These databases could reside in different cities—Hong Kong, New York, and Paris, for example. The users don't know that they are accessing information that is located on different machine types or in different locations. The server, on the other hand, doesn't know that different types of clients are accessing its information because all of the clients, regardless of what types of machines they are, are using a common language and a common interface to talk to the server. Another benefit is modularity. Client/server applications can be divided into front ends and back ends, with the front end responsible for data presentation and user queries and the back end responsible for data storage and crunching. Different developers may write the separate yet interlocking pieces. This division of labor is crucial for the next generation of network applications, which includes mail-enabled applications and multimedia applications.

Client/server is finally here, and as corporations look to off-load their mainframes, PC LANs and client/server will play increasingly important roles. Not all of these applications need to be on a grand scale, where a DB2 database is eliminated in favor of a PC SQL database. Instead, it could start much more simply, where an MIS department writes an application to enable Windows users to automate their mainframe logons. From there, they could add functionality using existing IBM application programming interfaces to download mainframe mail to the PC, for example. From there, MIS might write routines to retrieve sales figures from a host database.

# True Distributed Applications

How these applications will be distributed across an enterprise network is not trivial. On the simplest level, client/server is the answer, but the real problem isn't having many clients accessing one server—that's really not much different than the mainframe model. The real problem is having many clients and many servers. Not only do the clients communicate with the servers, but the servers must communicate with each other. The servers may not be the same type. The servers may be on PC LANs, minicomputers, or mainframes, each using its own flavor of operating system and transport protocols.

Today, these connections are generally made on a one-to-one basis. It's relatively simple, for example, to connect your NetWare LAN to your IBM mainframe. In this case, you'll use gateways. If the systems are more similar, say a PC LAN and UNIX, you might run a version of the PC LAN NOS on a UNIX server or use TCP/IP as a common transport. It's a little more difficult to extract data from DB2 to Oracle for NetWare; it's not as brainless as installing a peer-to-peer LAN, but it's not rocket science either.

Making one-to-one connections is like having interpreters in the United Nations each talking the delegates' own languages, instead of speaking a form of Esperanto. Without a common language, a great deal of work is duplicated. The challenge is settling on that common language. The "right" common language directly depends on your environment, only there's no clear-cut solution. Few environments are "largely" IBM anymore. Consider enabling that database connection, but now make it among DB2, Oracle for UNIX, and SQLBase on a PC LAN. TCP/IP? APPN? No pat answer exists; the solution must be decided on a case-by-case basis.

# Multimedia and Imaging Applications

Network applications are primitive. Word processing, spreadsheets, and some databases are really stand-alone applications. They involve text and numbers, and nothing more. They don't *need* networks. E-mail and some databases, on the other hand, *need* networks. Still, they involve text and numbers, and little more. The next generation of applications, however, will be truly network-intrinisic. As networked applications develop, the content becomes more complex. The next generation of applications will reintegrate the components of communications: words, pictures, and sound. *Multimedia* and *imaging* will play a big role in the future of networks and applications.

Imaging is undergoing a revolution akin to the network revolution that happened in the mid-1980s. Traditionally, imaging has been limited to the high-end systems where EDI is in full force or restricted to workgroup applications where bitmapped images, such as maps, are transmitted. It was largely a stand-alone application run on various proprietary systems. Imaging is becoming standards-based and is moving from stand-alone applications to the department. Imaging is being incorporated into everyday applications, such as databases, E-mail, and ordinary documents.

Imagine the possibilities if a real estate agent could show prospective buyers photographs of houses for sale without having the prospective buyers drive to the site. The agent could simply call up a record in a database that listed the salient facts plus included good-resolution photographs. (Images can be incorporated into databases today, but not so elegantly.) Now imagine the agent being able to incorporate a full-motion video of the properties, walking the buyers throughout the room, all while sitting at a computer terminal. Prospective buyers and agents can save time by narrowing the buyers' choices before leaving the office.

Now imagine the power of incorporating still and full-motion video images in other applications. The content and meaning of mail, databases, or other applications can be vastly improved with the addition of sound and pictures. With videoconferencing and other multimedia applications in place, businesspeople don't have to leave their offices to have face-to-face meetings with others who are not in their offices. Multimedia can significantly change how education is conducted. Students no longer have to be in the same room with the professor, making it more convenient for people to learn and gain expertise.

Implementing imaging and multimedia applications will require a large amount of work. Databases, for example, don't handle large blocks of unstructured data very well. The BLOB data type is one answer, but new architectures may have to be invented. E-mail must be restructured to better accommodate multimedia components. Multimedia applications are CPU and bandwidth hogs. Powerful workstations will be necessary. As the price of desktop MIPS decreases, imaging can become more widespread. Compression techniques and the speed of the underlying transport must be vastly improved.

Because of the bandwidth requirements, LANs and WANs must be carefully designed to handle the load. Current network bandwidth will be insufficient when such applications become widespread, and FDDI, now largely viewed as a backbone technology, will become essential for those who want image capabilities. Unlike with character-based applications, any inefficiency will become painfully clear to the users of multimedia.

# The Evolution of Networks— What's Next?

Networks will extend beyond the doors of the workplace. Once established as staples of business, networks will move into the home. Personal communications networks will enable people to be connected to their home or work computers at all times. Networks will be used in the home. Companies will move beyond their enterprise networks, and build global networks to connect their suppliers and customers.

# Personal Communications Networks

Network users are tethered by cable. You can move the keyboard only as far as the cord allows you; you can move the PC only as far as the LAN cable allows. You can place network workstations only where a LAN cable exists. People were once tethered by the telephone cord and wire, but cordless phones and cellular phones now let them roam. The same advances will come for networking. *Mobile* or *personal communications* networking is key to users of portable, laptop, notebook, and palmtop computers.

With a network connection built onto the computer's motherboard and the ability to access a wireless network facility, users are no longer constrained by cable. Integrated LAN chips are just beginning. IBM and National Semiconductor are working on chips to be integrated onto motherboards. Apple ships its high-end PowerBooks with integrated Ethernet chips, and all Macs have either LocalTalk or Ethernet. Other vendors use the notebooks' parallel ports to attach a LAN card. Vendors are also solving the problem of connecting the notebook to the LAN in other ways, including integrated cellular modems. Integrated LAN support makes it easier for users to do their work off-line, make a wired or wireless link to the network server, download or upload information, and continue working (see Figure 11.2).

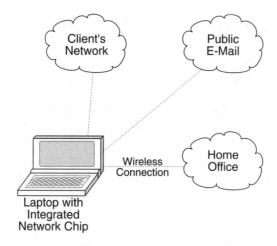

*Figure 11.2.   A personal communications network.*

Notebooks and nomadic networking are synergistic. Laptops and notebooks enable computer users to be freed from their desktop computers; wireless networking will provide the connection back to home base when it is necessary. On the local level, radio and infrared can be used. On the remote level, cellular modems and the telephone system can be used. The Federal Communications Commission is looking at redistributing the frequencies so that data communications can have a larger share of the spectrum. Public wireless services will be offered in the future, and service is likely to come from the traditional cellular phone service providers.

Roadblocks to personal communications include wireless transmission itself. Wireless LANs are in the very earliest stages, and performance and throughput must improve significantly. Standards work is being conducted, but because of the need to gain agreement among the hundreds of members of the IEEE committee, the pace will be slow. Even with well-engineered products, wireless transmission is slower than wire-based transmission. Also, few people are experienced with designing or managing wireless networks.

# Networks to the Home

An offshoot of metropolitan area networks is networks to the home. Today, the telephone and the television are the media-based information services in the home. The telephone is limited to sound, and with a modem it can be used for data. The television, although multimedia, is not interactive. Potential exists for integrating multimedia services and delivering them to the home much the way telephone service or television programming is delivered today (see Figure 11.3).

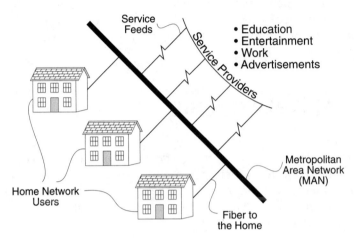

*Figure 11.3.* *Networks to the home.*

If the telephone companies run fiber directly to each subscriber's premise, whether a business or home, a great information revolution can occur. Today, the vast majority of phone networks are fiber anyway, and the last mile is often copper. Fiber needs to be run on this last mile, paving the way for these bandwidth-hungry applications.

With such an infrastructure, people at home can access information services such as individualized education, job training, entertainment, and (of course) advertising. Universities could broadcast classes over metropolitan area networks directly to television sets in homes. Students would not have to physically go to classrooms to learn. Such networks could be used to improve business's productivity. For example, if a problem occurs with a part, the drawing of the diagram could be transmitted to the expert engineer, no matter where the engineer was. The engineer could solve the problem, thereby saving many hours of work. Broadcast companies can provide entertainment programming, which could be far more customized to a viewer's preferences than is possible today. Such entertainment and education won't be one-sided as television is. With a computer attached to the television, people can interact with the programming or education services, and in the participation, will learn more.

Many obstacles exist to networking to the home, politics being the greatest. The cable television companies, the broadcast television networks, and the telephone companies all want to provide information and entertainment services to home users. All three have a delivery infrastructure in place. Such services are absolutely crucial in maintaining America's productivity as other countries—particularly Japan—will install fiber to every household and office by early next century, and subsequently could have such information-rich services.

# Global Networking

Corporations are embroiled in building networks that connect computers within their own locations, but the next connectivity step is to connect their enterprise networks to their suppliers' and customers' enterprise networks. This will enable global communications. For this to occur, networking must hit critical mass, where a large enough installed base of networks exists for customers and suppliers to be able to connect.

An internetwork of customers and suppliers saves time and labor, enabling the company to become more flexible and efficient. Companies do not have to maintain a centralized structure if their business practices are inherently decentralized. Global networks enable a company to let its business practices dictate its computing structure, rather than allowing its computing practices to control its business structure.

In such a configuration, just-in-time business is possible (see Figure 11.4). For example, a publishing company can enable its advertisers to dial into its network to place advertising insertion orders. No longer do advertisers have to obtain the order forms, fill them out, and fax them back. Writers can dial into the network and download articles; editors can upload articles, edit them, and return them. Such an editorial network permits writers and editors to be located wherever it is best for their jobs and lives, which may not necessarily be at the company's headquarters. Production of the books and magazines may occur at the most appropriate location. Such a network can connect the publishing company to its printers so that editorial and advertising pages can be downloaded directly to the printer, rather than printing them out, pasting the pages down, and sending them express mail to a remote printer. Printers may be located domestically or internationally, and pages could be delivered within the same time frame.

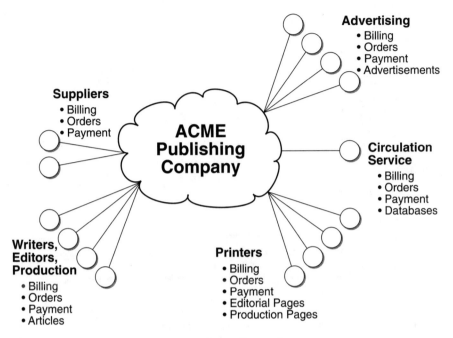

*Figure 11.4.* *Interconnecting a company's suppliers and customers.*

With just-in-time business, a company could reduce its inventory overhead by ordering supplies automatically. For example, when a particular component of the manufacturing process drops below a predefined threshold, the computer system calls an order in to the parts manufacturer. Human intervention—and human error—are eliminated. (Computer error is not eliminated, however.) Similarly, invoices could be generated and sent automatically, again eliminating the need for human intervention. Invoices can be paid by automatically transferring funds from banks.

Much has to be accomplished before such global, just-in-time networks can be built. As communications are increased, the risks increase (see Figure 11.5). Risk spirals when you build a company-wide or company-to-company network. Both technology and business risks exist. On the business side, careful negotiations between the company, its suppliers, and customers must occur. They must draw lines of demarcation and implement stringent security procedures so that the partners can access only the appropriate applications and not jeopardize the security of the system. Technology risks include a high reliance on technology. If the technology fails, your business can be severely disabled.

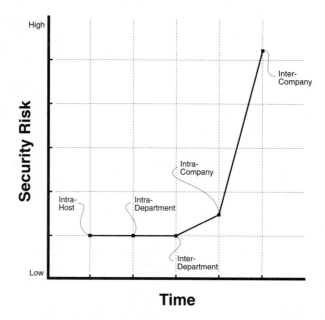

***Figure 11.5.*** *The relationship between communication and risk.*

For company-to-company communications to become widespread, international and domestic wide area networking services must improve so that large volumes of data can be exchanged automatically. Today, international wide area services are largely limited to X.25, which is a slow and overhead-intensive service. Leased lines are too expensive to be practical. Less expensive services are required. ISDN, little used in the United States, is one option. Frame relay, a burgeoning service both in the United States and in Europe, is another.

Many business applications will be built on the OSI application protocols, which are largely unfinished. OSI's FTAM file transfer protocol can be used for simple transactions, but more complex transactions require more complex protocols. For example, OSI Electronic Document Interchange (EDI) and Office Document Architecture (ODA) define a standard syntax for documents such as purchase orders and invoices. Underneath, OSI's X.400 messaging standards will provide at least some of the transport, and X.500 directory services will enable companies to more easily locate their trading partners in a global network. X.400 and X.500 will be the two most important OSI applications in a global context.

# Build Your Enterprise-Wide Network

What currently goes through wire, which is chiefly voice, will go through the air, and what currently goes through the air, which is chiefly video, will go through wires. The phone will become wireless, mobile, and small enough to fit in your pocket. Computer video will run over fiber in a switched digital system as convenient as today's telephone system. Nicholas Negroponte of MIT's Media Lab so neatly outlined this in a vision referred to as the Negroponte Switch.[1]

The Negroponte Switch is happening today (see Figure 11.6). The telephone companies are exploring SMDS and SONET so that their public services can accommodate high-speed transmissions that include voice, video, and data. Silicon is rapidly being miniaturized, and powerful laptop computers now fit in your palm. Cellular phones too are becoming smaller and lighter. A computer or telephone in the palm of the hand greatly empowers the user. Now plug into a wireless network, and the mobile user gains all of the benefits of being in the office.

*What currently goes through the wire will go through air, and what currently goes through air will go through wire.* What does this mean to the typical corporation in the throes of evaluating the benefits and risks of downsizing, enterprise-wide networking, client/server applications, and the new array of wide area network services? The information landscape is undergoing a fundamental change, a revolution. They way that people work, learn, and live will be irrevocably altered by computers and computer networks.

Your company is not immune to these changes. Enterprise networks are in their infancy, and end-user companies, integrators, and computer manufacturers are struggling to understand and build enterprise-wide networks. While the problems are being resolved—which include network management, WAN services, security, applications, and a lack of expertise—your company can stand to gain a significant competitive edge by jumping into the fray and building such a network. Your company can directly communicate with your business partners and enable your employees to gain access to information at any time. Building such a network is not without risks, but it is at these earliest stages that you can reap the greatest benefits. Approach the situation with both caution and abandon, making decisions carefully and implementing with intensity.

---

[1]George Gilder. "Into The Telecosm." *Harvard Business Review*, March/April 1991.

**Communications Today**

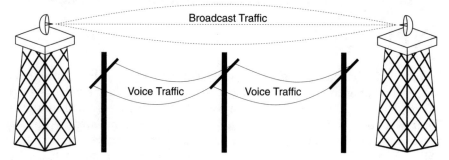

**Communications Tomorrow**

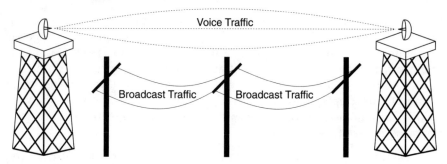

*Figure 11.6.    The Negroponte Switch.*

Having networks that span offices and homes, both domestically and internationally, can bring about a revolution in society as great as the advent of the telephone, television, or automobile. Fifty years ago, few people could imagine the changes that these technologies wrought. It is difficult, yet exciting, to imagine the impact networks will likely have in even the next 25 years.

# Network Standards Organizations

## ANSI

American National Standards Institute (ANSI)
1430 Broadway
New York, NY 10018
(212) 354-3300

## Federal Information Processing Standard (FIPS)

U.S. Department of Commerce
National Technical Information and Service
5285 Port Royal Road
Springfield, VA 22161
(703) 487-4650

## Consultative Committee for International Telegraphy and Telephony (CCITT)

(Inside the United States)
U.S. Department of Commerce
National Technical Information and Service
5285 Port Royal Road
Springfield, VA 22161
(703) 487-4650

(Outside the United States)
General Secretariat
International Telecommunications Union
Place des Natins
1121 Geneva 20, Switzerland
41 22 995111

## International Organization for Standardization (ISO)

(Inside the United States)
American National Standards Institute
1430 Broadway
New York, NY 10018
(212) 354-3300

(Outside the United States)
Central Secretariat
1 Rue de Varembe, CH-1211
Geneva, Switzerland
41 22 341240

## IEEE

Institute of Electronic and Electrical Engineers (IEEE)
345 East 47th St.
New York, NY 10017
(212) 705-7900

## NIST

National Institute of Technology and Standards (NIST)
Technology Building
Gaithersburg, MD 20899
(301) 921-2731

# Vendor List

3Com
5400 Bayfront Plaza
Santa Clara, CA  95052
(408) 764-5000

AT&T Network Systems
1 Speedwell Ave.
Morristown, NJ  07960
(800) 247-1212

Accton Technology
46750 Fremont Blvd., #104
Fremont, CA  94538
(510) 226-9800

Advanced Computer Communications
315 Bollay Dr.
Santa Barbara, CA  93117
(805) 685-4455

Advanced Logic Research
9401 Jeronimo
Irvine, CA  92718
(714) 581-6770

Andrew
19021 20th Ave. N.E.
Bothell, WA  98011
(206) 485-8200

Artisoft
691 East River Rd.
Tucson, AZ  85704
(602) 293-4000

Asante Technologies
404 Tasman Dr.
Sunnyvale, CA 94089
(408) 752-8388

Ascom Timeplex
400 Chestnut Ridge Rd.
Woodcliff Lake, NJ 07675
(201) 391-1111

Attachmate
13231 S.E. 36th St.
Bellevue, CA 98006
(206) 644-4010

BICC Communication
103 Millbury St.
Auburn, MA 01501
(508) 832-8650

Banyan Systems
120 Flanders Rd.
Westboro, MA 01581
(508) 898-1000

Beame & Whiteside Software
P.O. Box 8130
Dundas, Ontario L9H3E7
(416) 765-0822

Beyond
38 Sidney St.
Cambridge, MA 02139
(617) 621-0095

Borland International
1800 Green Hills Rd.
Scotts Valley, CA 95066
(408) 438-8400

Bytex
Four Technology Dr.
Westborough, MA 01581-1760
(508) 366-8000

CHI/COR Information Management
300 South Wacker Dr.
Chicago, IL 60606
(312) 322-0150

cisco Systems
501 E. Middlefield Rd.
Mountain View, CA 94043
(415) 326-1941

Cabletron Systems
35 Industrial Way, P.O. Box 5005
Rochester, NH 03878-0505
(603) 332-9400

California Microwave
985 Almanor Ave.
Sunnyvale, CA 94086
(408) 720-6471

Cayman Systems
26 Landsdowne St.
Cambridge, MA 02139
(617) 494-1999

Centel Federal Systems
11400 Commerce Park Dr.
Reston, VA 22091
(703) 758-7000

Ciprico
2800 Campus Dr.
Plymouth, MN 55441
(612) 551-4000

Comdisco Systems
919 E. Hillsdale Blvd.
Foster City, CA 94404
(415) 574-5800

Compaq Computer
20555 SH 249
Houston, TX 77070
(713) 370-0670

CrossCom
140 Locke Dr.
Marlboro, MA  01752
(508) 481-4060

Datability
1 Palmer Terrace
Carlstadt, NJ  07072
(201) 438-2400

David Systems
701 E. Evelyn Ave.
Sunnyvale, CA  94086
(408) 720-8000

DCA
1000 Alderman Dr.
Alpharetta, GA  30202
(404) 442-4000

DigiBoard
6400 Flying Cloud Dr.
Eden Prairie, MN  55344
(612) 943-9020

Digital Equipment
146 Main St., MLO 6A-3/T96
Maynard, MA  01754
(508) 493-5111

Dolphin Networks
4405 International Blvd.
Suite B-108
Norcross, GA  30093
(404) 279-7050

Eicon Technology
2196 32nd Ave.
Lachine, Quebec  H8J 3H7
(514) 631-2592

FTP Software
26 Princess St.
Wakefield, MA  01880
(617) 246-0900

Frontier Technologies
10201 N. Port Washington Rd., 13 W.
West Mequon, WI 53092
(414) 241-4555

Gandalf Systems
9 N. Olney Ave.
Cherry Hill, NJ 08003
(609) 424-9400

Gupta Technologies
1040 Marsh Rd.
Menlo Park, CA 94025
(415) 321-9500

Hewlett-Packard
3404 E. Harmony Rd.
Fort Collins, CO 80525
(303) 229-3800

Hughes LAN Systems
1225 Charleston
Mountain View, CA 94043
(415) 966-7300

IBM
1133 Westchester Ave.
White Plains, NY 10604
(914) 642-5474

ICOT
3801 Zanker Rd.
San Jose, CA 95150
(408) 433-3300

ISOCOR
12011 San Vicente Blvd.
Los Angeles, CA 90049
(310) 476-2671

Imara Systems
1110 N. Glebe Rd.
Arlington, VA 22201
(703) 516-4422

Information Builders
1250 Broadway
New York, NY  10001
(212) 736-4433

Informix Software
4100 Bohannon Dr.
Menlo Park, CA  94025
(415) 926-6300

InterConnections
14711 N.E. 29th Pl.
Bellevue, WA  98007
(206) 881-5773

Internetix
8903 Presidential Pkwy., Suite 210
Upper Marlboro, MD  20772
(301) 420-7900

Isicad
1920 W. Corporate Way
Anaheim, CA  92803
(714) 533-8910

Kalpana
3100 Patrick Henry Dr.
Santa Clara, CA  95054
(408) 988-1600

Magnalink Communications
63 Nahatan St.
Norwood, MA  02062
(617) 255-9400

Micom
4100 Los Angeles Ave.
Simi Valley, CA  93063
(805) 583 8600

Microsoft
1 Microsoft Way
Redmond, WA  98052
(206) 882-8080

Microwave Radio
20 Alpha Rd.
Chelmsford, MA 01824
(508) 250-1110 x704

Network Equipment Technologies
800 Saginaw Dr.
Redwood City, CA 94063
(415) 366-4400

Network General
4200 Bohannon Dr.
Menlo Park, CA 94025
(415) 688-2700

Network Products
1440 W. Colorado Blvd.
Pasadena, CA 91105
(818) 441-6504

Novell
122 E. 1700 St.
Provo, UT 84606
(801) 429-7000

Open Connect Systems
2033 Chennault Dr.
Carrollton, TX 75006
(214) 490-4090

Oracle
500 Oracle Pkwy.
Redwood Shores, CA 94065
(415) 506-7000

Phaser Systems
651 Gateway Blvd.
South San Francisco, CA 94080
(415) 952-6300

Plexcom
2255 Agate Ct.
Simi Valley, CA 93065
(805) 522-3333

ProTools
14976 N.W. Greenbrier Pkwy.
Beaverton, OR 97006
(503) 645-5400

Process Software
959 Concord St.
Framingham, MA 01701
(508) 879-6994

RND-RAD Network Devices
7711 Center Ave.
Huntington Beach, CA 92647
(714) 891-1446

Racal-Datacom
155 Swanson Rd.
Boxborough, MA 01719
(508) 263-9929

Raycom Systems
16525 Sherman Way, Unit C-8
Van Nuys, CA 91406
(818) 909-4186

Remedy
1965 Landings Dr.
Mountain View, CA 94043
(415) 903-5200

Retix
2401 Colorado Ave.
Santa Monica, CA 90404
(310) 828-3400

SNMP Research
3001 Kimberlin Heights Rd.
Knoxville, TN 37920
(615) 573-1434

Shiva
One Cambridge Center
Cambridge, MA 02142
(617) 252-6300

Siecor
489 Siecor Park, P.O. Box 489
Hickory, NC  28603
(704) 327-5000

Standard Microsystems
80 Arkay Dr.
Hauppauge, NY  11788
(516) 435-6255

Star-Tek
71 Lyman St.
Northboro, MA  01532
(508) 393-9393

SunConnect
2550 Garcia Ave.
Mountain View, CA  94043

SynOptics Communications
4401 Great American Pkwy.
Santa Clara, CA  95052
(408) 988-2400

TGV
603 Mission St.
Santa Cruz, CA  95060
(408) 427-4366

Tangram Systems
5511 Capital Center Dr., Suite 400
Raleigh, NC  27606
(919) 851-6000

Tektronix
P.O. Box 1197
Redmond, OR  97756
(503) 923-0333

Telebit
1315 Chesapeake Terrace
Sunnyvale, CA  94089
(408) 734-4333

Thomas-Conrad
1908-R Kramer Ln.
Austin, TX  78758
(800) 332-8683

Tricord Systems
3750 Annapolis Ln.
Minneapolis, MN  55447
(612) 557-9005

Triton Technologies
200 Middlesex Tpke.
Iselin, NJ  08830
(908) 855-9440

US Robotics
8100 N. McCormick Blvd.
Skokie, IL  60076
(708) 982-5001

Vitalink Communications
6607 Kaiser Dr.
Fremont, CA  94555
(510) 794-1100

Wall Data
17769 N.E. 782 Pl.
Redmond, WA  98052
(206) 883-4777

Wandel & Goltermann
2200 Gateway Centre Blvd.
Morrisville, NC  27560
(800) 346-6332

Wellfleet Communications
15 Crosby Dr.
Bedford, MA  01730
(617) 275-2400

Xyplex
330 Codman Hill Rd.
Boxborough, MA  01719
(508) 264-9900

**1Base5**   The IEEE 802.3 standard for 1Mbps Starlan. Starlan runs at 1Mbps over coaxial cable.

**10Base2**   An implementation of the IEEE 802.3 EtherNet standard on thin coaxial cable. Thin EtherNet, Thinnet or cheapernet, as it is commonly called, runs at 10Mbps. The maximum segment length is 200 meters.

**10Base5**   An implementation of the IEEE 802.3 EtherNet standard on thick coaxial cable. Thick, or standard EtherNet, as it is commonly called, runs at 10Mbps. The maximum segment length is 500 meters.

**10BaseF0**   The IEEE 802.3 draft for running EtherNet over fiber-optic cable. 10BaseF is an older draft standard.

**10BaseT**   An implementation of the IEEE 802.3 EtherNet standard on unshielded twisted-pair telephone wiring. It uses a star-wired configuration, runs at 10Mbps, and has a maximum segment length of 100 meters.

**3+**   3Com's network operating system implementing Microsoft's MS-Net and Xerox's XNS network protocols. 3Com no longer sells 3+.

**3+Open**   3Com's network operating system based on Microsoft's OS/2 LAN Manager. 3Com no longer sells 3+Open.

**802.1**   Defined by the IEEE for hardware-level network management. It includes the spanning tree algorithm for MAC-layer bridges and the Heterogeneous LAN Management specification for managing EtherNet and Token-Ring wiring hubs.

**802.2**   Defined by the IEEE for the logical link control (LLC) standard.

**802.3**   Defined by the IEEE, the 802.3 standards govern carrier sense multiple access/collision detection networks, and more specifically EtherNet. The 802.3 series consists of 1Base5 Starlan, 10Base2 thin EtherNet, 10Base5 thick EtherNet, and 10BaseT UTP EtherNet. The IEEE is working on 10BaseF0 for fiber EtherNet.

**802.4**   Defined by the IEEE, the 802.4 standard defines the use of the token bus network access method.

**802.5**   Defined by the IEEE, the 802.5 standard defines a logical ring network that uses a token-passing access method. Token Ring comes in 4Mbps and 16Mbps speeds.

**802.6**   Defined by the IEEE, the 802.6 standard defines metropolitan area networks. The MAN standard implements a distributed queue, dual bus access method over a fiber-optic medium. Defined by the IEEE, the 802.7 standard defines broadband networks.

**802.9**   Near completion, the IEEE 802.9 standard defines integrated digital and video networking.

**802.11**   When finalized by the IEEE, the 802.11 standard will define wireless networking.

**access method**   The set of rules by which the network arbitrates access among the nodes. Collision Sense Multiple Access Collision Detection and token passing are two network access methods.

**accounting management**   Reports for the costs of network resources. Accounting management is one of the five categories of network management defined by the ISO.

**acquisition costs**   The cost related to a network's initial planning, purchasing, and installation.

**address**   A unique identifier assigned to network devices so that they can independently send and receive messages.

**Address Resolution Protocol (ARP)**   Within TCP/IP, the protocol that determines whether a packet's source and destination addresses are in data link control (DLC) or Internet Protocol (IP) format. ARP is necessary for proper packet routing.

**Advanced Program-to-Program Networking (APPN)**   The protocol in IBM's Systems Application Architecture (SAA) that provides peer-to-peer access, enabling a PC to communicate directly with a mainframe. APPC is essential for distributed computing within an IBM environment. Also called Advanced Peer-to-Peer Communications (APPC).

**American National Standards Institute (ANSI)** The principal group in the United States for defining standards. ANSI represents the U.S. in ISO.

**AppleShare** Apple Computer's networking system implementing the AppleTalk protocol stack.

**AppleTalk** Apple Computer's protocol stack for connecting computers. AppleTalk includes physical specifications for LocalTalk, EtherTalk, and TokenTalk, network and transport functions (Datagram Delivery Protocol, AppleTalk Session Protocol), and the Name Binding Protocol. It also governs file and printer access.

**AppleTalk Filing Protocol (AFP)** In an AppleTalk network, the protocol that governs remote file access.

**application layer** The seventh and uppermost layer of the OSI model, the application layer enables users to transfer files, send mail, and so on. It is the only layer with which users can communicate directly.

**application programming interface (API)** A set of programming functions, calls, and interfaces that provide access to a particular network layer.

**ARCnet** A 2.5Mbps token-passing network running over coaxial cable. ARCnet was designed by Datapoint Corporation.

**asynchronous transfer mode (ATM)** The method of data transmission used by Broadband ISDN. Specified as 53-octet fixed-length packets transmitted over a packet-switched network. Also called *cell relay*.

**back end** The database engine functions, which include storing, manipulating, and protecting data.

**backbone** The main "spine" or segment of a campus network. Departmental networks are attached as "ribs" to the central backbone.

**bandwidth on demand** A new concept in which the user can call up more bandwidth as the application warrants. It enables users to pay only for bandwidth that they use, when they use it.

**Basic Rate ISDN (BRI)** Two bearer channels (B) of 64Kbps for bulk data transfer plus a data link (D) 16Kbps channel for control and signalling information.

**bridge** A device operating at the OSI's medium-access layer that connects similar networks—for example EtherNet to EtherNet—and is transparent to upper-layer devices and protocols.

**Broadband ISDN** A class of emerging high-speed data and voice services.

**broadcast** A message addressed to the destination addresses of all nodes on a network.

**brouter**    A device that can transparently bridge protocols as well as perform network-layer routing. It is a hybrid of a bridge and a router.

**bus topology**    A network architecture in which all of the nodes are connected to a single cable.

**campus network**    Connects LANs in multiple departments within a single building or campus of a corporation. Campus networks are still local area networks, but they may cover several miles.

**campus wiring system**    The part of the structured wiring system that connects multiple buildings to a centralized main distribution facility, local exchange carrier, or other point of demarcation. Also referred to as the *backbone*.

**cascaded star**    A network topology in which several data centers or hubs are set up for redundancy. Also called a *tree*.

**CCITT (Consultative Committee for International Telegraphy and Telephony)**    An international group that defines data communication standards.

**cell relay**    A form of packet transmission that will be used in Broadband ISDN networks. It uses 53-octet cells. Cell relay is also called asynchronous transfer mode.

**charge-back**    The traditional model of cost accounting in which the user or department is charged for every transaction.

**client**    A device that requests network services from a server.

**coaxial cable**    A type of cable in which the inner conductor is a solid wire surrounded by insulation, wrapped in metal screen. Its axis of curvature coincides with the inner conductors, hence the name *coaxial*. Also called *coax*.

**common carrier**    A licensed, private utility company that provides data and voice communication services for a fee.

**Common Management Information Protocol (CMIP)**    The OSI management information protocol for network management.

**Common Management Information Protocol over LLC (CMOL)**    The version of HLM proposed by IBM and 3Com. The Heterogeneous LAN Management specification is an 802.1 undertaking for the joint management of EtherNet and Token-Ring networks.

**Common Management Information Protocol over TCP/IP (CMOT)**    The spec for running CMIP over a TCP/IP transport, instead of an OSI transport. It is not widely used.

**compression**   A technique to "squash" files, making them smaller to optimize bandwidth utilization.

**concentrator**   A multiport repeater or hub that brings together the connections from multiple network nodes.

**Connectionless Network Protocol (CLNP)**   An OSI transport protocol, similar to TCP/IP, that uses the datagram method to route network messages by including addressing information in each. Efficient for LANs.

**Connection-Oriented Network Service (CONS)**   An OSI transport protocol, it allows the transport layer to bypass the Connectionless Network Protocol when a single logical X.25 network is used.

**controlled access unit (CAU)**   A Token Ring multistation access unit (MAU or hub) that is capable of being managed.

**corporate utility**   A model of cost accounting that is more appropriate than a charge-back model for enterprise-wide networks. The network is considered a utility, like water or electricity, and its usage is charged on a flat rate.

**Data Access Language (DAL)**   Apple's database query language. It is based on SQL; however, it provides far greater functionality.

**Data Encryption Standard (DES)**   The United States government standard for scrambling and adding security codes called *keys*, which cannot be deciphered by unauthorized users.

**data-link layer**   Layer 2 of the OSI model. It defines how data is packetized and transmitted to and from each node. It is divided into two sublayers: medium access control and logical link control.

**database server**   A database application that follows the client-server model dividing an application into a front end and a back end. The front end, running on the user's computer, displays the data and interacts with the user. The back end, running on a server, preserves data integrity and handles most of the processor-intensive work.

**DECnet**   Digital Equipment Corporation's network system. In 1991, DEC incorporated support for TCP/IP and OSI, as well as its proprietary DECnet protocols, into the system.

**departmental LAN**   Used by a small group of people working toward a similar goal. The departmental LAN's primary purpose is to share local resources, such as applications, data, and printers.

**directory services**   A White Pages-like directory of the users and resources that are located on an enterprise-wide network. The OSI's X.500 and Banyan's StreetTalk are examples.

**distributed computing**   Portions of the applications and the data are broken up and distributed among the server and client computers. In the older model, all applications and data resided on the same computer.

**distributed database**   A database application where there are many clients as well as many servers.

**distributed queue dual bus (DQDB)**   The medium access method of the IEEE 802.6 standard for metropolitan area networks.

**downsizing**   The process of moving or porting mission-critical applications down from a mainframe to a PC LAN.

**dual-attach station (DAS)**   In FDDI, a station that is connected to both rings by two fibers. DAS provides the greatest fault tolerance. Critical components, such as concentrators, routers, and file servers, generally use DAS connections.

**dynamic data exchange (DDE)**   Microsoft's specification that enables applications to communicate with each other without human intervention.

**E-1**   In Europe, the basic telecommunications carrier, which operates at 2.048Mbps.

**electromagnetic interference/radio frequency interference (EMI/RFI)**   A form of noise on data transmission that reduces data integrity. EMI is caused by motors, machines, and other generators of electromagnetic radiation. RFI is caused by radio waves.

**electronic data interchange (EDI)**   An OSI standard, the method of electronically exchanging business documents, such as purchase orders, bills of lading, and invoices.

**electronic mail**   An application that enables users to send files and messages over their computers. Also called E-mail.

**encapsulation**   Encasing one protocol in another's format. Also called *tunnelling*.

**end system**   In Internet terminology, a host computer.

**End System to Intermediate System (ES-IS)**   An OSI routing protocol that provides the capabilities for hosts (end systems) and routers (intermediate systems) to find each other. ES-IS does not handle the router-to-router protocols; IS-IS does.

**Enterprise Management Architecture**   Digital Equipment Corp.'s umbrella architecture for managing enterprise-wide networks. It is a distributed approach.

**enterprise-wide network**   A network that connects every computer in every location and runs the company's mission-critical applications.

**EtherNet**   A 10Mbps CSMA/CD network that runs over coax, thin coax, twisted-pair, and fiber-optic cable. DIX or Blue Book EtherNet is the DEC specification; 802.3 is the IEEE's.

**EtherTalk**   Apple's implementation of EtherNet.

**fast packet**   A technique for asynchronously transferring data across the network.

**fault management**   The detection, isolation, and correction of network faults. One of the five categories of network management defined by ISO.

**fault tolerance**   The ability of a system to continue operating in the event of a fault.

**Fiber Distributed Data Interface (FDDI)**   The ANSI specification for a 100Mbps fiber-optic network implemented on dual, counter-rotating rings. FDDI-I is specified for data networking only. FDDI-II, which is yet to be finalized, will specify the transmission of both voice and data.

**fiber-optic cable**   Glass or plastic fiber cable used to transmit signals in the form of light. It is composed of an outer protective sheath, cladding, and the optical fiber. It comes in single mode and multimode.

**File Transfer, Access, and Management (FTAM)**   The OSI protocol for file transfer and remote file access.

**File Transfer Protocol (FTP)**   The TCP/IP protocol for file transfer.

**filtering**   In bridging, the process by which particular source and destination addresses are prevented from crossing the bridge.

**flow control**   A process by which a router controls the progress of packets through the network.

**forwarding**   The process by which a MAC-layer copies a packet from one "side" of the network to another after it has been filtered.

**fractional T-1**   Dividing the 1.544 T-1 bandwidth into increments of 64Kbps.

**frame relay**   A CCITT standard for a low-overhead packet switching protocol that provides dynamic bandwidth allocation at speeds up to 2Mbps.

**front end**   A client application for presenting, manipulating, and displaying data. It works with a back end or engine.

**gateway**   In OSI terminology, a hardware and software device that connects two dissimilar systems. It operates at the fourth through the seventh layers of the OSI model. In Internet terminology, a gateway is called a *router*.

**global network**   Spans all departments, campuses, branch offices, and subsidiaries of a corporation. Global networks are international, and bring with them the problems of dealing with multiple languages, cultures, standards, and telephone companies.

**Government OSI Profile (GOSIP)**   The United States government's specification for OSI conformance. GOSIP support is required for all bids made on government contracting projects.

**hardware independence**   The ability of a software program to run independently of the underlying hardware. For example, through ODI and NDIS, both NetWare and LAN Manager can run independently of the network hardware.

**Heterogeneous LAN Management (HLM)**   An IEEE 802.1 specification for jointly managing mixed EtherNet and Token Ring networks with the same objects.

**heterogeneous network**   A network made up of a multitude of different types of workstations, operating systems, and applications.

**High-Level Language API (HLLAPI)**   A set of tools developed by IBM to help developers write SAA applications.

**homogeneous network**   A network comprised of similar components—one type of workstation, server, network operating system, and only a few applications.

**horizontal wiring subsystem**   The part of the structured wiring system that connects the users' computers in the departments. It is attached to the vertical wiring system.

**hub**   A wiring concentrator or multiport repeater that brings together the network connections from multiple nodes.

**incremental charges**   The cost of supporting routine changes to the network over a certain period, including adds, moves, deletes, and minor reconfigurations.

**Institute of Electronics and Electrical Engineers (IEEE)**   A standards-setting body that specifies data communications standards.

**Integrated Services Digital Network (ISDN)** The CCITT standard for carrying voice and data to the same destination. The specification is for 23 B channels plus one D channel.

**intermediate system** In Internet terminology, a router.

**Intermediate System to Intermediate System** An OSI routing protocol that provides dynamic routing between routers (intermediate systems).

**International Standards Organization (ISO)** A multinational standards-setting organization that formulates computer and communication standards, among others. ISO defined the seven-layer OSI model.

**Internet** A collection of more than 2,000 packet-switched networks located principally in the United States, but also in other parts of the world, all linked using the TCP/IP protocol.

**Internet Activities Board (IAB)** The coordinating committee for the Internet design, engineering, and management. The IAB has two main committees: the Internet Engineering Task Force (IETF) and the Internet Research Task Force (IRTF).

**Internet Protocol (IP)** Part of the TCP/IP stack. A session layer protocol that governs packet forwarding.

**internetwork** A collection of several networks, bridged or routed together so that all users and devices can communicate.

**interoperability** The ability of one manufacturer's computer equipment to operate alongside, communicate with, and exchange information with another vendor's computer equipment.

**inverted backbone** A network architecture in which the wiring hub and routers become the center of the network, and all subnetworks connect to this hub.

**IPX/SPX (Internetwork Packet Exchange/Sequenced Packet Exchange)** Novell's proprietary network and transport protocols for NetWare. IPX and SPX are based on XNS. IPX is an unreliable, connectionless protocol; SPX is a reliable, connection-oriented protocol.

**LAN Manager** Microsoft's network operating system. Today, LAN Manager runs on an OS/2 server, but Microsoft is moving it to Windows NT.

**LAN Server** IBM's implementation of Microsoft's OS/2 LAN Manager.

**LAN-aware** Applications that have file and record locking for use on a network.

**LAN-ignorant**   Applications that lack file and record locking, and cannot guarantee data integrity in a multiuser environment.

**LAN-intrinsic**   Applications that uniquely take advantage of a network's distributed intelligence. A client-server database is a LAN-intrinsic application. Also called *LAN-enabled*.

**leased line**   A private telephone line service.

**local area network (LAN)**   A group of computers, each equipped with the appropriate network adapter card and software, connected by cable, that share applications, data, and peripherals. All connections are made via cable, but without telephone services. A LAN typically spans a single building or campus.

**Local Area Transport (LAT)**   Digital Equipment's protocol for its terminal servers. Because it lacks a network layer, LAT must be bridged in an enterprise-wide network, not routed.

**LocalTalk**   Apple's physical layer standard for a 230Kbps network using CSMA/CD over unshielded twisted-pair telephone wire.

**logical link control (LLC)**   The upper portion of OSI Layer 2, which governs data transmission. Also known as the IEEE 802.2 standard.

**Logical Unit (LU)**   A suite of IBM protocols that govern session communication in an SNA environment. LU1, LU2, and LU3 provide control of host sessions. LU4 supports host-to-device and peer-to-peer communication between peripheral nodes. LU6.2 is the peer-to-peer protocol of APPN. LU7 is similar to LU2.

**mail-enabled applications**   A class of applications that incorporate E-mail's functionality but provide additional services, such as workflow automation or contact management software.

**main distribution facility**   The part of the structured wiring system that is located in the computer room. From this wiring room extends the campus subsystem, which runs to each building.

**management information base (MIB)**   A database of network parameters and identifiers used by the Simple Network Management Protocol as well as the Common Management Information Protocol.

**management information protocol**   The method of communication between a network manager and its agent.

**manager of managers**  A type of network management architecture in which one or more integrated management systems manage "lower-level" element manager systems, which in turn manage the devices.

**Manufacturing Automation Protocol (MAP)**  An OSI protocol for manufacturing equipment, originally developed by General Motors.

**medium access control (MAC)**  The lower sublayer of the data link layer (Layer 2), governing access to the particular type of transmission media.

**mesh**  A topology in which any site can communicate directly with any other site.

**Message Handling System (MHS)**  Novell's protocol for electronic mail management, storage, and exchange.

**Message Transfer Agent (MTA)**  In X.400 electronic messaging, the component that is responsible for storing and forwarding the messages to their destinations.

**metropolitan area network (MAN)**  An IEEE-specified network using the DQDB access method and capable of high-speed data communications over distances up to 80 kilometers.

**mission-critical application**  An application that is crucial to the business' continued operation.

**multimedia**  The incorporation of graphics, text, and sound into an application.

**multimode fiber**  A type of fiber-optic cable that uses LEDs to generate the light to transmit signals. A much less focused method of transmission than lasers, multimode fiber nonetheless is prevalent in data transmission, where shorter distances are necessary.

**multistation access unit (MAU)**  A multiport wiring hub for Token Ring networks. Managed MAUs are called *controlled access units*, or CAUs.

**Narrowband ISDN**  See *ISDN*.

**NetBIOS**  An IBM-developed protocol governing data exchange and network access.

**NetBEUI**  A Microsoft-developed protocol governing data exchange and network access. NetBEUI is used by LAN Manager networks.

**NetWare**  Novell's network operating system, a leader in PC LAN networks. It is based on Novell's IPX/SPX, but also accommodates TCP/IP and AFP as of version 3.11.

**NetWare loadable module (NLM)**   An application residing on a NetWare server that coexists with the core NetWare operating system. NLMs provide better performance than applications that run outside the protected mode of the Intel 386 or 486 chip.

**network**   A system of hardware and software connected so that data can be transmitted and end users can communicate.

**Network Driver Interface Specification (NDIS)**   A specification for generic device drivers for adapter cards used by LAN Manager networks.

**Network File System (NFS)**   Sun Microsystems' network operating system based on TCP/IP.

**network layer**   Layer 3 of the OSI model governing data routing.

**network operating system**   The software, running on a server, that governs access to the files and resources of the network by multiple users.

**object linking and embedding (OLE)**   Microsoft's specification for application-to-application exchange and communication. It is more powerful and easier to use than DDE.

**Open Data Link Interface (ODI)**   Novell's specification for network interface card device drivers.

**open shortest path first (OSPF)**   A routing protocol for TCP/IP routers that takes into account network loading and bandwidth when moving packets from their sources to their destinations.

**Open Systems Interconnection (OSI)**   The seven-layer protocol stack defined by ISO for data communications. The layers are as follows: physical, data-link, network, transport, session, application, and presentation.

**operational costs**   The cost of running the network on a daily basis.

**OS/2**   Microsoft's and IBM's multithreaded, multitasking, single-user operating system. Microsoft has given up development on OS/2; IBM is now responsible for its development.

**OS/2 Extended Edition**   IBM's version of Microsoft's OS/2 operating system. It includes a number of IBM extensions, including Database Manager and Communications Manager.

**outsourcing**   The process of subcontracting network operations and support to an organization outside your company.

**packet**   A collection of bits comprising data and control information, which is sent from one node to another.

**packet switching**   Data is segmented into packets and sent across a circuit shared by multiple subscribers. As the packet travels over the network, devices such as switches read the addresses and route the packet to its proper destination.

**peer-to-peer**   A data exchange method in which two or more nodes can initiate communication with each other.

**performance management**   A category of network management defined by the ISO. Performance management measures and records resources used on a LAN.

**physical layer**   OSI layer 1. The physical layer defines the protocols that govern transmission media and signals.

**point-to-point**   A direct connection between two points.

**presentation layer**   Layer 6 of the OSI model. The presentation layer involves data formatting and conversion.

**Primary Rate ISDN (PRI)**   A T-1 pipe that supports 23 B channels plus one D channel, which is normally written as 23B+D.

**propagation delay**   The time required for data to travel from the transmission point to the destination

**protocol**   A standardized set of rules that specify how a conversation is to take place, including the format, timing, sequencing, and error checking.

**proxy agent**   In network management, a piece of software that translates between an agent and a device that does not speak the same management information protocol. The proxy agent translates the data and communicates it to the manager.

**query language**   A programming language that enables users to retrieve information. SQL is one example.

**remote MIB (RMON)**   SNMP's facility for remotely monitoring agents.

**Remote Operations Service Element (ROSE)**   An OSI application layer protocol, it supports interactive applications in a distributed open systems environment. ROSE is the principal service for distributed processing in an OSI network.

**remote procedure call (RPC)**   A protocol or set of conventions that governs how an application activates a process on another node on the network and retrieves the results.

**repeater**   A physical layer device that regenerates, retimes, and amplifies electrical signals.

**request for comment (RFC)**   The Internet's notation for draft, experimental, and final standards.

**request for information (RFI)**   A document produced by an end-user company asking systems integrators to propose and design a system that will fulfill their business requirements.

**request for proposal (RFP)**   A document produced by an end-user company asking systems integrators to bid on a network design and specification.

**requirements analysis**   The process through which you define and evaluate the business needs of your network system. Also called the *needs analysis*.

**return on investment (ROI)**   This enables MIS to gauge the network's success from a business profit-and-loss standpoint. Calculate a ROI by subtracting the total cost of the network from the total benefit.

**RG-58**   50-ohm coaxial cable used for thin EtherNet.

**RG-62**   93-ohm coaxial cable used for ARCnet.

**ring topology**   A network configuration in which nodes are connected in a closed loop.

**risk analysis**   The process by which you analyze the business and technology risks of installing a new system.

**RJ-11**   Four-wire modular connectors used by the telephone system.

**RJ-45**   Eight-wire modular connector used by Starlan and some telephone systems.

**roll back**   A database application's ability to abort a transaction before it has been committed.

**roll forward**   A database's ability to recover from disasters. The database reads the transaction log and re-executes all of the readable and complete transactions.

**route discovery**   The process a router uses to discover information about the other devices on the network.

**router**   A network layer device that connects networks using the same network layer protocol, for example TCP/IP. A router uses a standardized protocol to efficiently move packets to their destination over an internetwork.

**routing**   The process of moving filtered packets among subnetworks on a large internetwork. Network layer routing is done through the use of a standardized routing protocol.

**Routing Information Protocol (RIP)**   The routing protocol used by most TCP/IP routers. It measures the shortest distance between the source and destination addresses by the lowest "hop" count.

**security management**   A level of network management defined by ISO, it prevents a network from invalid access.

**server**   A special-purpose computer that provides access to shared resources, such as files, printers, or applications.

**session**   A communications connection between two nodes.

**session layer**   OSI layer 5. The session layer defines the protocols governing communication between applications.

**shielded twisted-pair (STP)**   A pair of foil-encased copper wires, twisted around each other, and wrapped in an insulating shield. Used primarily in IBM networks.

**Simple Mail Transfer Protocol (SMTP)**   The TCP/IP protocol for E-mail transmission and reception.

**Simple Network Management Protocol (SNMP)**   A request-response type protocol that gathers management information. SNMP is most often used in TCP/IP networks.

**single-attach station (SAS)**   In FDDI, a device that is connected to only one ring, rather than both rings. SAS provides a lower degree of fault tolerance than dual-attach stations. SAS is typically used for workstations and other noncritical devices.

**single-mode fiber**   A type of fiber that uses lasers to transmit signals. Single mode fiber can transmit signals over great distances, and is primarily used in long-distance telephone networks.

**SNA mainframe gateway**   A device that connects a LAN to an IBM SNA mainframe.

**source routing**   Bridging similar LANs using MAC-layer bridges. Normally used with Token Ring LANs. With source routing, the frame contains information on its route through the network.

**source-explicit forwarding**   A feature that allows MAC-layer bridges to forward packets from only those source addresses specified by the administrator.

**spanning tree**   An IEEE 802.1D standard technique for configuring parallel MAC-layer EtherNet bridges. The spanning tree algorithm manages the loop created by the redundancy, which is illegal in the EtherNet specification.

**star topology**   A network topology in which nodes are connected in a hub and spoke configuration to a central device or location.

**Station Management (SMT)**   Part of ANSI's FDDI standard which specifies the network management features inherent in FDDI, including performance statistics, downloading software, and FDDI configuration.

**StreetTalk**   Banyan's distributed global naming and directory service for its network operating system, VINES.

**Structured Query Language**   An IBM and ANSI standard query language for extracting information from relational databases.

**structured wiring**   A planned cabling system which systematically lays out the wiring for an enterprise, including voice and data. IBM's Cabling System and AT&T Premises Distribution System are two such structured wiring designs.

**Switched 56**   Dial-up connections that use bandwidth in 56Kbps increments. A maximum of 24 channels can be dialed up, for a maximum bandwidth of 1.5Mbps.

**Switched Multimegabit Data Service (SMDS)**   A high-speed metropolitan area network service that is being introduced by carriers for T-1 and T-3 services.

**Synchronous Optical Network (SONET)**   SONET will establish a digital hierarchy throughout the world that will enable you to send data anywhere and be guaranteed that the message will be carried over a consistent transport scheme.

**System Application Architecture (SAA)**   IBM's set of rules for computer communications and application development. SAA is designed to help create programs that will run on a wide variety of IBM computing equipment.

**System Network Architecture (SNA)**   IBM's protocols for governing terminal-to-mainframe communications. It is the predecessor to SAA.

**systems integrator**   A company that is paid to combine disparate pieces of technology into a unified, working system for an end-user company.

**T-1**   A 1.544Mbps multichannel wide area transmission system. Can transport voice, video, data, and fax.

**T-2**    The equivalent of four T-1s, T-2 offers 6.3Mbps of bandwidth. Each T-2 link can carry at least 96 64Kbps circuits.

**T-3**    A T-3 circuit carries the equivalent of 28 T-1s in one multiplexed signal stream and provides 672 DS-0 channels.

**TCP/IP**    The protocol suite developed by ARPA. TCP/IP is used widely in the Internet and is gaining popularity in corporate networks.

**Technical Office Protocol (TOP)**    The OSI protocol stack for office automation.

**Telnet**    A TCP/IP protocol for terminal emulation.

**transceiver**    The device for transmitting and receiving packets to and from the wire. The transceiver is usually integrated directly onto the network adapter card.

**transparent bridging**    Bridging similar LANs using MAC-layer bridges. Normally used with EtherNet LANs. The frame does not know what path it will take; that path is determined by the bridges it passes through.

**transport layer**    OSI layer 4. The transport layer governs message structure and error checking. A transport layer provides reliable end-to-end data transport between two users.

**transport protocol**    A protocol that provides end-to-end data integrity and service quality on a network.

**Transmission Control Protocol (TCP)**    The TCP/IP protocol governing sequenced data.

**token**    A character sequence that mediates access on a token ring or token bus network.

**token passing**    A network access method that requires nodes to possess the electronic token before transmitting.

**Token Ring**    An IEEE 4Mbps or 16Mbps network using a ring topology and token access method. It works over UTP, STP, and fiber.

**tunneling**    Encasing one protocol in another's format. For example, AppleTalk packets are often enveloped in TCP/IP packet formats for transmission on an enterprise-wide network. Tunneling is also called *encapsulation*.

**twisted-pair**    A type of copper wiring in which two wires are twisted around each other, which reduces the amount of noise the cable absorbs.

**two-phase commit protocol**    In a distributed database, a two-phase commit protocol ensures data integrity by asking the multiple database engines for permission before committing each transaction.

**Type 1 cabling**   The IBM Cabling System's specification for a dual-pair shielded twisted-pair.

**Type 2 cabling**   The IBM Cabling System's specification for a six-pair shielded 22 AWG wire for voice transmission.

**Type 3 cabling**   The IBM Cabling System's specification for a single pair unshielded twisted-pair wire. Type 3 cabling is common telephone wire.

**Ultrix**   Digital Equipment Corp.'s implementation of UNIX.

**Unified Network Management Architecture (UNMA)**   AT&T's specification for an enterprise management system. UNMA relies on device-specific element management systems.

**UNIX**   A multitasking, multiuser operating system. Developed by Bell Labs and widely implemented in universities, UNIX is gaining popularity in corporate enterprise-wide networks.

**unshielded twisted-pair (UTP)**   Ordinary telephone wiring, UTP is a pair of foil-encased copper wires twisted around each other.

**user agent**   In X.400 mail systems, the component that provides the X.400 envelope, headers, and addressing before forwarding the message.

**User Datagram Protocol (UDP)**   The TCP/IP protocol used with applications such as network management. It is a connectionless transaction protocol.

**value-added reseller (VAR)**   A company that resells manufacturers' products, adding value by installing or customizing the system.

**VAX**   Digital Equipment Corp.'s line of minicomputer and workstation hardware.

**vertical wiring subsystem**   The part of the structured wiring system that connects the campus wiring system to the departmental wiring system. It runs in a building's risers.

**VINES**   Banyan's network operating system based on a UNIX core and TCP/IP protocols. Especially popular in large enterprise-wide networks.

**virtual circuit**   A communications link that appears to be a dedicated circuit and passes packets sequentially between devices over a packet-switched network.

**Virtual Terminal (VT)**   The OSI terminal emulation protocol.

**virus**   An undesirable executable program that attaches itself to another block of code in order to propagate.

**VMS**   Digital Equipment Corp.'s proprietary operating system for the VAX.

**vulnerability analysis**   A form of risk analysis in which you calculate the effects of a project's success or failure on your overall business.

**wide area network (WAN)**   Multiple LANs tied together via telephone services and/or fiber-optic cabling. WANs may span a city, state, country, or even the world.

**Windows**   Microsoft's DOS-based graphical user interface.

**Windows NT**   Microsoft's "New Technology" 32-bit, multitasking operating system slated to ship in 1993.

**wireless LANs**   Networks that do not use cable, but transmit signals through the air, either through radio or infrared signals.

**wiring closet**   A central location for data communications and voice equipment.

**workflow software**   A class of applications that helps information workers manage and route their work.

**X Window System**   A graphical user system most often implemented on UNIX. The Open Software Foundation's Motif is the most popular implementation of X Window.

**X.25**   The CCITT and OSI standard for packet-switching networks.

**X.400**   The OSI and CCITT standard for store-and-forward electronic messaging.

**X.500**   The OSI and CCITT protocol for directory services. The standard is still under development.

**Xerox Network System (XNS)**   Xerox's data communication protocols. XNS is the basis for 3Com's 3+ and Novell's NetWare.

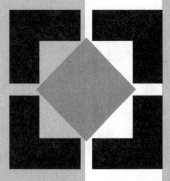

# Chapter 1: The Emergence of Enterprise-Wide Networking

Banyan Systems. "Directory Services & StreetTalk: A Technical Backgrounder." Westboro, MA: Banyan Systems, Oct. 1989.

Wayne Hall and Robert McCauley. "Planning and Maintaining a Corporate Network Utility." Maynard, MA: Digital Equipment Corporation, 1987.

Michael Hurwicz. "Banyan Tree Grows." *LAN Magazine*, Jan. 1990.

Ledgeway/Dataquest. "Network/Communications Support MarketTrends." 1991 Annual Edition. Framingham, MA: Ledgeway/Dataquest.

Market Intelligence Research Corp. "World Personal Computer Local Area Network Marketplace." Mountain View, CA: MIRC, 1990.

Monique Morrow. "Charting a Path Through the Protocol Maze." *LAN Technology*, Dec. 1990.

Monique Morrow. "Interop Achievement Award Application Form for Advanced Micro Devices." Mountain View, CA: Interop, 1990.

Robert Panza and Marc Holstein. "The Global Area." *LAN Magazine*, Nov. 1990.

Shyamala Reddy. "Airborne LAN." *LAN Magazine*, Apr. 1991.

Mark Schlack. "Can Banyan Grow VINES?" *Datamation*, May 15 1991.

Patricia Schnaidt. "Ray Noorda." *LAN Magazine*, Oct. 1991

# Chapter 2: Identifying the Business Issues and Requirements of Networking

Pete Abene, vice president, Network Engineering Services, Electronic Data Services, Plano, TX.

Dan Burger, Regional Director, Proteon, Westboro, MA.

David Korf, Director of Open Network Software, Digital Equipment Corporation.

Thomas Malone and John Rockart. "Computers, Networks and the Corporation." *Scientific American*, Sept. 1991.

Leo Spiegel, Executive Vice President, LANSystems, New York, NY.

# Chapter 3: Justifying and Budgeting the Enterprise-Wide Network

Pete Abene, Electronic Data Services.

David Ferris. "In-Depth Cost Analysis of PC Networks." Networld Boston Conference Manual 1991. Englewood Cliffs, NJ: Bruno/Blenheim, 1991.

David Korf, Digital Equipment Corp.

Frank Lynn & Associates. "Computer Industry Trends in the '90s: Three Perspectives." Chicago, IL: Frank Lynn & Associates, 1991.

Leo Spiegel, LANSystems.

Dr. Michael Treacy and The Index Group. "The Costs of Network Ownership." Cambridge, MA: The Index Group, 1989.

Jim Tyson. "LAN Cost Accounting." Networld Boston Conference Manual 1991.

# Chapter 4: High-Level Issues of Enterprise-Wide Network Design

Uyless Black. *OSI: A Model for Computer Communications Standards.* Englewood Cliffs, NJ: Prentice Hall, 1991.

Banyan Systems. "An Introduction to Symmetric Multiprocessing Technology." Aug. 1990.

Banyan Systems. "Directory Services & StreetTalk: A Technical Backgrounder." Oct. 1989.

Banyan Systems. "VINES Network Management." "VINES Security Features." "VINES Advanced Network Services." Aug. 1990.

Digital Equipment Corp. "Digital Unveils Fifth Generation of Networking." Maynard, MA: Digital Equipment Corp., June 3, 1991.

R.C. Dohrmann, A. Fermelia, D.J. Hardin, R.L. Hilton, P.M. MacIsaac, R.T. Marshall, M.D. McPeek, J.C.R. Morris, and R.K. Rosich. "Minimizing Communication Network Deployment Risks Through Simulation."Hughes Aircraft Company, Space and Communications Group, Colorado Engineering Laboratories, Aurora, CO, February 1991.

Michael Grieves. "LAN Manager: Stuck in Tomorrowland." *Data Communications,* February 1991.

Tom Henderson, President, Corporate Networks, Indianapolis, IN.

John Henshall and Sandy Shaw. *OSI Explained: End-to-End Computer Communication Standards.* New York: Ellis Horwood, 1990.

Dan Matthews, Springfield, Oregon Public Schools. "Interop Achievement Award Application Form for Oregon Public Schools," Interop 1991.

Monique Morrow. "Interop Achievement Award Application Form for Advanced Micro Devices." Interop 1990.

Mike Murray, general manager, David Thacher, senior product manager, Microsoft Networking Business Unit. "Microsoft Networking Strategy." Redmond, WA: Microsoft, Aug. 1991.

Tom Neiss, State University of New York Central Administration. "Interop Achievement Award Application Form," Interop 1991.

Novell. "NetWare v3.11 Product Line Press/Analyst Briefing." January-February 1991, Novell, Provo, UT.

Dr. Michael Treacy and The Index Group. "The Costs of Network Ownership." Cambridge, MA: The Index Group, 1989.

# Chapter 5: Designing the Local and Campus Internetwork

Scott Bradner. "Testing Multiprotocol Routers: How Fast is Fast Enough?" *Data Communications*, Feb. 1991.

John Kelley. "Boeing Banks on Twisted Pair." *LAN Technology*, Jan. 1990.

John Kelley. "The Boeing Company Implements Multi-Vendor Networking on a Grand Scale." *LAN Technology*, Feb. 1990.

Frank Leeds and Jim Chorey. "Cutting Cable Costs: The Facts About Coax." *LAN Technology*, March 1991.

Frank Leeds and Jim Chorey. "Twisted-Pair Wiring Made Simple." *LAN Technology*, Apr. 1991.

Nick Lippis and James Herman. "The Internetwork Decade." *Data Communications*, Jan. 1991.

Micom Communications. "The Demise of Data-Only Networks: A Marathon 1K Perspective." Simi Valley, CA: Micom Communications, June 20 1991.

William Morgan. "FDDI Design Guidelines: Today and Beyond the Year 2000." Morgan Hill, CA: W&J Partnership.

William Morris and Tony Beam. "How to Install Fiber-Optic Cable." *LAN Technology*, Dec. 1990.

Tony Nuciforo. "Wiring By Design." *LAN Magazine*, Nov. 1989.

San Sarto and Greg Campbell. "An Inside Look at Premises Wiring." *LAN Technology*, Feb. 1990.

Patricia Schnaidt. "The Dilemma." *LAN Magazine*, Sept. 1990.

SMDS Interest Group. "What Is SMDS?" "A Perspective on SMDS and IEEE 802.6 Market Size." "Some Potential User Applicatons." Mountain View, CA: SMDS Interest Group, Sept. 1991.

William Stallings. "What You Need to Know About Bridge Routing." *LAN Technology*, March 1990.

Everett Thiele. "Source Routing." *LAN Magazine*, Feb. 1988.

Kevin Tolly. "Remote Token Ring Bridges: Plug and Play or Plug and Pay?" *Data Communications*, Aug. 1991.

# Chapter 6: Building the Wide Area Network

Richard Caruso, vice president, information networking services, Bellcore. "Network Computing, Can The Network Really Become the Computer?" Keynote speech, Interop, Oct. 1991.

cisco Systems. "cisco Technology Directions: Routing for the New Wide-Area Netscape." Menlo Park, CA: cisco Systems, Sept. 1991.

Robert Davidson and Nathan Miller. *The Guide to SONET.* New York: Telecom Library, 1991.

Frank Henderson and Joseph McCoy. "Less is Faster." *LAN Magazine*, July 1991.

Gary Kessler. "Service for Your MAN." *LAN Magazine*, Oct. 1991.

Gary Kessler. "Simplifying SONET." *LAN Magazine*, July 1991.

Audrey MacLean, president and CEO, Adaptive, an NET Company, Redwood City, CA.

Network Equipment Technologies. "Frame Relay White Paper." Redwood City, CA: NET, July 1991.

Richard Rothwell, Dow Jones & Company. "How to Implement Frame Relay." Interop, Oct. 1991.

William Stalling. "Broadband ISDN: A Standards Update." *Network World*, March 18, 1991.

William Stallings. "Dash to Cell Relay." *LAN Magazine*, Sept. 1991.

Telco Systems. "LAN to WAN Internetworking." Norwood, MA: Telco Systems, 1991.

Trans-Formation, *SMDS Market,* Sept. 1990, Trans-Formation, Tulsa, OK.

# Chapter 7: Implementing and Testing the Enterprise-Wide Network

Pete Abene, Electronic Data Services.

Nina Burns. "Network 911." *LAN Magazine,* Nov. 1990.

Tom Henderson, Corporate Networks.

Tom Henderson. "The Practical Installers Checklist." Houston, TX: Business Systems Group.

Leo Spiegel, LANSystems.

Dean Wolf, Ernst & Young. "Outsourcing and Facilities Management." Networld Boston Conference Manual 1991.

# Chapter 8: Standards and Interoperability

Uyless Black. *OSI: A Model for Computer Communications Standards.*

Digital Equipment Corp. "Digital Unveils Fifth Generation of Networking." June 3, 1991.

Jerrold Grochow. *SAA: A Guide to Implementing IBM's Systems Application Architecture.* Yourdon Press Computing Series, Prentice Hall, 1991.

John Henshall and Sandy Shaw. *OSI Explained: End-to-End Computer Communication Standards.* New York: Ellis Horwood, 1990.

Michael Howard. "The Inside Scoop." *Interoperability,* Fall 1990.

Mike Hurwicz. "Software Brewing." *LAN Magazine,* Sept. 1990.

Warren Keuffel. "NetWise RPC." *LAN Magazine,* Sept. 1990.

David Korf, Digital Equipment Corp.

Robin Layland. "Token Ring Bridges and Routers: Heirs to the SNA Throne?" *Data Communications,* Nov. 21, 1990.

James Martin and Joe Leben. *DECnet Phase V: An OSI Implementation.* Bedford, MA: Digital Press, 1992.

Mike New, vice president of marketing, Attachmate, Redmond, WA.

Peter Stephenson. "Sweet TCP/IP Suite." *Interoperability*, Fall 1990.

Johna Till Johnson. "Video and LANs: Question of Balance." *Data Communications*, Aug. 1991.

# Chapter 9: Network Applications

Nina Burns, principal, Network Messaging Solutions, Menlo Park, CA.

Mike Hurwicz. "Start Your Engines." *LAN Magazine*, Dec. 1991.

Anand Jagannathan, founder and president, Reach Software, Sunnyvale, CA.

Frank Leeds and Matthew Kayes. "Improving DBMS Performance: The LAN Approach." *LAN Technology*, Nov. 1990.

Stan Levine, vice president of engineering, Automated Design Systems, Atlanta, GA.

Jamie Lewis and Craig Burton. "Workflow Automation." *Clarke-Burton Report*, Clarke Burton Corporation, Salt Lake City, UT, April 1991.

Lotus. "Lotus Announces Open Messaging Interface." Cambridge, MA: Lotus, Sept. 23, 1991.

Microsoft. "Client-Server Computing." Microsoft, 1991.

Microsoft. "Downsizing Corporate Information Systems." Microsoft, 1991.

Larry Palmer and Ricky Palmer. "Desktop Meeting." *LAN Magazine*, Nov. 1991.

Reach Software. "Workflow Automation White Paper." April 1991.

# Chapter 10: Network Management: Organizational and Practical

Pete Abene, Electronic Data Services.

Katherine Epes Barrett. "LAN Management: Where Does It Fit?" Networld Boston Conference Manual, 1991.

Business Research Group. "PC LAN Integration and Management: User Trends." Newton, MA: Business Research Group, 1991.

Elizabeth Dougherty. "Abuzz About Arrays." *LAN Magazine*, July 1991.

Mark Fedor, Michael Richards, and Martin Schoffstall. "Cutting Management Tasks Down to Size With SNMP." *LAN Technology*, March 1990.

James Herman. "Enterprise Management Vendors Shoot It Out." *Data Communications*, Nov. 1990.

Infonetics. "The Cost of LAN Downtime." San Jose, CA: Infonetics, Sept. 1989.

Greg Klien. "Developing a Corporate LAN Methodology." Networld Boston, Feb. 1991.

Alice LaPlante. "Taking a Second Look at the Concept of Outsourcing." *Infoworld*, IDC, May 13, 1991.

Farid Moslehi. "Reflections on Fault Tolerance." *LAN Technology*, Jan. 1992.

Leo Spiegel, LANSystems.

Eric Stral. "The New Role of the LAN Administrator." Networld Boston Conference Manual, Feb. 1991.

Lexel. "RMON White Paper." Lexel, Fullerton, CA.

# Chapter 11: The Future of Enterprise-Wide Networks

Andersen Consulting. *Trends in Information Technology: The Challenge of Business Integration*. Chicago, IL: Arthur Andersen, 1991.

George Gilder. "Into the Telecosm." *Harvard Business Review*, March-April 1991.

Gary Kessler. "IEEE 802.6 MAN." *LAN Magazine*, Apr. 1990.

John Leong, Carnegie-Mellon University, Pittsburgh, PA.

Nicholas Negroponte. "Products and Services for Computer Networks." *Scientific American*, Sept. 1991.

Mike New, vice president, Attachmate, Redmond, WA.

Bill Price and Jay Westrack. "Interop Achievement Award." Interop, Oct. 1991.

Mark Weiser. "The Computer for the 21st Century." *Scientific American*, Sept. 1991.

# Index

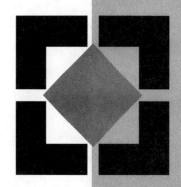

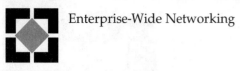

# D

# I

# N

## P

# Q

# R

## S

# T

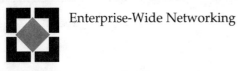

# X-Z

Name_____Phone (___)_____

Title_____

Company_____

Address _____ Suite/Box_____

City/State/Zip _____

**SAMS01**

‖‖‖‖‖

# BUSINESS REPLY MAIL

FIRST CLASS   PERMIT NO. 5548   HOUSTON, TEXAS

POSTAGE WILL BE PAID BY ADDRESSEE

***BSG***

P.O.Box 27966

Houston, Texas  77227-9902